P9-DFF-126

Yarringtons

Warson

Hymns of Faith

Tabernacle Publishing Company
Wheaton, Illinois 60187

Copyright © 1980 by Tabernacle Publishing Company
(A Division of Hope Publishing Company)
International Copyright Secured.   All Rights Reserved.
ISBN: 0-916642-14-3
1980

FOREWORD

During the past sixty-five years, the Tabernacle Publishing Company has published seven major hymnals, each one larger than the last. Each contained the best current expressions of our faith as well as all the standard historic hymns which are essential in the services of evangelical churches.

Hymns of Faith is both the biggest and the best in this series. It has sixty-four more pages than its predecessor. Without losing any of the traditional hymns and gospel songs that are important to this heritage, it has added the largest possible number of the fresh, joyful songs of praise and witness that have graced our singing generation. It also offers a larger page, easy-to-read words and music, and carefully selected keys for exuberant congregational singing.

The Scripture Readings (pages 570-596) are thoughtfully compiled to cover every emphasis of the church year. The King James version of the Bible was chosen, since it is the stated preference of most of the churches which have used our hymnals. A brand new feature—the scripture words under each title—will help congregations identify the biblical inspiration for each selection. Used in conjunction with the exhaustive Topical Index (pages 609-615), they will also aid ministers and musicians in choosing hymns for each service occasion.

We acknowledge with gratitude the invaluable help of our associate editors and the numerous advisers who helped compile the list of hymns from which the final index was chosen. This group included three hundred different denominational and independent pastors and church leaders who completed questionnaires which identified the strongest possible selections. As a result of their recommendations, three additional indexes have also been included. The first is a complete list of Scriptural Allusions in Hymns (pages 602-606). An Index of Authors, Composers and Sources (pages 598-601) also includes both birth and death dates and the page numbers on which their contributions appear. Lastly, an index with the names and addresses of all copyright owners and proprietors is included (pages 607-608) for ease in contacting these sources. All churches should be aware that it is illegal to reproduce any of the copyrighted words or music contained in this book. By the same token, we cannot grant permission for the use of someone else's copyrighted property and thus this index will facilitate contact with the appropriate owner.

Finally, we must speak our gratitude for the large group of poetic and musical witnesses whose works are included between the covers of this hymnal. They have made it possible for us to present so many diverse expressions of faith. For them and for ourselves, we express the hope that each selection will be used to glorify our Lord who gives us reason to sing!

The Publishers

CONTENTS

Our Great Savior 1

Behold . . . a friend of publicans and sinners! Luke 7:34

ROWLAND H. PRICHARD
ARR. BY ROBERT HARKNESS

J. WILBUR CHAPMAN

1. Je - sus! what a Friend for sin - ners! Je - sus! Lov - er of my soul;
2. Je - sus! what a Strength in weak - ness! Let me hide my - self in Him;
3. Je - sus! what a Help in sor - row! While the bil - lows o'er me roll,
4. Je - sus! what a Guide and Keep - er! While the tem-pest still is high,
5. Je - sus! I do now re-ceive Him, More than all in Him I find,

Friends may fail me, foes as - sail me, He, my Sav - ior, makes me whole.
Tempt-ed, tried, and some-times fail - ing, He, my Strength, my vic-t'ry wins.
E - ven when my heart is break-ing, He, my Com-fort, helps my soul.
Storms a - bout me, night o'er-takes me, He, my Pi - lot, hears my cry.
He hath grant - ed me for - give-ness, I am His, and He is mine.

Chorus

Hal - le - lu - jah! what a Sav - ior! Hal - le - lu - jah! what a Friend!

Sav - ing, help - ing, keep - ing, lov - ing, He is with me to the end.

Copyright 1910. Renewal 1938 extended. Hope Publishing Co., owner. All rights reserved.

2 How Great Thou Art

Great is the Lord, and greatly to be praised. Psa. 48:1

CARL BOBERG
TRANS. BY STUART K. HINE

Swedish Folk melody
ARR. BY STUART K. HINE

1. O Lord my God, when I in awe-some won-der Con-sid-er
2. When thro' the woods and for-est glades I wan-der And hear the
3. And when I think that God, His Son not spar-ing, Sent Him to
4. When Christ shall come with shout of ac-cla-ma-tion And take me

all the worlds Thy hands have made, I see the stars, I hear the roll-ing
birds sing sweet-ly in the trees, When I look down from loft-y moun-tain
die, I scarce can take it in, That on the cross, my bur-den glad-ly
home, what joy shall fill my heart! Then I shall bow in hum-ble ad-o-

Chorus

thun-der, Thy pow'r thro'-out the u-ni-verse dis-played.
gran-deur, And hear the brook and feel the gen-tle breeze.
bear-ing, He bled and died to take a-way my sin.
ra-tion, And there pro-claim, my God, how great Thou art.

Then sings my

soul, my Sav-ior God, to Thee; How great Thou art, how great Thou art! Then sings my

soul, my Sav-ior God, to Thee: How great Thou art, how great Thou art!

*Translator's original words are "works" and "mighty."

© Copyright 1953 by Stuart K. Hine, assigned to Manna Music, Inc.
© Copyright 1955 by MANNA MUSIC, INC., 2111 Kenmere Ave., Burbank, CA 91504.
International copyright secured. All rights reserved. Used by permission.

There's a Quiet Understanding 3

Where two or three are gathered in My name, there am I . . . Matt. 18:20

TEDD SMITH

TEDD SMITH

1. There's a qui - et un - der-stand - ing, when we're gath - ered in the Spir - it, It's a prom - ise that He gives us, when we gath-er in His name. There's a love we feel in Je - sus, there's a man - na that He feeds us, It's a prom - ise that He gives us When we gath-er in His name. Thank You, thank You, Lord.

2. And we know when we're to-geth - er, shar - ing love and un - der-stand - ing, That our broth - ers and our sis - ters feel the one-ness that He brings. Thank You, thank You, thank You, Je - sus, for the way You love and feed us, For the man - y ways You lead us,

[1] [2] (Repeat, ad lib.)

Copyright © 1973. Hope Publishing Co., owner. International copyright secured. All rights reserved.

4 My Tribute

To God only wise, be glory through Jesus Christ . . . Rom. 16:27

ANDRAÉ CROUCH

ANDRAÉ CROUCH

How can I say thanks for the things You have done for me?

Things so un-de-served, Yet You gave to prove Your love for me; The

voic-es of a mil-lion an-gels could not ex - press my gra-ti - tude.

All that I am, and ev - er hope to be; I owe it all to Thee.

Chorus

To God be the glo-ry, To God be the glo-ry,

© Copyright 1971 by LEXICON MUSIC, INC. ASCAP. All rights reserved. International copyright secured. Used by special permission.

5 Let's Just Praise the Lord

The Lord Jehovah is my strength and my song. . . Isa. 12:2

GLORIA GAITHER AND
WILLIAM J. GAITHER

WILLIAM J. GAITHER

Let's just praise the Lord! Praise the Lord! Let's just
lift our hearts* to heav-en and praise the
Lord; Let's just praise the Lord, Praise the Lord, Let's just
lift our hearts* to heav-en and praise the Lord!

Fine

*Alternate words "voice," "hands."
© Copyright 1972 by William J. Gaither. International copyright secured. All rights reserved. Used by permission.

1. O, we thank You for Your kind - ness, We thank You for Your
2. Just the pre - cious name of Je - sus is worth - y of our

love, We have been in heaven - ly plac - es, felt bless-ings from a -
praise. Let us bow our knees be - fore Him, our hands to heav - en

bove; We've been shar - ing all the good things, the fam - ily can af -
raise: When He comes in clouds of glo - ry, with Him to ev - er

D.C.

ford. Let's just turn our praise toward heav - en and praise the Lord.
reign, Let's just lift our hap - py voic - es, and praise His name.

6 I Just Came to Praise the Lord

While I live will I praise the Lord . . . Psa. 146:2

WAYNE ROMERO   WAYNE ROMERO

1. I just came to praise the Lord, I just came to praise the Lord;
2. I just came to thank the Lord, I just came to thank the Lord;
3. I just came to love the Lord, I just came to love the Lord;

I just came to praise His name, I just came to praise the Lord.
I just came to praise His name, I just came to thank the Lord.
I just came to praise His name, I just came to love the Lord.

He came in-to my life one ver-y spe-cial day, He came in-to my heart

to show me a bet-ter way; He said He would nev-er de-part,

And this is why I sing: I just came to praise the Lord.

© Copyright 1975 by Paragon Music Corp. (ASCAP), 803 18th Avenue, South, Nashville, Tennessee 37202. International copyright secured. Made in U.S.A. All rights reserved. Used by permission.

Praise, My Soul, the King of Heaven 7

Bless the Lord, O my soul, and forget not all his benefits. Psa. 103:2

HENRY FRANCIS LYTE

HENRY SMART

Same tune "Angels from the Realms of Glory"

1. Praise, my soul, the King of heav-en, To His feet your
2. Praise Him for His grace and fa-vor To our fa-thers
3. Fa-ther-like, He tends and spares us, Well our fee-ble
4. An-gels in the height, a-dore Him, You be-hold Him

trib-ute bring; Ran-somed, healed, re-stored, for-giv-en,
in dis-tress; Praise Him, still the same as ev-er,
frame He knows; In His hands He gen-tly bears us,
face to face; Saints tri-um-phant, bow be-fore Him,

Ev-er-more His praise oo sing. Al-le-lu-ia!
Slow to chide and swift to bless. Al-le-lu-ia!
Res-cues us from all our foes. Al-le-lu-ia!
Gath-ered in from ev-ery race. Al-le-lu-ia!

Al-le-lu-ia! Praise the ev-er-last-ing King!
Al-le-lu-ia! Glo-rious in His faith-ful-ness.
Al-le-lu-ia! Wide-ly yet His mer-cy flows!
Al-le-lu-ia! Praise with us the God of grace! A-men.

8 Bless His Holy Name

Bless the Lord, O my soul; and all that is within me. Psa. 103:1

PSALM 103
ANDRAÉ CROUCH

ANDRAÉ CROUCH

Bless the Lord, O my soul, and all that is with-in me, Bless His

Fine

ho - ly Name. He has done great things, He has done great

D.C. al Fine

things, He has done great things, Bless His ho - ly Name.

© Copyright 1973 by LEXICON MUSIC, INC. ASCAP. All rights reserved. International copyright secured. Used by special permission.

9 The Lord's My Shepherd

The Lord is my shepherd; I shall not want. Psa. 23:1

PSALM 23
Scottish Psalter, 1650
WILLIAM WHITTINGHAM AND OTHERS

JESSIE S. IRVINE
ARR. BY DAVID GRANT

1. The Lord's my Shep - herd, I'll not want; He makes me down to lie
2. My soul He doth re - store a - gain; And me to walk doth make
3. Yea, though I walk through death's dark vale, Yet will I fear no ill;
4. My ta - ble Thou hast fur - nish - ed In pres - ence of my foes;
5. Good-ness and mer - cy all my life Shall sure - ly fol - low me;

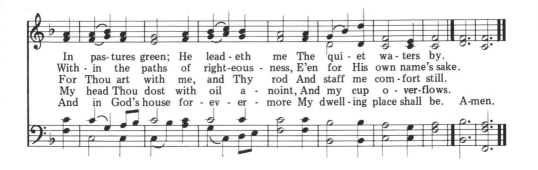

In pas-tures green; He lead-eth me The qui-et wa-ters by.
With-in the paths of right-eous-ness, E'en for His own name's sake.
For Thou art with me, and Thy rod And staff me com-fort still.
My head Thou dost with oil a-noint, And my cup o-ver-flows.
And in God's house for-ev-er-more My dwell-ing place shall be. A-men.

When Morning Gilds the Skies 10

My voice shalt Thou hear in the morning, O Lord. Psa. 5:3

Katholisches Gesangbuch, Würzburg, 1828
TRANS. BY EDWARD CASWALL

JOSEPH BARNBY

1. When morn-ing gilds the skies, My heart a-wak-ing cries:
2. The night be-comes as day When from the heart we say:
3. Sing, suns and stars of space, Sing, ye that see His face,
4. Be this while life is mine My can-ti-cle di-vine:

May Je-sus Christ be praised! A-like at work or prayer
May Je-sus Christ be praised! The pow'rs of dark-ness fear
Sing, Je-sus Christ be praised! Let all the earth a-round
May Je-sus Christ be praised! Be this th'e-ter-nal song,

To Je-sus I re-pair: May Je-sus Christ be praised!
When this sweet chant they hear: May Je-sus Christ be praised!
Ring joy-ous with the sound: May Je-sus Christ be praised!
Through all the a-ges long: May Je-sus Christ be praised! A-men.

11 A Mighty Fortress Is Our God

God is our refuge and strength. Psa. 46:1

PSALM 46
MARTIN LUTHER
TRANS. BY FREDERICK H. HEDGE

MARTIN LUTHER

1. A might-y for-tress is our God, A bul-wark nev-er fail-ing;
2. Did we in our own strength con-fide, Our striv-ing would be los-ing,
3. And though this world, with dev-ils filled, Should threat-en to un-do us,
4. That word a-bove all earth-ly powers, No thanks to them, a-bid-eth;

Our help-er He, a-mid the flood Of mor-tal ills pre-vail-ing:
Were not the right Man on our side, The man of God's own choos-ing:
We will not fear, for God hath willed His truth to tri-umph through us:
The Spir-it and the gifts are ours Through him who with us sid-eth:

For still our an-cient foe Doth seek to work us woe; His craft and power are
Dost ask who that may be? Christ Je-sus, it is He; Lord Sab-a-oth His
The Prince of Dark-ness grim, We trem-ble not for him; His rage we can en-
Let goods and kin-dred go, This mor-tal life al-so; The bod-y they may

great, And, armed with cru-el hate, On earth is not his e-qual.
name, From age to age the same, And He must win the bat-tle.
dure, For lo, his doom is sure; One lit-tle word shall fell him.
kill: God's truth a-bid-eth still; His king-dom is for-ev-er. A-men.

All Creatures of Our God and King 12

All Thy works shall praise Thee, O Lord. Psa. 145:10

ST. FRANCIS OF ASSISI
TRANS. BY WILLIAM H. DRAPER

Geistliche Kirchengesäng, Cologne, 1623

1. All crea-tures of our God and King, Lift up your voice and with us sing
2. Thou rush-ing wind that art so strong, Ye clouds that sail in heav'n a - long,
3. Thou flow-ing wa - ter, pure and clear, Make mu-sic for thy Lord to hear,
4. And all ye men of ten-der heart, For-giv - ing oth-ers, take your part,
5. Let all things their Cre-a - tor bless, And wor-ship Him in hum-ble - ness,

Al-le - lu - ia, Al-le-lu - ia! Thou burn-ing sun with gold-en beam,
O praise Him, Al-le-lu - ia! Thou ris-ing morn in praise re - joice,
Al-le - lu - ia, Al-le-lu - ia! Thou fire so mas-ter-ful and bright,
O sing ye, Al-le-lu - ia! Ye who long pain and sor-row bear,
O praise Him, Al-le-lu - ia! Praise, praise the Fa-ther, praise the Son,

Thou sil - ver moon with soft - er gleam, O praise Him, O praise Him,
Ye lights of eve - ning, find a voice, O praise Him, O praise Him,
That giv - est man both warmth and light, O praise Him, O praise Him,
Praise God and on Him cast your care, O praise Him, O praise Him,
And praise the Spir - it, three in one, O praise Him, O praise Him,

Al-le - lu - ia, al - le - lu - ia, al - le - lu - ia!
Al-le - lu - ia, al - le - lu - ia, al - le - lu - ia!
Al-le - lu - ia, al - le - lu - ia, al - le - lu - ia!
Al-le - lu - ia, al - le - lu - ia, al - le - lu - ia!
Al-le - lu - ia, al - le - lu - ia, al - le - lu - ia! A-men.

Copyright 1923 J. Curwen & Sons. Ltd. Used by permission.

13 Spirit of God, Descend upon My Heart

If we live in the Spirit, let us also walk in the Spirit. Gal. 5:25

GEORGE CROLY

FREDERICK C. ATKINSON

1. Spir - it of God, de - scend up - on my heart; Wean it from
2. I ask no dream, no proph - et ec - sta - sies, No sud - den
3. Hast Thou not bid us love Thee, God and King? All, all Thine
4. Teach me to feel that Thou art al - ways nigh; Teach me the
5. Teach me to love Thee as Thine an - gels love, One ho - ly

earth, through all its puls - es move; Stoop to my weak - ness, might - y
rend - ing of the veil of clay, No an - gel vis - it - ant, no
own, soul, heart and strength and mind. I see Thy cross—there teach my
strug - gles of the soul to bear, To check the ris - ing doubt, the
pas - sion fill - ing all my frame; The bap - tism of the heav'n - de-

as Thou art, And make me love Thee as I ought to love.
o - p'ning skies; But take the dim - ness of my soul a - way.
heart to cling: O let me seek Thee, and O let me find.
reb - el sigh; Teach me the pa - tience of un - an - swered prayer.
scend - ed Dove, My heart an al - tar, and Thy love the flame. A - men.

14 The King of Love My Shepherd Is

I am the good shepherd . . . I lay down My life for the sheep. John 10:14, 15

HENRY W. BAKER
Based on PSALM 23

JOHN B. DYKES

1. The King of love my Shep-herd is, Whose good-ness fail - eth nev - er;
2. Where streams of liv - ing wa - ter flow My ran-somed soul He lead - eth,
3. Per - verse and fool - ish oft I strayed But yet 'in love He sought me.
4. In death's dark vale I fear no ill With Thee, dear Lord, be - side me;
5. And so through all the length of days Thy good-ness fail - eth nev - er:

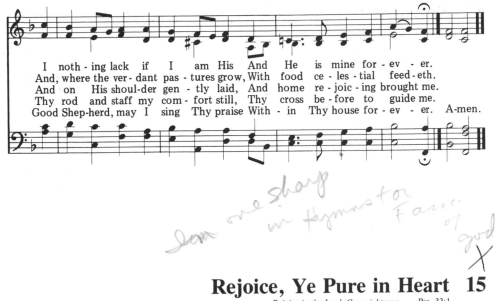

I noth-ing lack if I am His And He is mine for-ev-er.
And, where the ver-dant pas-tures grow, With food ce-les-tial feed-eth.
And on His shoul-der gen-tly laid, And home re-joic-ing brought me.
Thy rod and staff my com-fort still, Thy cross be-fore to guide me.
Good Shep-herd, may I sing Thy praise With-in Thy house for-ev-er. A-men.

Rejoice, Ye Pure in Heart 15

Rejoice in the Lord, O ye righteous . . . Psa. 33:1

EDWARD H. PLUMPTRE   ARTHUR H. MESSITER

1. Re - joice, ye pure in heart, Re - joice, give thanks, and sing;
2. Bright youth and snow-crowned age, Strong men and maid - ens fair,
3. With all the an - gel choirs, With all the saints on earth,
4. Yes, on through life's long path, Still chant - ing as ye go;
5. Still lift your stand - ard high, Still march in firm ar - ray;

Your fes - tal ban - ner wave on high, The cross of Christ your King.
Raise high your free, ex - ult - ing song, God's won - drous praise de - clare.
Pour out the strains of joy and bliss, True rap - ture, no - blest mirth!
From youth to age, by night and day, In glad - ness and in woe.
As war - riors through the dark - ness toil Till dawns the gold - en day.

Chorus

Re - joice, re - joice, Re - joice, give thanks, and sing! A - men.
Re - joice, re - joice,

16 This Is My Father's World

The morning stars sang together, and all the sons of God shouted for joy. Job 38:7

MALTBIE D. BABCOCK

FRANKLIN L. SHEPPARD

1. This is my Fa-ther's world, And to my lis-tening ears All
2. This is my Fa-ther's world, The birds their car-ols raise, The
3. This is my Fa-ther's world, O let me ne'er for-get That

na-ture sings, and round me rings The mu-sic of the spheres.
morn-ing light, the lil-y white, De-clare their Mak-er's praise.
though the wrong seems oft so strong, God is the Rul-er yet.

This is my Fa-ther's world: I rest me in the thought Of
This is my Fa-ther's world: He shines in all that's fair; In the
This is my Fa-ther's world: Why should my heart be sad? The

rocks and trees, of skies and seas—His hand the won-ders wrought.
rus-tling grass I hear Him pass, He speaks to me ev-ery-where.
Lord is King: let the heav-ens ring! God reigns: let earth be glad! A-men.

All Glory, Laud and Honor 17

Blessed is the King of Israel that cometh in the name of the Lord. John 12:13

Theodulph of Orleans
Trans. by John M. Neale

Melchior Teschner

1. All glo - ry, laud and hon - or To Thee, Re - deem - er, King,
2. The com - pa - ny of an - gels Are prais - ing Thee on high,
3. To Thee, be - fore Thy pas - sion, They sang their hymns of praise;

To whom the lips of chil - dren Made sweet ho - san - nas ring:
And mor - tal men and all things Cre - at - ed make re - ply:
To Thee, now high ex - alt - ed, Our mel - o - dy we raise:

Thou art the King of Is - rael, Thou Da - vid's roy - al Son,
The peo - ple of the He - brews With palms be - fore Thee went:
Thou didst ac - cept their prais - es— Ac - cept the praise we bring,

Who in the Lord's name com - est, The King and bless - ed One!
Our praise and prayer and an - thems Be - fore Thee we pre - sent.
Who in all good de - light - est, Thou good and gra - cious King! A - men.

18 Declare His Glory

They shall declare my glory among the Gentiles. Isa. 66:19

E. MARGARET CLARKSON

DONALD P. HUSTAD

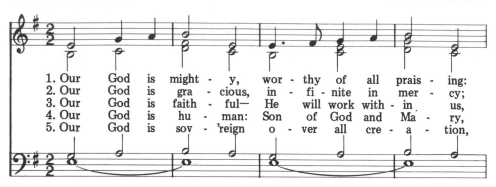

1. Our God is might - y, wor - thy of all prais - ing:
2. Our God is gra - cious, in - fi - nite in mer - cy;
3. Our God is faith - ful— He will work with - in us,
4. Our God is hu - man: Son of God and Ma - ry,
5. Our God is sov - 'reign o - ver all cre - a - tion,

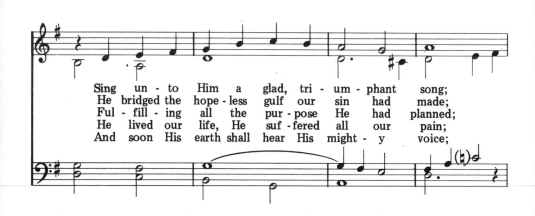

Sing un - to Him a glad, tri - um - phant song;
He bridged the hope - less gulf our sin had made;
Ful - fill - ing all the pur - pose He had planned;
He lived our life, He suf - fered all our pain;
And soon His earth shall hear His might - y voice;

He is the Lord, su - preme in earth and heav - en;
He gave His Son to pur - chase our sal - va - tion—
Cleans - ing our hearts and fill - ing with His Spir - it,
He bids us go to min - is - ter His mer - cy,
With shout of joy the King shall come in splen - dor—

Copyright © 1980. Hope Publishing Co., owner. International copyright secured. All rights reserved.

To Him all strength and maj-es-ty be - long.
In Je - sus Christ we meet God un - a - fraid!
Mak - ing us strong to keep His last com - mand.
To be to men God's Word made flesh a - gain.
Lift up your hearts, con - fess Him and re - joice!

Chorus

De -clare His glo - ry a - mong the na -tions; Through all cre-

a - tion His tri -umph sing, 'Till all earth's peo - ples

bow in ad -o - ra -tion And Je -sus Christ be ev -er -last-ing King.

19 In the Garden

Mary Magdalene came and told the disciples that she had seen the Lord. John 20:18

C. AUSTIN MILES   C. AUSTIN MILES

1. I come to the gar-den a - lone, While the dew is still on the
2. He speaks, and the sound of His voice Is so sweet the birds hush their
3. I'd stay in the gar-den with Him Though the night a-round me be

ros - es; And the voice I hear, fall - ing on my ear, The
sing - ing, And the mel - o - dy that He gave to me With-
fall - ing, But He bids me go; through the voice of woe, His

Chorus

Son of God dis - clos - es.
in my heart is ring - ing. And He walks with me, and He
voice to me is call - ing.

talks with me, And He tells me I am His own, And the

joy we share as we tar - ry there, None oth - er has ev - er known.

Copyright 1912 by Hall-Mack Co. © Renewal 1940, The Rodeheaver Co. All rights reserved. Used by permission.

All Hail the Power of Jesus' Name 20

He hath . . . a name written, King of Kings, and Lord of Lords. Rev. 19:16

EDWARD PERRONET
ADAPT. BY JOHN RIPPON

(CORONATION)
OLIVER HOLDEN

1. All hail the power of Je - sus' name! Let an - gels pros - trate fall;
2. Ye cho - sen seed of Is - rael's race, Ye ran - somed from the fall,
3. Let ev - ery kin - dred, ev - ery tribe, On this ter - res - trial ball,
4. O that with yon - der sa - cred throng We at His feet may fall!

Bring forth the roy - al di - a - dem, And crown Him Lord of all;
Hail Him who saves you by His grace, And crown Him Lord of all;
To Him all maj - es - ty as - cribe, And crown Him Lord of all;
We'll join the ev - er - last - ing song, And crown Him Lord of all;

Bring forth the roy - al di - a - dem, And crown Him Lord of all!
Hail Him who saves you by His grace, And crown Him Lord of all!
To Him all maj - es - ty as - cribe, And crown Him Lord of all!
We'll join the ev - er - last - ing song, And crown Him Lord of all!

1st time parts

He Is Lord 21

That at the name of Jesus every knee should bow . . . and every tongue confess that Jesus Christ is Lord. Phil. 2:10, 11

Based on Philippians 2:11

2nd - unison

Traditional

Reverently

He is Lord, He is Lord, He is ris - en from the dead and He is

Lord; Ev - ery knee shall bow, ev - ery tongue con - fess that Je - sus Christ is Lord.

22 Blessed Be the Name

Blessed be the name of the Lord. Job 1:21

Source unknown
ARR. BY RALPH E. HUDSON AND
WILLIAM J. KIRKPATRICK

WILLIAM H. CLARK
Refrain, RALPH E. HUDSON

1. All praise to Him who reigns a - bove In maj - es - ty su - preme,
2. His name a - bove all names shall stand, Ex - alt - ed more and more,
3. Re - deem - er, Sav - ior, Friend of man Once ru - ined by the fall,
4. His name shall be the Coun - sel - or, The might - y Prince of Peace,

Who gave His Son for man to die, That He might man re - deem!
At God the Fa - ther's own right hand, Where an - gel hosts a - dore.
Thou hast de - vised sal - va - tion's plan, For Thou hast died for all.
Of all earth's king - doms Con - quer - or, Whose reign shall nev - er cease.

Chorus

Bless-ed be the name, bless-ed be the name, Bless-ed be the name of the Lord;

Bless-ed be the name, bless-ed be the name, Bless-ed be the name of the Lord.

Come, Christians, Join to Sing 23

O come, let us sing unto the Lord. Psa. 95:1

CHRISTIAN H. BATEMAN

Traditional Spanish melody
ARR. BY DAVID EVANS

1. Come, Chris-tians, join to sing Al - le - lu - ia! A - men!
2. Come, lift your hearts on high, Al - le - lu - ia! A - men!
3. Praise yet our Christ a - gain, Al - le - lu - ia! A - men!

Loud praise to Christ our King; Al - le - lu - ia! A - men!
Let prais - es fill the sky; Al - le - lu - ia! A - men!
Life shall not end the strain; Al - le - lu - ia! A - men!

Let all, with heart and voice, Be - fore His throne re - joice;
He is our Guide and Friend; To us He'll con - de - scend;
On heav - en's bliss - ful shore His good - ness we'll a - dore,

Praise is His gra - cious choice: Al - le - lu - ia! A - men!
His love shall nev - er end: Al - le - lu - ia! A - men!
Sing - ing for - ev - er - more, "Al - le - lu - ia! A - men!"

24 Praise Ye the Triune God

I will . . . praise Thy name for Thy lovingkindness. Psa. 138:2

ELIZABETH R. CHARLES

FRIEDRICH F. FLEMMING

1. Praise ye the Fa - ther! for His lov - ing kind - ness, Ten - der - ly
2. Praise ye the Sav - ior! great is His com - pas - sion, Gra - cious - ly
3. Praise ye the Spir - it! Com - fort - er of Is - rael, Sent of the

cares He for His err - ing chil - dren; Praise Him, ye an - gels,
cares He for His cho - sen peo - ple; Young men and maid - ens,
Fa - ther and the Son to bless us; Praise ye the Fa - ther,

praise Him in the heav - ens, Praise ye Je - ho - vah!
ye old men and chil - dren, Praise ye the Sav - ior!
Son and Ho - ly Spir - it, Praise ye the tri - une God! A - men.

25 Jesus, Thy Blood and Righteousness

He hath clothed me with the garments of salvation . . . Isa. 61:10

NIKOLAUS L. VON ZINZENDORF
TRANS. BY JOHN WESLEY

William Gardiner's *Sacred Melodies*, 1815

1. Je - sus, Thy blood and right-eous-ness My beau - ty are, my glo - rious dress;
2. Bold shall I stand in Thy great day, For who aught to my charge shall lay?
3. Lord, I be - lieve Thy pre - cious blood, Which, at the mer - cy seat of God
4. Lord, I be - lieve were sin - ners more Than sands up - on the o - cean shore,

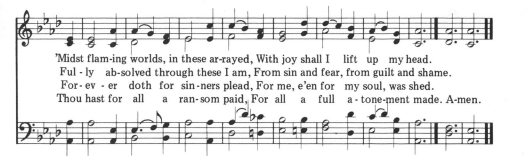

'Midst flam-ing worlds, in these ar-rayed, With joy shall I lift up my head.
Ful - ly ab-solved through these I am, From sin and fear, from guilt and shame.
For- ev - er doth for sin-ners plead, For me, e'en for my soul, was shed.
Thou hast for all a ran-som paid, For all a full a - tone-ment made. A-men.

O Love That Will Not Let Me Go   26

The Lord hath appeared . . . saying, Yea, I have loved thee with an everlasting love. Jer. 31:3

GEORGE MATHESON   ALBERT L. PEACE

1. O Love that will not let me go, I rest my wea - ry
2. O Light that fol - l'west all my way, I yield my flick - 'ring
3. O Joy that seek - est me through pain, I can - not close my
4. O Cross that lift - est up my head, I dare not ask to

soul in Thee; I give Thee back the life I owe, That
torch to Thee; My heart re - stores its bor - rowed ray, That
heart to Thee; I trace the rain - bow through the rain, And
fly from Thee; I lay in dust life's glo - ry dead, And

in Thine o - cean depths its flow May rich - er, full - er be.
in Thy sun-shine's blaze its day May bright-er, fair - er be.
feel the prom - ise is not vain That morn shall tear - less be.
from the ground there blos - soms red Life that shall end - less be. A - men.

27 Guide Me, O Thou Great Jehovah

This God is our God . . . He will be our guide even unto death. Psa. 48:14

WILLIAM WILLIAMS
TRANS. BY PETER WILLIAMS AND
WILLIAM WILLIAMS

JOHN HUGHES

1. Guide me, O Thou great Je - ho - vah, Pil - grim through this bar - ren land;
2. O - pen now the crys - tal foun - tain, Whence the healing stream doth flow;
3. When I tread the verge of Jor - dan, Bid my anx - ious fears sub - side;

I am weak, but Thou art might - y; Hold me with Thy pow'r - ful hand;
Let the fire and cloud - y pil - lar Lead me all my jour - ney through;
Death of death, and hell's de - struc - tion, Land me safe on Ca - naan's side;

Bread of heav - en, Bread of heav - en, Feed me till I want no
Strong De - liv - erer, strong De - liv - erer, Be Thou still my strength and
Songs of prais - es, songs of prais - es I will ev - er give to

more, (want no more,) Feed me till I want no more.
shield, (strength and shield,) Be Thou still my strength and shield.
Thee, (give to Thee,) I will ev - er give to Thee. A - men.

Music copyright used by permission of Mrs. Dilys S. Webb, Glamorganshire.

Come, Thou Fount of Every Blessing 28

Blessed be the Lord, who daily loadeth us with benefits. Psa. 68:19

ROBERT ROBINSON
ADAPT. BY E. MARGARET CLARKSON

Traditional American melody
John Wyeth's *Repository of Sacred Music*, 1813

1. Come, Thou Fount of ev - ery bless - ing, Tune my heart to sing Thy grace;
2. Hith - er - to Thy love has blest me; Thou hast bro't me to this place;
3. O to grace how great a debt - or Dai - ly I'm con-strained to be!

Streams of mer - cy, nev - er ceas - ing, Call for songs of loud - est praise.
And I know Thy hand will bring me Safe - ly home by Thy good grace.
Let Thy good - ness, like a fet - ter, Bind my wan-dering heart to Thee:

Teach me some me - lo - dious son - net, Sung by flam - ing tongues a - bove;
Je - sus sought me when a stran - ger, Wan-dering from the fold of God;
Prone to wan - der, Lord, I feel it, Prone to leave the God I love;

Praise His name—I'm fixed up - on it—Name of God's re - deem-ing love.
He, to res - cue me from dan - ger, Bought me with His pre-cious blood.
Here's my heart, O take and seal it; Seal it for Thy courts a - bove. A-men.

29 Joyful, Joyful, We Adore Thee

All Thy works shall praise Thee, O Lord . . . Psa. 145:10

HENRY VAN DYKE

LUDWIG VAN BEETHOVEN

1. Joy-ful, joy-ful, we a-dore Thee, God of glo-ry, Lord of love;
2. All Thy works with joy sur-round Thee, Earth and heav'n re-flect Thy rays,
3. Thou art giv-ing and for-giv-ing, Ev-er bless-ing, ev-er blest,
4. Mor-tals join the might-y cho-rus Which the morn-ing stars be-gan;

Hearts un-fold like flow'rs be-fore Thee, Open-ing to the sun a-bove.
Stars and an-gels sing a-round Thee, Cen-ter of un-bro-ken praise.
Well-spring of the joy of liv-ing, O-cean-depth of hap-py rest!
Fa-ther love is reign-ing o'er us, Broth-er love binds man to man.

Melt the clouds of sin and sad-ness; Drive the dark of doubt a-way;
Field and for-est, vale and moun-tain, Flow-ery mead-ow, flash-ing sea,
Thou our Fa-ther, Christ our Broth-er— All who live in love are Thine;
Ev-er sing-ing, march we on-ward, Vic-tors in the midst of strife;

Giv-er of im-mor-tal glad-ness, Fill us with the light of day!
Chant-ing bird and flow-ing foun-tain Call us to re-joice in Thee.
Teach us how to love each oth-er, Lift us to the joy di-vine.
Joy-ful mu-sic leads us sun-ward In the tri-umph song of life. A-men.

From "The Poems of Henry Van Dyke;" copyright, 1911, by Charles Scribner's Sons, 1939 by Tertius Van Dyke. Reprinted by permission of the publishers.

Crown Him with Many Crowns 30

. . . And on His head were many crowns . . . Rev. 19:12

MATTHEW BRIDGES AND
GODFREY THRING

GEORGE J. ELVEY

1. Crown Him with man - y crowns, The Lamb up - on His throne;
2. Crown Him the Son of God Be - fore the worlds be - gan,
3. Crown Him the Lord of life, Who tri - umphed o'er the grave,
4. Crown Him the Lord of love! Be - hold His hands and side,

Hark! how the heav'n - ly an - them drowns All mu - sic but its own!
And ye, who tread where He hath trod, Crown Him the Son of Man;
And rose vic - to - rious in the strife For those He came to save;
Those wounds, yet vis - i - ble a - bove, In beau - ty glo - ri - fied:

A - wake, my soul, and sing Of Him who died for thee, And
Who ev - ery grief hath known That wrings the hu - man breast, And
His glo - ries now we sing, Who died and rose on high, Who
All hail, Re - deem - er, hail! For Thou hast died for me: Thy

hail Him as thy match-less King Thro' all e - ter - ni - ty.
takes and bears them for His own, That all in Him may rest.
died e - ter - nal life to bring, And lives that death may die.
praise and glo - ry shall not fail Thro' - out e - ter - ni - ty. A - men.

31 My Jesus, I Love Thee

We love Him because He first loved us. I John 4:19

WILLIAM R. FEATHERSTONE

ADONIRAM J. GORDON

1. My Je - sus, I love Thee, I know Thou art mine; For Thee all the
2. I love Thee, be - cause Thou hast first lov - ed me, And pur - chased my
3. I'll love Thee in life, I will love Thee in death, And praise Thee as
4. In man - sions of glo - ry and end - less de - light, I'll ev - er a -

fol - lies of sin I re - sign; My gra - cious Re - deem - er, my Sav - ior art
par - don on Cal - va - ry's tree; I love Thee for wear - ing the thorns on Thy
long as Thou lend - est me breath; And say when the death - dew lies cold on my
dore Thee in heav - en so bright; I'll sing with the glit - ter - ing crown on my

Thou; If ev - er I loved Thee, my Je - sus, 'tis now.
brow; If ev - er I loved Thee, my Je - sus, 'tis now.
brow; If ev - er I loved Thee, my Je - sus, 'tis now.
brow; If ev - er I loved Thee, my Je - sus, 'tis now. A - men.

32 There's a Wideness in God's Mercy

Thou, O Lord, art a God . . . plenteous in mercy and truth. Psa. 86:15

FREDERICK W. FABER

LIZZIE S. TOURJÉE

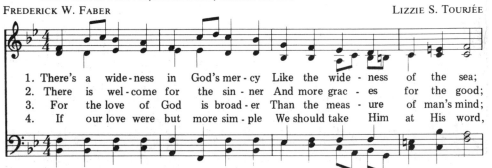

1. There's a wide - ness in God's mer - cy Like the wide - ness of the sea;
2. There is wel - come for the sin - ner And more grac - es for the good;
3. For the love of God is broad - er Than the meas - ure of man's mind;
4. If our love were but more sim - ple We should take Him at His word,

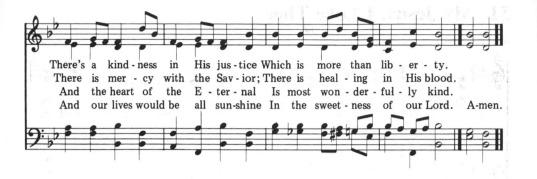

There's a kind-ness in His jus-tice Which is more than lib-er-ty.
There is mer-cy with the Sav-ior; There is heal-ing in His blood.
And the heart of the E-ter-nal Is most won-der-ful-ly kind.
And our lives would be all sun-shine In the sweet-ness of our Lord. A-men.

My Faith Looks Up to Thee 33

Looking unto Jesus the author and finisher of our faith. Heb. 12:2

RAY PALMER   LOWELL MASON

1. My faith looks up to Thee, Thou Lamb of Cal-va-ry,
2. May Thy rich grace im-part Strength to my faint-ing heart,
3. While life's dark maze I tread, And griefs a-round me spread,
4. When ends life's tran-sient dream, When death's cold, sul-len stream

Sav-ior di-vine! Now hear me while I pray, Take all my
My zeal in-spire; As Thou hast died for me, O may my
Be Thou my guide; Bid dark-ness turn to day, Wipe sor-row's
Shall o'er me roll; Blest Sav-ior, then, in love, Fear and dis-

guilt a-way, O let me from this day Be whol-ly Thine!
love to Thee Pure, warm, and change-less be, A liv-ing fire!
tears a-way, Nor let me ev-er stray From Thee a-side.
trust re-move; O bear me safe a-bove, A ran-somed soul! A-men.

34 A Quiet Place

Be still, and know that I am God . . . Psa. 46:10

RALPH CARMICHAEL

RALPH CARMICHAEL

There is a qui-et place, far from the rap - id pace, where God can soothe my

trou-bled mind; Shel-tered by tree and flow'r, there in my qui - et hour with

Him, my cares are left be - hind. Wheth-er a gar -den small, or on a

moun-tain tall, New strength and cour - age there I find; Then from this

qui - et place I go pre-pared to face A new day with love for all man-kind.

© Copyright 1967 by LEXICON MUSIC, INC. ASCAP. All rights reserved. International copyright secured. Used by special permission.

Holy, Holy 35

Holy, holy, holy, Lord God Almighty, which was, and is, and is to come. Rev. 4:8

JIMMY OWENS   JIMMY OWENS

1. Ho-ly, ho-ly, ho-ly, ho-ly, Ho-ly, ho-ly,
2. Gra-cious Fa-ther, gra-cious Fa-ther, We're so blest to be your
3. Pre-cious Je-sus, pre-cious Je-sus, We're so glad that you've re-
4. Ho-ly Spir-it, Ho-ly Spir-it, Come and fill our hearts a-
5. Ho-ly, ho-ly, ho-ly, ho-ly, Ho-ly, ho-ly,

Lord God al-might-y; And we lift our hearts be-fore You as a
chil-dren, gra-cious Fa-ther; And we lift our heads be-fore You as a
deemed us, pre-cious Je-sus; And we lift our hands be-fore You as a
new, Ho-ly Spir-it; And we lift our voice be-fore You as a
Lord God al-might-y; And we lift our hearts be-fore You as a

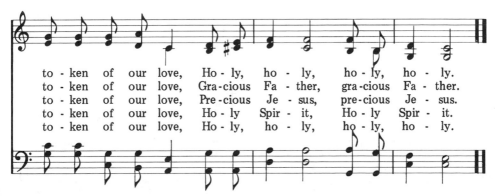

to-ken of our love, Ho-ly, ho-ly, ho-ly, ho-ly.
to-ken of our love, Gra-cious Fa-ther, gra-cious Fa-ther.
to-ken of our love, Pre-cious Je-sus, pre-cious Je-sus.
to-ken of our love, Ho-ly Spir-it, Ho-ly Spir-it.
to-ken of our love, Ho-ly, ho-ly, ho-ly, ho-ly.

© Copyright 1972 by LEXICON MUSIC, INC. ASCAP. All rights reserved. International copyright secured. Used by special permission.

36 For the Beauty of the Earth

Every good gift and every perfect gift is from above. James 1:17

FOLLIOTT S. PIERPOINT

CONRAD KOCHER
ARR. BY WILLIAM H. MONK

1. For the beau-ty of the earth, For the glo-ry
2. For the beau-ty of each hour Of the day and
3. For the joy of ear and eye, For the heart and
4. For the joy of hu-man love, Broth-er, sis-ter,
5. For each per-fect gift of Thine To our race so

of the skies, For the love which from our birth
of the night, Hill and vale, and tree, and flow'r,
mind's de-light, For the mys-tic har-mo-ny
par-ent, child, Friends on earth and friends a-bove,
free-ly giv'n, Grac-es hu-man and di-vine,

O-ver and a-round us lies, Lord of all, to
Sun and moon and stars of light, Lord of all, to
Link-ing sense to sound and sight, Lord of all, to
For all gen-tle thoughts and mild, Lord of all, to
Flow'rs of earth and buds of heav'n, Lord of all, to

Thee we raise This our hymn of grate-ful praise.
Thee we raise This our hymn of grate-ful praise.
Thee we raise This our hymn of grate-ful praise.
Thee we raise This our hymn of grate-ful praise.
Thee we raise This our hymn of grate-ful praise. A-men.

Praise to the Lord, the Almighty 37

For then shalt thou have thy delight in the Almighty. Job 22:26

JOACHIM NEANDER
TRANS. BY CATHERINE WINKWORTH

Stralsund Gesangbuch, 1665

1. Praise to the Lord, the Al-might-y, the King of cre-a-tion! O my soul, praise Him, for He is thy health and sal-va-tion! All ye who hear, Now to His tem-ple draw near; Join me in glad ad-o-ra-tion!

2. Praise to the Lord, who o'er all things so won-drous-ly reign-eth, Shel-ters thee un-der His wings, yea, so gen-tly sus-tain-eth! Hast thou not seen How thy de-sires e'er have been Grant-ed in what He or-dain-eth?

3. Praise to the Lord, who doth pros-per thy work and de-fend thee; Sure-ly His good-ness and mer-cy here dai-ly at-tend thee. Pon-der a-new What the Al-might-y can do, If with His love He be-friend thee.

4. Praise to the Lord! O let all that is in me a-dore Him! All that hath life and breath, come now with prais-es be-fore Him! Let the A-men Sound from His peo-ple a-gain: Glad-ly for aye we a-dore Him. A-men.

38 Grace Greater Than Our Sin

Where sin abounded, grace did much more abound. Rom. 5:20

JULIA H. JOHNSTON

DANIEL B. TOWNER

1. Mar-vel-ous grace of our lov-ing Lord, Grace that ex-ceeds our
2. Sin and de-spair like the sea waves cold, Threat-en the soul with
3. Dark is the stain that we can-not hide, What can a-vail to
4. Mar-vel-ous, in-fi-nite, match-less grace, Free-ly be-stowed on

sin and our guilt, Yon-der on Cal-va-ry's mount out-poured,
in-fi-nite loss; Grace that is great-er, yes, grace un-told,
wash it a-way? Look! there is flow-ing a crim-son tide;
all who be-lieve; All who are long-ing to see His face,

Chorus

There where the blood of the Lamb was spilt.
Points to the ref-uge, the might-y cross. Grace, grace,
Whit-er than snow you may be to-day. Mar-vel-ous grace,
Will you this mo-ment His grace re-ceive?

God's grace, Grace that will par-don and cleanse with-in; Grace,
in-fi-nite grace, Mar-vel-ous

grace, God's grace, Grace that is great-er than all our sin.
grace, in-fi-nite grace,

Copyright 1910. Renewal 1938 extended. Hope Publishing Co., owner. All rights reserved.

His compassions fail not. They are new every morning. Lam. 3:22, 23

THOMAS O. CHISHOLM   WILLIAM M. RUNYAN

1. Great is Thy faith-ful-ness, O God my Fa-ther, There is no shad-ow of
2. Sum-mer and win-ter, and springtime and har-vest, Sun, moon and stars in their
3. Par-don for sin and a peace that en-dur-eth, Thy own dear pres-ence to

turn-ing with Thee; Thou chang-est not, Thy com-pas-sions they fail not;
cours-es a-bove Join with all na-ture in man-i-fold wit-ness
cheer and to guide; Strength for to-day and bright hope for to-mor-row,

Chorus

As Thou hast been Thou for-ev-er wilt be.
To Thy great faith-ful-ness, mer-cy and love. Great is Thy faith-ful-ness!
Bless-ings all mine, with ten thou-sand be-side!

Great is Thy faith-ful-ness! Morn-ing by morn-ing new mer-cies I see; All I have

need-ed Thy hand hath pro-vid-ed—Great is Thy faith-ful-ness, Lord, un-to me!

Copyright 1923. Renewal 1951 extended. Hope Publishing Co., owner. All rights reserved.

40 How Big Is God

The heavens shall praise Thy wonders, O Lord. Psa. 89:5

STUART HAMBLEN   STUART HAMBLEN

1. Tho' man may strive to go be-yond the reef of space, To crawl be-
2. As win-ter's chill may cause the ti-ny seed to fall, To lie a-

yond the dis-tant glim-m'ring stars; This world's a room so small with-in my
sleep till waked by sum-mer's rain; The heart grown cold will warm and throb with

Mas-ter's house, The o-pen sky but a por-tion of His yard.
life a-new, The Mas-ter's touch will bring the glow a-gain.

Chorus

How big is God! How big and wide His vast do-main, To try to

tell these lips can on-ly start; He's big e-nough to rule His might-y

© Copyright 1959 by Hamblen Music Company. International copyright secured. All rights reserved. Used by permission.

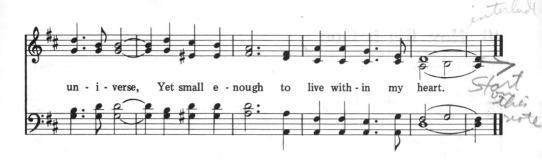

un - i - verse, Yet small e - nough to live with - in my heart.

interlude

Start this note

Jesus, Revealed in Me 41

For me to live is Christ . . . Phil. 1:21

GIPSY SMITH

E. EDWIN YOUNG

1. Christ, the Trans-form-ing Light, Touch-es this heart of mine,
2. Here, Lord, I bring my heart, My love, my strength, my will,
3. Life is no long-er mine, I yield it all to Thee;
4. Tri - um-phant peace is mine, Now Je - sus reigns with - in;

Pierc-ing the dark-est night, Mak-ing His glo-ry shine.
Cleanse me in ev - ery part, With all Thy Spir-it fill.
Fill me, that I may shine, Un til Thy face I see.
He giv-eth joy di - vine, And vic-t'ry o - ver sin.

Chorus

Oh, to re-flect His grace, Caus-ing the world to see
His grace, to see

Love that will glow, till oth - ers shall know Je - sus, re-vealed in me.

Copyright 1931. Renewal 1959. Hope Publishing Co., owner. All rights reserved.

42 His Name is Wonderful

His name shall be called Wonderful . . . Isa. 9:6

AUDREY MIEIR   AUDREY MIEIR

His name is Won-der-ful, His name is Won-der-ful, His name is Won-der-ful, Je-sus, my Lord; He is the might-y King, Mas-ter of ev-ery-thing, His name is Won-der-ful, Je-sus, my Lord.

He's the great Shep-herd, the Rock of all a-ges, Al-might-y God is He; Bow down be-fore Him, Love and a-

© Copyright 1959 by MANNA MUSIC, INC., 2111 Kenmere Ave., Burbank, CA 91504. International copyright secured. All rights reserved. Used by permission.

dore Him,   His   name   is   Won-der-ful,   Je - sus,   my   Lord.

The Threefold Truth   43

Christ both died, and rose . . . that he might be Lord . . . Rom. 14:9

FRED PRATT GREEN

JACK SCHRADER

1. This   is   the   three-fold   truth   On   which   our   faith   de - pends;
2. Made   sa - cred   by   long   use,   New-mint - ed   for   our   time,
3. On   this   we   fix   our   minds   As,   kneel - ing   side   by   side,
4. By   this   we   are   up - held   When doubt   or   grief   as - sails
5. This   is   the   three-fold   truth   Which,   if   we   hold   it   fast,

And   with   this   joy - ful   cry   Wor - ship be - gins   and   ends:
Our   lit - ur - gies   sum   up   The   hope   we   have   in   Him:
We   take   the   bread   and   wine   From   Him,   the   Cru - ci - fied:
Our   Christ - ian   for - ti - tude,   And   on - ly   grace   a - vails:
Chang - es   the   world   and   us,   And   brings   us   home   at   last:

Christ has   died!   Christ   is   ris - en! Christ will   come   a - gain!

Copyright © 1980 by Agape (a division of Hope Publishing Co.). International copyright secured. All rights reserved.

44 Revive Us Again

Wilt Thou not revive us again: that Thy people may rejoice in Thee? Psa. 85:6

WILLIAM P. MACKAY

JOHN J. HUSBAND

1. We praise Thee, O God, for the Son of Thy love, For Je-sus who
2. We praise Thee, O God, for Thy Spir-it of light, Who has shown us our
3. All glo-ry and praise to the Lamb that was slain, Who has borne all our
4. Re-vive us a-gain, fill each heart with Thy love; May each soul be re-

Chorus

died and is now gone a-bove.
Sav-ior and scat-tered our night.
sins, and has cleansed ev-ery stain. Hal-le-lu-jah! Thine the glo-ry, Hal-le-
kin-dled with fire from a-bove.

lu-jah! A-men; Hal-le-lu-jah! Thine the glo-ry; Re-vive us a-gain.

45 O for a Thousand Tongues to Sing

My tongue shall speak of Thy . . . praise all the day long. Psa. 35:28

CHARLES WESLEY

CARL G. GLÄSER
ARR. BY LOWELL MASON

1. O for a thou-sand tongues to sing My great Re-deem-er's praise,
2. Je-sus! the name that charms our fears, That bids our sor-rows cease,
3. He breaks the power of can-celed sin, He sets the pris-oner free;
4. Hear Him, ye deaf; His praise, ye dumb, Your loos-ened tongues em-ploy;
5. My gra-cious Mas-ter and my God, As-sist me to pro-claim,

The glo - ries of my God and King, The tri-umphs of His grace.
'Tis mu - sic in the sin-ner's ears, 'Tis life and health and peace.
His blood can make the foul-est clean; His blood a-vailed for me.
Ye blind, be-hold your Sav - ior come; And leap, ye lame, for joy.
To spread thro' all the earth a - broad, The hon - ors of Thy name. A - men.

Fairest Lord Jesus 46

Thou art fairer than the children of men . . . Psa. 45:2

Gesangbuch, Münster, 1677
Trans. anonymous
St. 4, trans. by Joseph A. Seiss

H. A. Hoffmann von Fallersleben's
Schlesische Volkslieder, 1842
Arr. by Richard S. Willis

1. Fair - est Lord Je - sus! Ru - ler of all na - ture,
2. Fair are the mead - ows, Fair - er still the wood - lands,
3. Fair is the sun - shine, Fair - er still the moon - light,
4. Beau - ti - ful Sav - ior! Lord of the na - tions!

O Thou of God and man the Son! Thee will I cher - ish,
Robed in the bloom - ing garb of spring: Je - sus is fair - er,
And all the twink - ling star - ry host: Je - sus shines bright - er,
Son of God and Son of Man! Glo - ry and hon - or,

Thee will I hon - or, Thou, my soul's glo - ry, joy, and crown!
Je - sus is pur - er, Who makes the woe-ful heart to sing.
Je - sus shines pur - er, Than all the an-gels heav'n can boast.
Praise, ad - o - ra - tion, Now and for - ev - er - more be Thine! A - men.

47 Like a River Glorious

Then had Thy peace been as a river . . . Isa. 48:18

FRANCES R. HAVERGAL

JAMES MOUNTAIN

1. Like a riv-er glo-rious Is God's per-fect peace, O-ver all vic-to-rious
2. Hid-den in the hol-low Of His bless-ed hand, Nev-er foe can fol-low,
3. Ev-ery joy or tri-al Fall-eth from a-bove, Traced up-on our di-al

In its bright in-crease; Per-fect, yet it flow-eth Full-er ev-ery day,
Nev-er trai-tor stand; Not a surge of wor-ry, Not a shade of care,
By the Sun of Love. We may trust Him ful-ly All for us to do;

Chorus

Per-fect, yet it grow-eth Deep-er all the way.
Not a blast of hur-ry Touch the spir-it there. Stayed up-on Je-ho-vah,
They who trust Him whol-ly Find Him whol-ly true.

Hearts are ful-ly blest; Find-ing, as He prom-ised, Per-fect peace and rest.

Copyright used by permission of Marshall, Morgan and Scott.

48 O God, Our Help in Ages Past

Lord, thou hast been our dwelling place in all generations. Psa. 90:1

PSALM 90
ISAAC WATTS

WILLIAM CROFT

1. O God, our help in a-ges past, Our hope for years to come,
2. Un-der the shad-ow of Thy throne Still may we dwell se-cure;
3. Be-fore the hills in or-der stood, Or earth re-ceived her frame,
4. A thou-sand a-ges in Thy sight Are like an eve-ning gone;
5. O God, our help in a-ges past, Our hope for years to come,

Our shel - ter from the storm - y blast, And our e - ter - nal home!
Suf - fi - cient is Thine arm a - lone, And our de - fense is sure.
From ev - er - last - ing Thou art God, To end - less years the same.
Short as the watch that ends the night, Be - fore the ris - ing sun.
Be Thou our guide while life shall last, And our e - ter - nal home! A-men.

Ye Servants of God, Your Master Proclaim 49

Salvation. and glory. and honor. and power. unto the Lord our God. Rev. 19:1

CHARLES WESLEY   WILLIAM CROFT

1. Ye serv - ants of God, your Mas - ter pro - claim, And pub - lish a-
2. God rul - eth on high, al - might - y to save; And still He is
3. Sal - va - tion to God who sits on the throne, Let all cry a
4. Then let us a - dore and give Him His right, All glo - ry and

broad His won - der - ful name; The name all vic - to - rious of
nigh— His pres - ence we have; The great con - gre - ga - tion His
loud, and hon - or the Son; The prais - es of Je - sus the
pow'r, all wis - dom and might; All hon - or and bless - ing, with

Je - sus ex - tol; His king - dom is glo - rious, He rules o - ver all.
tri - umph shall sing, As - crib - ing sal - va - tion to Je - sus our King.
an - gels pro - claim, Fall down on their fac - es and wor - ship the Lamb.
an - gels a - bove, And thanks nev - er ceas - ing, and in - fi - nite love. A - men.

50 Worthy Is the Lamb

Worthy is the Lamb that was slain . . . Rev. 5:12

STEPHEN LEDDY   STEPHEN LEDDY

Unison

1. Wor - thy is the Lamb who died in awe - some grief;
2. Wor - thy is the Lamb who paid the price of death;
3. Wor - thy is the Lamb, though dead all else should be;
4. Wor - thy is the Lamb to live my life a - lone;

Wor - thy is the Lamb who saved a dy - ing thief.
Wor - thy is the Lamb who gave my soul its breath;
Wor - thy is the Lamb to live in you and me;
Wor - thy is the Lamb to make my soul His own,

Wor - thy is the Lamb to make up for my fall; Yes,
Wor - thy is the Lamb to grant my life the call; Yes,
Wor - thy is the Lamb to take our bit - ter gall; Yes,
Wor - thy is the Lamb to change our lives, like Paul; Yes,

wor - thy is the Lamb, praise God, He is all!
wor - thy is the Lamb, praise God, He is all!
wor - thy is the Lamb, praise God, He is all!
wor - thy is the Lamb, praise God, He is all!

Copyright. © 1967. Hope Publishing Co., owner. International copyright secured. All rights reserved.

My Hope Is in the Lord 51

Christ in you, the hope of glory. Col. 1:27

Norman J. Clayton

Norman J. Clayton

1. My hope is in the Lord Who gave Him-self for me,
2. No mer-it of my own His an-ger to sup-press,
3. And now for me He stands Be-fore the Fa-ther's throne,
4. His grace has planned it all, 'Tis mine but to be-lieve,

And paid the price of all my sin at Cal-va-ry.
My on-ly hope is found in Je-sus' right-eous-ness.
He shows His wound-ed hands, and names me as His own.
And rec-og-nize His work of love and Christ re-ceive.

Chorus

For me He died, For me He lives,
For me He died, For me He lives,

And ev-er-last-ing life and light He free-ly gives.

Copyright 1945 by Norman J. Clayton. © Renewed 1973 by Norman Clayton Publishing Co. Used by permission.

52 Rejoice, the Lord Is King

But we see Jesus . . . crowned with glory and honor. Heb. 2:9

CHARLES WESLEY

JOHN DARWALL

1. Re - joice, the Lord is King: Your Lord and King a - dore! Re -
2. Je - sus the Sav - ior reigns, The God of truth and love; When
3. His king - dom can - not fail, He rules o'er earth and heav'n; The
4. Re - joice in glo - rious hope! Our Lord the Judge shall come, And

joice, give thanks, and sing, And tri - umph ev - er - more: Lift up your
He had purged our stains He took His seat a - bove: Lift up your
keys of death and hell Are to our Je - sus giv'n: Lift up your
take his serv - ants up To their e - ter - nal home. Lift up your

heart, lift up your voice! Re - joice, a - gain I say, re - joice!
heart, lift up your voice! Re - joice, a - gain I say, re - joice!
heart, lift up your voice! Re - joice, a - gain I say, re - joice!
heart, lift up your voice! Re - joice, a - gain I say, re - joice! A - men.

53 All People That on Earth Do Dwell

Make a joyful noise unto the Lord, all ye lands. Psa. 100:1

PSALM 100
WILLIAM KETHE

Genevan Psalter, 1551
LOUIS BOURGEOIS

1. All peo - ple that on earth do dwell, Sing to the Lord with cheer - ful voice;
2. The Lord, ye know, is God in - deed; With - out our aid He did us make;
3. O en - ter then His gates with praise, Ap - proach with joy His courts un - to;
4. For why? The Lord our God is good, His mer - cy is for - ev - er sure;

Him serve with fear, His praise forth tell, Come ye be-fore Him and re - joice.
We are His flock, He doth us feed, And for His sheep He doth us take.
Praise, laud, and bless His name al-ways, For it is seem-ly so to do.
His truth at all times firm-ly stood, And shall from age to age en - dure. A-men.

Come, Thou Almighty King 54

Give unto the Lord the glory due unto His name . . . Psa. 29:2

Source unknown

FELICE DE GIARDINI

1. Come, Thou Al - might - y King, Help us Thy name to sing,
2. Come, Thou In - car - nate Word, Gird on Thy might - y sword,
3. Come, Ho - ly Com - fort - er, Thy sa - cred wit - ness bear
4. To Thee, great One in Three, E - ter - nal prais - es be

Help us to praise: Fa - ther, all glo - ri - ous, O'er all vic -
Our prayer at - tend: Come, and Thy peo - ple bless, And give Thy
In this glad hour: Thou who al - might - y art, Now rule in
Hence, ev - er - more! Thy sov - ereign maj - es - ty May we in

to - ri - ous, Come, and reign o - ver us, An - cient of Days.
word suc - cess: Spir - it of ho - li - ness, On us de - scend.
ev - ery heart, And ne'er from us de - part, Spir - it of pow'r.
glo - ry see, And to e - ter - ni - ty Love and a - dore! A - men.

55 Holy, Holy, Holy!

Holy, holy, holy, Lord God almighty. Rev. 4:8

REGINALD HEBER   JOHN B. DYKES

1. Ho - ly, ho - ly, ho - ly! Lord God Al - might - y!
2. Ho - ly, ho - ly, ho - ly! all the saints a - dore Thee,
3. Ho - ly, ho - ly, ho - ly! though the dark - ness hide Thee,
4. Ho - ly, ho - ly, ho - ly! Lord God Al - might - y!

Ear - ly in the morn - ing our song shall rise to Thee;
Cast - ing down their gold - en crowns a - round the glass - y sea;
Though the eye of sin - ful man Thy glo - ry may not see,
All Thy works shall praise Thy name, in earth, and sky, and sea;

Ho - ly, ho - ly, ho - ly! mer - ci - ful and might - y!
Cher - u - bim and ser - a - phim fall - ing down be - fore Thee,
On - ly Thou art ho - ly; there is none be - side Thee,
Ho - ly, ho - ly, ho - ly! mer - ci - ful and might - y!

God in three per - sons, bless - ed Trin - i - ty!
Which wert and art, and ev - er - more shalt be.
Per - fect in pow'r, in love, and pu - ri - ty.
God in three per - sons, bless - ed Trin - i - ty! A - men.

Love Divine, All Loves Excelling 56

Above all these things put on charity, which is the bond of perfectness. Col. 3:14

CHARLES WESLEY

JOHN ZUNDEL

1. Love di - vine, all loves ex - cel - ling, Joy of heav'n, to earth come down;
2. Breathe, O breathe Thy lov - ing Spir - it In - to ev - ery trou-bled breast!
3. Come, Al - might - y to de - liv - er, Let us all Thy life re - ceive;
4. Fin - ish then Thy new cre - a - tion, Pure and spot-less let us be;

Fix in us Thy hum - ble dwell-ing, All Thy faith - ful mer-cies crown
Let us all in Thee in - her - it, Let us find the prom-ised rest.
Sud - den - ly re - turn, and nev - er, Nev - er - more Thy tem-ples leave:
Let us see Thy great sal - va - tion Per - fect - ly re - stored in Thee:

Je - sus, Thou art all com - pas - sion, Pure, un-bound-ed love Thou art;
Take a - way the love of sin - ning, Al - pha and O - me - ga be;
Thee we would be al - ways bless-ing, Serve Thee as Thy hosts a - bove,
Changed from glo - ry in - to glo - ry, Till in heav'n we take our place,

Vis - it us with Thy sal - va - tion; En - ter ev - ery trem-bling heart.
End of faith, as its be - gin - ning, Set our hearts at lib - er - ty.
Pray, and praise Thee with-out ceas-ing, Glo - ry in Thy per-fect love.
Till we cast our crowns be-fore Thee, Lost in won-der, love, and praise. A-men.

57 And Can It Be That I Should Gain

While we were yet sinners, Christ died for us. Rom. 5:8

CHARLES WESLEY

THOMAS CAMPBELL

1. And can it be that I should gain An in - t'rest in the
2. 'Tis mys - tery all! Th' Im - mor - tal dies! Who can ex - plore His
3. He left His Fa - ther's throne a - bove, So free, so in - fi -
4. Long my im - pris - oned spir - it lay Fast bound in sin and
5. No con - dem - na - tion now I dread; Je - sus, and all in

Sav - ior's blood? Died He for me, who caused His pain? For me, who
strange de - sign? In vain the first - born ser - aph tries To sound the
nite His grace; Emp - tied Him - self of all but love, And bled for
na - ture's night; Thine eye dif - fused a quick-'ning ray, I woke, the
Him, is mine! A - live in Him, my liv - ing Head, And clothed in

Him to death pur - sued? A - maz - ing love! how can it be That
depths of love di - vine! 'Tis mer - cy all! let earth a - dore, Let
Ad - am's help - less race; 'Tis mer - cy all, im - mense and free; For,
dun - geon flamed with light; My chains fell off, my heart was free; I
right - eous - ness di - vine, Bold I ap - proach th'e - ter - nal throne, And

Chorus

Thou, my God, shouldst die for me?
an - gel minds in - quire no more.
rose, went forth and fol - lowed Thee. A - maz - ing love! how
claim the crown, through Christ my own. A - maz - ing love!

can it be That Thou, my God, shouldst die for me. A - men.

How can it be That Thou, my God,

No Other Plea 58

While we were yet sinners, Christ died for us. Rom. 5:8

LIDIE H. EDMUNDS

Norse melody
ARR. BY WILLIAM J. KIRKPATRICK

1. My faith has found a rest - ing place, Not in de - vice nor creed;
2. E - nough for me that Je - sus saves, This ends my fear and doubt;
3. My heart is lean - ing on the Word, The writ - ten Word of God,
4. My great Phy - si - cian heals the sick, The lost He came to save,

I trust the Ev - er - liv - ing One, His wounds for me shall plead.
A sin - ful soul I come to Him, He'll nev - er cast me out.
Sal - va - tion by my Sav - ior's name, Sal - va - tion through His blood.
For me His pre - cious blood He shed, For me His life He gave.

Chorus

I need no oth - er ar - gu - ment, I need no oth - er plea,

It is e - nough that Je - sus died, And that He died for me.

59 Praise Him! Praise Him!

Praise Him according to His excellent greatness. Psa. 150:2

FANNY J. CROSBY   CHESTER G. ALLEN

1. Praise Him! praise Him! Je - sus, our bless - ed Re - deem - er! Sing, O Earth, His
2. Praise Him! praise Him! Je - sus, our bless - ed Re - deem - er! For our sins He
3. Praise Him! praise Him! Je - sus, our bless - ed Re - deem - er! Heav'n - ly por - tals

won - der - ful love pro - claim! Hail Him! hail Him! high - est arch - an - gels in glo - ry;
suf - fered, and bled and died; He our Rock, our hope of e - ter - nal sal - va - tion,
loud with ho - san - nas ring! Je - sus, Sav - ior, reign - eth for - ev - er and ev - er;

Strength and hon - or give to His ho - ly name! Like a shep - herd Je - sus will
Hail Him! hail Him! Je - sus the Cru - ci - fied. Sound His prais - es! Je - sus who
Crown Him! crown Him! Proph - et and Priest and King! Christ is com - ing! o - ver the

Chorus

guard His chil - dren, In His arms He car - ries them all day long:
bore our sor - rows; Love un - bound - ed, won - der - ful, deep and strong: Praise Him! praise Him!
world vic - to - rious, Pow'r and glo - ry un - to the Lord be - long:

tell of His ex - cel - lent great - ness; Praise Him! praise Him! ev - er in joy - ful song!

O Worship the King, All Glorious Above 60

O Lord my God . . . Thou art clothed with honor and majesty. Psa. 104:1

PSALM 104
WILLIAM KETHE
ADAPT. BY ROBERT H. GRANT

William Gardiner's *Sacred Melodies,* 1815
ARR. FROM JOHANN M. HAYDN

1. O wor - ship the King, all glo - rious a - bove, O grate - ful - ly
2. O tell of His might, O sing of His grace, Whose robe is the
3. Thy boun - ti - ful care what tongue can re - cite? It breathes in the
4. Frail chil - dren of dust, and fee - ble as frail, In Thee do we

sing His pow'r and His love; Our Shield and De - fend - er, the An - cient of
light, whose can - o - py space. His char - iots of wrath the deep thun - der clouds
air, it shines in the light; It streams from the hills, it de - scends to the
trust, nor find Thee to fail; Thy mer - cies how ten - der! how firm to the

Days, Pa - vil - ioned in splen - dor and gird - ed with praise.
form, And dark is His path on the wings of the storm.
plain, And sweet - ly dis - tills in the dew and the rain.
end! Our Mak - er, De - fend - er, Re - deem - er and Friend. A - men.

61 The Lord's Prayer

After this manner therefore pray ye . . . Matt. 6:9

ALBERT HAY MALOTTE
ARR. BY FRED BOCK

MATT. 6:9-13

Our Fa - ther, which art in heav - en, hal - low - ed
be Thy name. Thy king-dom come,
Thy will be done on earth as it is in
heav - en. Give us this day our dai - ly bread, and for-

Copyright 1935 G. Schirmer. Inc. Used by permission.

give us our debts as we for- give our debt - ors. And

lead us not in - to temp - ta - tion, but de - liv - er us from

e - vil, for Thine is the King-dom and the Pow - er and the

Glo - ry, for - ev - er. A - men.

62 I Will Praise Him

Worthy is the Lamb that was slain . . . Rev. 5:12

MARGARET J. HARRIS

MARGARET J. HARRIS

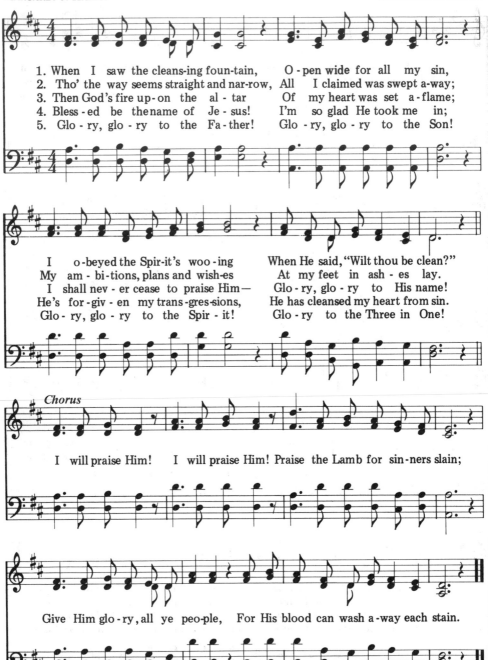

1. When I saw the cleans-ing foun-tain, O - pen wide for all my sin,
2. Tho' the way seems straight and nar-row, All I claimed was swept a-way;
3. Then God's fire up-on the al - tar Of my heart was set a-flame;
4. Bless - ed be the name of Je - sus! I'm so glad He took me in;
5. Glo - ry, glo - ry to the Fa-ther! Glo - ry, glo - ry to the Son!

I o-beyed the Spir-it's woo-ing When He said, "Wilt thou be clean?"
My am - bi-tions, plans and wish-es At my feet in ash - es lay.
I shall nev - er cease to praise Him— Glo - ry, glo - ry to His name!
He's for-giv - en my trans-gres-sions, He has cleansed my heart from sin.
Glo - ry, glo - ry to the Spir - it! Glo - ry to the Three in One!

Chorus

I will praise Him! I will praise Him! Praise the Lamb for sin-ners slain;

Give Him glo-ry, all ye peo-ple, For His blood can wash a-way each stain.

O Thou God of My Salvation 63

Thou art the God of my salvation . . . Psa. 25:5

Thomas Olivers

Daniel B. Towner

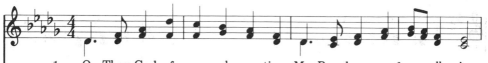

1. O Thou God of my sal - va - tion, My Re - deem - er from all sin;
2. Though un - seen, I love the Sav - ior, He hath brought sal - va - tion near;
3. While the an - gel choirs are cry - ing, "Glo - ry to the great I Am,"
4. An - gels now are hov - 'ring round us, Un - per - ceived a - mong the throng;

Moved by Thy di - vine com - pas - sion, Who hast died my heart to win;
Man - i - fests His pard - 'ning fa - vor; And when Je - sus doth ap - pear,
I with them will still be vy - ing—Glo - ry, glo - ry to the Lamb!
Won - d'ring at the love that crowned us, Glad to sing the ho - ly song;

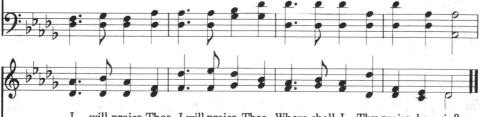

I will praise Thee, I will praise Thee, Where shall I Thy praise be - gin?
Soul and bod - y, soul and bod - y Shall His glo - rious im - age bear;
Oh, how pre - cious, oh, how pre - cious Is the sound of Je - sus' name!
Hal - le - lu - jah, hal - le - lu - jah, Love and praise to Christ be - long!

I will praise Thee, I will praise Thee, Where shall I Thy praise be - gin?
Soul and bod - y, soul and bod - y Shall His glo - rious im - age bear.
Oh, how pre - cious, oh, how pre - cious Is the sound of Je - sus' name!
Hal - le - lu - jah, hal - le - lu - jah, Love and praise to Christ be - long!

Copyright 1913. Renewal 1941 extended. Hope Publishing Co.. owner. All rights reserved.

64 To God Be the Glory

Give unto the Lord the glory due unto His name. Psa. 29:2

FANNY J. CROSBY

WILLIAM H. DOANE

1. To God be the glo-ry, great things He hath done, So loved He the world that He
2. O per-fect re-demp-tion, the pur-chase of blood, To ev-ery be-liev-er the
3. Great things He hath taught us, great things He hath done, And great our re-joic-ing thro'

gave us His Son, Who yield-ed His life an a-tone-ment for sin, And o-pened the
prom-ise of God; The vil-est of-fend-er who tru-ly be-lieves, That mo-ment from
Je-sus the Son; But pur-er, and high-er, and great-er will be Our won-der, our

Chorus

Life-gate that all may go in.
Je-sus a par-don re-ceives. Praise the Lord, praise the Lord, Let the earth hear His
trans-port, when Je-sus we see.

voice! Praise the Lord, praise the Lord, Let the peo-ple re-joice! O come to the

Fa-ther thro' Je-sus the Son, And give Him the glo-ry, great things He hath done.

Lord, We Praise You 65

Praise ye the Lord. Psa. 150:1

OTIS SKILLINGS   OTIS SKILLINGS

1. Lord, we praise You, Lord, we praise You; Lord, we praise You, We praise You, Lord.
2. Lord, we love You, Lord, we love You; Lord, we love You, We love You, Lord.
3. Al - le - lu - ia! Al - le - lu - ia! Al - le - lu - ia! We praise You, Lord.

© 1976 by Lillenas Publishing Co. All rights reserved. Used by permission.

Majestic Sweetness Sits Enthroned 66

But we see Jesus . . . crowned with glory and honor. Heb. 2:9

SAMUEL STENNETT   THOMAS HASTINGS

1. Ma - jes - tic sweet - ness sits en - throned Up - on the Sav - ior's
2. No mor - tal can with Him com - pare, A - mong the sons of
3. He saw me plunged in deep dis - tress, He flew to my re -
4. To Him I owe my life and breath, And all the joys I
5. Since from His boun - ty I re - ceive Such proofs of love di -

brow; His head with ra - diant glo - ries crowned, His
men; Fair - er is He than all the fair That
lief; For me He bore the shame - ful cross And
have; He makes me tri - umph o - ver death, And
vine, Had I a thou - sand hearts to give, Lord,

lips with grace o'er - flow, His lips with grace o'er - flow.
fill the heav'n - ly train, That fill the heav'n - ly train.
car - ried all my grief, And car - ried all my grief.
saves me from the grave, And saves me from the grave.
they should all be Thine, Lord, they should all be Thine. A-men.

67 Jesus Is Lord of All

For he is Lord of lords, and King of kings . . . Rev. 17:14

GLORIA GAITHER AND
WILLIAM J. GAITHER

WILLIAM GAITHER

1. All my to-mor-rows, all my past, Je-sus is Lord of
2. All of my con-flicts, all my thoughts, Je-sus is Lord of
3. All of my long-ings, all my dreams, Je-sus is Lord of

all. I've quit my strug-gles, con-tent-ment at last,
all. His love wins the bat-tles I could not have fought,
all. All of my fail-ures His pow-er re-deems,

Chorus

Je - sus is Lord of all.
Je - sus is Lord of all. King of kings, Lord of lords,
Je - sus is Lord of all.

Je - sus is Lord of all; All my pos-sess-ions and

all my life, Je - sus is Lord of all.

© Copyright 1973 by William J. Gaither. International copyright secured. All rights reserved. Used by permission.

Come, We That Love the Lord 68

Praise the Lord! Sing to the Lord a new song . . . Psa. 149:1

ISAAC WATTS

AARON WILLIAMS

1. Come, we that love the Lord, And let our joys be known; Join
2. Let those re - fuse to sing Who nev - er knew our God; But
3. The men of grace have found Glo - ry be - gun be - low; Ce -
4. The hill of Zi - on yields A thou - sand sa - cred sweets Be -
5. Then let our songs a - bound, And ev - ery tear be dry; We're

in a song with sweet ac - cord, And thus sur - round the throne.
chil - dren of the heav'n - ly King May speak their joys a - broad.
les - tial fruit on earth - ly ground From faith and hope may grow.
fore we reach the heav'n - ly fields, Or walk the gold - en streets.
march - ing thro' Em - man - uel's ground To fair - er worlds on high. A - men.

How Sweet the Name of Jesus Sounds 69

Unto you therefore which believe He is precious . . . 1 Pet. 2:7

JOHN NEWTON

ALEXANDER R. REINAGLE

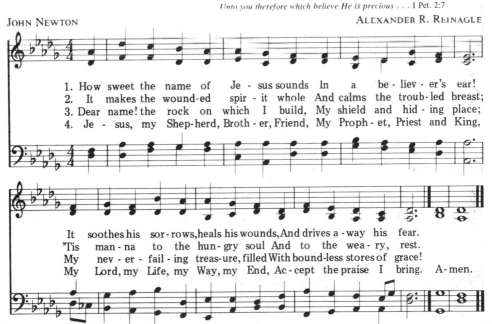

1. How sweet the name of Je - sus sounds In a be - liev - er's ear!
2. It makes the wound-ed spir - it whole And calms the troub-led breast;
3. Dear name! the rock on which I build, My shield and hid - ing place;
4. Je - sus, my Shep-herd, Broth - er, Friend, My Proph - et, Priest and King,

It soothes his sor - rows, heals his wounds, And drives a - way his fear.
'Tis man - na to the hun-gry soul And to the wea - ry, rest.
My nev - er - fail - ing treas-ure, filled With bound-less stores of grace!
My Lord, my Life, my Way, my End, Ac - cept the praise I bring. A - men.

70 The Name of Jesus

Wherefore God also hath . . . given Him a name which is above every name. Phil. 2:9

W. C. MARTIN

EDMUND S. LORENZ

1. The name of Je - sus is so sweet, I love its mu - sic to re-peat;
2. I love the name of Him whose heart Knows all my griefs and bears a part;
3. That name I fond - ly love to hear, It nev - er fails my heart to cheer;
4. No word of man can ev - er tell How sweet the name I love so well;

It makes my joys full and com-plete, The pre-cious name of Je - sus!
Who bids all anx - ious fears de-part I love the name of Je - sus!
Its mu - sic dries the fall - ing tear Ex-alt the name of Je - sus!
O let its prais - es ev - er swell, O praise the name of Je - sus!
The pre-cious name

Chorus

"Je - sus"—O how sweet the name, "Je - sus" ev - ery day the same;

"Je - sus"—let all saints pro-claim Its wor-thy praise for - ev - er!
Its wor - thy praise

There's Something About That Name 71

Thou shalt call His name Jesus . . . Matt. 1:23

GLORIA GAITHER AND
WILLIAM J. GAITHER

WILLIAM J. GAITHER

Je - sus, Je - sus, Je - sus; There's just some - thing a - bout that

name! Mas - ter, Sav - ior, Je - sus, Like the fra - grance

af - ter the rain; Je - sus, Je - sus, Je - sus, Let all

Heav - en and earth pro - claim: Kings and king-doms will

all pass a - way, But there's some - thing a - bout that name!

© Copyright 1970 by William J. Gaither. International copyright secured. All rights reserved. Used by permission.

72 The Unveiled Christ

And the veil of the temple was rent in the midst. Luke 23:45

N. B. HERRELL

N. B. HERRELL

1. Once our bless-ed Christ of beau - ty   Was veiled off from hu - man view;
2. Now He is with God the Fa - ther, In - ter - ced - ing there for you;
3. Ho - ly an - gels bow be-fore Him, Men of earth give prais - es   due;
4. Thro'-out time and end - less a - ges, Heights and depths of love so true;

But thro' suf-f'ring, death and sor - row He has rent the veil in two.
For He is the might - y con-qu'ror Since He rent the veil in two.
For He is the well - be - lov - ed Since He rent the veil in two.
He a - lone can be the giv - er Since He rent the veil in two.

Chorus

O be -hold the Man of Sor - rows, O be -hold Him in plain view;

Lo! He is the might - y con - qu'ror, Since He rent the veil in two.

Lo! He is the might - y con - qu'ror, Since He rent the veil in two.

Copyright 1916. Renewed 1944 by Nazarene Publishing House. Used by permission.

I Love Thy Kingdom, Lord 73

Lord, I have loved the habitation of Thy house. Psa. 26:8

TIMOTHY DWIGHT

AARON WILLIAMS

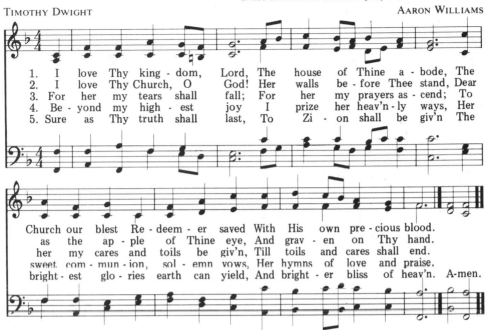

1. I love Thy king-dom, Lord, The house of Thine a-bode, The
2. I love Thy Church, O God! Her walls be-fore Thee stand, Dear
3. For her my tears shall fall; For her my prayers as-cend; To
4. Be-yond my high-est joy I prize her heav'n-ly ways, Her
5. Sure as Thy truth shall last, To Zi-on shall be giv'n The

Church our blest Re-deem-er saved With His own pre-cious blood.
as the ap-ple of Thine eye, And grav-en on Thy hand.
her my cares and toils be giv'n, Till toils and cares shall end.
sweet com-mun-ion, sol-emn vows, Her hymns of love and praise.
bright-est glo-ries earth can yield, And bright-er bliss of heav'n. A-men.

Blest Be the Tie That Binds 74

For ye are all one in Christ Jesus. Gal. 3:28

JOHANN G. NAGELI
ARR. BY LOWELL MASON

JOHN FAWCETT

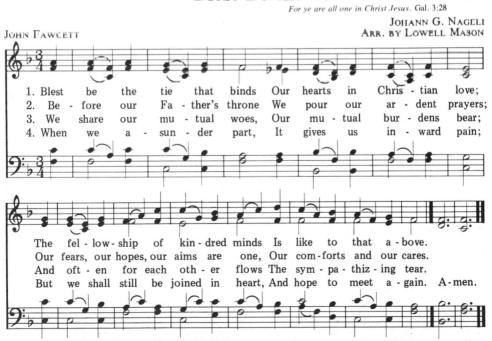

1. Blest be the tie that binds Our hearts in Chris-tian love;
2. Be-fore our Fa-ther's throne We pour our ar-dent prayers;
3. We share our mu-tual woes, Our mu-tual bur-dens bear;
4. When we a-sun-der part, It gives us in-ward pain;

The fel-low-ship of kin-dred minds Is like to that a-bove.
Our fears, our hopes, our aims are one, Our com-forts and our cares.
And oft-en for each oth-er flows The sym-pa-thiz-ing tear.
But we shall still be joined in heart, And hope to meet a-gain. A-men.

75 The Family of God

And ye shall be my sons and daughters, saith the Lord Almighty. II Cor. 6:18

GLORIA GAITHER AND
WILLIAM J. GAITHER

WILLIAM J. GAITHER

I'm so glad I'm a part of the fam-ily of

God—I've been washed in the foun-tain, cleansed by His blood!

Joint heirs with Je-sus as we trav-el this sod, For I'm

Fine

part of the fam-ily, the fam-ily of God.

© Copyright 1970 by William J. Gaither. International copyright secured. All rights reserved. Used by permission.

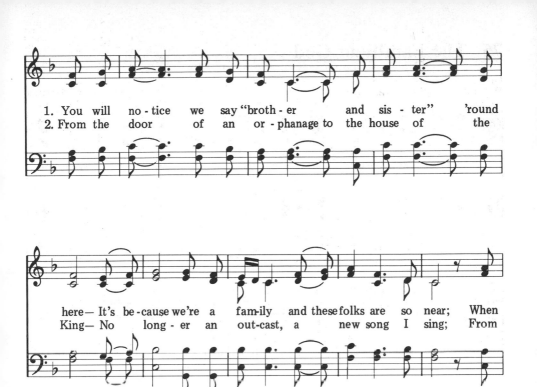

1. You will no-tice we say "broth-er and sis-ter" 'round
2. From the door of an or-phanage to the house of the

here— It's be-cause we're a fam-ily and these folks are so near; When
King— No long-er an out-cast, a new song I sing; From

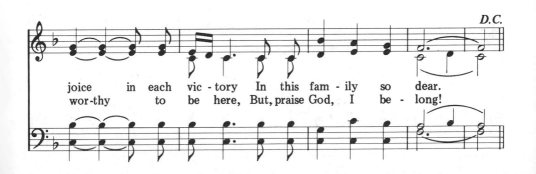

one has a heart-ache we all share the tears, And re-
rags un-to rich-es, from the weak to the strong, I'm not

D.C.

joice in each vic-tory In this fam-i-ly so dear.
wor-thy to be here, But, praise God, I be - long!

76 Glorious Things of Thee Are Spoken

Glorious things are spoken of thee, O city of God. Psa. 87:3

JOHN NEWTON   FRANZ JOSEPH HAYDN

1. Glo - rious things of thee are spo - ken, Zi - on, cit - y of our God;
2. See the streams of liv - ing wa - ters, Spring-ing from e - ter-nal love,
3. Round each hab - i - ta - tion hov-ering, See the cloud and fire ap - pear
4. Sav - ior, if of Zi - on's cit - y, I through grace a mem-ber am,

He whose word can - not be bro - ken Formed thee for His own a - bode;
Well sup - ply thy sons and daugh-ters, And all fear of want re - move:
For a glo - ry and a cov - ering, Show - ing that the Lord is near!
Let the world de - ride or pit - y, I will glo - ry in Thy name;

On the Rock of A - ges found-ed, What can shake thy sure re - pose?
Who can faint, while such a riv - er Ev - er will their thirst as - suage?
Thus de - riv - ing from their ban - ner Light by night and shade by day;
Fad - ing is the world's best pleas-ure, All its boast-ed pomp and show;

With sal - va - tion's walls sur-round-ed, Thou mayst smile at all thy foes.
Grace which, like the Lord, the Giv - er, Nev - er fails from age to age.
Safe they feed up - on the man - na Which He gives them when they pray.
Sol - id joys and last - ing treas-ure None but Zi - on's chil-dren know. A-men.

Other foundation can no man lay than that is laid . . . Jesus Christ. I Cor. 3:11

SAMUEL J. STONE

SAMUEL S. WESLEY

1. The Church's one foun-da-tion Is Je-sus Christ her Lord;
2. E-lect from ev-ery na-tion, Yet one o'er all the earth,
3. Though with a scorn-ful won-der Men see her sore op-pressed,
4. 'Mid toil and trib-u-la-tion, And tu-mult of her war,
5. Yet she on earth hath un-ion With God, the Three in One,

She is His new cre-a-tion, By wa-ter and the word:
Her char-ter of sal-va-tion, One Lord, one faith, one birth;
By schisms rent a-sun-der, By her-e-sies dis-tressed:
She waits the con-sum-ma-tion Of peace for-ev-er-more;
And mys-tic sweet com-mun-ion With those whose rest is won:

From heav'n He came and sought her To be His ho-ly bride;
One ho-ly name she bless-es, Par-takes one ho-ly food,
Yet saints their watch are keep-ing, Their cry goes up, "How long?"
Till with the vi-sion glo-rious Her long-ing eyes are blest,
O hap-py ones and ho-ly! Lord, give us grace that we,

With His own blood He bought her, And for her life He died.
And to one hope she press-es, With ev-ery grace en-dued.
And soon the night of weep-ing Shall be the morn of song.
And the great Church vic-to-rious Shall be the Church at rest.
Like them, the meek and low-ly, On high may dwell with Thee. A-men.

78 Sweet, Sweet Spirit

Behold, how good and how pleasant it is for brethren to dwell together in unity! Psa. 133:1

DORIS AKERS   DORIS AKERS

1. There's a sweet, sweet Spir - it in this place, And I
2. There are bless - ings you can - not re - ceive Till you

know that it's the Spir - it of the Lord; There are
know Him in His full - ness, and be - lieve. You're the

sweet ex - pres - sions on each face, And I
one to pro - fit when you say, "I am

know they feel the pres - ence of the Lord.
going to walk with Je - sus all the way."

© Copyright 1962 by MANNA MUSIC, INC., 2111 Kenmere Ave., Burbank, CA 91504. International copyright secured. All rights reserved. Used by permission.

Chorus

Sweet Ho - ly Spir - it, Sweet heav-en-ly Dove, Stay right here

with us, Fill - ing us with your love, And for these

bless - ings we lift our hearts in praise; With-out a

doubt we'll know that we have been re - vived When we shall leave this place.

79 Come, Holy Spirit

In the last days . . . I will pour out of my Spirit upon all flesh. Acts 2:17

JOHN W. PETERSON   JOHN W. PETERSON

1. The Ho - ly Spir - it came at Pen - te - cost, He came in
   The ear - ly Chris-tians scat - tered o'er the world, They preached the
2. Then in an age when dark - ness gripped the earth, "The just shall
   In lat - er years the great re - viv - als came, When saints would

1. might - y full - ness then; His wit - ness thro' be - liev - ers won the lost,
   Gos - pel fear - less - ly; Tho' some were mar - tyred and to li - ons hurled,
2. live by faith" was learned; The Ho - ly Spir - it gave the Church new birth
   seek the Lord and pray; O, once a - gain we need that ho - ly flame

1
1. And mul - ti - tudes were born a - gain.
2. As ref - or - ma - tion fires burned.

2
They marched a - long in vic - to - ry!
To meet the chal - lenge of to - day!

Chorus

Come, Ho - ly Spir - it, Dark is the hour, We need your fill - ing, Your

love and your might - y pow'r; Move now a - mong us, Stir us, we

© Copyright 1971 by Singspiration, Inc. Arr. © 1979 by Singspiration, Division of The Zondervan Corporation. All rights reserved. Used by permission.

pray, Come, Ho - ly Spir - it, Re - vive the church to - day!

Coda

Re - vive the church to - day! Re - vive the church to - day!

Breathe on Me, Breath of God 80

He breathed on them, and saith, Receive ye the Holy Ghost. John 20:22

EDWIN HATCH

ROBERT JACKSON

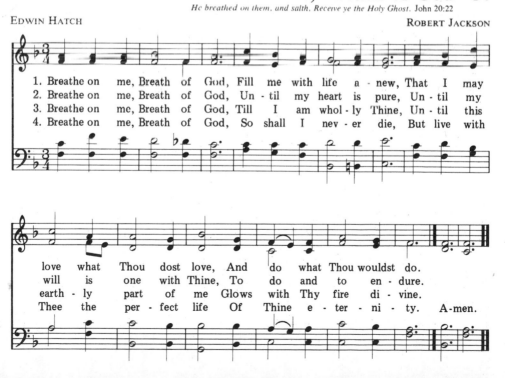

1. Breathe on me, Breath of God, Fill me with life a - new, That I may
2. Breathe on me, Breath of God, Un - til my heart is pure, Un - til my
3. Breathe on me, Breath of God, Till I am whol - ly Thine, Un - til this
4. Breathe on me, Breath of God, So shall I nev - er die, But live with

love what Thou dost love, And do what Thou wouldst do.
will is one with Thine, To do and to en - dure.
earth - ly part of me Glows with Thy fire di - vine.
Thee the per - fect life Of Thine e - ter - ni - ty. A - men.

81 Holy Spirit, Faithful Guide

For as many as are led by the Spirit of God . . . Rom. 8:14

MARCUS M. WELLS

MARCUS M. WELLS

1. { Ho - ly Spir - it, faith - ful Guide, Ev - er near the Chris-tian's side;
   { Gen - tly lead us by the hand, Pil-grims in a des - ert land;

2. { Ev - er pres - ent, tru - est Friend, Ev - er near Thine aid to lend,
   { Leave us not to doubt and fear, Grop-ing on in dark-ness drear;

3. { When our days of toil shall cease, Wait-ing still for sweet re - lease,
   { Noth-ing left but heav'n and prayer, Won-d'ring if our names were there;

Wea - ry souls for - e'er re - joice, While they hear that sweet - est voice,
When the storms are rag - ing sore, Hearts grow faint, and hopes give o'er.
Wad - ing deep the dis - mal flood, Plead - ing naught but Je - sus' blood,

Whis-p'ring soft - ly, "Wan -d'rer, come! Fol - low Me, I'll guide thee home."
Whis - per soft - ly, "Wan -d'rer, come! Fol - low Me, I'll guide thee home."
Whis - per soft - ly, "Wan -d'rer, come! Fol - low Me, I'll guide thee home."

82 Holy Spirit, Light Divine

He . . . shall also quicken your mortal bodies by His Spirit. Rom. 8:11

LOUIS M. GOTTSCHALK
ARR. BY EDWIN P. PARKER

ANDREW REED, ALT.

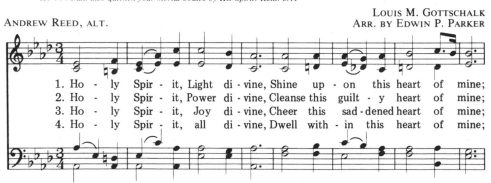

1. Ho - ly Spir - it, Light di - vine, Shine up - on this heart of mine;
2. Ho - ly Spir - it, Power di - vine, Cleanse this guilt - y heart of mine;
3. Ho - ly Spir - it, Joy di - vine, Cheer this sad -dened heart of mine;
4. Ho - ly Spir - it, all di - vine, Dwell with - in this heart of mine;

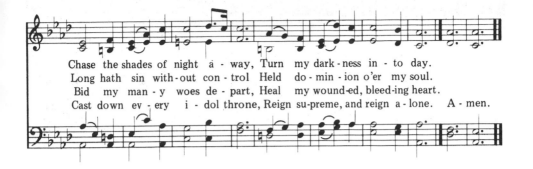

Chase the shades of night a - way, Turn my dark - ness in - to day.
Long hath sin with-out con - trol Held do - min - ion o'er my soul.
Bid my man - y woes de - part, Heal my wound-ed, bleed-ing heart.
Cast down ev - ery i - dol throne, Reign su-preme, and reign a - lone. A - men.

Spirit of the Living God 83

I will pour out in those days of my Spirit . . . Acts 2:18

DANIEL IVERSON   DANIEL IVERSON

Spir - it of the liv - ing God, Fall fresh on me. Spir - it of the

liv - ing God, Fall fresh on me. Melt me, mold me, fill me,

use me. Spir - it of the liv - ing God, Fall fresh on me.

Copyright 1935. Renewal 1963 by Daniel Iverson.
Assigned to Moody Bible Institute. Moody Press. Used by permission.

84 Bring Your Vessels, Not a Few

Go, borrow thee vessels . . . borrow not a few. II Kings 4:3

LELIA N. MORRIS

LELIA N. MORRIS

1. Are you look-ing for the full-ness of the bless-ing of the Lord
2. Bring your emp-ty earth-en ves-sels, clean thro' Je-sus' pre-cious blood,
3. Like the cruse of oil un-fail-ing is. His grace for-ev-er-more,

In your heart and life to-day? Claim the prom-ise of your Fa-ther,
Come, ye need-y, one and all; And in hu-man con-se-cra-tion
And His love un-chang-ing still; And ac-cord-ing to His prom-ise

come ac-cord-ing to His word, in the bless-ed old time way.
wait be-fore the throne of God, 'Till the Ho-ly Ghost shall fall.
with the Ho-ly Ghost and pow'r, He will ev-'ry ves-sel fill.

Chorus

He will fill your heart to-day to o-ver-flow-ing, As the
Lord com-mand-eth you, "Bring your ves-sels, not a few;" He will

Copyright 1912. Renewal 1940 extended. Hope Publishing Co., owner. All rights reserved.

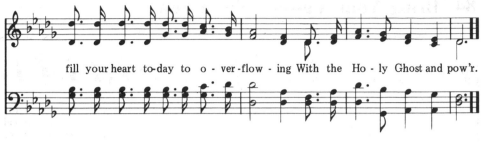

fill your heart to-day to o - ver-flow - ing With the Ho - ly Ghost and pow'r.

Fill Me Now 85

. . . Be filled with the Spirit. Eph. 5:18

ELWOOD H. STOKES

JOHN R. SWENEY

1. Hov - er o'er me, Ho - ly Spir - it, Bathe my trem - bling heart and brow;
2. Thou canst fill me, gra - cious Spir - it, Though I can - not tell Thee how;
3. I am weak - ness, full of weak - ness, At Thy sa - cred feet I bow;
4. Cleanse and com - fort, bless and save me, Bathe, O bathe my heart and brow;

Fill me with Thy hal - lowed pres - ence, Come, O come and fill me now.
But I need Thee, great - ly need Thee, Come, O come and fill me now.
Blest di - vine, e - ter - nal Spir - it, Fill with pow'r and fill me now.
Thou art com - fort - ing and sav - ing, Thou art sweet - ly fill - ing now.

Chorus

Fill me now, fill me now, Je - sus, come and fill me now;

Fill me with Thy hal - lowed pres - ence, Come, O come and fill me now.

86 Blessed Quietness

He shall give you another Comforter, that He may abide with you forever. John 14:16

MANIE P. FERGUSON

W. S. MARSHALL
ARR. BY JAMES M. KIRK

1. Joys are flow-ing like a riv-er, Since the Com-fort-er has come;
2. Bring-ing life and health and glad-ness, All a-round this heav'n-ly Guest,
3. Like the rain that falls from heav-en, Like the sun-light from the sky,
4. See, a fruit-ful field is grow-ing, Bless-ed fruit of right-eous-ness;
5. What a won-der-ful sal-va-tion, Where we al-ways see His face!

He a-bides with us for-ev-er, Makes the trust-ing heart His home.
Ban-ished un-be-lief and sad-ness, Changed our wea-ri-ness to rest.
So the Ho-ly Ghost is giv-en, Com-ing on us from on high.
And the streams of life are flow-ing In the lone-ly wil-der-ness.
What a per-fect hab-i-ta-tion, What a qui-et rest-ing place!

Chorus

Bless-ed qui-et-ness, ho-ly qui-et-ness, What as-sur-ance in my soul!

On the storm-y sea He speaks peace to me, How the bil-lows cease to roll!

Turn Your Eyes upon Jesus 87

Look unto Me, and be ye saved, all the ends of the earth. Isa. 45:22

Helen H. Lemmel   Helen H. Lemmel

1. O soul, are you wea-ry and troub-led? No light in the
2. Through death in-to life ev-er-last-ing He passed,and we
3. His word shall not fail you— He prom-ised; Be-lieve Him and

dark-ness you see? There's light for a look at the Sav-ior,
fol-low Him there; O-ver us sin no more hath do-min-ion—
all will be well: Then go to a world that is dy-ing,

And life more a-bun-dant and free!
For more than con-qu'rors we are!
His per-fect sal-va-tion to tell!

Chorus

Turn your eyes up-on Je-sus, Look full in His won-der-ful face; And the things of

earth will grow strange-ly dim In the light of His glo-ry and grace.

Copyright 1922. Renewal 1950 by H. H. Lemmel. Assigned to Singspiration, Inc. All rights reserved. Used by permission.

88 Heavenly Father, We Appreciate You

My soul doth magnify the Lord . . . Luke 1:46

Source Unknown   Source Unknown

1. Heav'n-ly Fa-ther, we ap-pre-ci-ate You; Heav'n-ly
2. Son of God, we mag-ni-fy You; Son of
3. Ho-ly Spir-it, what a com-fort You are; Ho-ly

Fa-ther, we ap-pre-ci-ate You. We
God, we mag-ni-fy You. You've
Spir-it, what a com-fort You are. You

love You, a-dore You, We bow down be-fore You;
saved us from sin, gave a new life with-in;
lead us, You guide us, You dwell right in-side us;

Heav'n-ly Fa-ther, we ap-pre-ci-ate You.
Son of God, we mag-ni-fy You.
Ho-ly Spir-it, what a com-fort You are.

Where the Spirit of the Lord Is 89

Where the Spirit of the Lord is . . . II Cor. 3:17

STEPHEN R. ADAMS

STEPHEN R. ADAMS

Where the Spir-it of the Lord is, there is peace; Where the

Spir-it of the Lord is, there is love. There is com-fort in life's

dark-est hour, there is light and life; There is help and

pow-er in the Spir-it, in the Spir-it of the Lord.

© 1976 by Dimension Music, a division of The Benson Company, 365 Great Circle Road, Nashville, TN 37228. International copyright secured. All rights reserved. Printed by permission.

90 The Comforter Has Come

I will pray the Father, and He will give you another Comforter. John 14:16

FRANK BOTTOME   WILLIAM J. KIRKPATRICK

1. O spread the ti-dings 'round wher-ev-er man is found, Wher-
2. The long, long night is past, the morn-ing breaks at last, And
3. Lo, the great King of kings with heal-ing in His wings, To
4. O bound-less love di-vine! how shall this tongue of mine To

ev-er hu-man hearts and hu-man woes a-bound; Let ev-ery Chris-tian
hushed the dread-ful wail and fu-ry of the blast, As o'er the gold-en
ev-ery cap-tive soul a full de-liv-'rance brings; And through the va-cant
wond-'ring mor-tals tell the match-less grace di-vine—That I, a child of

tongue pro-claim the joy-ful sound: The Com-fort-er has come!
hills the day ad-vanc-es fast! The Com-fort-er has come!
cells the song of tri-umph rings; The Com-fort-er has come!
hell, should in His im-age shine! The Com-fort-er has come!

Chorus

The Com-fort-er has come, the Com-fort-er has come! The

Ho-ly Ghost from Heav'n, the Fa-ther's pro-mise giv'n; O spread the ti-dings

'round wher-ev-er man is found—The Com-fort-er has come!

Channels Only 91

A vessel unto honor . . . and fit for the Master's use . . . II Tim. 2:21

MARY E. MAXWELL

ADA R. GIBBS

1. How I praise Thee, pre-cious Sav-ior, That Thy love laid hold of me;
2. Emp-tied that Thou should-est fill me, A clean ves-sel in Thy hand;
3. Wit-ness-ing Thy pow'r to save me, Set-ting free from self and sin;
4. Je-sus, fill now with Thy Spir-it Hearts that full sur-ren-der know;

Thou hast saved and cleansed and filled me That I might Thy chan-nel be.
With no pow'r but as Thou giv-est Gra-cious-ly with each com-mand.
Thou who bought me to pos-sess me, In Thy full-ness, Lord, come in.
That the streams of liv-ing wa-ter From our in-ner man may flow.

Chorus

Chan-nels on-ly, bless-ed Mas-ter, But with all Thy won-drous pow'r

Flow-ing through us, Thou canst use us Ev-ery day and ev-ery hour.

92 Sweet Hour of Prayer

Now Peter and John went up together . . . at the hour of prayer. Acts 3:1

WILLIAM WALFORD   WILLIAM B. BRADBURY

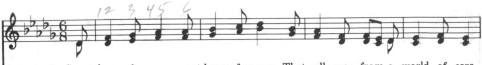

1. Sweet hour of prayer, sweet hour of prayer, That calls me from a world of care,
2. Sweet hour of prayer, sweet hour of prayer, Thy wings shall my pe - ti - tion bear,
3. Sweet hour of prayer, sweet hour of prayer, May I thy con - so - la - tion share,

And bids me at my Fa-ther's throne Make all my wants and wish - es known;
To Him whose truth and faith-ful - ness En - gage the wait - ing soul to bless;
Till, from Mount Pis-gah's loft - y height, I view my home, and take my flight:

In sea - sons of dis-tress and grief, My soul has oft - en found re - lief,
And since He bids me seek His face, Be - lieve His word and trust His grace,
This robe of flesh I'll drop, and rise To seize the ev - er - last - ing prize;

And oft es-caped the tempt - er's snare, By thy re - turn, sweet hour of prayer.
I'll cast on Him my ev - 'ry care, And wait for thee, sweet hour of prayer.
And shout, while pass-ing through the air, Fare-well, fare-well, sweet hour of prayer!

'Tis the Blessed Hour of Prayer   93

He shall call upon me, and I will answer Him . . . Psa. 91:15

FANNY J. CROSBY

WILLIAM H. DOANE

1. 'Tis the bless-ed hour of prayer, when our hearts low-ly bend,
2. 'Tis the bless-ed hour of prayer, when the Sav-ior draws near,
3. 'Tis the bless-ed hour of prayer, when the tempt-ed and tried
4. At the bless-ed hour of prayer, trust-ing Him we be-lieve

And we gath-er to Je-sus, our Sav-ior and Friend; If we
With a ten-der com-pas-sion His chil-dren to hear; When He
To the Sav-ior who loves them their sor-row con-fide; With a
That the bless-ings we're need-ing we'll sure-ly re-ceive; In the

come to Him in faith, His pro-tec-tion to share, What a balm for the
tells us we may cast at His feet ev-ery care, What a balm for the
sym-pa-thiz-ing heart He re-moves ev-ery care, What a balm for the
full-ness of this trust we shall lose ev-ery care; What a balm for the

Chorus

wea-ry! O how sweet to be there! Bless-ed hour of prayer, Bless-ed

hour of prayer; What a balm for the wea-ry! O how sweet to be there!

94 Leave It There

The righteous cry, and the Lord heareth . . . Psa. 34:17

C. ALBERT TINDLEY   C. ALBERT TINDLEY

1. If the world from you with-hold of its sil - ver and its gold, And you
2. If your bod - y suf - fers pain and your health you can't re - gain, And your
3. When your en - e - mies as - sail and your heart be - gins to fail, Don't for-
4. When your youth-ful days are gone and old age is steal-ing on, And your

have to get a - long with mea - ger fare, Just re - mem - ber, in His Word,
soul is al - most sink - ing in de - spair, Je - sus knows the pain you feel,
get that God in heav - en an-swers prayer; He will make a way for you
bod - y bends be - neath the weight of care, He will nev - er leave you then,

how He feeds the lit - tle bird—Take your bur-den to the Lord and leave it there.
He can save and He can heal—Take your bur-den to the Lord and leave it there.
and will lead you safe - ly thro'—Take your bur-den to the Lord and leave it there.
He'll go with you to the end—Take your bur-den to the Lord and leave it there.

Chorus

Leave it there,   leave it there,   Take your bur-den to the
Leave it there,   leave it there,

Copyright 1916. Renewal 1944 extended. Hope Publishing Co., owner. All rights reserved.

Lord and leave it there; (leave it there;) If you trust and nev-er doubt, He will
sure-ly bring you out—Take your bur-den to the Lord and leave it there.

From Every Stormy Wind That Blows 95

I will commune with thee from above the mercy seat. Exo. 25:22

HUGH STOWELL

THOMAS HASTINGS

1. From ev - ery storm - y wind that blows, From ev - ery swell - ing
2. There is a place where Je - sus sheds The oil of glad - ness
3. There is a scene where spir - its blend, Where friend holds fel - low-
4. Ah! whith - er could we flee for aid, When tempt - ed, des - o -
5. Ah! there on ea - gle wings we soar, And sin and sense mo -

tide of woes, There is a calm, a sure re - treat:
on our heads; A place than all be - side more sweet:
ship with friend; Though sun - dered far, by faith they meet
late, dis - mayed; Or how the hosts of hell de - feat,
lest no more: And heav'n comes down our souls to greet,

'Tis found be - neath the mer - cy seat.
It is the blood - bought mer - cy seat.
A - round one com - mon mer - cy seat.
Had suf - f'ring saints no mer - cy seat.
While glo - ry crowns the mer - cy seat. A - men.

96 Tell It to Jesus

Praying always with all prayer and supplication in the Spirit . . . Eph. 6:18

JEREMIAH E. RANKIN

EDMUND S. LORENZ

1. Are you wea - ry, are you heav - y - heart - ed? Tell it to Je - sus,
2. Do the tears flow down your cheeks un - bid - den? Tell it to Je - sus,
3. Do you fear the gath - 'ring clouds of sor - row? Tell it to Je - sus,
4. Are you trou - bled at the thought of dy - ing? Tell it to Je - sus,

Tell it to Je - sus; Are you griev - ing o - ver joys de - part - ed?
Tell it to Je - sus; Have you sins that to men's eyes are hid - den?
Tell it to Je - sus; Are you anx - ious what shall be to - mor - row?
Tell it to Je - sus; For Christ's com - ing king - dom are you sigh - ing?

Chorus

Tell it to Je - sus a - lone. Tell it to Je - sus, tell it to

Je - sus, He is a friend that's well-known; You've no oth - er

such a friend or broth - er, Tell it to Je - sus a - lone.

Did You Think to Pray? 97

In the morning will I direct my prayer unto Thee . . . Psa. 5:3

MARY ANN KIDDER

W. O. PERKINS

1. Ere you left your room this morn - ing, Did you think to pray?
2. When you met with great temp - ta - tion, Did you think to pray?
3. When your heart was filled with an - ger, Did you think to pray?
4. When sore tri - als came up - on you, Did you think to pray?

In the name of Christ our Sav - ior, Did you sue for lov - ing
By His dy - ing love and mer - it, Did you claim the Ho - ly
Did you plead for grace, my broth - er, That you might for - give an -
When your soul was bowed in sor - row, Balm of Gil - ead did you

Chorus

fa - vor, As a shield to - day?
Spir - it As your guide and stay?
oth - er Who had crossed your way?   Oh, how pray - ing rests the
bor - row, At the gates of day?

wea - ry! Prayer will change the night to day;

So in sor - row and in glad - ness, Don't for - get to pray.

98 Teach Me to Pray, Lord

Lord, teach us to pray . . . Luke 11:1

ALBERT S. REITZ   ALBERT S. REITZ

1. Teach me to pray, Lord, teach me to pray; This is my heart-cry
2. Pow-er in prayer, Lord, pow-er in prayer, Here 'mid earth's sin and
3. My weak-ened will, Lord, Thou canst re-new; My sin-ful na-ture
4. Teach me to pray, Lord, teach me to pray; Thou art my pat-tern,

day un-to day; I long to know Thy will and Thy way; Teach me to
sor-row and care; Men lost and dy-ing, souls in de-spair; O give me
Thou canst sub-due; Fill me just now with pow-er a-new, Pow-er to
day un-to day; Thou art my sure-ty, now and for aye; Teach me to

Chorus

pray, Lord, teach me to pray.
pow-er, pow-er in prayer! Liv-ing in Thee, Lord, and Thou in
pray and pow-er to do!
pray, Lord, teach me to pray.

me; Con-stant a-bid-ing, this is my plea; Grant me Thy

pow-er, bound-less and free: Pow-er with men and pow-er with Thee.

© Copyright 1925 A. S. Reitz. Renewal 1953 Broadman Press. All rights reserved. Used by permission.

The Beautiful Garden of Prayer

Be ye therefore sober, and watch unto prayer. I Pet. 4:7

ELEANOR ALLEN SCHROLL

JAMES H. FILLMORE

1. There's a gar-den where Je-sus is wait-ing, There's a place that is
2. There's a gar-den where Je-sus is wait-ing, And I go with my
3. There's a gar-den where Je-sus is wait-ing, And He bids you to

won-drous-ly fair; For it glows with the light of His pres-ence, 'Tis the
bur-den and care, Just to learn from His lips words of com-fort In the
come meet Him there; Just to bow, and re-ceive a new bless-ing, In the

Chorus

beau-ti-ful gar-den of prayer. O the beau-ti-ful gar-den, the

gar-den of prayer, O the beau-ti-ful gar-den of prayer; There my Sav-ior a-

waits, and He o-pens the gates To the beau-ti-ful gar-den of prayer.

Copyright 1920. Renewed 1948 by Nazarene Publishing House. Used by permission

100 What a Friend We Have in Jesus

By prayer . . . with thanksgiving let your requests be made known unto God. Phil. 4:6

JOSEPH M. SCRIVEN   CHARLES C. CONVERSE

1. What a Friend we have in Je - sus, All our sins and griefs to bear!
2. Have we tri - als and temp - ta - tions? Is there trou - ble an - y - where?
3. Are we weak and heav - y - la - den, Cum - bered with a load of care?

What a priv - i - lege to car - ry Ev - ery-thing to God in prayer!
We should nev - er be dis - cour - aged, Take it to the Lord in prayer.
Pre - cious Sav - ior, still our ref - uge— Take it to the Lord in prayer.

O what peace we of - ten for - feit, O what need-less pain we bear,
Can we find a friend so faith - ful Who will all our sor - rows share?
Do thy friends de - spise, for - sake thee? Take it to the Lord in prayer;

All be - cause we do not car - ry Ev - ery-thing to God in prayer!
Je - sus knows our ev - ery weak - ness, Take it to the Lord in prayer.
In His arms He'll take and shield thee, Thou wilt find a sol - ace there.

I Must Tell Jesus   101

For in that He himself hath suffered . . . He is able to succor them . . . Heb. 2:18

ELISHA A. HOFFMANN   ELISHA A. HOFFMANN

1. I must tell Je - sus all of my tri - als; I can - not bear these
2. I must tell Je - sus all of my trou - bles; He is a kind, com-
3. Tempt-ed and tried, I need a great Sav - ior, One who can help my
4. O how the world to e - vil al - lures me! O how my heart is

bur - dens a - lone; In my dis - tress He kind - ly will help me;
pas - sion - ate Friend; If I but ask Him, He will de - liv - er,
bur - dens to bear; I must tell Je - sus, I must tell Je - sus;
tempt - ed to sin! I must tell Je - sus, and He will help me

Chorus

He ev - er loves and cares for His own.
Make of my trou - bles quick - ly an end.   I must tell Je - sus!
He all my cares and sor - rows will share.
O - ver the world the vic - t'ry to win.

I must tell Je - sus! I can - not bear my bur - dens a - lone; I must tell

Je - sus! I must tell Je - sus! Je - sus can help me, Je - sus a - lone.

102 Lord, Listen to Your Children

The effectual fervent prayer of a righteous man availeth much. James 5:16

KEN MEDEMA

KEN MEDEMA

Chorus - parts

Lord, lis-ten to your chil-dren pray-ing, Lord, send your

Spir-it in this place; Lord, lis-ten to your chil-dren

Fine

pray - ing, Send us love, send us pow'r, send us grace.

unison

1. Some-thing's gon - na hap-pen like the world has nev - er known, When the
2. ℅ He's gon-na take o - ver, He's gon-na take con-trol, When the
3. ℅ You're gon - na know it when the Lord stretch-es out His hand, When the

peo - ple of the Lord get down to pray;
peo - ple of the Lord get down to pray;
peo - ple of the Lord get down to pray;

Copyright © 1973 CRESCENDO PUBLICATIONS, INC. BMI. All rights reserved. International copyright secured. Used by special permission.

A door's gon-na swing o - pen, and the walls come a-tum-bl-ing
He's gon-na move the moun-tain He's gon-na make the wa - ters
There's gon-na be a brand new song of vic - t'ry in this

D.C.

down, When the peo-ple of the Lord get down to pray.
roll, When the peo-ple of the Lord get down to pray.
land, When the peo-ple of the Lord get down to pray.

Lord, Speak to Me, That I May Speak 103

The things that thou hast heard of me . . . commit thou to faithful men. II Tim. 2:2

FRANCES R. HAVERGAL   ROBERT A. SCHUMANN

1. Lord, speak to me, that I may speak In liv - ing ech - oes of Thy tone;
2. O teach me, Lord, that I may teach The pre - cious things Thou dost im-part;
3. O fill me with Thy full - ness, Lord, Un - til my ver - y heart o'er-flow
4. O use me, Lord, use e - ven me, Just as Thou wilt and when and where;

As Thou hast sought, so let me seek Thy err - ing chil - dren lost and lone.
And wing my words, that they may reach The hid - den depths of many a heart.
In kind-ling thought and glow - ing word Thy love to tell, Thy praise to show.
Un - til Thy bless - ed face I see, Thy rest, Thy joy, Thy glo - ry share. A-men.

104 I Found the Answer

Praying always with all prayer . . . Eph. 6:18

JOHNNY LANGE   JOHNNY LANGE

1. I was weak and wear-y, I had gone a-stray, Walk-ing in the
2. I was sad and lone-ly, all my hopes were gone, Days were long and
3. Keep your Bi-ble with you, read it ev-ery day, Al-ways count your

dark-ness, I could-n't find my way; Then a light came shin-ing to
drear-y, I could-n't car-ry on; Then I found the cour-age to
bless-ings and al-ways stop to pray; Learn to keep be-liev-ing and

lead me from des-pair, All my sins for-giv-en, and I was free from care.
keep my head up high, Once a-gain I'm hap-py, and here's the rea-son why:
faith will see you through, Seek to know con-tent-ment, and it will come to you.

Chorus

I found the an-swer, I learned to pray! With faith to guide me,

I found the way; The sun is shin-ing for me each

Copyright © 1957 by BULLS-EYE MUSIC, INC., P.O. Box 1589, Hollywood, CA 90028. International copyright secured. All rights reserved. Used by permission.

day, I found the an - swer, I learned to pray!

Lord, I Have Shut the Door 105

And when thou hast shut thy door, pray to thy Father . . . Matt. 6:6

WILLIAM M. RUNYAN

WILLIAM M. RUNYAN

1. Lord, I have shut the door, Speak now the word Which in the
2. Lord, I have shut the door, Here do I bow; Speak, for my
3. In this blest qui - et - ness Clam - or - ings cease; Here in Thy
4. Lord, I have shut the door, Strength - en my heart; Yon - der a -

din and throng Could not be heard; Hushed now my in - ner heart,
soul at - tent Turns to Thee now. Re - buke Thou what is vain,
pres - ence dwells In - fi - nite peace; Yon - der, the strife and cry,
waits the task— I share a part. On - ly through grace be - stowed

Whis - per Thy will, While I have come a - part, While all is still.
Coun - sel my soul, Thy ho - ly will re - veal, My will con - trol.
Yon - der, the sin: Lord, I have shut the door, Thou art with - in!
May I be true; Here, while a - lone with Thee, My strength re - new. A-men.

Copyright 1923. Renewal 1951 extended. Hope Publishing Co., owner. All rights reserved.

106 Teach Me, Lord, to Wait

They that wait upon the Lord shall renew their strength. Isa. 40:31

ISAIAH 40
STUART HAMBLEN

STUART HAMBLEN

They that wait up-on the Lord shall re-new their

strength, They shall mount up with wings as ea-gles;

They shall run and not be wear-y, They shall

walk and not faint. Teach me, Lord, Teach me, Lord, to

© Copyright 1953 by Hamblen Music Company. International copyright secured. All rights reserved. Used by permission.

wait.   Teach me,   Lord, to wait

down on my knees Till in Your own good time   You an-swer my

pleas;   Teach me not to re - ly   on what oth - ers

D.C. al Fine

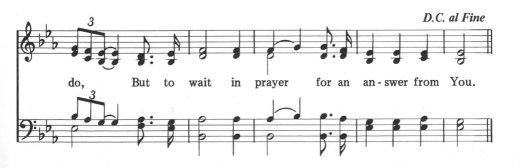

do,   But to wait in prayer   for an an-swer from You.

107 The Bible Stands

. . . The word of God, which liveth and abideth forever. I Pet. 1:23

Haldor Lillenas   Donald P. Hustad

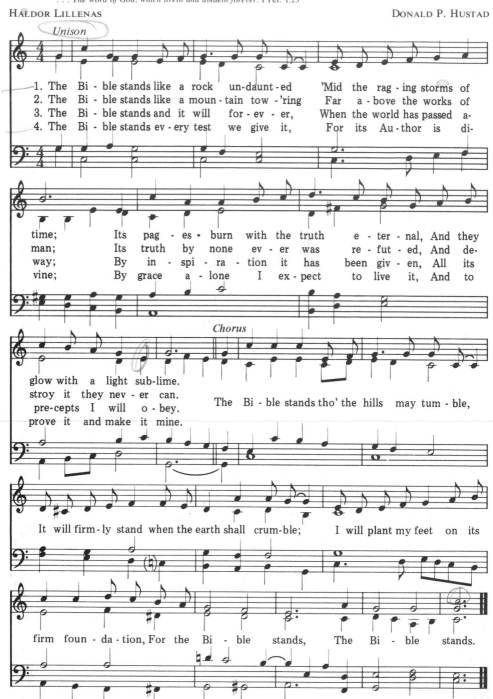

Unison

1. The Bi - ble stands like a rock un-daunt-ed 'Mid the rag-ing storms of
2. The Bi - ble stands like a moun-tain tow -'ring Far a-bove the works of
3. The Bi - ble stands and it will for-ev-er, When the world has passed a-
4. The Bi - ble stands ev-ery test we give it, For its Au-thor is di-

time; Its pag-es burn with the truth e-ter-nal, And they
man; Its truth by none ev-er was re-fut-ed, And de-
way; By in-spi-ra-tion it has been giv-en, All its
vine; By grace a-lone I ex-pect to live it, And to

Chorus

glow with a light sub-lime.
stroy it they nev-er can.   The Bi-ble stands tho' the hills may tum-ble,
pre-cepts I will o-bey.
prove it and make it mine.

It will firm-ly stand when the earth shall crum-ble; I will plant my feet on its

firm foun-da-tion, For the Bi-ble stands, The Bi-ble stands.

Words copyright 1917. Renewal 1945 extended. Hope Publishing Co., owner. Music copyright © 1974. Hope Publishing Co., owner.
All rights reserved.

Thy Word Have I Hid in My Heart 108

Thy word have I hid in mine heart . . . Psa. 119:11

From Psalm 119
Adapt. by Ernest O. Sellers

Ernest O. Sellers

1. Thy Word is a lamp to my feet, A light to my path al-
2. For - ev - er, O Lord, is Thy Word Es - tab-lished and fixed on
3. At morn-ing, at noon, and at night I ev - er will give Thee
4. Thro' Him whom Thy Word hath fore - told, The Sav - ior and Morn - ing

way, To guide and to save me from sin, And show me the
high; Thy faith - ful - ness un - to all men A - bid - eth for -
praise; For Thou art my por - tion, O Lord, And shall be thro'
Star, Sal - va - tion and peace have been brought To those who have

Chorus

heav'n - ly way.
ev - er nigh.   Thy Word have I hid in my heart (in my heart), That
all my days!
strayed a - far.

I might not sin a - gainst Thee (a - gainst Thee); That I might not

sin, That I might not sin, Thy Word have I hid in my heart.

109 Standing on the Promises

Whereby are given unto us exceeding great and precious promises . . . II Pet. 1:4

R. KELSO CARTER

R. KELSO CARTER

1. Stand-ing on the prom-is-es of Christ my King, Thro' e-ter-nal a-ges
2. Stand-ing on the prom-is-es that can-not fail, When the howl-ing storms of
3. Stand-ing on the prom-is-es of Christ the Lord, Bound to Him e-ter-nal-
4. Stand-ing on the prom-is-es I can-not fall, Lis-t'ning ev-ery mo-ment

let His prais-es ring; Glo-ry in the high-est, I will shout and sing,
doubt and fear as-sail, By the liv-ing Word of God I shall pre-vail,
ly by love's strong cord, O-ver-com-ing dai-ly with the Spir-it's sword,
to the Spir-it's call, Rest-ing in my Sav-ior as my all in all,

Chorus

Stand-ing on the prom-is-es of God. Stand-ing, stand - ing,
stand-ing on the prom-is-es,

Stand-ing on the prom-is-es of God my Sav-ior; Stand-ing,

stand - ing, I'm stand-ing on the prom-is-es of God.
stand-ing on the prom-is-es,

O Word of God Incarnate 110

The entrance of Thy words giveth light . . . Psa. 119:130

Neuvermehrtes Gesangbuch, Meiningen, 1693
WILLIAM W. HOW
ARR. BY FELIX MENDELSSOHN

1. O Word of God in-car-nate, O Wis-dom from on high,
O Truth un-changed, un-chang-ing, O Light of our dark sky;
We praise Thee for the ra-diance That from the hal-lowed page,
A lan-tern to our foot-steps, Shines on from age to age.

2. The Church from her dear Mas-ter Re-ceived the gift di-vine,
And still that light she lift-eth O'er all the earth to shine.
It is the gold-en cas-ket Where gems of truth are stored;
It is the heav'n-drawn pic-ture Of Christ, the liv-ing Word.

3. It float-eth like a ban-ner Be-fore God's host un-furled;
It shin-eth like a bea-con A-bove the dark-ling world.
It is the chart and com-pass That o'er life's surg-ing sea,
'Mid mists and rocks and quick-sands, Still guides, O Christ, to Thee.

4. O make Thy Church, dear Sav-ior, A lamp of pur-est gold,
To bear be-fore the na-tions Thy true light as of old.
O teach Thy wan-d'ring pil-grims By this their path to trace,
Till, clouds and dark-ness end-ed, They see Thee face to face. A-men.

111 How Firm a Foundation

Heaven and earth shall pass away: but My words shall not . . . Luke 21:33

Rippon's *Selection of Hymns*, 1787

Traditional American melody
Caldwell's *Union Harmony*, 1837

1. How firm a foun - da - tion, ye saints of the Lord,
2. "Fear not, I am with thee; O be not dis - mayed,
3. "When through the deep wa - ters I call thee to go,
4. "When through fier - y tri - als thy path - way shall lie,
5. "The soul that on Je - sus hath leaned for re - pose,

Is laid for your faith in His ex - cel - lent Word!
For I am thy God, and will still give thee aid;
The riv - ers of sor - row shall not o - ver - flow;
My grace, all suf - fi - cient, shall be thy sup - ply:
I will not, I will not de - sert to his foes;

What more can He say than to you He hath said,
I'll strength - en thee, help thee, and cause thee to stand,
For I will be with thee, thy trou - bles to bless,
The flame shall not hurt thee; I on - ly de - sign
That soul, though all hell should en - deav - or to shake,

To you who for ref - uge to Je - sus have fled?
Up - held by my right - eous, om - nip - o - tent hand.
And sanc - ti - fy to thee thy deep - est dis - tress.
Thy dross to con - sume, and thy gold to re - fine.
I'll nev - er, no, nev - er, no, nev - er for - sake!" A - men.

Thy Word Is Like a Garden, Lord 112

I rejoice at thy word, as one that findeth great spoil. Psa. 119:162

EDWIN HODDER

GOTTFRIED W. FINK

1. Thy Word is like a gar - den, Lord, With flow-ers bright and fair;
2. Thy Word is like a star - ry host: A thou-sand rays of light
3. Oh, may I love Thy pre - cious Word, May I ex-plore the mine,

And ev - ery one who seeks may pluck A love - ly clus - ter there.
Are seen to guard the trav - el - er, And make his path-way bright.
May I its fra - grant flow - ers glean, May light up - on me shine!

Thy Word is like a deep, deep mine, And jew - els rich and rare
Thy Word is like an ar - mor - y, Where sol-diers may re - pair,
Oh, may I find my ar - mor there! Thy Word my trust - y sword,

Are hid - den in its might - y depths For ev - ery search-er there.
And find, for life's long bat - tle - day, All need - ful weap-ons there.
I'll learn to fight with ev - ery foe The bat - tle of the Lord.

113 Break Thou the Bread of Life

He looked up to heaven, and blessed, and brake the loaves . . . Mark 6:41

MARY A. LATHBURY WILLIAM F. SHERWIN

1. Break Thou the bread of life, Dear Lord, to me, As Thou didst
2. Bless Thou the truth, dear Lord, To me, to me, As Thou didst
3. Thou art the bread of life, O Lord, to me, Thy ho - ly
4. O send Thy Spir - it, Lord, Now un - to me, That He may

break the loaves Be - side the sea; Be - yond the sa - cred page
bless the bread By Gal - i - lee; Then shall all bond - age cease,
Word the truth That sav - eth me; Give me to eat and live
touch my eyes And make me see: Show me the truth con - cealed

I seek Thee, Lord, My spir - it pants for Thee, O liv - ing Word.
All fet - ters fall; And I shall find my peace, My All in all.
With Thee a - bove; Teach me to love Thy truth, For Thou art love.
With - in Thy Word, And in Thy Book re-vealed I see the Lord. A-men.

114 Holy Bible, Book Divine

O how love I Thy law! it is my meditation all the day! Psa. 119:97

JOHN BURTON WILLIAM B. BRADBURY

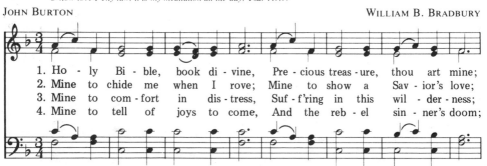

1. Ho - ly Bi - ble, book di - vine, Pre - cious treas - ure, thou art mine;
2. Mine to chide me when I rove; Mine to show a Sav - ior's love;
3. Mine to com - fort in dis - tress, Suf - f'ring in this wil - der - ness;
4. Mine to tell of joys to come, And the reb - el sin - ner's doom;

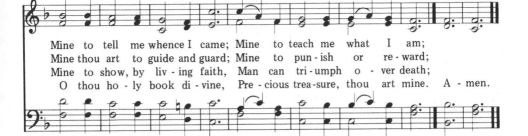

Mine to tell me whence I came; Mine to teach me what I am;
Mine thou art to guide and guard; Mine to pun-ish or re-ward;
Mine to show, by liv-ing faith, Man can tri-umph o-ver death;
O thou ho-ly book di-vine, Pre-cious trea-sure, thou art mine. A-men.

Wonderful Words of Life 115

Lord, to whom shall we go? Thou hast the words of eternal life. John 6:68

PHILIP P. BLISS   PHILIP P. BLISS

1. Sing them o-ver a-gain to me, Won-der-ful words of Life;
2. Christ, the bless-ed One, gives to all Won-der-ful words of Life;
3. Sweet-ly ech-o the gos-pel call, Won-der-ful words of Life;

Let me more of their beau-ty see, Won-der-ful words of Life.
Sin-ner, list to the lov-ing call, Won-der-ful words of Life.
Of-fer par-don and peace to all, Won-der-ful words of Life.

Words of life and beau-ty, Teach me faith and du-ty:
All so free-ly giv-en, Woo-ing us to Heav-en:
Je-sus, on-ly Sav-ior, Sanc-ti-fy for-ev-er:

Chorus

Beau-ti-ful words, won-der-ful words, Won-der-ful words of Life. Life.

116 Thou Didst Leave Thy Throne

He came unto His own and His own received Him not. John 1:11

EMILY E. S. ELLIOTT

TIMOTHY R. MATTHEWS

1. Thou didst leave Thy throne and Thy king - ly crown When Thou
2. Heav - en's arch - es rang when the an - gels sang, Pro -
3. The fox - es found rest and the birds their nest In the
4. Thou cam - est, O Lord, with the liv - ing Word That should
5. When the heav - ens shall ring, and the an - gels sing, At Thy

cam - est to earth for me; But in Beth - le - hem's home
claim - ing Thy roy - al de - gree; But in low - ly birth
shade of the for - est tree; But thy couch was the sod,
set Thy peo - ple free; But with mock - ing scorn,
com - ing to vic - to - ry, Let Thy voice call me home,

there was found no room For Thy ho - ly na - tiv - i - ty:
Thou didst come to earth, And in great hu - mil - i - ty:
O Thou Son of God, In the des - ert of Gal - i - lee:
and with crown of thorn, They bore Thee to Cal - va - ry:
say - ing, "Yet there is room, There is room at My side for thee:"

Chorus

1-4. O come to my heart, Lord Je - sus! There is room in my heart for Thee.
5. My heart shall re - joice, Lord Je - sus! When Thou com - est and call - est for me. A - men.

Joy to the World! The Lord Is Come 117

Make a joyful noise unto the Lord, all the earth . . . Psa. 98:4

ISAAC WATTS
Based on PSALM 98

GEORGE FREDERICK HANDEL
ARR. BY LOWELL MASON

1. Joy to the world! the Lord is come; Let earth receive her King; Let every heart prepare Him room, And heav'n and nature sing, And heav'n and nature sing, And heav'n, and heav'n and nature sing.

2. Joy to the earth! the Savior reigns; Let men their songs employ; While fields and floods, rocks, hills, and plains Repeat the sounding joy, Re-peat the sounding joy, Re-peat, re-peat the sounding joy.

3. No more let sins and sorrows grow, Nor thorns infest the ground; He comes to make His blessings flow Far as the curse is found, Far as the curse is found, Far as, far as the curse is found.

4. He rules the world with truth and grace, And makes the nations prove The glories of His righteousness, And wonders of His love, And wonders of His love, And wonders, wonders of His love.

118 It Came upon the Midnight Clear

Glory to God in the highest, and on earth peace . . . Luke 2:14

EDMUND H. SEARS

RICHARD S. WILLIS

1. It came up - on the mid - night clear, That glo - rious song of old,
2. Still through the clo - ven skies they come, With peace-ful wings un - furled,
3. And ye, be - neath life's crush-ing load, Whose forms are bend - ing low,
4. For lo, the days are has-tening on, By proph - et seen of old,

From an - gels bend - ing near the earth To touch their harps of gold:
And still their heav'n - ly mu - sic floats O'er all the wea - ry world:
Who toil a - long the climb - ing way With pain - ful steps and slow,
When, with the ev - er - cir - cling years, Shall come the time fore - told,

"Peace on the earth, good-will to men, From heav'n's all-gra - cious King": The
A - bove its sad and low - ly plains They bend on hov-ering wing: And
Look now! for glad and gold-en hours Come swift-ly on the wing: O
When the new heav'n and earth shall own The Prince of Peace their King, And

world in sol - emn still - ness lay To hear the an - gels sing.
ev - er o'er its Ba - bel sounds The bless - ed an - gels sing.
rest be - side the wea - ry road, And hear the an - gels sing.
the whole world send back the song Which now the an - gels sing.

Good Christian Men, Rejoice 119

Unto you is born this day . . . a Savior, which is Christ the Lord. Luke 2:11

Latin carol
Trans. by John M. Neale

Traditional German melody

1. Good Chris-tian men, re - joice With heart and soul and voice!
2. Good Chris-tian men, re - joice With heart and soul and voice!
3. Good Chris-tian men, re - joice With heart and soul and voice!

Give ye heed to what we say: Je - sus Christ is born to - day;
Now ye hear of end - less bliss; Je - sus Christ was born for this!
Now ye need not fear the grave; Je - sus Christ was born to save!

Ox and ass be - fore Him bow, And He is in the man - ger now.
He hath oped the heav'n - ly door, And man is blest for - ev - er - more.
Calls you one and calls you all To gain His ev - er - last - ing hall.

Christ is born to - day! Christ is born to - day!
Christ was born for this! Christ was born for this!
Christ was born to save! Christ was born to save!

120 The First Noel, the Angel Did Say

And there were in the same country shepherds abiding in the field . . . Luke 2:8

Traditional English carol

W. Sandys' *Christmas Carols*, 1833
ARR. BY JOHN STAINER

1. The first No - el, the an-gel did say, Was to cer-tain poor shepherds in
2. They look - ed up and saw a star Shin-ing in the east, be -
3. And by the light of that same star Three wise men came from
4. This star drew nigh to the north-west, O'er Beth - le - hem it
5. Then en - tered in those wise men three, Full rev - 'rent-ly up -
6. Then let us all with one ac - cord Sing prais - es to our

fields as they lay; In fields where they lay keep-ing their sheep, On a
yond them far, And to the earth it gave great light, And
coun - try far; To seek for a king was their in - tent, And to
took its rest, And there it did both stop and stay, Right
on their knee, And of - fered there in His pres - ence Their
heav'n - ly Lord, That hath made heav'n and earth of naught, And

Chorus

cold win-ter's night that was so deep.
so it con - tin - ued both day and night.
fol - low the star wher - ev - er it went.   No - el, No - el, No -
o - ver the place where Je - sus lay.
gold, and myrrh, and frank - in - cense.
with His blood man - kind hath bought.

el, No - el, Born is the King of Is - ra - el.

There's a Song in the Air 121

The Lord of hosts, He is the King of glory. Psa. 24:10

JOSIAH G. HOLLAND

KARL P. HARRINGTON

1. There's a song in the air! There's a star in the
2. There's a tu - mult of joy O'er the won - der - ful
3. In the light of that star Lie the a - ges im -
4. We re - joice in the light, And we ech - o the

sky! There's a moth - er's deep prayer, And a ba - by's low
birth, For the Vir - gin's sweet boy Is the Lord of the
pearled; And that song from a - far Has swept o - ver the
song That comes down thro' the night From the heav - en - ly

cry! And the star rains its fire while the beau - ti - ful sing,
earth. Ay! the star rains its fire while the beau - ti - ful sing,
world. Ev - ery hearth is a - flame, and the beau - ti - ful sing
throng. Ay! we shout to the love - ly e - van - gel they bring,

For the man - ger of Beth - le - hem cra - dles a King!
For the man - ger of Beth - le - hem cra - dles a King!
In the homes of the na - tions that Je - sus is King!
And we greet in His cra - dle our Sav - ior and King!

122 Silent Night! Holy Night!

And they . . . found Mary; and Joseph, and the babe lying in a manger. Luke 2:16

JOSEPH MOHR
TRANS. BY JOHN F. YOUNG

FRANZ GRÜBER

1. Si - lent night! ho - ly night! All is calm, all is bright
2. Si - lent night! ho - ly night! Shep - herds quake at the sight,
3. Si - lent night! ho - ly night! Son of God, love's pure light,

'Round yon vir - gin moth - er and Child, Ho - ly In - fant so ten - der and mild,
Glo - ries stream from heav - en a - far, Heav'n-ly hosts sing Al - le - lu - ia;
Ra - diant beams from Thy ho - ly face, With the dawn of re - deem - ing grace,

Sleep in heav - en - ly peace, Sleep in heav - en - ly peace.
Christ the Sav - ior is born, Christ the Sav - ior is born.
Je - sus, Lord, at Thy birth, Je - sus, Lord, at Thy birth. A - men.

123 I Heard the Bells on Christmas Day

And He shall speak peace unto the heathen . . . Zech. 9:10

HENRY W. LONGFELLOW

J. BAPTISTE CALKIN

1. I heard the bells on Christ-mas day Their old fa - mil - iar car - ols play,
2. I thought how, as the day had come, The bel - fries of all Chris - ten-dom
3. And in de - spair I bowed my head:"There is no peace on earth," I said,
4. Then pealed the bells more loud and deep:"God is not dead: nor doth He sleep;
5. Till, ring - ing, sing - ing on its way, The world re-volved from night to day,

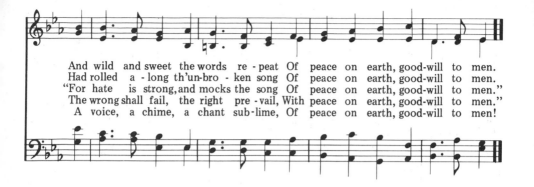

And wild and sweet the words re-peat Of peace on earth, good-will to men.
Had rolled a-long th'un-bro-ken song Of peace on earth, good-will to men.
"For hate is strong,and mocks the song Of peace on earth, good-will to men."
The wrong shall fail, the right pre-vail, With peace on earth, good-will to men."
A voice, a chime, a chant sub-lime, Of peace on earth, good-will to men!

Angels from the Realms of Glory 124

We . . . are come to worship Him. Matt. 2:2

JAMES MONTGOMERY

HENRY T. SMART

1. An-gels from the realms of glo-ry, Wing your flight o'er all the earth;
2. Shep-herds in the fields a-bid-ing, Watch-ing o'er your flocks by night,
3. Sag-es, leave your con-tem-pla-tions, Bright-er vi-sions beam a-far;
4. Saints be-fore the al-tar bend-ing, Watch-ing long in hope and fear,

Ye who sang cre-a-tion's sto-ry, Now pro-claim Mes-si-ah's birth:
God with man is now re-sid-ing, Yon-der shines the in-fant Light:
Seek the great De-sire of na-tions, Ye have seen His na-tal star:
Sud-den-ly the Lord, de-scend-ing, In His tem-ple shall ap-pear:

Chorus

Come and wor-ship, come and wor-ship, Wor-ship Christ, the new-born King. A-men.

125 Hark! the Herald Angels Sing

And suddenly there was . . . a multitude of the heavenly host praising God . . . Luke 2:13

CHARLES WESLEY

FELIX MENDELSSOHN
ARR. BY WILLIAM H. CUMMINGS

1. Hark! the her-ald an-gels sing, "Glo-ry to the new-born King:
2. Christ, by high-est heav'n a-dored; Christ, the ev-er-last-ing Lord!
3. Hail the heav'n-born Prince of Peace! Hail the Sun of Right-eous-ness!

Peace on earth, and mer-cy mild, God and sin-ners rec-on-ciled!"
Late in time be-hold Him come, Off-spring of the Vir-gin's womb:
Light and life to all He brings, Ris'n with heal-ing in His wings.

Joy-ful, all ye na-tions, rise, Join the tri-umph of the skies;
Veiled in flesh the God-head see; Hail th'in-car-nate De-i-ty,
Mild He lays His glo-ry by, Born that man no more may die,

With th'an-gel-ic host pro-claim, "Christ is born in Beth-le-hem!"
Pleased as man with men to dwell, Je-sus, our Em-man-u-el.
Born to raise the sons of earth, Born to give them sec-ond birth.

Hark! the her-ald an-gels sing, "Glo-ry to the new-born King." A-men.

1978

What Child Is This 126

Where is He that is born King of the Jews? Matt. 2:2

William C. Dix

Traditional English melody

1. What Child is this, who, laid to rest, On Ma-ry's lap is sleep-ing?
2. Why lies He in such mean es-tate Where ox and ass are feed-ing?
3. So bring Him in-cense, gold and myrrh, Come, peas-ant, king, to own Him;

Unison until chorus on 3rd vs

Whom an-gels greet with an-thems sweet, While shep-herds watch are keep-ing?
Good Chris-tian, fear; for sin-ners here The si-lent Word is plead-ing.
The King of kings sal-va-tion brings, Let lov-ing hearts en-throne Him.

Chorus

This, this is Christ the King, Whom shep-herds guard and an-gels sing:

This, this is Christ the King, The babe, the Son of Ma-ry.

127 Go, Tell It on the Mountain

. . . They made known abroad the saying . . . concerning this child. Luke 2:17

JOHN W. WORK, II   Traditional Spiritual

Unison

(Ref.) Go, tell it on the moun-tain, O-ver the hills and ev-ery-where;

Fine

Go, tell it on the moun - tain That Je-sus Christ is born.

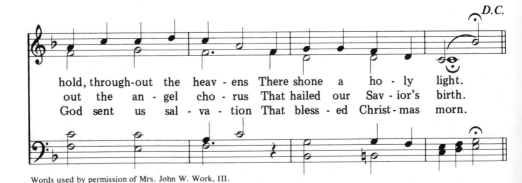

1. While shep-herds kept their watch-ing O'er si - lent flocks by night, Be-
2. The shep-herds feared and trem-bled When, lo! a-bove the earth Rang
3. Down in a low-ly man-ger Our hum-ble Christ was born, And

D.C.

hold, through-out the heav-ens There shone a ho-ly light.
out the an - gel cho - rus That hailed our Sav-ior's birth.
God sent us sal-va-tion That bless - ed Christ-mas morn.

Words used by permission of Mrs. John W. Work, III.

O Little Town of Bethlehem   128

Thou, Bethlehem . . . though thou be little . . . out of thee shall He come. Micah 5:2

PHILLIPS BROOKS   LEWIS H. REDNER

1. O lit-tle town of Beth-le-hem, How still we see thee lie!
2. For Christ is born of Ma - ry, And gath-ered all a - bove,
3. How si-lent-ly, how si-lent-ly The won-drous gift is giv'n!
4. O ho-ly Child of Beth-le-hem! De-scend to us, we pray;

A - bove thy deep and dream-less sleep The si - lent stars go by.
While mor-tals sleep, the an - gels keep Their watch of won-d'ring love,
So God im-parts to hu - man hearts The bless - ings of His heav'n.
Cast out our sin, and en - ter in; Be born in us to day.

Yet in thy dark streets shin - eth The ev - er - last - ing Light;
O morn - ing stars, to - geth - er Pro - claim the ho - ly birth!
No ear may hear His com - ing, But in this world of sin,
We hear the Christ - mas an - gels The great glad ti - dings tell;

The hopes and fears of all the years Are met in thee to - night.
And prais - es sing to God the King, And peace to men on earth.
Where meek souls will re - ceive Him still The dear Christ en - ters in.
O come to us, a - bide with us, Our Lord Em - man - u - el. A-men.

129 Little Baby Jesus

. . . Call His name Jesus, for He shall save His people from their sins. Matt. 1:21

BLAINE H. ALLEN

BLAINE H. ALLEN

Unison

1. Lit - tle Ba - by Je - sus, born in Beth - le - hem;
2. Lit - tle Ba - by Je - sus, born in Beth - le - hem;
3. Lit - tle Ba - by Je - sus, born in a sta - ble bare;
4. Lit - tle Ba - by Je - sus, born in Beth - le - hem;

Lit - tle Ba - by Je - sus, born in Beth - le - hem;
Lit - tle Ba - by Je - sus, born in Beth - le - hem;
Lit - tle Ba - by Je - sus, ly - ing in a man-ger there;
Lit - tle Ba - by Je - sus, born in Beth - le - hem;

Lit - tle Ba - by Je - sus, born to be The Sa - vior of the world for
Lit - tle Ba - by Je - sus, born to die, To suf - fer on the cross for
Lit - tle Ba - by Je - sus, King to be, The mas - ter of the earth, the
Lit - tle Ba - by Je - sus, do come in, Come right in - to my heart and

you and me; Lit - tle Ba - by Je - sus, born in Beth - le - hem.
you and I; Lit - tle Ba - by Je - sus, born in Beth - le - hem.
sky and sea; Lit - tle Ba - by Je - sus, born in Beth - le - hem.
save me from sin! Lit - tle Ba - by Je - sus, born in Beth-le - hem.

Copyright. © 1969. Hope Publishing Co.. owner. International copyright secured. All rights reserved.

O Come, All Ye Faithful 130

Let us now go even unto Bethlehem . . . Luke 2:15

Latin hymn
ATTR. TO JOHN F. WADE
TRANS. BY FREDERICK OAKELEY AND OTHERS

John F. Wade's *Cantus Diversi*, 1751

1. O come, all ye faith - ful, joy - ful and tri - um - phant,
2. God of God, and Light of Light be - got - ten,
3. Sing, choirs of an - gels, sing in ex - ul - ta - tion!
4. Yea, Lord, we greet Thee, born this hap - py morn - ing,

O come ye, O come ye to Beth - le - hem!
Lo, He ab - hors not the Vir - gin's womb;
O sing, all ye cit - i - zens of heav'n a - bove;
Je - sus, to Thee be all glo - ry giv'n;

Come and be - hold Him, born the King of an - gels;
Ver - y God, be - got - ten, not cre - a - ted;
Glo - ry to God, all glo - ry in the high - est;
Word of the Fa - ther, now in flesh ap - pear - ing;

Chorus

O come, let us a - dore Him, O come, let us a - dore Him,

O come, let us a - dore Him, Christ the Lord. A - men.

131 Away in a Manger

She brought forth her firstborn son . . . and laid Him in a manger. Luke 2:7

Source unknown

JAMES R. MURRAY

1. A - way in a man - ger, no crib for a bed, The lit - tle Lord
2. The cat - tle are low - ing, the poor ba - by wakes, But lit - tle Lord

Je - sus laid down His sweet head; The stars in the sky looked
Je - sus, no cry - ing He makes; I love Thee, Lord Je - sus, look

down where He lay, The lit - tle Lord Je - sus, a - sleep on the hay.
down from the sky, And stay by my cra - dle to watch lu - la - by.

132 From Heaven Above to Earth I Come

I bring you good tidings of great joy . . . Luke 2:10

MARTIN LUTHER
TRANS. BY CATHERINE WINKWORTH

Geystliche Lieder, Leipzig, 1539

1. From heav'n a - bove to earth I come To bear good news to ev - ery home;
2. "To you, this night is born a Child Of Ma - ry, cho - sen moth - er mild;
3. Ah, dear - est Je - sus, ho - ly Child, Make Thee a bed, soft, un - de - filed
4. Glo - ry to God in high - est heav'n, Who un - to man His Son hath giv'n.

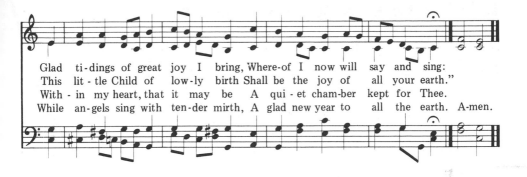

Glad ti-dings of great joy I bring, Where-of I now will say and sing:
This lit-tle Child of low-ly birth Shall be the joy of all your earth."
With-in my heart, that it may be A qui-et cham-ber kept for Thee.
While an-gels sing with ten-der mirth, A glad new year to all the earth. A-men.

Who Is This Boy? 133

Thou art the Christ, the Son of the living God. Matt. 16:16

St. 1. Source unknown
St. 2, 3, JOHN F. WILSON

JOHN F. WILSON

Unison

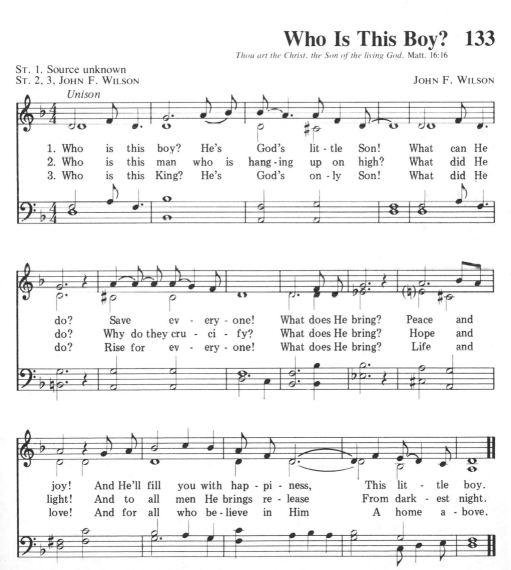

1. Who is this boy? He's God's lit-tle Son! What can He
2. Who is this man who is hang-ing up on high? What did He
3. Who is this King? He's God's on-ly Son! What did He

do? Save ev - ery - one! What does He bring? Peace and
do? Why do they cru - ci - fy? What does He bring? Hope and
do? Rise for ev - ery - one! What does He bring? Life and

joy! And He'll fill you with hap - pi - ness, This lit - tle boy.
light! And to all men He brings re - lease From dark - est night.
love! And for all who be - lieve in Him A home a - bove.

Copyright, © 1967. Hope Publishing Co., owner. International copyright secured. All rights reserved.

134 We Three Kings of Orient Are

Behold, there came wise men from the east . . . Matt. 2:1

JOHN H. HOPKINS

JOHN H. HOPKINS

1. We three kings of O - ri - ent are, Bear - ing gifts we
2. Born a King on Beth - le - hem's plain, Gold I bring to
3. Frank - in - cense to of - fer have I, In - cense owns a
4. Myrrh is mine; its bit - ter per - fume Breathes a life of
5. Glo - rious now be - hold Him a - rise, King and God and

trav - erse a - far Field and foun - tain, moor and moun - tain,
crown Him a - gain, King for - ev - er, ceas - ing nev - er
De - i - ty nigh; Prayer and prais - ing, all men rais - ing,
gath - er - ing gloom; Sor - rowing, sigh - ing, bleed - ing, dy - ing,
Sac - ri - fice; Al - le - lu - ia, Al - le - lu - ia!

Chorus

Fol - low - ing yon - der star.
O - ver us all to reign.
Wor - ship Him, God on high. O star of won - der,
Sealed in the stone - cold tomb.
Peals through the earth and skies.

star of night, Star with roy - al beau - ty bright, West - ward

lead - ing, still pro - ceed - ing, Guide us to thy per - fect light.

While Shepherds Watched Their Flocks 135

There were shepherds abiding in the field, keeping watch over their flocks . . . Luke 2:8

NAHUM TATE

GEORGE FREDERICK HANDEL
Arr. in Weyman's *Melodia Sacra*, 1815

1. While shep-herds watched their flocks by night, All seat - ed on the
2. "Fear not!" said he; for might - y dread Had seized their troub - led
3. "To you, in Da - vid's town this day, Is born of Da - vid's
4. "The heav'n-ly Babe you there shall find To hu - man view dis -
5. "All glo - ry be to God on high, And to the earth be

ground, The an - gel of the Lord came down, And
mind, "Glad ti - dings of great joy I bring To
line, The Sav - ior who is Christ the Lord, And
played, All mean - ly wrapped in swath - ing bands, And
peace: Good will hence - forth from heav'n to men, Be -

glo - ry shone a - round, And glo - ry shone a - round.
you and all man - kind, To you and all man - kind.
this shall be the sign: And this shall be the sign:
in a man - ger laid; And in a man - ger laid.
gin and nev - er cease, Be - gin and nev - er cease." A - men.

136 Angels We Have Heard on High

Glory to God in the highest and on earth peace . . . Luke 2:14

Traditional French carol

Traditional French melody

1. An - gels we have heard on high, Sweet - ly sing - ing o'er the plains,
2. Shepherds, why this ju - bi - lee? Why your joy - ous strains pro - long?
3. Come to Beth - le - hem, and see Him whose birth the an - gels sing;
4. See with - in a man - ger laid Je - sus, Lord of heav'n and earth!

And the moun-tains in re - ply Ech - o back their joy - ous strains.
Say what may the ti - dings be, Which in - spire your heav'n-ly song?
Come, a - dore on bend - ed knee Christ the Lord, the new - born King.
Ma - ry, Jo - seph, lend your aid, With us sing our Sav - ior's birth.

Chorus

Glo - - - ri - a in ex-cel-sis De - o,

Glo - - - ri - a in ex-cel-sis De - o.

Tell Me the Story of Jesus 137

He expounded unto them . . . the things concerning Himself. Luke 24:27

FANNY J. CROSBY

JOHN R. SWENEY

1. Tell me the sto-ry of Je - sus, Write on my heart ev-ery word;
2. Fast-ing a - lone in the des - ert, Tell of the days that are past,
3. Tell of the cross where they nailed Him, Writhing in an-guish and pain;

Ref. Tell me the sto - ry of Je - sus, Write on my heart ev-ery word;

Fine

Tell me the sto - ry most pre - cious, Sweet-est that ev - er was heard.
How for our sins He was tempt - ed, Yet was tri - um-phant at last.
Tell of the grave where they laid Him, Tell how He liv - eth a - gain.

Tell me the sto - ry most pre - cious, Sweet-est that ev - er was heard.

Tell how the an - gels in cho - rus Sang as they wel-comed His birth,
Tell of the years of His la - bor, Tell of the sor - row He bore,
Love in that sto - ry so ten - der Clear - er than ev - er I see:

D.C. for Refrain

"Glo - ry to God in the high - est! Peace and good ti - dings to earth."
He was de-spised and af - flict - ed, Home-less, re - ject - ed and poor.
Stay, let me weep while you whis - per, Love paid the ran - som for me.

138 One Day

When the fulness of the time was come, God sent forth His Son . . . Gal. 4:4

J. WILBUR CHAPMAN   CHARLES H. MARSH

1. One day when heav-en was filled with His prais-es, One day when
2. One day they led Him up Cal-va-ry's moun-tain, One day they
3. One day they left Him a-lone in the gar-den, One day He
4. One day the grave could con-ceal Him no long-er, One day the
5. One day the trum-pet will sound for His com-ing, One day the

sin was as black as could be, Je-sus came forth to be
nailed Him to die on the tree; Suf-fer-ing an-guish, de-
rest-ed, from suf-fer-ing free; An-gels came down o'er His
stone rolled a-way from the door; Then He a-rose, o-ver
skies with His glo-ry will shine; Won-der-ful day, my be-

born of a vir-gin, Dwelt a-mong men, my ex-am-ple is He!
spised and re-ject-ed, Bear-ing our sins, my Re-deem-er is He!
tomb to keep vig-il; Hope of the hope-less, my Sav-ior is He!
death He has con-quered; Now is as-cend-ed, my Lord ev-er-more!
lov-ed ones bring-ing; Glo-ri-ous Sav-ior, this Je-sus is mine!

Chorus

Liv-ing, He loved me; dy-ing, He saved me; Bur-ied, He

car-ried my sins far a-way; Ris-ing, He jus-ti-fied

Copyright 1910 by C. H. Marsh. © Renewed by Chas. H. Marsh. Assigned to The Rodeheaver Co. Used by permission.

free - ly for - ev - er: One day He's com - ing— O, glo - ri - ous day!

Wounded for Me 139

He was wounded for our transgressions . . . Isa. 53:5

St. 1, W. G. Ovens and
St. 2-5, Gladys W. Roberts

W. G. Ovens

1. Wound-ed for me, wound-ed for me, There on the cross
2. Dy - ing for me, dy - ing for me, There on the cross
3. Ris - en for me, ris - en for me, Up from the grave
4. Liv - ing for me, liv - ing for me, Up in the skies
5. Com - ing for me, com - ing for me, One day to earth

He was wound-ed for me; Gone my trans-gres-sions, and
He was dy - ing for me; Now in His death my re -
He has ris - en for me; Now ev - er - more from death's
He is liv - ing for me; Dai - ly He's plead-ing and
He is com-ing for me; Then with what joy His dear

now I am free, All be-cause Je - sus was wound-ed for me.
demp-tion I see, All be-cause Je - sus was dy - ing for me.
sting I am free, All be-cause Je - sus has ris - en for me.
pray - ing for me, All be-cause Je - sus is liv - ing for me.
face I shall see, O how I praise Him—He's com-ing for me!

140 The Ninety and Nine

Rejoice with me; for I have found my sheep which was lost. Luke 15:6

ELIZABETH C. CLEPHANE

IRA D. SANKEY

1. There were nine-ty and nine that safe - ly lay In the
2. "Lord, Thou hast here Thy nine-ty and nine; Are
3. But none of the ran-somed ev - er knew How
4. "Lord, whence are those blood-drops all the way That
5. But all thro' the moun-tains thun - der-riv'n, And

shel - ter of the fold, But one was out on the
they not e-nough for Thee?" But the Shep-herd made an-swer:
deep were the wa-ters crossed; Nor how dark was the night that the
mark out the moun-tain's track?" "They were shed for one who had
up from the rock-y steep, There a-rose a glad cry to the

hills a - way, Far off from the gates of gold— A -
"This of mine Has wan-dered a - way from me, And al -
Lord passed thro' Ere He found His sheep that was lost.
gone a - stray Ere the Shep-herd could bring him back." "Lord,
gate of heav'n, "Re - joice! I have found my sheep!" And the

way on the moun-tains wild and bare, A-way from the ten - der
though the road be rough and steep, I go to the des - ert to
Out in the des - ert He heard its cry — Sick and help-less and
whence are Thy hands so rent and torn?" "They're pierced to - night by
an - gels ech-oed a - round the throne, "Re-joice, for the Lord brings

Shep - herd's care, A - way from the ten - der Shep - herd's care.
find my sheep, I go to the des - ert to find my sheep."
read - y to die; Sick and help - less, and read - y to die.
man - y a thorn; They re pierced to - night by man - y a thorn,"
back His own! Re - joice, for the Lord brings back His own!"

Tell Me the Stories of Jesus 141

Suffer the little children to come unto me. Mark 10:14

WILLIAM H. PARKER

FREDERIC A. CHALLINOR

1. Tell me the sto - ries of Je - sus I love to hear; Things I would
2. First let me hear how the chil - dren Stood round His knee; And I shall
3. In - to the cit - y I'd fol - low The chil - dren's band, Wav - ing a

ask Him to tell me If He were here; Scenes by the way - side,
fan - cy His bless - ing Rest - ing on me: Words full of kind - ness,
branch of the palm tree High in my hand; One of His her - alds,

Tales of the sea, Sto - ries of Je - sus, Tell them to me.
Deeds full of grace, All in the love-light Of Je - sus' face.
Yes, I would sing Loud-est ho - san - nas! Je - sus is King.

142 Ten Thousand Angels

And He shall presently give me more than twelve legions of angels. Matt. 26:53

RAY OVERHOLT

RAY OVERHOLT

Slowly, with much feeling

1. They bound the hands of Je - sus in the gar - den where He prayed;
2. Up - on His pre - cious head they placed a crown of thorns;
3. When they nailed Him to the cross, His moth - er stood near by;
4. To the howl - ing mob He yield-ed; He did not for mer - cy cry.

They led Him thro' the streets in shame. They spat up - on the
They laughed and said, "Be - hold the King." They struck Him and they
He said, "Wom - an, be - hold thy son!" He cried, "I thirst for
The cross of shame He took a - lone. And when He cried, "It's

Sav - ior so pure and free from sin; They said,
cursed Him and mocked His ho - ly name. All a -
wa - ter," but they gave Him none to drink. Then the
fin - ished," He gave Him - self to die; Sal -

Chorus
f Faster

"Cru - ci - fy Him; He's to blame."
lone He suf - fered ev - ery - thing. He could have
sin - ful work of man was done.
va - tion's won - drous plan was done.

© 1959 by Lillenas Publishing Co. All rights reserved. Used by permission.

called ten thou-sand an-gels To de-stroy the world and set Him the world free. He could have called ten thou-sand an-gels, But He died a-lone, a-lone, for you and me.

rall.

'Tis Midnight; and on Olive's Brow 143

. . . They went out into the mount of Olives. Matt. 26:30

WILLIAM B. TAPPAN

WILLIAM B. BRADBURY

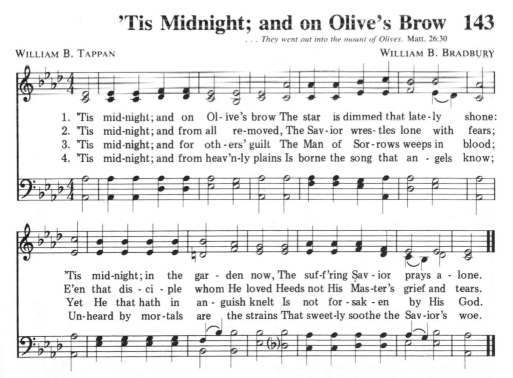

1. 'Tis mid-night; and on Ol-ive's brow The star is dimmed that late-ly shone:
2. 'Tis mid-night; and from all re-moved, The Sav-ior wres-tles lone with fears;
3. 'Tis mid-night; and for oth-ers' guilt The Man of Sor-rows weeps in blood;
4. 'Tis mid-night; and from heav'n-ly plains Is borne the song that an-gels know;

'Tis mid-night; in the gar-den now, The suf-f'ring Sav-ior prays a-lone.
E'en that dis-ci-ple whom He loved Heeds not His Mas-ter's grief and tears.
Yet He that hath in an-guish knelt Is not for-sak-en by His God.
Un-heard by mor-tals are the strains That sweet-ly soothe the Sav-ior's woe.

144 Ivory Palaces

... Out of the ivory palaces, whereby they have made thee glad. Psa. 45:8

HENRY BARRACLOUGH   HENRY BARRACLOUGH

1. My Lord has gar-ments so won-drous fine, And myrrh their tex-ture fills;
2. His life had al-so its sor-rows sore, For al-oes had a part;
3. His gar-ments too were in cas-sia dipped, With heal-ing in a touch;
4. In gar-ments glo-ri-ous He will come, To o-pen wide the door;

Its fra-grance reached to this heart of mine, With joy my be-ing thrills.
And when I think of the cross He bore, My eyes with tear-drops start.
Each time my feet in some sin have slipped, He took me from its clutch.
And I shall en-ter my heav'n-ly home, To dwell for-ev-er-more.

Chorus

Out of the i-vo-ry pal-a-ces, In-to a world of woe,

On-ly His great, e-ter-nal love Made my Sav-ior go.

Copyright 1915. Renewal 1943 extended. Hope Publishing Co., owner. All rights reserved.

He Died for Me 145

Who . . . bare our sins in His own body on the tree. I Pet. 2:24

JOHN NEWTON

EDWIN O. EXCELL

1. I saw One hang-ing on a tree, In ag-o-ny and blood;
2. Sure, nev-er till my lat-est breath, Can I for-get that look;
3. My con-science felt and owned the guilt, And plunged me in de-spair;
4. A sec-ond look He gave, which said, "I free-ly all for-give:

He fixed His lov-ing eyes on me, As near His cross I stood.
It seemed to charge me with His death, Though not a word He spoke.
I saw my sins His blood had spilt And helped to nail Him there.
This blood is for your ran-som paid, I die that you may live."

Chorus

O, can it be, up-on a tree The Sav-ior died for me?

My soul is thrilled, my heart is filled, To think He died for me!

Copyright 1917. Renewal 1944 in "Praiseworthy" by G. J. Excell Loftus, extended. Hope Publishing Co., owner. All rights reserved.

146 Jesus Paid It All

Though your sins be as scarlet, they shall be as white as snow. Isa. 1:18

ELVINA M. HALL

JOHN T. GRAPE

1. I hear the Sav-ior say, "Thy strength in-deed is small, Child of
2. Lord, now in-deed I find Thy pow'r and Thine a-lone Can
3. For noth-ing good have I Where-by Thy grace to claim— I'll
4. And when be-fore the throne I stand in Him com-plete, "Je-sus

Chorus

weak-ness, watch and pray, Find in Me thine all in all."
change the lep-er's spots And melt the heart of stone.
wash my gar-ments white In the blood of Cal-v'ry's Lamb. Je-sus paid it all,
died my soul to save," My lips shall still re-peat.

All to Him I owe; Sin had left a crim-son stain, He washed it white as snow.

147 Hallelujah! What a Savior!

A man of sorrows and acquainted with grief . . . Isa. 53:3

PHILIP P. BLISS

PHILIP P. BLISS

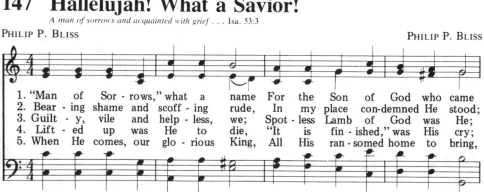

1. "Man of Sor-rows," what a name For the Son of God who came
2. Bear-ing shame and scoff-ing rude, In my place con-demned He stood;
3. Guilt-y, vile and help-less, we; Spot-less Lamb of God was He;
4. Lift-ed up was He to die, "It is fin-ished," was His cry;
5. When He comes, our glo-rious King, All His ran-somed home to bring,

Ru - ined sin - ners to re - claim! Hal - le - lu - jah! what a Sav - ior!
Sealed my par - don with His blood; Hal - le - lu - jah! what a Sav - ior!
"Full a - tone - ment" can it be? Hal - le - lu - jah! what a Sav - ior!
Now in heav'n ex - alt - ed high; Hal - le - lu - jah! what a Sav - ior!
Then a - new this song we'll sing: Hal - le - lu - jah! what a Sav - ior!

Lead Me to Calvary 148

Consider Him that endured such contradiction of sinners against Himself. Heb. 12:3

JENNIE E. HUSSEY   WILLIAM J. KIRKPATRICK

1. King of my life, I crown Thee now, Thine shall the glo - ry be;
2. Show me the tomb where Thou wast laid, Ten - der - ly mourned and wept;
3. Let me, like Ma - ry thro' the gloom, Come with a gift to Thee;
4. May I be will - ing, Lord, to bear Dai - ly my cross for Thee;

Lest I for - get Thy thorn-crowned brow, Lead me to Cal - va - ry.
An - gels in robes of light ar - rayed Guard - ed Thee whilst Thou slept.
Show to me now the emp - ty tomb, Lead me to Cal - va - ry.
E - ven Thy cup of grief to share, Thou hast borne all for me.

Chorus

Lest I for - get Geth - sem - a - ne; Lest I for - get Thine ag - o - ny;

Lest I for - get Thy love for me, Lead me to Cal - va - ry.

Copyright 1921. Renewal 1949 extended. Hope Publishing Co., owner. All rights reserved.

149 Blessed Redeemer

They were come to the place called Calvary . . . Luke 23:33

AVIS B. CHRISTIANSEN

HARRY D. LOES

1. Up Cal-vary's moun-tain one dread-ful morn, Walked Christ my Sav - ior,
2. "Fa - ther, for-give them!" thus did He pray, E'en while His life-blood
3. O how I love Him, Sav - ior and Friend, How can my prais - es

wea - ry and worn; Fac-ing for sin - ners death on the cross,
flowed fast a - way; Pray-ing for sin - ners while such woe—
ev - er find end! Thro' years un - num-bered on heav - en's shore,

Chorus

That He might save them from end-less loss.
No one but Je - sus ev - er loved so. Bless - ed Re-deem - er!
My tongue shall praise Him for - ev - er - more.

pre-cious Re-deem - er! Seems now I see Him on Cal-va-ry's tree;

Wound-ed and bleed-ing, for sin-ners plead-ing, Blind and un-heed-ing—dy-ing for me!

© 1921 and renewed 1949 by John T. Benson, Jr. Copyright extended. International copyright secured. All rights reserved. Printed by permission of The Benson Company, 365 Great Circle Road, Nashville, TN 37228.

Let Me Live at Calvary 150

I am crucified with Christ . . . Gal. 2:20

PAUL HUTCHENS   PAULINE HUTCHENS WILSON

1. The world calls it "waste," when I yield to the Lord All my
2. For life is not meas-ured by fame or suc-cess, Nor by
3. The fra-grance of love I would pour on His head, In de-

heart and life and love; It knows not the gains of the
gifts with which I part; 'Tis meas-ured in-stead by the
vo-tion warm and true, As He gave His life for my

self - life are loss, 'Tis blind - ed to the wealth a - bove.
life that He gives To oth - ers, thro' my yield - ed heart.
sins on the cross— Oh, great - er love none ev - er knew.

Chorus

Lord, let me live at Cal - v'ry, All my sin re - move;

May Thy life be seen in me, Let me ra - di - ate Thy love.

Copyright 1947. Renewal 1975. Hope Publishing Co., owner. All rights reserved.

151 When I See My Savior

And the people stood beholding. Luke 23:35

MAUD FRAZER

ROBERT HARKNESS

1. When I see my Sav - ior, hang - ing on Cal - va - ry,
2. I can see the blood - drops, red 'neath His thorn - y crown,
3. "Why hast thou for - sak - en?"—list to that sad, sad moan!

Bear - ing there for sin - ners bit - ter - est ag - o - ny,
From the cru - el nail - wounds now they are fall - ing down;
Oh, His heart was bro - ken, suf - fer - ing there a - lone:

Grat - i - tude o'er - whelms me, makes mine eyes grow dim,
Lord, when I would wan - der from Thy love a - way,
Bro - ken then that mor - tals ne'er need cry in vain

All my ran - somed be - ing cap - tive is to Him,
Let me see those blood - drops shed for me that day.
For God's love and com - fort, in the hour of pain.

Copyright 1911. Renewal 1939 extended. Hope Publishing Co., owner. All rights reserved.

There Is a Green Hill Far Away 152

Wherefore Jesus also . . . suffered without the gate. Heb. 13:12

CECIL F. ALEXANDER

GEORGE C. STEBBINS

1. There is a green hill far a - way, Out - side a cit - y wall,
2. We may not know, we can - not tell What pains He had to bear;
3. He died that we might be for - giv'n, He died to make us good,
4. There was no oth - er good e - nough To pay the price of sin;

Where the dear Lord was cru - ci - fied, Who died to save us all.
But we be - lieve it was for us He hung and suf - fered there.
That we might go at last to heav'n, Saved by His pre - cious blood.
He on - ly could un - lock the gate Of heav'n and let us in.

Chorus

O dear - ly, dear - ly has He loved, And we must love Him too;

And trust in His re - deem - ing blood, And try His works to do.

153 At the Cross

Surely He hath borne our griefs, and carried our sorrows. Isa. 53:4

Isaac Watts
Refrain, Ralph E. Hudson

Ralph E. Hudson

1. A-las! and did my Sav-ior bleed?And did my Sov-'reign die?
2. Was it for crimes that I have done He groaned up-on the tree?
3. Well might the sun in dark-ness hide, And shut his glo-ries in,
4. But drops of grief can ne'er re-pay The debt of love I owe:

Would He de-vote that sa-cred head For sin-ners such as I?
A-maz-ing pit-y! grace un-known! And love be-yond de-gree!
When Christ, the might-y Mak-er, died For man the crea-ture's sin.
Here, Lord, I give my-self a-way, 'Tis all that I can do!

Chorus

At the cross, at the cross where I first saw the light, And the

bur-den of my heart rolled a-way,(rolled a-way,) It was there by faith

I re-ceived my sight, And now I am hap-py all the day!

Beneath the Cross of Jesus 154

Now there stood by the cross of Jesus . . . John 19:25

ELIZABETH C. CLEPHANE   FREDERICK C. MAKER

1. Be - neath the cross of Je - sus I fain would take my stand—
2. Up - on that cross of Je - sus Mine eye at times can see
3. I take, O cross, thy shad - ow For my a - bid - ing place;

The shad - ow of a might - y Rock With - in a wea - ry land;
The ver - y dy - ing form of One Who suf - fered there for me;
I ask no oth - er sun - shine than The sun - shine of His face;

A home with - in the wil - der - ness, A rest up - on the way,
And from my smit - ten heart with tears Two won - ders I con - fess—
Con - tent to let the world go by, To know no gain nor loss,

From the burn - ing of the noon - tide heat, And the bur - den of the day.
The won - ders of re - deem - ing love And my un - wor - thi - ness.
My sin - ful self my on - ly shame, My glo - ry all the cross. A - men.

155 Here Comes Jesus

When the right time came, . . . God . . . sent his Son. Gal. 4:4

VERSE 1 Traditional
VERSES 2, 3, 4 BY CORDELIA SPITZER

Traditional melody
adapted by WILLIAM J. FLOYD

1. Here comes Je - sus, see Him walk-ing on the wa - ter,
2. Here comes Je - sus, see Him feed the hun - gry peo - ple,
3. Here comes Je - sus, see Him cleanse the lep - er,
4. Here comes Je - sus, see Him walk-ing up to Cal - va - ry,

He'll lift you up and He'll help you to stand;
He'll fill your life till you hun - ger no more;
He'll heal your heart and will give you His aid;
He's go-ing to die for you and me;

Oh, here comes Je - sus, He's the Mas - ter of the waves that roll.
Oh, here comes Je - sus, He's the an - swer to your ev - ery need.
Oh, here comes Je - sus, He's the great Phy - si - cian;
Oh, here comes Je - sus, He's the ran - som for the guilt - y one;

Here comes Je - sus, let Him take your hand.
Here comes Je - sus, He will your life re - store.
Here comes Je - sus, don't be a - fraid.
Here comes Je - sus, to set us free!

Copyright © 1971 by Hope Publishing Co. International copyright secured. All rights reserved.

Jesus Only, Let Me See 156

They saw no man, save Jesus only. Matt. 17:8

Oswald J. Smith

Daniel B. Towner

1. For sal - va - tion full and free, Pur-chased once on Cal - va - ry,
2. He my guide from day to day, As I jour - ney on life's way;
3. May my mod - el ev - er be Christ the Lord, and none save He,
4. He shall reign from shore to shore, His the glo - ry ev - er - more—

Christ a - lone shall be my plea— Je - sus! Je - sus on - ly.
Close be - side Him let me stay— Je - sus! Je - sus on - ly.
That the world may see in me Je - sus! Je - sus on - ly.
Heav'n and earth shall bow be - fore Je - sus! Je - sus on - ly.

Chorus

Je - sus on - ly, let me see, Je - sus on - ly, none save He,

Then my song shall ev - er be— Je - sus! Je - sus on - ly!

Copyright 1914. Renewal 1942 extended. Hope Publishing Co., owner. All rights reserved.

157 The Old Rugged Cross

Who for the joy that was set before Him endured the cross, despising the shame . . . Heb. 12:2

GEORGE BENNARD   GEORGE BENNARD

1. On a hill far a-way stood an old rug-ged cross, The em-blem of
2. O that old rug-ged cross, so de-spised by the world, Has a won-drous at-
3. In the old rug-ged cross, stained with blood so di-vine, A won-drous
4. To the old rug-ged cross I will ev-er be true, Its shame and re-

suf-fering and shame; And I love that old cross where the dear-est and best
trac-tion for me; For the dear Lamb of God left His glo-ry a-bove
beau-ty I see; For 'twas on that old cross Je-sus suf-fered and died
proach glad-ly bear; Then He'll call me some day to my home far a-way,

Chorus

For a world of lost sin-ners was slain.
To bear it to dark Cal-va-ry.
To par-don and sanc-ti-fy me. So I'll cher-ish the old rug-ged
Where His glo-ry for-ev-er I'll share. cross, the

cross, Till my tro-phies at last I lay down; I will cling to the
old rug-ged cross,

old rug-ged cross, And ex-change it some day for a crown.
cross, the old rug-ged cross,

Copyright 1913 by George Bennard. © Renewed 1941. The Rodeheaver Co. Used by permission.

When I Survey the Wondrous Cross 158

What things were gain to me, those I counted loss for Christ. Phil. 3:7

ISAAC WATTS

LOWELL MASON
Based on plainsong melody

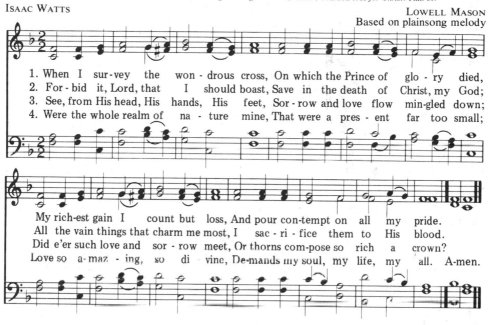

1. When I sur-vey the won-drous cross, On which the Prince of glo-ry died,
2. For-bid it, Lord, that I should boast, Save in the death of Christ, my God;
3. See, from His head, His hands, His feet, Sor-row and love flow min-gled down;
4. Were the whole realm of na-ture mine, That were a pres-ent far too small;

My rich-est gain I count but loss, And pour con-tempt on all my pride.
All the vain things that charm me most, I sac-ri-fice them to His blood.
Did e'er such love and sor-row meet, Or thorns com-pose so rich a crown?
Love so a-maz-ing, so di-vine, De-mands my soul, my life, my all. A-men.

Alas! and Did My Savior Bleed? 159

... He was bruised for our iniquities. Isa. 53:5

ISAAC WATTS

HUGH WILSON

1. A-las! and did my Sav-ior bleed, And did my Sov-'reign die? Would
2. Was it for crimes that I have done, He groaned up-on the tree? A-
3. Well might the sun in dark-ness hide And shut his glo-ries in, When
4. But drops of grief can ne'er re-pay The debt of love I owe; Here,

He de-vote that sa-cred head For sin-ners such as I?
maz-ing pit-y! grace un-known! And love be-yond de-gree!
God, the might-y Mak-er, died For man the crea-ture's sin.
Lord, I give my-self a-way; 'Tis all that I can do. A-men.

160 There Is a Fountain Filled with Blood

In that day there shall be a fountain opened . . . for sin and for uncleanness. Zech. 13:1

Traditional American melody
ARR. BY LOWELL MASON

WILLIAM COWPER

1. There is a foun-tain filled with blood Drawn from Im-man-uel's veins;
2. The dy-ing thief re-joiced to see That foun-tain in his day;
3. Dear dy-ing Lamb, Thy pre-cious blood Shall nev-er lose its pow'r,
4. E'er since by faith I saw the stream Thy flow-ing wounds sup-ply,
5. When this poor lisp-ing, stamm'ring tongue Lies si-lent in the grave,

And sin-ners, plunged be-neath that flood, Lose all their guilt-y stains:
And there may I, though vile as he, Wash all my sins a-way:
Till all the ran-somed Church of God Be saved, to sin no more,
Re-deem-ing love has been my theme, And shall be till I die:
Then in a no-bler, sweet-er song, I'll sing Thy pow'r to save:

Lose all their guilt-y stains, Lose all their guilt-y stains; And
Wash all my sins a-way, Wash all my sins a-way; And
Be saved, to sin no more, Be saved, to sin no more; Till
And shall be till I die, And shall be till I die; Re-
I'll sing Thy pow'r to save, I'll sing Thy pow'r to save; Then

sin-ners, plunged be-neath that flood, Lose all their guilt-y stains.
there may I, though vile as he, Wash all my sins a-way.
all the ran-somed Church of God Be saved, to sin no more.
deem-ing love has been my theme, And shall be till I die.
in a no-bler, sweet-er song I'll sing Thy pow'r to save. A-men.

O Sacred Head, Now Wounded 161

When they had platted a crown of thorns, they put it upon His head . . . Matt. 27:29

ATTR. TO BERNARD OF CLAIRVAUX
TRANS. (GERMAN) BY PAUL GERHARDT
TRANS. (ENGLISH) BY JAMES W. ALEXANDER

HANS LEO HASSLER
ARR. BY J. S. BACH

1. O   sa-cred Head, now wound-ed, With grief   and   shame weighed down,
2. What Thou, my Lord, hast suf-fered Was all   for   sin-ners'   gain;
3. What lan-guage shall I   bor-row To thank Thee, dear-est   friend,

Now   scorn-ful-ly   sur-round-ed   With thorns, Thine on-ly   crown:
Mine, mine was the trans-gres-sion, But Thine the dead-ly   pain.
For   this Thy dy-ing sor-row, Thy pit-y   with-out   end?

O   sa-cred Head, what   glo-ry, What bliss till now was   Thine!
Lo,   here I   fall,   my Sav-ior! 'Tis I   de-serve Thy   place;
O   make me Thine for-ev-er; And should I faint-ing   be,

Yet, though de-spised and   go-ry, I   joy   to call Thee mine.
Look on   me with Thy   fa-vor, Vouch-safe to   me Thy grace.
Lord, let   me nev-er,   nev-er Out-live my love to Thee. A-men.

162 In the Cross of Christ I Glory

God forbid that I should glory, save in the cross . . . Gal. 6:14

JOHN BOWRING

ITHAMAR CONKEY

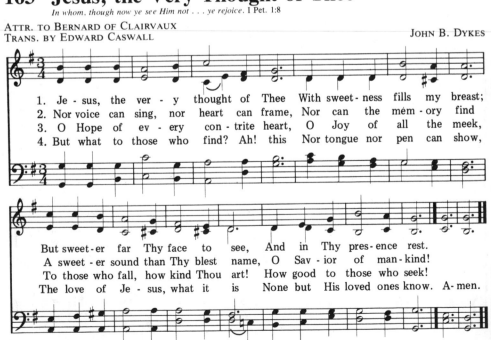

1. In the cross of Christ I glo-ry, Tow'r-ing o'er the wrecks of time;
2. When the woes of life o'er-take me, Hopes de-ceive, and fears an-noy,
3. When the sun of bliss is beam-ing Light and love up-on my way,
4. Bane and bless-ing, pain and pleas-ure, By the cross are sanc-ti-fied;

All the light of sa-cred sto-ry Gath-ers round its head sub-lime.
Nev-er shall the cross for-sake me: Lo! it glows with peace and joy.
From the cross the ra-diance stream-ing Adds more lus-ter to the day.
Peace is there that knows no meas-ure, Joys that thro' all time a-bide. A-men.

163 Jesus, the Very Thought of Thee

In whom, though now ye see Him not . . . ye rejoice. I Pet. 1:8

ATTR. TO BERNARD OF CLAIRVAUX
TRANS. BY EDWARD CASWALL

JOHN B. DYKES

1. Je-sus, the ver-y thought of Thee With sweet-ness fills my breast;
2. Nor voice can sing, nor heart can frame, Nor can the mem-ory find
3. O Hope of ev-ery con-trite heart, O Joy of all the meek,
4. But what to those who find? Ah! this Nor tongue nor pen can show,

But sweet-er far Thy face to see, And in Thy pres-ence rest.
A sweet-er sound than Thy blest name, O Sav-ior of man-kind!
To those who fall, how kind Thou art! How good to those who seek!
The love of Je-sus, what it is None but His loved ones know. A-men.

I Know That My Redeemer Liveth 164

. . . My Redeemer liveth, and . . . He shall stand at the latter day upon the earth. Job 19:25

JESSIE B. POUNDS

JAMES H. FILLMORE

1. I know that my Re-deem-er liv - eth, And on the earth
2. I know His prom-ise nev-er fail - eth, The word He speaks,
3. I know my man-sion He pre-par - eth, That where He is

1. And on the earth

a - gain shall stand; I know e-ter-nal life He giv - eth, That grace and
it can-not die; Tho' cru-el death my flesh as-sail - eth, Yet I shall
there I may be; O won-drous thought, for me He car - eth, And He at

1. That

pow'r are in His hand.
see Him by and by.
last will come for me.
grace and pow'r

Chorus

I know, I know that Je-sus
I know, I know

liv - eth, And on the earth a-gain shall stand. I know, I
And on the earth I

know that life He giv - eth, That grace and pow'r are in His hand.
know, I know

165 Christ the Lord Is Risen Today

Now is Christ risen . . . and become the first fruits of them that slept. I Cor. 15:20

CHARLES WESLEY

Arr. from *Lyra Davidica*, London, 1708

1. Christ the Lord is risen to-day, Al - le - lu - ia!
2. Lives a - gain our glo - rious King; Al - le - lu - ia!
3. Love's re - deem - ing work is done, Al - le - lu - ia!
4. Soar we now where Christ has led, Al - le - lu - ia!

Sons of men and an - gels say: Al - le - lu - ia!
Where, O death, is now thy sting? Al - le - lu - ia!
Fought the fight, the bat - tle won; Al - le - lu - ia!
Fol-lowing our ex - alt - ed Head; Al - le - lu - ia!

Raise your joys and tri - umphs high, Al - le - lu - ia!
Dy - ing once, He all doth save: Al - le - lu - ia!
Death in vain for - bids Him rise; Al - le - lu - ia!
Made like Him, like Him we rise; Al - le - lu - ia!

Sing, ye heav'ns, and earth re - ply, Al - le - lu - ia!
Where thy vic - to - ry, O grave? Al - le - lu - ia!
Christ has o - pened Par - a - dise. Al - le - lu - ia!
Ours the cross, the grave, the skies. Al - le - lu - ia! A-men.

Christ Arose! 166

The angel of the Lord . . . rolled back the stone from the door. Matt. 28:2

ROBERT LOWRY   ROBERT LOWRY

1. Low in the grave He lay—Je-sus my Sav-ior! Wait-ing the com-ing day—
2. Vain-ly they watch His bed—Je-sus my Sav-ior! Vain-ly they seal the dead—
3. Death can-not keep his prey—Je-sus my Sav-ior! He tore the bars a-way—

Chorus

Je - sus my Lord!
Je - sus my Lord! Up from the grave He a-rose, With a
Je - sus my Lord! He a-rose,

might - y tri-umph o'er His foes; He a-rose a vic-tor from the
He a-rose!

dark do-main, And He lives for-ev-er with His saints to reign. He a-

rose! He a-rose!
He a-rose! He a-rose! Hal-le-lu-jah! Christ a-rose!

167 He Lives

. . . That I may know Him, and the power of His resurrection. Phil. 3:10

ALFRED H. ACKLEY   ALFRED H. ACKLEY

1. I serve a ris-en Sav-ior, He's in the world to-day; I know that He is
2. In all the world a-round me I see His lov-ing care, And tho' my heart grows
3. Re-joice, re-joice, O Christ-ian, lift up your voice and sing E - ter-nal hal - le-

liv - ing, what - ev - er men may say; I see His hand of mer - cy, I
wea - ry, I nev - er will de - spair; I know that He is lead - ing thro'
lu - jahs to Je - sus Christ the King! The Hope of all who seek Him, the

hear His voice of cheer, And just the time I need Him He's al - ways near.
all the storm - y blast, The day of His ap - pear - ing will come at last.
Help of all who find, None oth - er is so lov - ing, so good and kind.

Chorus

He lives, He lives, Christ Je - sus lives to - day! He walks with me and
He lives, He lives,

talks with me a - long life's nar - row way. He lives, He lives, sal-
He lives, He lives,

Copyright 1933 by Homer A. Rodeheaver. © Renewed 1961. The Rodeheaver Co. All rights reserved. Used by permission.

va-tion to im - part! You ask me how I know He lives? He lives within my heart.

O Jesus, I Have Promised   168

If any man serve Me, let him follow Me . . . John 12:26

JOHN E. BODE

ARTHUR H. MANN

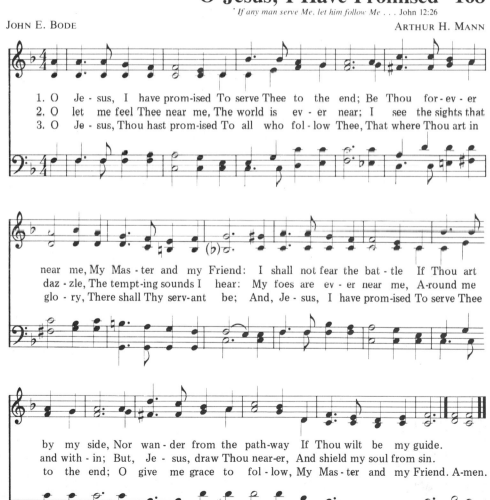

1. O Je - sus, I have prom-ised To serve Thee to the end; Be Thou for - ev - er
2. O let me feel Thee near me, The world is ev - er near; I see the sights that
3. O Je - sus, Thou hast prom-ised To all who fol - low Thee, That where Thou art in

near me, My Mas - ter and my Friend: I shall not fear the bat - tle If Thou art
daz - zle, The tempt-ing sounds I hear: My foes are ev - er near me, A-round me
glo - ry, There shall Thy serv-ant be; And, Je - sus, I have prom-ised To serve Thee

by my side, Nor wan - der from the path-way If Thou wilt be my guide.
and with - in; But, Je - sus, draw Thou near-er, And shield my soul from sin.
to the end; O give me grace to fol - low, My Mas - ter and my Friend. A-men.

Music copyright used by permission of E. R. Goodliffe, Somerset.

169 Because He Lives

Because I live, ye shall live also. John 14:19

GLORIA GAITHER AND
WILLIAM J. GAITHER

WILLIAM J. GAITHER

1. God sent His Son, they called Him Je - sus; He came to love,
2. How sweet to hold a new-born ba - by, And feel the pride
3. And then one day I'll cross the riv - er; I'll fight life's fi -

heal, and for - give; He lived and died to buy my
and joy He gives; But great - er still the calm as -
nal war with pain; And then as death gives way to

par - don, An emp - ty grave is there to prove my Sav - ior lives.
sur - ance, This child can face un - cer - tain days be - cause He lives.
vic - tory, I'll see the lights of glo - ry and I'll know He lives.

Chorus

Be - cause He lives I can face to - mor - row; Be - cause He lives
all fear is gone; Be - cause I know He holds the fu - ture,

© Copyright 1971 by William J. Gaither. International copyright secured. All rights reserved. Used by permission.

And life is worth the liv - ing just be - cause He lives.

Now I Belong to Jesus 170

Whether we live, therefore, or die, we are the Lord's. Rom. 14:8

NORMAN J. CLAYTON   NORMAN J. CLAYTON

1. Je - sus my Lord will love me for - ev - er, From Him no pow'r of e - vil can
2. Once I was lost in sin's deg - ra - da - tion, Je - sus came down to bring me sal -
3. Joy floods my soul for Je - sus has saved me, Freed me from sin that long had en -

sev - er, He gave His life to ran som my soul, Now I be - long to Him;
va - tion, Lift - ed me up from sor - row and shame, Now I be - long to Him;
slaved me, His pre - cious blood He gave to re - deem, Now I be - long to Him;

Chorus

Now I be - long to Je - sus, Je - sus be - longs to me,

Not for the years of time a - lone, But for e - ter - ni - ty.

Copyright 1938 and 1943 by Norman J. Clayton. © Renewed 1966, 1971, Norman Clayton Publishing Co. Used by permission.

171 Easter Song

He is not here: for He is risen, as He said. Matt. 28:6

ANNE HERRING   ANNE HERRING

Hear the bells ring-ing, they're sing-ing that we can be born a-gain. Hear the bells ring-ing, they're sing-ing "Christ is ris-en from the dead." The an-gel up on the tomb-stone said "He is ris-en just as He said.

© 1974 Latter Rain Music (ASCAP) used by permission.

172 Come, Ye Faithful, Raise the Strain

Thou hast ascended on high, Thou hast led captivity captive. Psa. 68:18

JOHN OF DAMASCUS
TRANS. BY JOHN M. NEALE

ARTHUR S. SULLIVAN

1. Come, ye faith-ful, raise the strain Of tri-um-phant glad-ness;
2. 'Tis the spring of souls to-day, Christ hath burst His pris-on,
3. "Al-le-lu-ia!" now we cry To our King Im-mor-tal,

God hath brought His peo-ple forth In-to joy from sad-ness.
And from three day's sleep in death As a sun hath ris-en.
Who, tri-um-phant, burst the bars Of the tomb's dark por-tal;

Now re-joice, Je-ru-sa-lem, And with true af-fec-tion
All the win-ter of our sins, Long and dark, is fly-ing
"Al-le-lu-ia!" with the Son, God the Fa-ther prais-ing;

Wel-come in un-wea-ried strains Je-sus' res-ur-rec-tion.
From His light, to whom we give Laud and praise un-dy-ing.
"Al-le-lu-ia!" yet a-gain To the Spir-it rais-ing. A-men.

All Hail the Power of Jesus' Name 173

He hath . . . a name written, King of Kings, and Lord of Lords. Rev. 19:16

EDWARD PERRONET
ADAPT. BY JOHN RIPPON

(DIADEM)
JAMES ELLOR

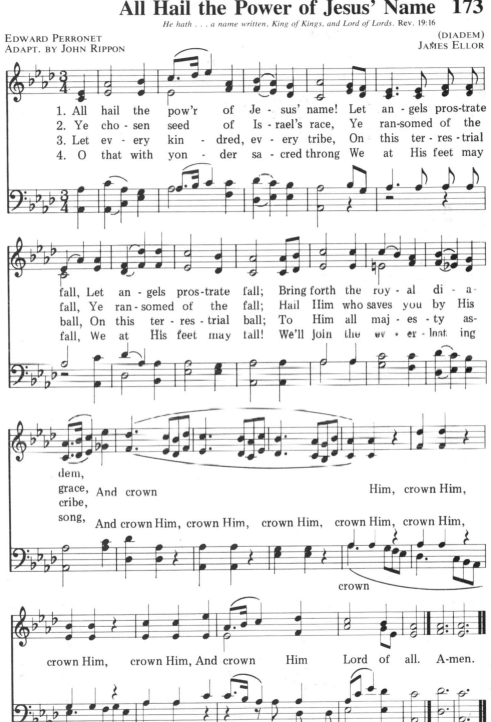

1. All hail the pow'r of Je - sus' name! Let an - gels pros-trate
2. Ye cho - sen seed of Is - rael's race, Ye ran-somed of the
3. Let ev - ery kin - dred, ev - ery tribe, On this ter - res-trial
4. O that with yon - der sa - cred throng We at His feet may

fall, Let an - gels pros-trate fall; Bring forth the roy - al di - a-
fall, Ye ran - somed of the fall; Hail Him who saves you by His
ball, On this ter - res - trial ball; To Him all maj - es - ty as-
fall, We at His feet may fall! We'll join the ev - er - last - ing

dem,
grace, And crown
cribe,
song, And crown Him, crown Him, crown Him, crown Him, crown Him,

Him, crown Him,

crown

crown Him, crown Him, And crown Him Lord of all. A-men.

Him,

And crown Him

174 In Tenderness He Sought Me

Rejoice with me; for I have found my sheep which was lost. Luke 15:6

W. SPENCER WALTON

ADONIRAM J. GORDON

1. In ten-der-ness He sought me, Wea-ry and sick with sin,
2. He washed the bleed-ing sin-wounds And poured in oil and wine;
3. He point-ed to the nail-prints, For me His blood was shed,
4. I'm sit-ting in His pres-ence, The sun-shine of His face,
5. So while the hours are pass-ing All now is per-fect rest;

And on His shoul-ders brought me Back to His fold a-gain. While
He whis-pered to as-sure me, "I've found thee, thou art Mine;" I
A mock-ing crown so thorn-y Was placed up-on His head: I
While with a-dor-ing won-der His bless-ings I re-trace: It
I'm wait-ing for the morn-ing, The bright-est and the best, When

an-gels in His pres-ence sang Un-til the courts of heav-en rang.
nev-er heard a sweet-er voice; It made my ach-ing heart re-joice!
won-dered what He saw in me To suf-fer such deep ag-o-ny.
seems as if e-ter-nal days Are far too short to sound His praise.
He will call us to His side, To be with Him, His spot-less bride.

Chorus

O the love that sought me! O the blood that bought me! O the grace that

brought me to the fold, Won-drous grace that brought me to the fold!

Wonderful Story of Love 175

And to know the love of Christ, which passeth knowledge . . . Eph. 3:19

J. M. DRIVER   J. M. DRIVER

1. Won-der-ful sto-ry of love; Tell it to me a - gain; Won-der-ful
2. Won-der-ful sto-ry of love; Tho' you are far a - way; Won-der-ful
3. Won-der-ful sto-ry of love; Je - sus pro-vides a rest; Won-der-ful

sto-ry of love; Wake the im-mor-tal strain! An-gels with rap-ture an-nounce it,
sto-ry of love; Still He doth call to - day; Call-ing from Cal - va - ry's moun-tain,
sto-ry of love; For all the pure and blest, Rest in those man-sions a - bove us,

Shep-herds with won - der re - ceive it; Sin - ner, O won't you be - lieve it?
Down from the crys - tal bright foun-tain, E'en from the dawn of cre - a - tion,
With those who've gone on be - fore us, Sing - ing the rap - tur - ous cho - rus,

Chorus

Won-der-ful sto-ry of love. Won - der - ful! Won - der -
Won-der-ful sto-ry of love; Won-der-ful sto - ry of

ful! Won - der - ful! Won-der - ful sto - ry of love!
love; Won-der-ful sto - ry of love;

176 Without Him

The Son of man is come to save that which was lost. Matt. 18:11

MYLON R. LeFevre   MYLON R. LeFevre

1. With - out Him I could do noth - ing, With - out Him
2. With - out Him I could be dy - ing, With - out Him

I'd sure - ly fail; With - out Him I would be drift - ing
I'd be en - slaved; With - out Him life would be hope - less,

Chorus

Like a ship with - out a sail. Je - sus, O Je - sus,
But with Je - sus, thank God, I'm saved.

Do you know Him to - day? You can't turn Him a - way. O

Je - sus, O Je - sus, With - out him, How lost I would be.

© Copyright 1963 by LeFevre Sing Publishing Company. International copyright secured. All rights reserved. Used by permission.

Something Beautiful 177

If any man be in Christ, he is a new creature. II Cor. 5:17

GLORIA GAITHER

WILLIAM J. GAITHER

Some - thing beau - ti - ful, some - thing good;

All my con - fu - sion He un - der - stood;

All I had to of - fer Him was bro - ken - ness and

strife, But He made some - thing beau - ti - ful of my life.

© Copyright 1971 by William J. Gaither. International copyright secured. All rights reserved. Used by permission.

178 Yesterday, Today and Tomorrow

Chirst died for our sins according to the scriptures . . . . I Cor. 15:3

JACK WYRTZEN

DON WYRTZEN

Yes-ter-day He died for me, yes-ter-day, yes-ter-day, Yes-ter-day He

died for me, yes-ter-day, Yes-ter-day He died for me, died for me—

This is his-to-ry. To-day He lives for me, to-day,

to-day, To-day He lives for me, to-day, To-day He

lives for me, lives for me— This is vic-to-ry.

© Copyright 1966 by Singspiration, Inc. All rights reserved. Used by permission.

179 A Child of the King

We are the children of God; and if children, then heirs. Rom. 8:16, 17

HARRIET E. BUELL

JOHN B. SUMNER

1. My Fa - ther is rich in hous - es and lands, He hold - eth the
2. My Fa - ther's own Son, the Sav - ior of men, Once wan - dered on
3. I once was an out - cast stran - ger on earth, A sin - ner by
4. A tent or a cot - tage, why should I care? They're build-ing a

wealth of the world in His hands! Of ru - bies and dia - monds, of
earth as the poor - est of them; But now He is reign - ing for -
choice, and an al - ien by birth; But I've been a - dopt - ed, my
pal - ace for me o - ver there; Though ex - iled from home, yet

sil - ver and gold, His cof - fers are full, He has rich - es un - told.
ev - er on high, And will give me a home in heav'n by and by.
name's writ - ten down, An heir to a man - sion, a robe, and a crown.
still I may sing: All glo - ry to God, I'm a child of the King.

Chorus

I'm a child of the King, A child of the King:

With Je - sus my Sav - ior, I'm a child of the King.

A Shelter in the Time of Storm   180

A man shall be . . . like the shadow of a great rock in a weary land. Isa. 32:2

VERNON J. CHARLESWORTH
ADAPT. BY IRA D. SANKEY

IRA D. SANKEY

1. The Lord's our rock, in Him we hide, A shel-ter in the time of storm;
2. A shade by day, de-fense by night, A shel-ter in the time of storm;
3. The rag-ing storms may round us beat, A shel-ter in the time of storm;
4. O Rock di-vine, O Ref-uge dear, A shel-ter in the time of storm;

Se-cure what-ev-er ill be-tide, A shel-ter in the time of storm.
No tears a-larm, no foes af-fright, A shel-ter in the time of storm.
We'll nev-er leave our safe re-treat, A shel-ter in the time of storm.
Be Thou our help-er ev-er near, A shel-ter in the time of storm.

Chorus

O, Je-sus is a rock in a wea-ry land, A wea-ry land, a wea-ry land;

O, Je-sus is a rock in a wea-ry land, A shel-ter in the time of storm.

181 Accepted in the Beloved

. . . He hath made us accepted in the Beloved. Eph. 1:6

CIVILLA D. MARTIN

WENDELL P. LOVELESS

1. "In the Be-lov-ed" ac-cept-ed am I, Ris-en, as-cend-ed, and
2. "In the Be-lov-ed"—how safe my re-treat, In the Be-lov-ed ac-
3. "In the Be-lov-ed" I went to the tree, There, in His Per-son, by

seat-ed on high; Saved from all sin thro' His in-fi-nite grace,
count-ed com-plete; "Who can con-demn me?" In Him I am free,
faith I may see In-fi-nite wrath roll-ing o-ver His head,

Chorus

With the re-deemed ones ac-cord-ed a place.
Sav-ior and Keep-er for-ev-er is He. "In the Be-lov-ed,"God's
In-fi-nite grace, for He died in my stead.

mar-vel-ous grace Calls me to dwell in this won-der-ful place; God sees my

Sav-ior and then He sees me "In the Be-lov-ed,"ac-cept-ed and free.

Copyright 1930. Renewal 1958. Hope Publishing Co., owner. All rights reserved.

All Because of Calvary 182

This is my blood . . . which is shed for the remission of sins. Matt. 26:28

WENDELL P. LOVELESS

WENDELL P. LOVELESS

All my sins are gone, All be-cause of
All my sins are gone,

Cal - va - ry; Life is filled with song,
Life is filled with

All be-cause of Cal - va - ry; Christ my Sav - ior lives,
song Christ my Sav - ior

Lives from sin to set me free; Some day He's com - ing, O
lives

won - drous, bless - ed day, All, yes, all be - cause of Cal - va - ry.

Copyright 1940. Renewal 1968. Hope Publishing Co., owner. All rights reserved.

might be easier to direct
3/4 instead of 6/8

183 Heaven Came Down and Glory Filled My Soul

If any man be in Christ, he is a new creature. II Cor. 5:17

JOHN W. PETERSON

JOHN W. PETERSON

1. O what a won-der-ful, won-der-ful day— Day I will
2. Born of the Spir-it with life from a-bove In-to God's
3. Now I've a hope that will sure-ly en-dure Aft-er the

nev-er for-get; Aft-er I'd wan-dered in dark-ness a-way,
fam-ily di-vine, Jus-ti-fied ful-ly thro' Cal-va-ry's love,
pass-ing of time; I have a fu-ture in heav-en for sure,

Je-sus my Sav-ior I met. O what a ten-der, com-pas-sion-ate friend—
O what a stand-ing is mine! And the trans-ac-tion so quick-ly was made
There in those man-sions sub-lime. And it's be-cause of that won-der-ful day

He met the need of my heart; Shad-ows dis-pel-ling, With
When as a sin-ner I came, Took of the of-fer Of
When at the cross I be-lieved; Rich-es e-ter-nal And

© Copyright 1961 by Singspiration, Inc. All rights reserved. Used by permission.

joy I am tell - ing, He made all the dark - ness de - part!
grace He did prof - fer— He saved me, O praise His dear name!
bless - ings su - per - nal From His pre - cious hand I re - ceived.

Chorus

Heav - en came down and glo - ry filled my soul, (filled my soul,)

When at the cross the Sav - ior made me whole; (made me whole;) My

sins were washed a - way And my night was turned to day—

Heav - en came down and glo - ry filled my soul! (filled my soul!)

184 The Old Rugged Cross Made the Difference

The law of the Spirit of life in Christ Jesus has made me free . . . Rom. 8:2

GLORIA GAITHER AND
WILLIAM J. GAITHER

WILLIAM J. GAITHER

1. 'Twas a life filled with aim-less des-per-a-tion,
2. Bar-ren walls ech-oed harsh-ness and an-ger,
3. There's a room filled with sad, ash-en fa-ces,

With-out hope walk'd the shell of a man;
Lit-tle feet ran in ter-ror to hide;
With-out hope death has wrapp'd them in gloom;

Then a hand with a nail-print stretch'd down-ward,
Now those walls ring with love, warmth and laugh-ter,
But at the side of a saint there's re-joic-ing,

Just one touch, then a new life be-gan.
Since the Giv-er of life moved in-side.
For life can't be seal'd in a tomb.

© Copyright 1970 by William J. Gaither. International copyright secured. All rights reserved. Used by permission.

Chorus

And the old rug - ged cross made the dif - ference

In a life bound for heart - ache and de - feat;

I will praise Him for - ev - er and ev - er,

For the cross made the dif - ference for me.

185 All Things in Jesus

Of His fulness have all we received, and grace for grace. John 1:16

HARRY D. LOES   HARRY D. LOES

1. Friends all a-round us are try-ing to find What the heart yearns for, by
2. Some car-ry bur-dens whose weight has for years Crushed them with sor-row and
3. No oth-er name stirs the joy chords with-in, And thro' none else is re-
4. Je-sus is all this sad world needs to-day; Blind-ly men strive, for sin

sin un-der-mined; I have the se-cret, I know where 'tis found:
blind-ed with tears; Yet One stands read-y to help them just now,
mis-sion of sin; He knows the pain of the heart sore-ly tried,
dark-ens the way. O to draw back the grim cur-tains of night—

Chorus

On-ly in Je-sus true pleas-ures a-bound.
If they with faith and in pen-i-tence bow.
All of its needs will in Him be sup-plied.   All that I want is in
One glimpse of Je-sus, and all will be bright.

Je - sus;   He sat-is-fies,   joy He sup-plies;
Je-sus, in Je - sus;   with the   free-ly

Life would be worth-less with-out   Him,   All things in Je-sus I find.
                     with-out Him, with-out Him,

Copyright 1915. Renewal 1943 extended. Hope Publishing Co., owner. All rights reserved.

Since I Have Been Redeemed 186

Let the redeemed of the Lord say so . . . Psa. 107:2

EDWIN O. EXCELL

EDWIN O. EXCELL

1. I have a song I love to sing, Since I have been re-deemed,
2. I have a Christ who sat - is - fies, Since I have been re-deemed;
3. I have a wit - ness bright and clear, Since I have been re-deemed,
4. I have a home pre - pared for me, Since I have been re-deemed,

Of my Re - deem - er, Sav - ior, King, Since I have been re-deemed.
To do His will my high - est prize, Since I have been re-deemed.
Dis - pel - ling ev - ery doubt and fear, Since I have been re-deemed.
Where I shall dwell e - ter - nal - ly, Since I have been re-deemed.

Chorus

Since I have been re - deemed, Since I have been re-
Since I have been re-deemed, Since I have been re-deemed,

deemed, I will glo - ry in His name; Since I have been re-
Since I have been re-deemed, Since

deemed, I will glo - ry in my Sav - ior's name.
I have been re - deemed,

187 At Calvary

And When they were come to . . . Calvary, there they crucified Him. Luke 23:33

WILLIAM R. NEWELL

DANIEL B. TOWNER

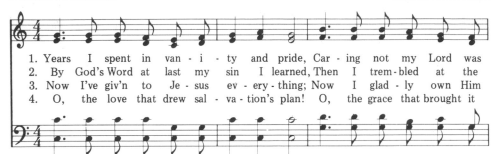

1. Years I spent in van - i - ty and pride, Car - ing not my Lord was
2. By God's Word at last my sin I learned, Then I trem - bled at the
3. Now I've giv'n to Je - sus ev - ery - thing; Now I glad - ly own Him
4. O, the love that drew sal - va - tion's plan! O, the grace that brought it

cru - ci - fied, Know - ing not it was for me He died On Cal - va - ry.
law I'd spurned, Till my guilt - y soul im - plor - ing turned To Cal - va - ry.
as my King; Now my rap - tured soul can on - ly sing Of Cal - va - ry.
down to man! O, the might - y gulf that God did span At Cal - va - ry!

Chorus

Mer - cy there was great, and grace was free; Par - don there was mul - ti -

plied to me; There my bur - dened soul found lib - er - ty, At Cal - va - ry.

I Belong to the King 188

. . . We are the children of God. Rom. 8:16

IDA R. SMITH

J. LINCOLN HALL

1. I be-long to the King, I'm a child of His love, I shall dwell in His
2. I be-long to the King, and He loves me, I know, For His mer-cy and
3. I be-long to the King, and His prom-ise is sure, That we all shall be

pal-ace so fair; For He tells of its bliss in yon heav-en a-bove, And His
kind-ness, so free, Are un-ceas-ing-ly mine where-so-ev-er I go, And my
gath-ered at last In His king-dom a-bove, by life's wa-ters so pure, When this

chil-dren its splen-dors shall share.
ref-uge un-fail-ing is He.
life with its tri-als is past.

Chorus

I be-long to the King, I'm a
child of His love, And He nev-er for-sak-eth His own; He will call me some
day to His pal-ace a-bove, I shall dwell by His glo-ri-fied throne.

189 A New Name in Glory

Rejoice, because your names are written in heaven. Luke 10:20

C. AUSTIN MILES

C. AUSTIN MILES

1. I was once a sin-ner, but I came Par-don to re-ceive
2. I was hum-bly kneel-ing at the cross, Fear-ing naught but God's
3. In the Book 'tis writ-ten, "Saved by Grace," O the joy that came

from my Lord: This was free-ly giv-en, and I found
an-gry frown; When the heav-ens o-pened and I saw
to my soul! Now I am for-giv-en, and I know

That He al-ways kept His word (kept His word).
That my name was writ-ten down (writ-ten down).
By the blood I am made whole (am made whole).

Chorus

There's a new name writ-ten down in glo-ry, And it's

Copyright 1910 by Hall-Mack Co. © Renewed 1938. The Rodeheaver Co. Used by permission.

190 I Love to Tell the Story

And they sang a new song saying, Thou art worthy . . . Rev. 5:9

A. CATHERINE HANKEY   WILLIAM G. FISCHER

1. I love to tell the sto - ry Of un - seen things a -
2. I love to tell the sto - ry, More won - der - ful it
3. I love to tell the sto - ry, 'Tis pleas - ant to re -
4. I love to tell the sto - ry, For those who know it

bove, Of Je - sus and His glo - ry, Of Je - sus and His
seems Than all the gold - en fan - cies Of all our gold - en
peat What seems, each time I tell it, More won - der - ful - ly
best Seem hun - ger - ing and thirst - ing To hear it like the

love. I love to tell the sto - ry Be - cause I know 'tis
dreams. I love to tell the sto - ry, It did so much for
sweet. I love to tell the sto - ry, For some have nev - er
rest. And when, in scenes of glo - ry, I sing the new, new

true; It sat - is - fies my long - ings As noth - ing else can do.
me; And that is just the rea - son I tell it now to thee.
heard The mes - sage of sal - va - tion From God's own Ho - ly Word.
song, 'Twill be the old, old sto - ry That I have loved so long.

Chorus

I love to tell the sto - ry, 'Twill be my theme in glo - ry,

To tell the old, old sto-ry Of Je-sus and His love.

Christ Liveth in Me   191

Nevertheless I live; yet not I, but Christ liveth in me . . . Gal. 2:20

DANIEL W. WHITTLE

JAMES McGRANAHAN

1. Once far from God and dead in sin, No light my heart could see,
2. As rays of light from yon-der sun The flow'rs of earth set free,
3. As lives the flow'r with-in the seed, As in the cone the tree,
4. With long-ing all my heart is filled That like Him I may be,

But in God's Word the light I found—Now Christ liv-eth in me.
So life and light and love came forth From Christ liv-ing in me.
So, praise the God of truth and grace, His Spir-it dwell-eth in me.
As on the won-drous thought I dwell, That Christ liv-eth in me.

Chorus

Christ liv-eth in me, Christ liv-eth in me;
Christ liv-eth in me, Christ liv-eth in

O what a sal-va-tion this— That Christ liv-eth in me.
me; O

192 Altogether Lovely

Yea, He is altogether lovely. S. of S. 5:16

WENDELL P. LOVELESS

WENDELL P. LOVELESS

Al - to - geth - er love - ly, He is al - to - geth - er love - ly, And the fair - est of ten thou - sand, This won - der - ful Friend di - vine; He gave Him - self to save me, Now He lives in heav'n to keep me, He is al - to - geth - er love - ly, Is this won - der - ful Sav - ior of mine.

Copyright 1931. Renewal 1959. Hope Publishing Co.. owner. All rights reserved.

The Light of the World Is Jesus 193

I am the light of the world . . . John 8.12

PHILIP P. BLISS

PHILIP P. BLISS

1. The whole world was lost in the dark-ness of sin; The Light of the
2. No dark-ness have we who in Je - sus a - bide, The Light of the
3. Ye dwell - ers in dark-ness with sin-blind-ed eyes, The Light of the
4. No need of the sun-light in heav - en, we're told, The Light of the

world is Je - sus; Like sun-shine at noon-day His glo - ry shone in,
world is Je - sus; We walk in the Light when we fol - low our Guide,
world is Je - sus; Go wash at His bid-ding and light will a - rise,
world is Je - sus; The Lamb is the Light in the Cit - y of Gold,

Chorus

The Light of the world is Je - sus. Come to the Light, 'tis

shin - ing for thee; Sweet-ly the Light has dawned up - on me;

Once I was blind, but now I can see; The Light of the world is Je - sus.

194 He's Everything to Me

When I consider Thy heavens . . . what is man, that Thou art mindful of him? Psa. 8:3, 4

RALPH CARMICHAEL   RALPH CARMICHAEL

1. In the stars His hand-i-work I see,   On the wind He speaks in maj-es-ty,
2. I will cel - e - brate na -tiv - i - ty   For it has a place in his-to-ry,

Though He ruleth o - ver land and sea,   What is that to   me?   What is that to
Sure, He came to set His people free,

me?   Till by faith I met Him face to face, And I felt the won-der of His grace,

Then I knew that He was more than just a God who did-n't care, who lived a-way out

there, And now He walks be-side me day by day,   Ev -er watch-ing o'er me lest I stray,

© Copyright 1964 by LEXICON MUSIC, INC. ASCAP. All rights reserved. International copyright secured. Used by special permission.

Helping me to find that narrow way, He's everything to me.

Glory to His Name 195

. . . Having made peace by the blood of His cross. Col. 1:20

ELISHA A. HOFFMAN

JOHN H. STOCKTON

1. Down at the cross where my Savior died, Down where for cleansing from
2. I am so wondrous-ly saved from sin, Jesus so sweetly a-
3. O precious foun-tain that saves from sin, I am so glad I have
4. Come to this foun-tain so rich and sweet; Cast your poor soul at the

sin I cried, There to my heart was the blood applied; Glory to His name!
bides with-in, There at the cross where He took me in; Glory to His name!
en-tered in; There Jesus saves me and keeps me clean; Glory to His name!
Sav-ior's feet; Plunge in to-day and be made com-plete; Glory to His name!

Chorus

Glory to His name, Glory to His name;

There to my heart was the blood applied; Glory to His name!

196 Trust and Obey

If ye continue in My word, then are ye My disciples indeed. John 8:31

John H. Sammis

Daniel B. Towner

1. When we walk with the Lord in the light of His Word,
2. Not a shad - ow can rise, not a cloud in the skies,
3. Not a bur - den we bear, not a sor - row we share,
4. But we nev - er can prove the de - lights of His love
5. Then in fel - low - ship sweet we will sit at His feet,

What a glo - ry He sheds on our way! While we do His good
But His smile quick - ly drives it a - way; Not a doubt nor a
But our toil He doth rich - ly re - pay; Not a grief nor a
Un - til all on the al - tar we lay; For the fa - vor He
Or we'll walk by His side in the way; What He says we will

will He a - bides with us still, And with all who will
fear, not a sigh nor a tear, Can a - bide while we
loss, not a frown nor a cross, But is blest if we
shows and the joy He be - stows Are for them who will
do, where He sends we will go— Nev - er fear, on - ly

Chorus

trust and o - bey. Trust and o - bey, for there's no oth - er

way To be hap - py in Je - sus, But to trust and o - bey.

Blessed Assurance 197

I will sing praises unto my God while I have any being. Psa. 146:2

FANNY J. CROSBY

PHOEBE P. KNAPP

1. Bless - ed as - sur - ance, Je - sus is mine! O, what a fore - taste of
2. Per - fect sub - mis - sion, per - fect de - light, Vi - sions of rap - ture now
3. Per - fect sub - mis - sion, all is at rest, I in my Sav - ior am

glo - ry di - vine! Heir of sal - va - tion, pur - chase of God,
burst on my sight; An - gels de - scend - ing, bring from a - bove
hap - py and blest; Watch - ing and wait - ing, look - ing a - bove,

Chorus

Born of His Spir - it, washed in His blood.
Ech - oes of mer - cy, whis - pers of love.
Filled with His good - ness, lost in His love.

This is my sto - ry, this is my

song, Prais - ing my Sav - ior all the day long; This is my sto - ry,

this is my song, Prais - ing my Sav - ior all the day long.

198 Dwelling in Beulah Land

Thy land (shall be called) Beulah; for the Lord delighteth in thee. Isa. 62:4

C. AUSTIN MILES

C. AUSTIN MILES

1. Far a - way the noise of strife up - on my ear is
2. Far be - low the storm of doubt up - on the world is
3. Let the storm - y breez - es blow, their cry can - not a -
4. View - ing here the works of God, I sink in con - tem -

fall - ing, Then I know the sins of earth be - set on ev - ery
beat - ing, Sons of men in bat - tle long the en - e - my with -
larm me; I am safe - ly shel - tered here, pro - tect - ed by God's
pla - tion, Hear - ing now His bless - ed voice, I see the way He

hand: Doubt and fear and things of earth in vain to me are
stand: Safe am I with - in the cas - tle of God's word re -
hand: Here the sun is al - ways shin - ing, here there's naught can
planned: Dwell - ing in the Spir - it, here I learn of full sal -

call - ing, None of these shall move me from Beu - lah Land.
treat - ing, Noth - ing then can reach me — 'tis Beu - lah Land.
harm me, I am safe for - ev - er in Beu - lah Land.
va - tion, Glad - ly will I tar - ry in Beu - lah Land.

Copyright 1911 by Hall-Mack Co. © Renewed 1939, The Rodeheaver Co. Used by permission.

Chorus

I'm liv-ing on the moun-tain, un-der-neath a cloud-less sky, I'm drink-ing at the foun-tain that nev-er shall run dry; O yes! I'm feast-ing on the man-na from a boun-ti-ful sup-ply, For I am dwell-ing in Beu-lah Land.

Praise God!

199 'Twas a Glad Day When Jesus Found Me

Rejoice with me; for I have found my sheep which was lost. Luke 15:6

ALBERT S. REITZ   ALBERT S. REITZ

1. I was lost in sin when Je - sus found me, But He res - cued me,
2. O the bells of heav - en now are ring - ing, For I hear their tones
3. O the joy when we shall meet in glo - ry, In the man - sions of

all glo - ry to His name! And the cords of world - ly
with - in my ran - somed soul; And my heart is filled with
my Fa - ther's home a - bove; And thro' end - less a - ges

pleas - ure bound me, Till He saved me from sin and shame.
joy - ful sing - ing Since the Sav - ior hath made me whole.
tell the sto - ry Of the Sav - ior's re - deem - ing love.

Chorus

'Twas a glad day when Je - sus found me, When His strong arms were

thrown a - round me; When my sins He bur - ied in the deep - est sea,

Copyright 1918. Renewal 1946 extended. Hope Publishing Co., owner. All rights reserved.

And my soul He filled with joy and vic - to - ry, 'Twas a

glad day, O hal - le - lu - jah! 'Twas a glad day He claimed His own; I will

shout a glad ho - san - na in glo - ry When I see Him up - on His throne.

Amazing Grace! 200

God is able to make all grace abound toward you . . . II Cor. 9:8

JOHN NEWTON
St. 4, Source unknown

Traditional American melody
ARR. BY EDWIN O. EXCELL

1. A - maz - ing grace! how sweet the sound That saved a wretch like me!
2. 'Twas grace that taught my heart to fear, And grace my fears re - lieved;
3. Through man - y dan - gers, toils and snares, I have al - read - y come;
4. When we've been there ten thou - sand years, Bright shin - ing as the sun,

I once was lost, but now am found, Was blind, but now I see.
How pre - cious did that grace ap - pear The hour I first be - lieved!
'Tis grace hath brought me safe thus far, And grace will lead me home.
We've no less days to sing God's praise Than when we first be - gun.

201 He Included Me

Whosoever will, let him take the water of life freely. Rev. 22:17

JOHNSON OATMAN, JR.   HAMPTON H. SEWELL

1. I am so hap-py in Christ to-day, That I go sing-ing a-
2. Glad-ly I read, "Who-so-ev-er may Come to the foun-tain of
3. Ev-er God's Spi-rit is say-ing, "Come!" Hear the Bride say-ing, "No
4. "Free-ly come drink," words the soul to thrill! O with what joy they my

long my way; Yes, I'm so hap-py to know and say,
life to-day;" But when I read it I al-ways say,
long-er roam;" But I am sure while they're call-ing home,
heart do fill! For when He said, "Who-so-ev-er will,"

Chorus

"Je-sus in-clud-ed me too."
"Je-sus in-clud-ed me too."
Je-sus in-clud-ed me too.   Je-sus in-clud-ed me,
Je-sus in-clud-ed me too.

Yes, He in-clud-ed me,   When the Lord said "Who-so-ev-er,"

He in-clud-ed me; Je-sus in-clud-ed me, Yes, He in-clud-ed me,

© 1913 and renewed 1941 by John T. Benson, Jr. Copyright extended. International copyright secured. All rights reserved. Printed by permission of The Benson Company, 365 Great Circle Road, Nashville, TN 37228.

When the Lord said "Who - so - ev - er," He in - clud - ed me.

Fully Surrendered 202

Yield yourselves unto God, as those that are alive from the dead . . . Rom. 6:13

ALFRED C. SNEAD

GEORGE C. STEBBINS

1. Ful - ly sur-rend - ered, Lord, I would be, Ful - ly sur-rend - ered, dear Lord, to Thee; All on the al - tar laid, Sur-rend - er ful - ly made, Thou hast my ran - som paid, I yield to Thee.

2. Ful - ly sur-rend - ered—life, time and all, All Thou hast giv'n me held at Thy call. Speak but the word to me, Glad - ly I'll fol - low Thee, Now and e - ter - nal - ly O - bey my Lord.

3. Ful - ly sur-rend - ered— sil - ver and gold, His, Who hath giv'n me rich - es un - told. All, all be - long to Thee, For Thou didst pur - chase me, Thine ev - er - more to be, Je - sus my Lord.

4. Ful - ly sur-rend - ered, Lord, I am Thine; Ful - ly sur-rend - ered, Sav - ior di - vine; Live Thou Thy life in me, All ful - ness dwells in Thee, Not I, but Christ in me, Christ all in all.

Copyright 1936. Renewal 1964. Hope Publishing Co., owner. All rights reserved.

203 The Stranger of Galilee

And Jesus, walking by the sea of Galilee . . . Matt. 4:18

LELIA N. MORRIS   LELIA N. MORRIS

1. In fan-cy I stood by the shore, one day, Of the
2. His look of com-pas-sion, His words of love, They shall
3. I heard Him speak peace to the an-gry waves, Of that
4. Come ye who are driv-en, and tem-pest-tossed, And His

beau-ti-ful mur-m'ring sea; I saw the great crowds as they
nev-er for-got-ten be, When sin-sick and help-less He
tur-bu-lent, rag-ing sea; And lo! at His word are the
gra-cious sal-va-tion see; He'll qui-et life's storms with His

thronged the way Of the Stran-ger of Gal-i-lee; I
saw me there, This Stran-ger of Gal-i-lee; He
wa-ters stilled, This Stran-ger of Gal-i-lee; A
"Peace, be still!" This Stran-ger of Gal-i-lee; He

saw how the man who was blind from birth, In a
showed me His hand and His riv-en side, And He
peace-ful, a qui-et, and ho-ly calm, Now and
bids me to go and the sto-ry tell— What He

Used by permission of the copyright owner. Boston Music Company, Boston, Mass. by arrangement with Standard Publishing Company.

mo-ment was made to see; The lame was made whole by the match-less skill
whisp-ered "It was for thee!" My bur-den fell off at the pierc-ed feet
ev - er a-bides with me; He hold-eth my life in His might-y hands,
ev - er to you will be, If on-ly you let Him with you a-bide,

Chorus

Of the Stran-ger of Gal - i - lee.
Of the Stran-ger of Gal - i - lee. And I felt I could love Him for -
This Stran-ger of Gal - i - lee.
This Stran-ger of Gal - i - lee. (4 v.) Oh, my friend, won't you love Him for -

ev - er, So gra-cious and ten - der was He! I
ev - er? So gra-cious and ten - der is He! Ac -

claimed Him that day as my Sav - ior, This Strang-er of Gal - i - lee.
cept Him to-day as your Sav - ior, This Strang-er of Gal - i - lee.

204 When Love Shines In

For God . . . hath shined in our hearts. II Cor. 4:6

CARRIE E. BRECK

WILLIAM J. KIRKPATRICK

1. Je - sus comes with pow'r to glad - den, When love shines in,
2. How the world will grow with beau - ty, When love shines in,
3. Dark - est sor - row will grow bright - er, When love shines in,
4. We may have un - fad - ing splen - dor, When love shines in,

Ev - ery life that woe can sad - den, When love shines in. .
And the heart re - joice in du - ty, When love shines in.
And the heav - iest bur - den light - er, When love shines in.
And a friend-ship true and ten - der, When love shines in.

Love will teach us how to pray, Love will drive the gloom a - way,
Tri - als may be sanc - ti - fied, And the soul in peace a - bide,
'Tis the glo - ry that will throw Light to show us where to go;
When earth's vic - t'ries shall be won, And our life in heav'n be - gun;

Turn our dark - ness in - to day— When love shines in.
Life will all be glo - ri - fied— When love shines in.
O the heart shall bless - ing know— When love shines in.
There will be no need of sun— When love shines in.

Chorus

When love shines in,   When love   shines   in,
When love, when love shines in,   When love shines in,

How the heart is tuned to sing-ing, When love   shines   in,   When

love shines in,   When love   shines   in,
love, when love shines in,   When love shines in,

Joy and peace to oth-ers bring-ing—When love shines   in!

205 Wonderful Grace of Jesus

For ye know the grace of our Lord Jesus Christ . . . II Cor. 8:9

HALDOR LILLENAS

HALDOR LILLENAS

1. Won - der - ful grace of Je - sus, Great - er than all my sin;
2. Won - der - ful grace of Je - sus, Reach - ing to all the lost,
3. Won - der - ful grace of Je - sus, Reach - ing the most de - filed,

How shall my tongue de - scribe it, Where shall its praise be - gin?
By it I have been par - doned, Saved to the ut - ter - most;
By its trans-form - ing pow - er Mak - ing him God's dear child,

Tak - ing a - way my bur - den, Set - ting my spir - it free,
Chains have been torn a - sun - der, Giv - ing me lib - er - ty,
Pur - chas - ing peace and heav - en For all e - ter - ni - ty—

For the won - der - ful grace of Je - sus reach - es me.
For the won - der - ful grace of Je - sus reach - es me.
And the won - der - ful grace of Je - sus reach - es me.

Chorus

Won - der - ful the match-less grace of Je - sus, the match-less grace of Je - sus, Deep - er than the

Copyright 1918. Renewal 1946 extended. Hope Publishing Co., owner. All rights reserved.

206 It's a Miracle

Such mighty works are wrought by His hands. Mark 6:2

GLORIA GAITHER AND
WILLIAM J. GAITHER

WILLIAM J. GAITHER

1. What drives the stars with-out mak-ing a sound? Why don't they
2. Who shows the birds how to make a good nest? How can the

crash when they're spin-ning a-round? What holds me up when the
geese fly so far with-out rest? Why do the ducks go

world's up-side down? I know it's a mir-a-cle. Who tells the
south and not west? I know it's a mir-a-cle. What makes a

o-ceans where to stop on the sand? What keeps the wa-ter back from
brown seed so ti-ny and dry, Burst in-to green,

drown-ing the land? Who makes the rules I don't un-der-stand?
grow up so high, And shoot out blos-soms of red by and by?

© Copyright 1975 by William J. Gaither. International copyright secured. All rights reserved. Used by permission.

Peace Like a River 207

The fruit of the Spirit is love, joy, peace . . . Gal. 5:22

Traditional   Traditional

1. I've got peace like a riv-er, I've got peace like a
2. I've got love like an o-cean, I've got love like an
3. I've got joy like a foun-tain, I've got joy like a

riv-er, I've got peace like a riv-er in my soul, I've got
o-cean, I've got love like an o-cean in my soul, I've got
foun-tain, I've got joy like a foun-tain in my soul, I've got

peace like a riv-er, I've got peace like a riv-er,
love like an o-cean, I've got love like an o-cean,
joy like a foun-tain, I've got joy like a foun-tain,

I've got peace like a riv-er in my soul. (my soul)
I've got love like an o-cean in my soul. (my soul)
I've got joy like a foun-tain in my soul. (my soul)

208 Saved!

For there is none other name under heaven . . . whereby we must be saved. Acts 4:12

Oswald J. Smith

Roger M. Hickman

Unison

1. Saved! saved! saved! my sins are all for-giv'n; Christ is
2. Saved! saved! saved! by grace and grace a-lone; O, what
3. Saved! saved! saved! O, joy be-yond com-pare! Christ my

mine! I'm on my way to heav'n; Once a guilt-y
won-drous love to me was shown, In my stead Christ
life and I His con-stant care; Yield-ing all and

sin-ner, lost, un-done, Now a child of God, saved thro' His Son.
Je-sus bled and died, Bore my sins, for me was cru-ci-fied.
trust-ing Him a-lone, Liv-ing now each mo-ment as His own.

Chorus - parts

Saved! I'm saved thro' Christ, my all in all; Saved! I'm saved, what-
my all in all;

ev-er may be-fall; He died up-on the cross for me, He bore the aw-ful

Copyright 1918. Renewal 1946 extended. Hope Publishing Co., owner. All rights reserved.

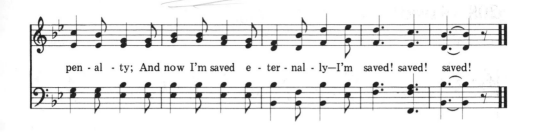

pen - al - ty; And now I'm saved e - ter - nal - ly—I'm saved! saved! saved!

Showers of Blessing 209

There shall be showers of blessing . . . Ezek. 34:26

Daniel W. Whittle

James McGranahan

1. There shall be show-ers of bless - ing: This is the prom-ise of love;
2. There shall be show-ers of bless - ing — Pre-cious re - viv-ing a - gain;
3. There shall be show-ers of bless - ing: Send them up - on us, O Lord;
4. There shall be show-ers of bless - ing: O, that to - day they might fall,

There shall be sea - sons re - fresh - ing, Sent from the Sav - ior a - bove.
O - ver the hills and the val - leys, Sound of a - bun-dance of rain.
Grant to us now a re - fresh - ing, Come, and now hon - or Thy Word.
Now as to God we're con - fess - ing, Now, as on Je - sus we call!

Chorus

Show ers of bless - ing, Show - ers of bless - ing we need:
Show - ers, show - ers of bless - ing,

Mer - cy - drops 'round us are fall - ing, But for the show - ers we plead.

210 I Have Christ in My Heart

This know also, that in the last days perilous times shall come. II Tim. 3:1

WENDELL P. LOVELESS   WENDELL P. LOVELESS

What though wars may come, with march - ing feet and beat of the drum, For
I have Christ in my heart; my heart, What though na - tions rage, as we ap-proach the
end of the age, For I have Christ in my heart. God is still on the throne, Al-
might - y God is He; And He cares for His own through all e - ter - ni - ty.
So let come what may, what - ev - er it is, I on - ly say That

Copyright 1940. Renewal 1968. Hope Publishing Co., owner. All rights reserved.

I have Christ in my heart, I have Christ in my heart.
in my heart,

Close to Thee 211

Lo, I am with you alway . . . Matt. 28:20

FANNY J. CROSBY

SILAS J. VAIL

1. Thou, my ev - er - last - ing por - tion, More than friend or life to me;
2. Not for ease or world - ly pleas - ure, Nor for fame my prayer shall be;
3. Lead me thro' the vale of shad - ows, Bear me o'er life's fit - ful sea;

All a - long my pil - grim jour - ney, Sav - ior, let me walk with Thee.
Glad - ly will I toil and suf - fer, On - ly let me walk with Thee.
Then the gate of life e - ter - nal May I en - ter, Lord, with Thee.

Chorus

Close to Thee, close to Thee, Close to Thee, close to Thee;

All a - long my pil - grim jour - ney, Sav - ior, let me walk with Thee.
Glad - ly will I toil and suf - fer, On - ly let me walk with Thee.
Then the gate of life e - ter - nal May I en - ter, Lord, with Thee.

212 I've Discovered the Way of Gladness

When he had found one pearl of great price . . . Matt. 13:46

FLOYD W. HAWKINS

FLOYD W. HAWKINS

1. Man-kind is search-ing ev-ery day In quest of some-thing new; But
2. I've found the Pearl of great-est price, "E - ter - nal life" so fair; 'Twas

I have found the "liv - ing way," The path of pleas-ures true.
through the Sav - ior's sac - ri - fice, I found this jew - el rare.

Chorus

Lower voices

High voices

I've dis - cov-ered the way of glad-ness, I've dis - cov-ered the way of joy,

Lower voices

Duet

I've dis - cov-ered re - lief from sad - ness, 'Tis a hap-pi-ness with-out al - loy;

Parts

I've dis - cov-ered the fount of bless - ing, I've dis - cov-ered the "Liv-ing Word";

Copyright 1937. Renewed 1965 by Lillenas Publishing Co. Used by permission

'Twas the great-est of all dis-cov-er-ies When I found Je-sus my Lord.

He Lifted Me 213

He brought me up also out of an horrible pit . . . Psa. 40:2

CHARLES H. GABRIEL   CHARLES H. GABRIEL

1. In lov-ing kind-ness Je-sus came My soul in mer-cy to re-claim,
2. He called me long be-fore I heard, Be-fore my sin-ful heart was stirred,
3. His brow was pierced with man-y a thorn, His hands by cru-el nails were torn,
4. Now on a high-er plane I dwell, And with my soul I know 'tis well;

And from the depths of sin and shame 'Thro' grace He lift-ed me.
But when I took Him at His word, For-giv'n He lift-ed me.
When from my guilt and grief, for-lorn, In love He lift-ed me.
Yet how or why, I can-not tell, He should have lift-ed me.

(He lift-ed me.)

Chorus

From sink-ing sand He lift-ed me, With ten-der hand He lift-ed me,

From shades of night to plains of light, O praise His name, He lift-ed me!

214 O Happy Day

This day is salvation come to this house . . . Luke 19:9

PHILIP DODDRIDGE

EDWARD F. RIMBAULT

1. O hap-py day that fixed my choice On Thee, my Sav-ior and my God!
2. O hap-py bond, that seals my vows To Him who mer-its all my love!
3. 'Tis done: the great trans-ac-tion's done; I am my Lord's and He is mine;
4. Now rest, my long di-vid-ed heart; Fixed on this bliss-ful cen-ter, rest;

Well may this glow-ing heart re-joice, And tell its rap-tures all a-broad.
Let cheer-ful an-thems fill His house, While to that sa-cred shrine I move.
He drew me, and I fol-lowed on, Charmed to con-fess the voice di-vine.
Nor ev-er from my Lord de-part, With Him of ev-ery good pos-sessed.

Chorus   *Fine*

Hap-py day, hap-py day, When Je-sus washed my sins a-way!

D.S.

He taught me how to watch and pray, And live re-joic-ing ev-ery day;

The Solid Rock 215

Other foundation can no man lay than that is laid, which is Jesus Christ. I Cor. 3:11

EDWARD MOTE

WILLIAM B. BRADBURY

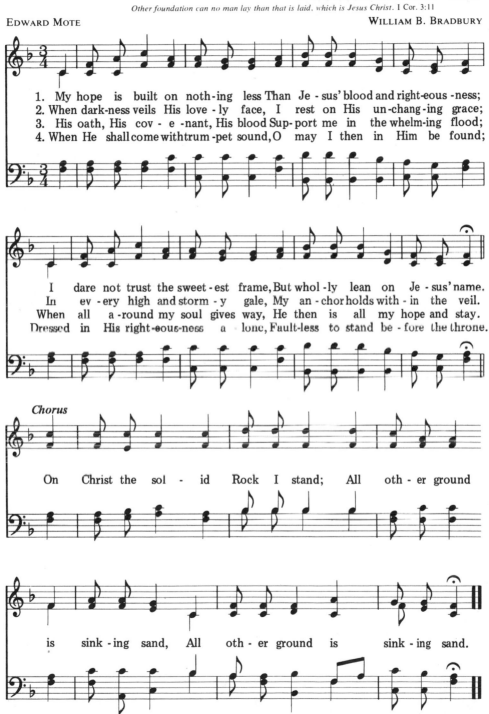

1. My hope is built on noth-ing less Than Je - sus' blood and right-eous -ness;
2. When dark-ness veils His love - ly face, I rest on His un-chang-ing grace;
3. His oath, His cov - e -nant, His blood Sup-port me in the whelm-ing flood;
4. When He shall come with trum -pet sound, O may I then in Him be found;

I dare not trust the sweet -est frame, But whol -ly lean on Je - sus' name.
In ev -ery high and storm - y gale, My an -chor holds with - in the veil.
When all a -round my soul gives way, He then is all my hope and stay.
Dressed in His right-eous-ness a - lone, Fault-less to stand be - fore the throne.

Chorus

On Christ the sol - id Rock I stand; All oth - er ground is sink - ing sand, All oth - er ground is sink - ing sand.

216 No, Not One!

There is a friend that sticketh closer than a brother. Prov. 18:24

JOHNSON OATMAN, JR.

GEORGE C. HUGG

1. There's not a friend like the low-ly Je-sus, No, not one! no, not one!
2. No friend like Him is so high and ho-ly, No, not one! no, not one!
3. There's not an hour that He is not near us, No, not one! no, not one!
4. Did ev-er saint find this friend for-sake him? No, not one! no, not one!
5. Was e'er a gift like the Sav-ior giv-en? No, not one! no, not one!

None else could heal all our soul's dis-eas-es, No, not one! no, not one!
And yet no friend is so meek and low-ly, No, not one! no, not one!
No night so dark but His love can cheer us, No, not one! no, not one!
Or sin-ner find that He would not take him? No, not one! no, not one!
Will He re-fuse us a home in heav-en? No, not one! no, not one!

Chorus

Je-sus knows all a-bout our strug-gles, He will guide till the day is done;

There's not a friend like the low-ly Je-sus, No, not one! no, not one!

Jesus Is All the World to Me   217

I have called you friends. John 15:15

WILL L. THOMPSON   WILL L. THOMPSON

1. Je - sus is all the world to me, My life, my joy, my all;
2. Je - sus is all the world to me, My Friend in tri - als sore;
3. Je - sus is all the world to me, And true to Him I'll be;
4. Je - sus is all the world to me, I want no bet - ter friend;

He is my strength from day to day, With - out Him I would fall.
I go to Him for bless - ings, and He gives them o'er and o'er.
O, how could I this Friend de - ny, When He's so true to me?
I trust Him now, I'll trust Him when Life's fleet - ing days shall end.

When I am sad to Him I go, No oth - er one can cheer me so;
He sends the sun-shine and the rain, He sends the har-vest's gold - en grain;
Fol - low - ing Him I know I'm right, He watch - es o'er me day and night;
Beau - ti - ful life with such a Friend; Beau - ti - ful life that has no end;

When I am sad He makes me glad, He's my Friend.
Sun - shine and rain, har - vest of grain, He's my Friend.
Fol - low - ing Him by day and night, He's my Friend.
E - ter - nal life, e - ter - nal joy, He's my Friend.

218 Take the Name of Jesus with You

. . . Do all in the name of the Lord Jesus. Col. 3:17

LYDIA BAXTER

WILLIAM H. DOANE

1. Take the name of Je - sus with you, Child of sor - row and of
2. Take the name of Je - sus ev - er, As a shield from ev - ery
3. O the pre - cious name of Je - sus! How it thrills our souls with
4. At the name of Je - sus bow - ing, Fall - ing pros - trate at His

woe; It will joy and com - fort give you, Take it,
snare; If temp - ta - tions 'round you gath - er, Breathe that
joy, When His lov - ing arms re - ceive us, And His
feet, King of kings in heav'n we'll crown Him, When our

Chorus

then, wher - e'er you go.
ho - ly name in prayer. Pre - cious name, O how
songs our tongues em - ploy. Pre - cious name,
jour - ney is com - plete.

sweet! Hope of earth and joy of heav'n; Pre - cious
O how sweet!

name, O how sweet! Hope of earth and joy of heav'n.
Pre - cious name, O how sweet, how sweet!

He Hideth My Soul 219

I will put thee in a clift of the rock, and will cover thee with My hand. Exo. 33:22

Fanny J. Crosby

William J. Kirkpatrick

1. A won-der-ful Sav-ior is Je-sus my Lord, A won-der-ful
2. A won-der-ful Sav-ior is Je-sus my Lord, He tak-eth my
3. With num-ber-less bless-ings each mo-ment He crowns, And, filled with His
4. When clothed in His bright-ness, trans-port-ed I rise To meet Him in

Sav-ior to me; He hid-eth my soul in the cleft of the rock, Where
bur-den a-way; He hold-eth me up, and I shall not be moved, He
full-ness di-vine, I sing in my rap-ture, O glo-ry to God For
clouds of the sky, His per-fect sal-va-tion, His won-der-ful love, I'll

Chorus

riv-ers of pleas-ure I see.
giv-eth me strength as my day.
such a Re-deem-er as mine!   He hid-eth my soul in the cleft of the rock
shout with the mil-lions on high.

That shad-ows a dry, thirst-y land; He hid-eth my life in the depths of His love,

And cov-ers me there with His hand, And cov-ers me there with His hand.

220 Fill My Cup, Lord

Whosoever drinketh of the water that I shall give him shall never thirst. John 4:14

RICHARD BLANCHARD

RICHARD BLANCHARD
ARR. BY EUGENE CLARK

1. Like the wom-an at the well I was seek-ing For things that could not
2. There are mil-lions in this world who are crav-ing The pleas-ure earth-ly
3. So, my broth-er, if the things this world gave you Leave hun-gers that won't

sat-is-fy. And then I heard my Sav-ior speak-ing: "Draw from my
things af-ford. But none can match the won-drous treas-ure That I
pass a-way. My bless-ed Lord will come and save you If you

Chorus

well that nev-er shall run dry." Fill my cup, Lord, I lift it
find in Je-sus Christ, my Lord.
kneel to Him and hum-bly pray.

up, Lord. Come and quench this thirst-ing of my soul. Bread of heav-en,

feed me till I want no more; Fill my cup, fill it up and make me whole.

Copyright 1959 by Richard Blanchard. Assigned to Sacred Songs. © 1964 by Sacred Songs. Arr. © 1971 by Word, Inc., owner.
Used by permission.

Happiness Is to Know the Savior 221

Blessed is everyone that feareth the Lord . . . happy shalt thou be . . . Psa. 128:1, 2

IRA F. STANPHILL

IRA F. STANPHILL

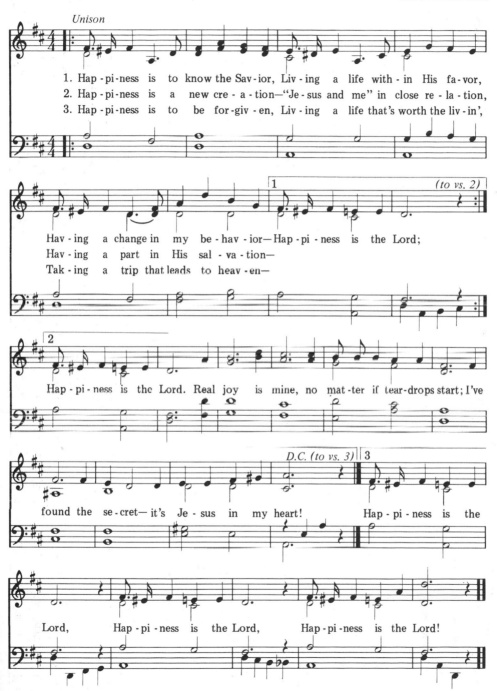

1. Hap-pi-ness is to know the Sav-ior, Liv-ing a life with-in His fa-vor,
2. Hap-pi-ness is a new cre-a-tion—"Je-sus and me" in close re-la-tion,
3. Hap-pi-ness is to be for-giv-en, Liv-ing a life that's worth the liv-in',

Hav-ing a change in my be-hav-ior—Hap-pi-ness is the Lord;
Hav-ing a part in His sal-va-tion—
Tak-ing a trip that leads to heav-en—

Hap-pi-ness is the Lord. Real joy is mine, no mat-ter if tear-drops start; I've

found the se-cret—it's Je-sus in my heart! Hap-pi-ness is the

Lord, Hap-pi-ness is the Lord, Hap-pi-ness is the Lord!

© Copyright 1968 by Singspiration, Inc. All rights reserved. Used by permission.

222 Saved by the Blood

Unto Him that . . . washed us from our sins in His own blood. Rev, 1:5

S. J. HENDERSON

DANIEL B. TOWNER

1. Saved by the blood of the Cru-ci-fied One! Now ran-somed from sin and a new work be-gun, Sing praise to the Fa-ther and praise to the Son, Saved by the blood of the Cru-ci-fied One!

2. Saved by the blood of the Cru-ci-fied One! The an-gels re-joic-ing be-cause it is done; A child of the Fa-ther, joint heir with the Son, Saved by the blood of the Cru-ci-fied One!

3. Saved by the blood of the Cru-ci-fied One! The Fa-ther— He spake, and His will— it was done; Great price of my par-don, His own pre-cious Son; Saved by the blood of the Cru-ci-fied One!

4. Saved by the blood of the Cru-ci-fied One! All hail to the Fa-ther, all hail to the Son, All hail to the Spir-it, the great Three in One! Saved by the blood of the Cru-ci-fied One!

Chorus

Saved! Saved! My sins are all par-doned, my guilt is all gone!
Saved, I'm saved! glo-ry, I'm saved!

Saved! saved! I am saved by the blood of the Cru-ci-fied One!
Saved, I'm saved! glo-ry, I'm saved!

It Is Well with My Soul 223

Bless the Lord, O my soul, and forget not all His benefits . . . Psa. 103:2

HORATIO G. SPAFFORD

PHILIP P. BLISS

1. When peace like a riv - er at - tend - eth my way, When sor - rows like
2. Though Sa - tan should buf - fet, tho' tri - als should come, Let this blest as -
3. My sin— O, the bliss of this glo - ri - ous thought, My sin—not in
4. And, Lord, haste the day when the faith shall be sight, The clouds be rolled

sea - bil - lows roll; What - ev - er my lot, Thou hast taught me to say,
sur - ance con - trol, That Christ has re - gard - ed my help - less es - tate,
part but the whole, Is nailed to the cross and I bear it no more,
back as a scroll, The trump shall re - sound and the Lord shall de - scend,

Chorus

"It is well, it is well with my soul."
And hath shed His own blood for my soul. It is well with my
Praise the Lord, praise the Lord, O my soul! It is well
"E - ven so"— it is well with my soul.

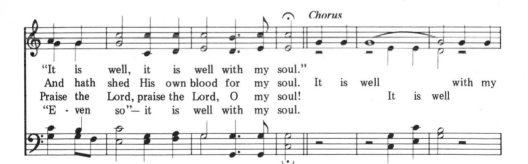

soul, It is well, it is well with my soul.
with my soul,

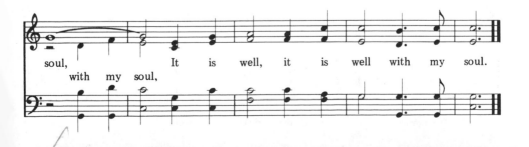

224 He Keeps Me Singing

We know that we have passed from death to life . . . I John 3:14

LUTHER B. BRIDGERS

LUTHER B. BRIDGERS

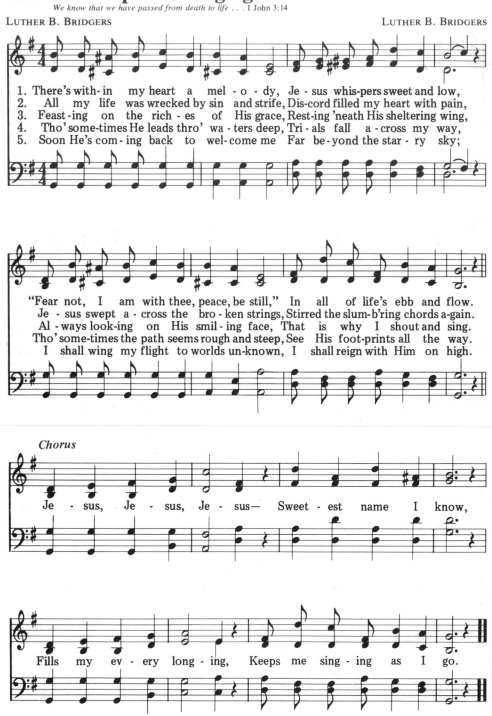

1. There's with-in my heart a mel - o - dy, Je - sus whis-pers sweet and low,
2. All my life was wrecked by sin and strife, Dis-cord filled my heart with pain,
3. Feast-ing on the rich - es of His grace, Rest-ing 'neath His sheltering wing,
4. Tho' some-times He leads thro' wa - ters deep, Tri - als fall a - cross my way,
5. Soon He's com - ing back to wel - come me Far be - yond the star - ry sky;

"Fear not, I am with thee, peace, be still," In all of life's ebb and flow.
Je - sus swept a - cross the bro - ken strings, Stirred the slum-b'ring chords a-gain.
Al - ways look-ing on His smil - ing face, That is why I shout and sing.
Tho' some-times the path seems rough and steep, See His foot-prints all the way.
I shall wing my flight to worlds un-known, I shall reign with Him on high.

Chorus

Je - sus, Je - sus, Je - sus— Sweet - est name I know,

Fills my ev - ery long - ing, Keeps me sing - ing as I go.

© Copyright 1910. Renewal 1937 Broadman Press. All rights reserved. Used by permission.

I Am His and He Is Mine 225

I am persuaded that (nothing) shall be able to separate us from the love of God . . . Rom. 8:38, 39

GEORGE W. ROBINSON

JAMES MOUNTAIN

all in unison

Ladies
Men

1. Loved with ev - er - last - ing love, Led by grace that love to know;
2. Heav'n a - bove is soft - er blue, Earth a - round is sweet - er green!
3. Things that once were wild a - larms Can - not now dis - turb my rest;

all

4. His for - ev - er, on - ly His; Who the Lord and me shall part?

Gra - cious Spir - it from a - bove, Thou hast taught me it is so!
Some-thing lives in ev - 'ry hue Christ - less eyes have nev - er seen:
Closed in ev - er - last - ing arms, Pil - lowed on the lov - ing breast.
Ah, with what a rest of bliss Christ can fill the lov - ing heart!

O, this full and per - fect peace! O, this trans - port all di - vine!
Birds with glad - der songs o'er - flow, Flow'rs with deep - er beau - ties shine,
O, to lie for - ev - er here, Doubt and care and self re - sign,
Heav'n and earth may fade and flee, First - born light in gloom de - cline;

1. | 2.

In a love which can - not cease, I am His, and He is mine. mine.
Since I know, as now I know, I am His, and He is mine. mine.
While He whis - pers in my ear, I am His, and He is mine. mine.
But while God and I shall be, I am His, and He is mine. mine.

Copyright used by permission of Marshall, Morgan and Scott.

226 He Took My Sins Away

Behold the Lamb of God, which taketh away the sin of the world. John 1:29

MARGARET J. HARRIS

MARGARET J. HARRIS

1. I came to Jesus, weary, worn, and sad, He took my sins away, He
2. The load of sin was more than I could bear, He took them all away, He
3. No condemnation have I in my heart, He took my sins away, He
4. If you will come to Jesus Christ today, He'll take your sins away, He'll

took my sins away. And now His love has made my heart so
took them all away. And now on Him I roll my every
took my sins away. His perfect peace He did to me im-
take your sins away. And keep you happy in His love each

Chorus

glad, He took my sins away.
care, He took my sins away.
part, He took my sins away.   He took my sins away, He
day, He'll take your sins away.

took my sins away, And keeps me singing every day!

I'm so glad He took my sins away. He took my sins away.

He Touched Me 227

Jesus put forth His hand and touched him, saying, I will; be thou clean. Matt. 8:3

WILLIAM J. GAITHER   WILLIAM J. GAITHER

1. Shack-led by a heav-y bur-den, 'Neath a load of
2. Since I met this bless-ed Sav-ior, Since He cleansed and

guilt and shame; Then the hand of Je - sus touched me,
made me whole; I will nev - er cease to praise Him,

Chorus

And now I am no long-er the same. He touched me, O, He
I'll shout it while e - ter-ni-ty rolls;

touched me, And O, the joy that floods my soul; Some-thing

hap-pened, and now I know, He touched me and made me whole.

© Copyright 1963 by William J. Gaither. International copyright secured. All rights reserved. Used by permission.

228 In My Heart There Rings a Melody

Singing and making melody in your heart to the Lord. Eph. 5:19

ELTON M. ROTH

ELTON M. ROTH

1. I have a song that Je - sus gave me, It was sent from heav'n a - bove; There nev - er was a sweet - er mel - o - dy, 'Tis a mel - o - dy of love.

2. I love the Christ who died on Cal - v'ry, For He washed my sins a - way; He put with - in my heart a mel - o - dy, And I know it's there to stay.

3. 'Twill be my end - less theme in glo - ry, With the an - gels I will sing; 'Twill be a song with glo - rious har - mo - ny, When the courts of heav - en ring.

Chorus

In my heart there rings a mel - o - dy, There rings a mel - o - dy with heav - en's har - mo - ny; In my heart there rings a mel - o - dy; There rings a mel - o - dy of love.

Copyright 1924. Renewal 1951. Hope Publishing Co., owner. All rights reserved.

I Know Whom I Have Believed 229

For I know whom I have believed . . . II Tim. 1:12

DANIEL W. WHITTLE

JAMES MCGRANAHAN

1. I know not why God's won-drous grace To me He hath made known,
2. I know not how this sav-ing faith To me He did im-part,
3. I know not how the Spir-it moves, Con-vinc-ing men of sin,
4. I know not when my Lord may come, At night or noon-day fair,

Nor why, un-wor-thy, Christ in love Re-deemed me for His own.
Nor how be-liev-ing in His Word Wrought peace with-in my heart.
Re-veal-ing Je-sus through the Word, Cre-at-ing faith in Him.
Nor if I'll walk the vale with Him, Or "meet Him in the air."

Chorus

But "I know whom I have be-liev-ed, And am per-suad-ed that He is

a-ble To keep that which I've com-mit-ted Un-to Him a-gainst that day."

230 Higher Ground

I press toward the mark for the prize . . . Phil. 3:14

JOHNSON OATMAN, JR.

CHARLES H. GABRIEL

1. I'm press-ing on the up-ward way, New heights I'm gain-ing ev-ery
2. My heart has no de-sire to stay Where doubts a-rise and fears dis-
3. I want to live a-bove the world, Though Sa-tan's darts at me are
4. I want to scale the ut-most height, And catch a gleam of glo-ry

day; Still pray-ing as I'm on-ward bound, "Lord, plant my
may; Though some may dwell where these a-bound, My prayer, my
hurled; For faith has caught the joy-ful sound, The song of
bright; But still I'll pray till heav'n I've found, "Lord, lead me

Chorus

feet on high-er ground."
aim is high-er ground. Lord, lift me up and let me stand
saints on high-er ground.
on to high-er ground."

By faith on heav-en's ta-ble-land, A high-er plane

than I have found; Lord, plant my feet on high-er ground.

His Sheep Am I 231

He maketh me to lie down in green pastures . . . Psa. 23:2

ORIEN JOHNSON   ORIEN JOHNSON

In God's green pas - tures feed - ing, by His cool wa - ters lie;

Soft in the eve - ning walk my Lord and I. All the

sheep of His pas - tures fare so won - drous - ly fine, His sheep am I.

1. Wa - ters cool,   Pas - tures green,
2. Dark the night,   Rough the way,

In the val - ley,   On the moun - tain

In the eve - ning walk my Lord and I;
Step by step my Lord and I.

In the eve - ning walk my Lord and I;
Step by step my Lord and I.

© Copyright 1956 by Orien Johnson. Assigned to Sacred Songs (A division of Word, Inc.). All rights reserved. Used by permission.

232 Calvary Covers It All

Blessed is he whose . . . sin is covered. Psa. 32:1

MRS. WALTER G. TAYLOR   MRS. WALTER G. TAYLOR

1. Far dear-er than all that the world can im-part Was the mes-sage that
2. The stripes that He bore and the thorns that He wore Told His mer-cy and
3. How match-less the grace, when I looked on the face Of this Je-sus, my
4. How bless-ed the thought, that my soul by Him bought, Shall be His in the

came to my heart; How that Je-sus a-lone for my sin did a-tone,
love ev-er-more; And my heart bowed in shame as I called on His name,
cru-ci-fied Lord; My re-demp-tion com-plete I then found at His feet,
glo-ry on high; Where with glad-ness and song I'll be one of the throng,

Chorus

And Cal-va-ry cov-ers it all. Cal-va-ry cov-ers it all, My past with its sin and stain; My guilt and de-spair Je-sus took on Him there, And Cal-va-ry cov-ers it all.

Copyright 1934 by Mrs. Walter Taylor. © Renewed 1962, The Rodeheaver Co., owner. All rights reserved. Used by permission.

Sunshine in My Soul 233

For God, who commanded the light to shine out of darkness, hath shined in our hearts . . . II Cor. 4:6

ELIZA E. HEWITT   JOHN R. SWENEY

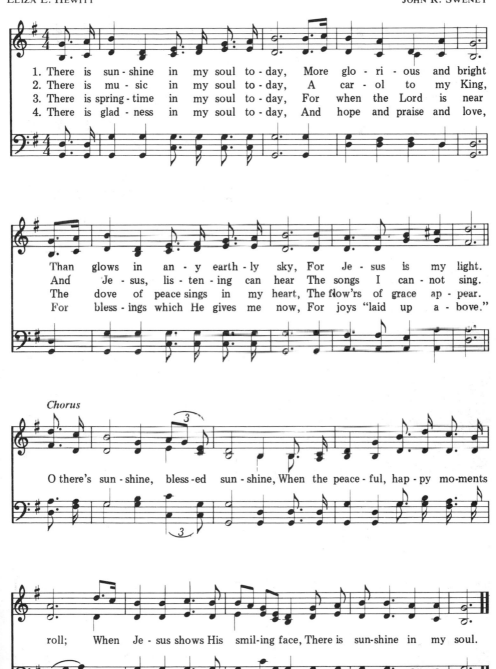

1. There is sun-shine in my soul to-day, More glo-ri-ous and bright
2. There is mu-sic in my soul to-day, A car-ol to my King,
3. There is spring-time in my soul to-day, For when the Lord is near
4. There is glad-ness in my soul to-day, And hope and praise and love,

Than glows in an-y earth-ly sky, For Je-sus is my light.
And Je-sus, lis-ten-ing can hear The songs I can-not sing.
The dove of peace sings in my heart, The flow'rs of grace ap-pear.
For bless-ings which He gives me now, For joys "laid up a-bove."

Chorus

O there's sun-shine, bless-ed sun-shine, When the peace-ful, hap-py mo-ments roll; When Je-sus shows His smil-ing face, There is sun-shine in my soul.

234 I Will Sing the Wondrous Story

And they sing the song . . . of the Lamb, saying, Great and marvelous are Thy works. Rev. 15:3

Francis H. Rowley   Peter P. Bilhorn

1. I will sing the won-drous sto - ry Of the Christ who died for me,
2. I was lost but Je - sus found me, Found the sheep that went a - stray,
3. I was bruised but Je - sus healed me; Faint was I from man - y a fall;
4. Days of dark - ness still come o'er me, Sor-row's paths I oft - en tread,

How He left His home in glo - ry For the cross of Cal - va - ry.
Threw His lov - ing arms a - round me, Drew me back in - to His way.
Sight was gone, and fears pos-sessed me, But He freed me from them all.
But the Sav - ior still is with me; By His hand I'm safe - ly led.

Chorus

Yes, I'll sing the won-drous sto - ry Of the
Yes, I'll sing the won-drous sto - ry

Christ who died for me, Sing it with the saints in
Of the Christ who died for me, Sing it with

glo ry Gath-ered by the crys-tal sea.
the saints in glo - ry, Gath-ered by the crys-tal sea.

"Whosoever" Meaneth Me 235

Whosoever believeth in Him . . . should have everlasting life. John 3:16

J. Edwin McConnell

J. Edwin McConnell

1. I am hap-py to-day and the sun shines bright, The clouds have been
2. All my hopes have been raised, O His name be praised, His glo-ry has
3. O what won-der-ful love, O what grace di-vine, That Je-sus should

rolled a - way; For the Sav - ior said "Who - so - ev - er will" May
filled my soul; I've been lift - ed up and from sin set free, His
die for me! I was lost in sin, for the world I pined, But

Chorus

come with Him to stay (to stay).
blood hath made me whole (me whole). "Who-so-ev-er" sure-ly mean-eth me,
now I am set free (set free).

Sure-ly mean-eth me, O sure-ly mean-eth me; "Who-so-ev-er"

sure-ly mean-eth me, "Who-so-ev-er" mean-eth me.
mean-eth me.

© 1913 and renewed 1941 by John T. Benson, Jr. Copyright extended. International copyright secured. All rights reserved. Printed by permission of The Benson Company, 365 Great Circle Road, Nashville, TN 37228.

236 Nailed to the Cross

Took it out of the way, nailing it to His cross. Col. 2:14

CARRIE E. BRECK

GRANT COLFAX TULLAR

1. There was One who was will-ing to die in my stead, That a
2. He is ten-der and lov-ing and pa-tient with me, While He
3. I will cling to my Sav-ior and nev-er de-part; I will

soul so un-wor-thy might live; And the path to the cross He was
cleans-es my heart of the dross; But "there's no con-dem-na-tion"— I
joy-ful-ly jour-ney each day With a song on my lips and a

Chorus

will-ing to tread, All the sins of my life to for-give.
know I am free, For my sins are all nailed to the cross. They are nailed to the cross,
song in my heart, That my sins have been tak-en a-way.

They are nailed to the cross, O how much He was will-ing to bear! With what

an-guish and loss Je-sus went to the cross! But He car-ried my sins with Him there.

I'd Rather Have Jesus 237

I count all things but loss for the excellency of the knowledge of Christ Jesus . . . Phil. 3:8

RHEA F. MILLER   GEORGE BEVERLY SHEA

1. I'd rath-er have Je-sus than sil-ver or gold, I'd rath-er be
2. I'd rath-er have Je-sus than men's ap - plause, I'd rath-er be
3. He's fair-er than lil-ies of rar-est bloom, He's sweet-er than

His than have rich-es un-told; I'd rath-er have Je-sus than
faith-ful to His dear cause; I'd rath-er have Je-sus than
hon-ey from out the comb; He's all that my hun-ger-ing

hous-es or lands, I'd rath-er be led by His nail-pierced hand
world-wide fame, I'd rath-er be true to His ho-ly name
spir-it needs, I'd rath-er have Je-sus and let Him lead

Than to be the king of a vast do-main Or be held in sin's dread sway; I'd

rath-er have Je-sus than an-y-thing This world af-fords to-day.

© Copyright—1922 Rhea F. Miller—Renewal 1950; Assigned to Chancel Music, Inc. Copyright 1939 George Beverly Shea—Renewal 1966; Assigned to Chancel Music, Inc. International copyright secured. Printed in U.S.A. All rights reserved including right of public performance for profit. Used by permission.

238 Jesus Said That Whosoever Will

Whosoever will, let him take of the water of life freely. Rev. 22:17

ARTHUR J. PANKRATZ   ARTHUR J. PANKRATZ

Je - sus said that who - so - ev - er will, who - so - ev - er will,

who - so - ev - er will, Je - sus said that who - so - ev - er will,

who - so - ev - er will may come. I'm so glad that He in - clud - ed me,

He in - clud - ed me, He in - clud - ed me; I'm so glad that

He in - clud - ed me When Je - sus said that who - so - ev - er will may come!

Copyright 1940. Renewal 1968. Hope Publishing Co., owner. All rights reserved.

I've Found a Friend 239

Greater love hath no man than this, that a man lay down his life for his friends. John 15:13

JAMES G. SMALL

GEORGE C. STEBBINS

1. I've found a Friend, O such a Friend! He loved me ere I knew Him;
2. I've found a Friend, O such a Friend! He bled, He died to save me;
3. I've found a Friend, O such a Friend! So kind and true and ten - der,

He drew me with the cords of love, And thus He bound me to Him.
And not a - lone the gift of life, But His own self He gave me.
So wise a Coun - sel - or and Guide, So might - y a De - fend - er!

And round my heart still close - ly twine Those ties which naught can sev - er,
Naught that I have my own I call, I hold it for the Giv - er;
From Him who loves me now so well, What pow'r my soul can sev - er?

For I am His and He is mine, For - ev - er and for - ev - er.
My heart, my strength, my life, my all Are His, and His for - ev - er.
Shall life or death, or earth or hell? No! I am His for - ev - er.

240 Leaning on the Everlasting Arms

The eternal God is thy refuge, and underneath are the everlasting arms. Deut. 33:27

ELISHA A. HOFFMAN

ANTHONY J. SHOWALTER

1. What a fel-low-ship, what a joy di-vine, Lean-ing on the ev-er-
2. O how sweet to walk in this pil-grim way, Lean-ing on the ev-er-
3. What have I to dread, what have I to fear, Lean-ing on the ev-er-

last-ing arms; What a bless-ed-ness, what a peace is mine,
last-ing arms; O, how bright the path grows from day to day,
last-ing arms? I have bless-ed peace with my Lord so near,

Chorus

Lean-ing on the ev-er-last-ing arms. Lean - ing,
Lean-ing on the ev-er-last-ing arms. Lean-ing on Je-sus,
Lean-ing on the ev-er-last-ing arms.

lean - ing, Safe and se-cure from all a-larms; Lean -
lean-ing on Je-sus, Lean-ing on

ing, lean - ing, Lean-ing on the ev-er-last-ing arms.
Je-sus, lean-ing on Je-sus,

It Took a Miracle 241

Greater love hath no man than this . . . John 15:13

JOHN W. PETERSON   JOHN W. PETERSON

1. My Fa - ther is om - nip - o - tent, And that you can't de - ny;
2. Tho' here His glo - ry has been shown, We still can't ful - ly see
3. The Bi - ble tells us of His pow'r And wis - dom all way thro';

A God of might and mir - a - cles— 'Tis writ - ten in the sky.
The won - ders of His might, His throne, 'Twill take e - ter - ni - ty.
And ev - ery lit - tle bird and flow'r Are tes - ti - mo - nies, too.

Chorus

It took a mir - a - cle to put the stars in place, It took a
mir - a - cle to hang the world in space; But when He saved my soul,
Cleansed and made me whole, It took a mir - a - cle of love and grace!

Copyright 1948. Renewal 1976 by John W. Peterson. Assigned to Singspiration, Division of The Zondervan Corporation. All rights reserved. Used by permission.

242 Jesus Has Lifted Me

I will extol Thee, O Lord; for Thou hast lifted me up. Psa. 30:1

AVIS B. CHRISTIANSEN   HALDOR LILLENAS

1. Out of the depths to the glo-ry a-bove, I have been lift-ed in won-der-ful love; From ev-ery fet-ter my spir-it is free— For Je-sus has lift-ed me!

2. Out of the world in-to heav-en-ly rest, In-to the land of the ran-somed and blest; There in the glo-ry with Him I shall be— For Je-sus has lift-ed me!

3. Out of my-self in-to Him I a-dore, There to a-bide in His love ev-er-more; Thro' end-less a-ges His glo-ry to see— My Je-sus has lift-ed me!

Chorus

Je-sus has lift-ed me! Je-sus has lift-ed me! lift-ed me! lift-ed me!
Out of the night in-to glo-ri-ous light, Yes, Je-sus has lift-ed me! lift-ed me!

Copyright 1918. Renewal 1946 extended. Hope Publishing Co., owner. All rights reserved.

Jesus Loves Even Me 243

I will love him, and will manifest myself to him. John 14:21

PHILIP P. BLISS

PHILIP P. BLISS

1. I am so glad that our Fa - ther in heav'n Tells of His
2. Though I for - get Him and wan - der a - way, Still He doth
3. Oh, if there's on - ly one song I can sing, When in His

love in the Book He has giv'n; Won - der - ful things in the
love me wher - ev - er I stray; Back to His dear lov - ing
beau - ty I see the great King, This shall my song in e -

Bi - ble I see— This is the dear - est, that Je - sus loves me.
arms would I flee, When I re - mem - ber that Je - sus loves me.
ter - ni - ty be: "Oh, what a won - der that Je - sus loves me!"

Chorus

I am so glad that Je - sus loves me, Je - sus loves me, Je - sus loves me;

I am so glad that Je - sus loves me, Je - sus loves e - ven me.

244 Springs of Living Water

He would have given thee living water. John 4:10

JOHN W. PETERSON   JOHN W. PETERSON

1. I thirst-ed in the bar-ren land of sin and shame, And
2. How sweet the liv-ing wat-er from the hills of God, It
3. O sin-ner, won't you come to-day to Cal-va-ry, A

noth-ing sat-is-fy-ing there I found; But to the bless-ed cross of
makes me glad and hap-py all the way; Now glo-ry, grace and bless-ing
foun-tain there is flow-ing deep and wide; The Sav-ior now in-vites you

Christ one day I came, Where springs of liv-ing wat-er did a-bound.
mark the path I've trod, I'm shout-ing "Hal-le-lu-jah" ev-ery day.
to the wat-er free, Where thirst-ing spir-its can be sat-is-fied.

Chorus

Drink-ing at the springs of liv-ing wa-ter, Hap-py now am
Hap-py

Copyright 1950 by Singspiration, Inc. All rights reserved. Used by permission.

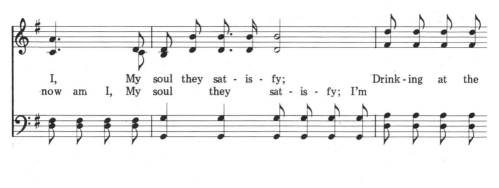

I, My soul they sat - is - fy; Drink - ing at the
now am I, My soul they sat - is - fy; I'm

springs of liv - ing wa - ter, O won - der - ful and boun - ti - ful sup - ply.

Greater Is He That Is in Me 245

Greater is He that is in you, than he that is in the world. I John 4:4

LANNY WOLFE

LANNY WOLFE

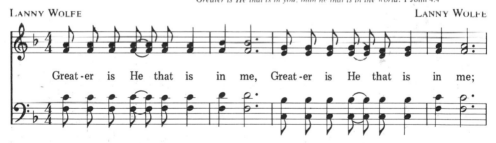

Great - er is He that is in me, Great - er is He that is in me;

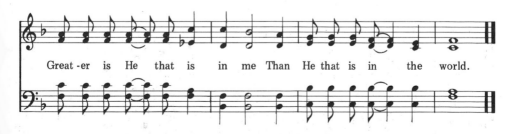

Great - er is He that is in me Than He that is in the world.

© 1973 by Lanny Wolfe Music, a division of The Benson Company, 365 Great Circle Road, Nashville, TN 38229. International copyright secured. All rights reserved. Printed by permission.

246 Constantly Abiding

I will never leave thee, nor forsake thee. Heb. 13:5

ANNE S. MURPHY

ANNE S. MURPHY

1. There's a peace in my heart that the world nev-er gave, A peace it can
2. All the world seemed to sing of a Sav-ior and King, When peace sweetly
3. This treas-ure I have in a tem-ple of clay, While here on His

not take a - way; Tho' the tri - als of life may sur-round like a cloud,
came to my heart; Troub-les all fled a - way and my night turned to day,
foot-stool I roam: But He's com-ing to take me some glo - ri - ous day,

Chorus

I've a peace that has come there to stay! Con - stant-ly a-
Bless-ed Je - sus, how glorious Thou art! Con-stant-ly a - bid - ing,
O - ver there to my heav-en - ly home!

bid - ing, Je - sus is mine;
con-stant-ly a - bid - ing, Je - sus is mine, yes, Je - sus is mine;

Con - stant-ly a-bid - ing, rap - ture di-
Con-stant-ly a - bid - ing, con-stant-ly a-bid-ing, rap-ture di-vine, O

Copyright 1908. Renewed 1935 by Nazarene Publishing House. Used by permission.

vine; He nev - er leaves me lone - ly, whis-pers,
rap-ture di - vine; He nev - er leaves me, nev-er leaves me lone-ly, whis-pers,

O so kind: "I will nev - er leave thee," Je - sus is mine.
whis-pers, O so kind: nev - er leave thee, Je-sus, Je - sus is mine.

More Love to Thee 247

This I pray, that your love may abound yet more and more. Phil. 1:9

ELIZABETH P. PRENTISS WILLIAM H. DOANE

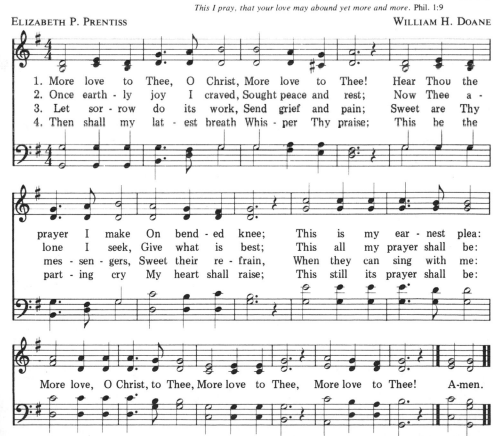

1. More love to Thee, O Christ, More love to Thee! Hear Thou the
2. Once earth - ly joy I craved, Sought peace and rest; Now Thee a -
3. Let sor - row do its work, Send grief and pain; Sweet are Thy
4. Then shall my lat - est breath Whis - per Thy praise; This be the

prayer I make On bend - ed knee; This is my ear - nest plea:
lone I seek, Give what is best; This all my prayer shall be:
mes - sen - gers, Sweet their re - frain, When they can sing with me:
part - ing cry My heart shall raise; This still its prayer shall be:

More love, O Christ, to Thee, More love to Thee, More love to Thee! A-men.

248 Through It All

All things work together for good to them that love God . . . Rom. 8:28

ANDRAÉ CROUCH   ANDRAÉ CROUCH

1. I've had man - y   tears   and sor - rows,   I've had ques - tions
2. I've   been to lots   of plac - es,   And I've seen   a
3. I   thank God for   the moun - tains,   And I thank Him

for to - mor - row,   There've been times I   did - n't know right from
lot   of fac - es,   There've been times I   felt   so all   a -
for   the val - leys,   I   thank Him for   the storms He brought me

wrong;   But in   ev - ery sit - u -   a - tion God gave
lone;   But   in   my lone - ly   hours,   Yes, those
through;   For   if   I'd nev - er   had a prob - lem, I

bless - ed con - so -   la - tion That   my   tri - als   come to
pre - cious lone - ly   hours,   Je - sus   let   me   know that
would - n't   know that   He could   solve them, I'd   nev - er   know what

© Copyright 1971 by MANNA MUSIC, INC., 2111 Kenmere Ave., Burbank, CA 91504. International copyright secured. All rights reserved. Used by permission.

on - ly make me strong.
I was His own. Through it all,
faith in God could do.

Through it all, I've learned to trust in Je - sus, I've

learned to trust in God; Through it all, Through it all,

I've learned to de - pend up - on His Word.

249 Wonderful, Wonderful Jesus

And he hath put a new song in my mouth. Psa. 40:3

ANNA B. RUSSELL   ERNEST O. SELLERS

1. There is nev-er a day so drear-y, There is nev-er a night so
2. There is nev-er a cross so heav-y, There is nev-er a weight of
3. There is nev-er a care or bur-den, There is nev-er a grief or
4. There is nev-er a guilt-y sin-ner, There is nev-er a wan-d'ring

long, But the soul that is trust-ing Je-sus Will some-where
woe, But that Je-sus will help to car-ry Be-cause He
loss, But that Je-sus in love will light-en When car-ried
one, But that God can in mer-cy par-don Thro' Je-sus

Chorus

find a song.
lov-eth so.
to the cross.   Won-der-ful, won-der-ful Je-sus! In the
Christ, His Son.

heart He im-plant-eth a song;   A song of de-liv-'rance,

im-plant-eth a song;

of cour-age, of strength—In the heart He im-plant-eth a song.

'Tis So Sweet to Trust in Jesus 250

That we should be to the praise of His glory, who first trusted in Christ. Eph. 1:12

LOUISA M. R. STEAD   WILLIAM J. KIRKPATRICK

1. 'Tis so sweet to trust in Je-sus, Just to take Him at His word;
2. O how sweet to trust in Je-sus, Just to trust His cleans-ing blood;
3. Yes, 'tis sweet to trust in Je-sus, Just from sin and self to cease;
4. I'm so glad I learned to trust Thee, Pre-cious Je-sus, Sav-ior, Friend;

Just to rest up-on His prom-ise; Just to know, "Thus saith the Lord."
Just in sim-ple faith to plunge me 'Neath the heal-ing, cleans-ing flood!
Just from Je-sus sim-ply tak-ing Life and rest, and joy in peace.
And I know that Thou art with me, Wilt be with me to the end.

Chorus

Je-sus, Je-sus, how I trust Him! How I've proved Him o'er and o'er!

Je-sus, Je-sus, pre-cious Je-sus! O for grace to trust Him more!

251 Jesus Loves Me

Who shall separate us from the love of Christ? Rom. 8:35

ANNA B. WARNER

WILLIAM B. BRADBURY

1. Je - sus loves me! this I know, For the Bi - ble
2. Je - sus loves me! He who died Heav - en's gate to
3. Je - sus loves me! He will stay Close be - side me

tells me so; Lit - tle ones to Him be - long, They are weak but
o - pen wide; He will wash a - way my sin, Let His lit - tle
all the way; Thou hast bled and died for me, I will hence-forth

Chorus

He is strong. Yes, Je - sus loves me! Yes, Je - sus
child come in.
live for Thee.

loves me! Yes, Je - sus loves me! The Bi - ble tells me so.

Jesus Never Fails 252

I will never leave thee nor forsake thee. Heb. 13:5

ARTHUR A. LUTHER   ARTHUR A. LUTHER

1. Earth-ly friends may prove un-true, Doubts and fears as-sail;
2. Though the sky be dark and drear, Fierce and strong the gale,
3. In life's dark and bit-ter hour Love will still pre-vail;

One still loves and cares for you, One who will not fail.
Just re-mem-ber He is near, And He will not fail.
Trust His ev-er-last-ing pow'r— Je-sus will not fail.

Chorus

Je-sus nev-er fails, Je-sus nev-er fails;

Heav'n and earth may pass a-way, But Je-sus nev-er fails.

Copyright 1927. Renewal 1955 by A. A. Luther. Assigned to Singspiration, Inc. All rights reserved. Used by permission.

253 Just When I Need Him Most

God is our refuge and strength, a very present help in trouble. Psa. 46:1

WILLIAM C. POOLE

CHARLES H. GABRIEL

1. Just when I need Him Je-sus is near, Just when I fal-ter,
2. Just when I need Him Je-sus is true, Nev-er for-sak-ing
3. Just when I need Him Je-sus is strong, Bear-ing my bur-dens
4. Just when I need Him He is my all, An-swer-ing when up-

just when I fear; Read-y to help me, read-y to cheer,
all the way through; Giv-ing for bur-dens pleas-ures a-new,
all the day long; For all my sor-row giv-ing a song,
on Him I call; Ten-der-ly watch-ing lest I should fall,

Chorus

Just when I need Him most. Just when I need Him most,

Just when I need Him most; Je-sus is near to

com-fort and cheer, Just when I need Him most.

Copyright 1908 by Chas. H. Gabriel. © Renewed 1936, The Rodeheaver Co., owner. Used by permission.

Jesus Is the Sweetest Name I Know 254

Far above . . . every name that is named . . . Eph. 1:21

LELA B. LONG

LELA B. LONG

1. There have been names that I have loved to hear, But nev - er has there
2. There is no name in earth or heav'n a - bove, That we should give such
3. And some day I shall see Him face to face To thank and praise Him

been a name so dear To this heart of mine, as the name di-vine, The
hon - or and such love As the bless - ed name, let us all ac-claim, That
for His won-drous grace, Which He gave to me, when He made me free, The

Chorus

pre-cious, pre-cious name of Je - sus.
won-drous, glo-rious name of Je - sus. Je - sus is the sweet-est name I
bless - ed Son of God called Je - sus.

know, And He's just the same as His love - ly name, And that's the rea - son

why I love Him so; Oh, Je - sus is the sweet - est name I know.

255 What a Wonderful Savior

. . . And know that this is indeed the Christ, the Savior of the world. John 4:42

ELISHA A. HOFFMAN   ELISHA A. HOFFMAN

1. Christ has for sin a-tone-ment made, What a won-der-ful Sav-ior!
2. I praise Him for the cleans-ing blood, What a won-der-ful Sav-ior!
3. He cleansed my heart from all its sin, What a won-der-ful Sav-ior!
4. He walks be-side me in the way, What a won-der-ful Sav-ior!

We are re-deemed! the price is paid! What a won-der-ful Sav-ior!
That rec-on-ciled my soul to God; What a won-der-ful Sav-ior!
And now He reigns and rules there-in; What a won-der-ful Sav-ior!
And keeps me faith-ful day by day, What a won-der-ful Sav-ior!

Chorus

What a won-der-ful Sav-ior is Je-sus, my Je-sus!

What a won-der-ful Sav-ior is Je-sus, my Lord!

My Savior's Love 256

God, who is rich in mercy, for His great love wherewith He loved us . . . Eph. 2:4

CHARLES H. GABRIEL   CHARLES H. GABRIEL

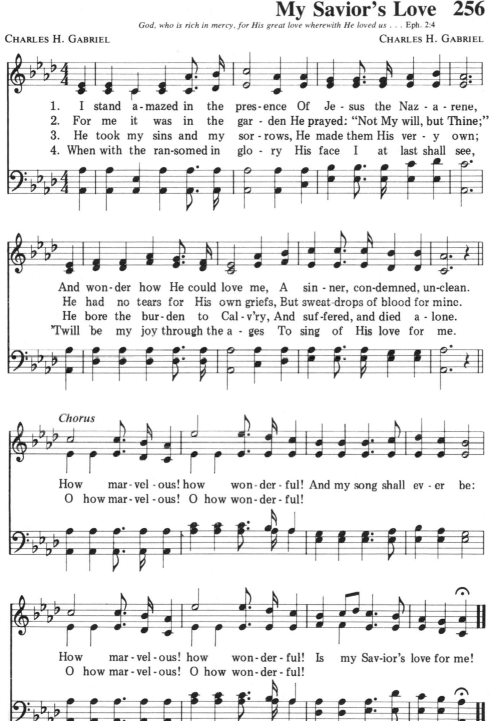

1. I stand a-mazed in the pres-ence Of Je-sus the Naz-a-rene,
2. For me it was in the gar-den He prayed: "Not My will, but Thine;"
3. He took my sins and my sor-rows, He made them His ver-y own;
4. When with the ran-somed in glo-ry His face I at last shall see,

And won-der how He could love me, A sin-ner, con-demned, un-clean.
He had no tears for His own griefs, But sweat-drops of blood for mine.
He bore the bur-den to Cal-v'ry, And suf-fered, and died a-lone.
'Twill be my joy through the a-ges To sing of His love for me.

Chorus

How mar-vel-ous! how won-der-ful! And my song shall ev-er be:
O how mar-vel-ous! O how won-der-ful!

How mar-vel-ous! how won-der-ful! Is my Sav-ior's love for me!
O how mar-vel-ous! O how won-der-ful!

257 Only a Sinner

For by grace are ye saved through faith . . . Eph. 2:8

James M. Gray

Daniel B. Towner

1. Naught have I got-ten but what I re-ceived; Grace hath be-stowed it since
2. Once I was fool-ish, and sin ruled my heart, Caus-ing my foot-steps from
3. Tears un-a-vail-ing, no mer-it had I; Mer-cy had saved me, or
4. Suf-fer a sin-ner whose heart o-ver-flows, Lov-ing his Sav-ior to

I have be-lieved; Boast-ing ex-clud-ed, pride I a-base; I'm
God to de-part; Je-sus hath found me, hap-py my case; I
else I must die; Sin had a-larmed me, fear-ing God's face; But
tell what he knows; Once more to tell it would I em-brace—I'm

Chorus

on-ly a sin-ner saved by grace!
now am a sin-ner saved by grace!
now I'm a sin-ner saved by grace!
on-ly a sin-ner saved by grace!

On-ly a sin-ner saved by grace!

On-ly a sin-ner saved by grace! This is my sto-ry, to

God be the glo-ry— I'm on-ly a sin-ner saved by grace!

My Sins Are Blotted Out, I Know! 258

Be converted, that your sins may be blotted out . . . Acts 3:19

MERRILL DUNLOP

MERRILL DUNLOP

1. What a won-drous mes-sage in God's Word! My sins are blot-ted out, I know! If I trust in His re-deem-ing blood, My sins are blot-ted out, I know!
2. Once my heart was black, but now what joy, My sins are blot-ted out, I know! I have peace that noth-ing can de-stroy, My sins are blot-ted out, I know!" My
3. I shall stand some-day be-fore my King, My sins are blot-ted out, I know! With the ran-somed host I then shall sing: "My sins are blot-ted out, I know!"

Chorus

My sins are blot-ted out, I know! I know! My sins are blot-ted out, I know! I know! They are bur-ied in the depths of the deep-est sea: My sins are blot-ted out, I know! I know!

Copyright 1927. Renewal 1955 by Merrill Dunlop. Assigned to Singspiration, Inc. All rights reserved. Used by permission.

259 Since Jesus Came into My Heart

If any man be in Christ, he is a new creature . . . II Cor. 5:17

RUFUS H. McDANIEL

CHARLES H. GABRIEL

1. What a won-der-ful change in my life has been wrought Since Je-sus came
2. I have ceased from my wand-'ring and go - ing a - stray, Since Je - sus came
3. There's a light in the val - ley of death now for me, Since Je - sus came
4. I shall go there to dwell in that Cit - y, I know, Since Je - sus came

in - to my heart! I have light in my soul for which long I have sought,
in - to my heart! And my sins, which were man - y, are all washed a - way,
in - to my heart! And the gates of the Cit - y be - yond I can see,
in - to my heart! And I'm hap - py, so hap - py, as on - ward I go,

Chorus

Since Je - sus came in - to my heart! Since Je - sus came in - to my
Since Je - sus came in, came

heart, Since Je - sus came in - to my heart, Floods of joy o'er my
in - to my heart, Since Je - sus came in, came in - to my heart,

soul like the sea bil - lows roll, Since Je - sus came in - to my heart.

Copyright 1914 by Chas. H. Gabriel. © Renewed 1942, The Rodeheaver Co. Used by permission.

Precious Hiding Place 260

For ye were as sheep going astray . . . I Pet. 2:25

AVIS B. CHRISTIANSEN

WENDELL P. LOVELESS

1. I was stray-ing when Christ found me In the night so dark and cold;
2. With His nail-scarred hand He bro't me To the shel-ter of His love;
3. Tho' the night be dark a-round me, I am safe, for He is near;

Ten-der-ly His arm went round me, And He bore me to His fold.
Of His grace and will He taught me, And of heav'n-ly rest a-bove.
Nev-er shall my foes con-found me, While the Sav-ior's voice I hear.

Chorus

Pre-cious hid-ing place, Pre-cious hid-ing place, In the shel-ter of His love; Not a doubt or fear, Since my Lord is near, And I'm shel-tered in His love.

Copyright 1928. Renewal 1956. Hope Publishing Co.. owner. All rights reserved.

261 He Is So Precious to Me

Unto you therefore which believe He is precious. I Pet. 2:7

CHARLES H. GABRIEL   CHARLES H. GABRIEL

1. So pre-cious is Je-sus, my Sav-ior, my King, His praise all the
2. He stood at my heart's door 'mid sun-shine and rain, And pa-tient-ly
3. I stand on the moun-tain of bless-ing at last, No cloud in the
4. I praise Him be-cause He ap-point-ed a place Where some day, thro'

day long with rap-ture I sing; To Him in my weak-ness for
wait-ed an en-trance to gain; What shame that so long He en-
heav-ens a shad-ow to cast; His smile is up-on me, the
faith in His won-der-ful grace, I know I shall see Him, shall

strength I can cling, For He is so pre-cious to me.
treat-ed in vain, For He is so pre-cious to me.
val-ley is past, For He is so pre-cious to me.
look on His face, For He is so pre-cious to me.

Chorus

For He is so pre-cious to me,   For He is so
     so pre-cious to me,

pre-cious to me;   'Tis heav-en be-low
     so pre-cious to me;

my Re - deem - er to know, For He is so pre - cious to me.

Cleanse Me 262

Search me, O God, and know my heart . . . Psa. 139:23

J. EDWIN ORR   Traditional Maori melody

1. Search me, O God, and know my heart to - day; Try me, O
2. I praise Thee, Lord, for cleans - ing me from sin; Ful - fill Thy
3. Lord, take my life and make it whol - ly Thine; Fill my poor
4. O Ho - ly Spir - it, re - viv - al comes from Thee; Send a re-

Sav - ior, know my thoughts, I pray. See if there be some wick - ed
Word and make me pure with - in. Fill me with fire where once I
heart with Thy great love di - vine. Take all my will, my pas - sion,
viv - al— start the work in me. Thy Word de - clares Thou wilt sup-

way in me; Cleanse me from ev - ery sin and set me free.
burned with shame; Grant my de - sire to mag - ni - fy Thy name.
self and pride; I now sur - ren - der, Lord— in me a - bide.
ply our need; For bless - ings now, O Lord, I hum - bly plead.

263 Nor Silver nor Gold

Redeemed . . . with the precious blood of Christ. I Pet. 1:18, 19

JAMES M. GRAY   DANIEL B. TOWNER

1. Nor sil-ver nor gold hath ob-tained my re-demp-tion, Nor rich-es of
2. Nor sil-ver nor gold hath ob-tained my re-demp-tion, The guilt on my
3. Nor sil-ver nor gold hath ob-tained my re-demp-tion, The ho-ly com-
4. Nor sil-ver nor gold hath ob-tained my re-demp-tion, The way in-to

earth could have saved my poor soul; The blood of the cross is my
con-science too heav-y had grown; The blood of the cross is my
mand-ment for-bade me draw near; The blood of the cross is my
heav-en could not thus be bought; The blood of the cross is my

on-ly foun-da-tion, The death of my Sav-ior now mak-eth me whole.
on-ly foun-da-tion, The death of my Sav-ior could on-ly a-tone.
on-ly foun-da-tion, The death of my Sav-ior re-mov-eth my fear.
on-ly foun-da-tion, The death of my Sav-ior re-demp-tion hath wrought.

Chorus

I am re-deemed, but not with sil-ver; I am
I am re-deemed,

bought, but not with gold; Bought with a price—
I am bought, Bought with a price—

the blood of Je - sus, Pre -cious price of love un - told.

Nothing But the Blood 264

The blood of Jesus Christ His Son cleanseth us from all sin. I John 1:7

ROBERT LOWRY   ROBERT LOWRY

1. What can wash a - way my sin? Noth - ing but the blood of Je - sus;
2. For my par - don this I see— Noth - ing but the blood of Je - sus;
3. Noth - ing can for sin a - tone— Noth - ing but the blood of Je - sus;
4. This is all my hope and peace— Noth - ing but the blood of Je - sus;

What can make me whole a - gain? Noth - ing but the blood of Je - sus.
For my cleans - ing, this my plea— Noth - ing but the blood of Je - sus.
Naught of good that I have done— Noth - ing but the blood of Je - sus.
This is all my right - eous - ness— Noth - ing but the blood of Je - sus.

Chorus

O! pre - cious is the flow That makes me white as snow;

No oth - er fount I know, Noth - ing but the blood of Je - sus.

265 Redeemed

In whom we have redemption through His blood . . . Eph. 1:7

FANNY J. CROSBY

WILLIAM J. KIRKPATRICK

1. Redeemed, how I love to pro-claim it! Redeemed by the blood of the Lamb;
2. Redeemed and so hap-py in Je-sus, No lan-guage my rap-ture can tell;
3. I think of my bless-ed Re-deem-er, I think of Him all the day long;
4. I know I shall see in His beau-ty The King in whose law I de-light;

Redeemed thro' His in-fi-nite mer-cy, His child, and for-ev-er, I am.
I know that the light of His pres-ence With me doth con-tin-ual-ly dwell.
I sing, for I can-not be si-lent; His love is the theme of my song.
Who lov-ing-ly guardeth my foot-steps, And giv-eth me songs in the night.

Chorus

Re-deemed, re-deemed, Redeemed by the blood of the Lamb;
re-deemed, re-deemed,

Re-deemed, re-deemed, His child, and for-ev-er, I am.
re-deemed, re-deemed,

The Great Physician 266

He hath sent Me to heal the broken-hearted . . . Luke 4:18

WILLIAM HUNTER

JOHN H. STOCKTON

1. The great Phy - si - cian now is near—The sym - pa - thiz - ing Je - sus;
2. Your man - y sins are all for - giv'n— O hear the voice of Je - sus;
3. All glo - ry to the dy - ing Lamb— I now be - lieve in Je - sus;
4. And when to that bright world a - bove We rise to be with Je - sus,

He speaks the droop-ing heart to cheer—O hear the voice of Je - sus!
Go on your way in peace to heav'n And wear a crown with Je - sus.
I love the bless - ed Sav - ior's name, I love the name of Je - sus.
We'll sing a - round the throne of love His name, the name of Je - sus.

Chorus

Sweet-est note in ser - aph song, Sweet-est name on mor - tal tongue,

Sweet - est car - ol ev - er sung— Je - sus, bless - ed Je - sus!

267 Shepherd of Love

Our Lord Jesus, that great shepherd of the sheep . . . Heb. 13:20

JOHN W. PETERSON   JOHN W. PETERSON

1. Shep - herd of love, You knew I had lost my way;
Shep - herd of love, You cared that I'd gone a - stray.

2. Shep - herd of love— Sav - ior and Lord and Guide,
Shep - herd of love, For - ev - er I'll stay by your side.

You sought and found me, placed a - round me

Strong arms that car - ried me home; No foe can harm me

D.C. al Fine

or a - larm me, Nev - er a - gain will I roam.

© Copyright 1966. Arr. © 1979 by Singspiration. Division of The Zondervan Corporation. All rights reserved. Used by permission.

There Is Power in the Blood 268

In whom we have redemption through His blood . . . Col. 1:14

Lewis E. Jones

1. Would you be free from the bur-den of sin? There's pow'r in the blood,
2. Would you be free from your pas-sion and pride? There's pow'r in the blood,
3. Would you be whit-er, much whit-er than snow? There's pow'r in the blood,
4. Would you do serv-ice for Je-sus your King? There's pow'r in the blood,

pow'r in the blood; Would you o'er e-vil a vic-to-ry win? There's
pow'r in the blood; Come for a cleans-ing to Cal-va-ry's tide? There's
pow'r in the blood; Sin-stains are lost in its life-giv-ing flow; There's
pow'r in the blood; Would you live dai-ly His prais-es to sing? There's

Chorus

won-der-ful pow'r in the blood. There is pow'r, pow'r, won-der-work-ing pow'r
there is

In the blood of the Lamb; There is pow'r, pow'r,
In the blood of the Lamb; there is

won-der-work-ing pow'r In the pre-cious blood of the Lamb.

269 The Blood Will Never Lose Its Power

Thou . . . hast redeemed us to God by Thy blood . . . Rev. 5:9

ANDRAÉ CROUCH   ANDRAÉ CROUCH

1. The blood that Je - sus shed for me, 'Way back on
2. It soothes my doubts and calms my fears, And it dries

Cal - va - ry; The blood that gives me strength from day to
all my tears; The blood that gives me strength from day to

day, It will nev - er lose its power.
day, It will nev - er lose its power.

Chorus

It reach - es to the high - est moun - tain. It flows to the

© Copyright 1966 by MANNA MUSIC, INC., 2111 Kenmere Ave., Burbank CA 91504. International copyright secured. All rights reserved. Used by permission.

low - est val - ley. The blood that gives me strength from
day to day, It will nev - er lose its power.

That's the Name I Love 270

Wherefore God also hath . . . given Him a name which is above every name. Phil. 2:9

E. MARGARET CLARKSON   E. MARGARET CLARKSON

1. Je - sus, Je - sus, Je - sus, That's the Name I love.
2. Je - sus, Je - sus, Je - sus, That's the Name I love.
3. Je - sus, Je - sus, Je - sus, That's the Name I love.
4. Je - sus, Je - sus, Je - sus, That's the Name I love.

He's my shep - herd, I'm His lamb, He's the One I love!
He is with me all the day: He's the One I love!
He will wash my sins a - way; He's the One I love!
He's my Sav - ior, I'm His child, He's the One I love!

Copyright © 1975. Hope Publishing Co.. owner. International copyright secured. All rights reserved.

271 Why Do I Sing About Jesus?

Therefore my heart greatly rejoiceth: and with my song will I praise Him. Psa. 28:7

ALBERT A. KETCHUM

ALBERT A. KETCHUM

1. Deep in my heart there's a glad - ness, Je - sus has saved me from
2. On - ly a glimpse of His good - ness, That was suf - fi - cient for
3. He is the fair - est of fair ones, He is the Lil - y, the

sin! Praise to His name—what a Sav - ior! Cleans - ing with-
me; On - ly one look at the Sav - ior, Then was my
Rose; Riv - ers of mer - cy sur - round Him, Grace, love and

Chorus – Unison or Two Parts

out and with - in.
spir - it set free. Why do I sing a - bout Je - sus?
pit - y He shows.

Why is He pre - cious to me? He is my Lord and my

Sav - ior, Dy - ing! He set me free!
(set me free!)

Copyright 1923. Renewal 1951. Hope Publishing Co., owner. All rights reserved.

'Twas Jesus' Blood 272

The Son of man came . . . to give his life a ransom for man. Matt. 20:28

HARRY D. LOES

HARRY D. LOES

1. A sin - ner, lost, con - demned was I, Doomed an e - ter - nal death to
2. I ne'er could be at peace with God, But for the cleans - ing, crim - son
3. No doubt-er's scorn or creed of man Can shake my faith in Cal - v'ry's

die; But Je - sus died for me, He bore sin's pen - al - ty; On Cal-v'ry's
flood, No one but Christ could win A - tone-ment for all sin— He signed my
plan; His blood re-deemed my soul, It made me pure and whole; By faith my

Chorus

hill was lift - ed high.
par - don with His blood. 'Twas Je - sus' blood that ran-somed me,
life in Him be - gan.

From chains of sin He set me free. While a - ges roll,

my song shall be: 'Twas Je - sus' blood that ran-somed me.

Copyright 1941. Renewal 1969. Hope Publishing Co., owner. All rights reserved.

273 Since the Fullness of His Love Came In

To know the love of Christ, which passeth knowledge . . . Eph. 3:19

ELIZA E. HEWITT

BENTLEY D. ACKLEY

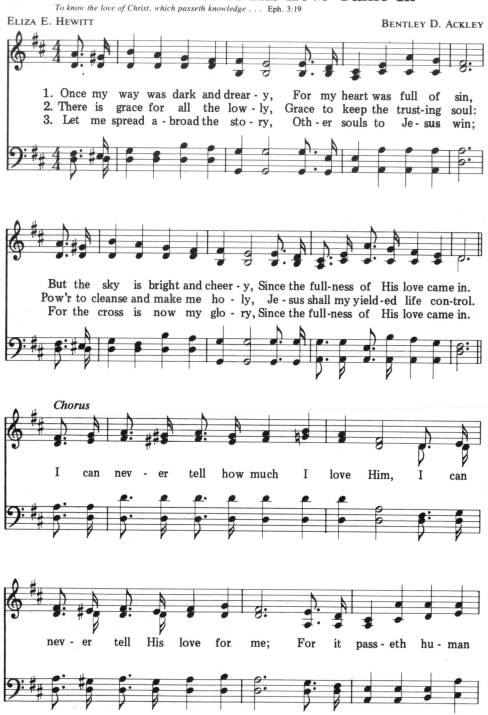

1. Once my way was dark and drear - y, For my heart was full of sin,
2. There is grace for all the low - ly, Grace to keep the trust-ing soul:
3. Let me spread a - broad the sto - ry, Oth - er souls to Je - sus win;

But the sky is bright and cheer - y, Since the full-ness of His love came in.
Pow'r to cleanse and make me ho - ly, Je - sus shall my yield-ed life con-trol.
For the cross is now my glo - ry, Since the full-ness of His love came in.

Chorus

I can nev - er tell how much I love Him, I can

nev - er tell His love for me; For it pass - eth hu - man

Copyright 1916. Renewal 1944 extended. Hope Publishing Co., owner. All rights reserved.

274 Saved, Saved!

He is able also to save them to the uttermost . . . Heb. 7:25

JACK P. SCHOLFIELD

JACK P. SCHOLFIELD

1. I've found a friend who is all to me, His
2. He saves me from ev-ery sin and harm, Se-
3. When poor and need-y and all a-lone, In

love is ev-er true; I love to tell how He
cures my soul each day; I'm lean-ing strong on His
love He said to me, "Come un-to me and I'll

lift-ed me, And what His grace can do for you.
might-y arm; I know He'll guide me all the way.
lead you home, To live with me e-ter-nal-ly."

Chorus

Saved by His pow'r di-vine, Saved to new life sub-lime!
Saved by His pow'r, Saved to new life,

Life now is sweet and my joy is com-plete, For I'm saved, saved, saved!

Satisfied 275

He satisfieth the longing soul, and filleth the hungry soul with goodness. Psa. 107:9

CLARA T. WILLIAMS

RALPH E. HUDSON

1. All my life long I had pant-ed For a drink from some cool spring
2. Feed-ing on the husks a-round me Till my strength was al-most gone,
3. Poor I was, and sought for rich-es, Some-thing that would sat-is-fy;
4. Well of wa-ter, ev-er spring-ing, Bread of life, so rich and free,

That I hoped would quench the burn-ing Of the thirst I felt with-in.
Longed my soul for some-thing bet-ter, On-ly still to hun-ger on.
But the dust I gath-ered round me On-ly mocked my soul's sad cry.
Un-told wealth that nev-er fail-eth, My Re-deem-er is to me.

Chorus

Hal-le-lu-jah! I have found Him—Whom my soul so long has craved!

Je-sus sat-is-fies my long-ings; Thro' His blood I now am saved.

276 Ring the Bells of Heaven

Joy shall be in heaven over one sinner that repenteth . . . Luke 15:7

WILLIAM O. CUSHING

GEORGE F. ROOT

1. Ring the bells of heav - en! there is joy to - day For a
2. Ring the bells of heav - en! there is joy to - day, For the
3. Ring the bells of heav - en! spread the feast to - day! An - gels,

soul re - turn - ing from the wild! See! the Fa - ther meets him
wan - d'rer now is rec - on - ciled; Yes, a soul is res - cued
swell the glad tri - um - phant strain! Tell the joy - ful ti - dings,

out up - on the way, Wel - com - ing His wea - ry, wan - d'ring child.
from his sin - ful way, And is born a - new a ran - somed child.
bear it far a - way! For a pre - cious soul is born a - gain.

Chorus

Glo - ry! glo - ry! how the an - gels sing; Glo - ry!

glo - ry! how the loud harps ring! 'Tis the ran - somed ar - my,

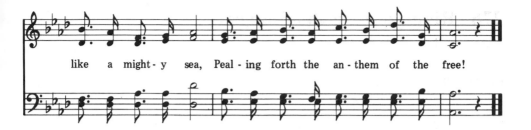

like a might-y sea, Peal-ing forth the an-them of the free!

The Sweetest Name 277

Wherefore God also hath . . . given Him a name which is above every name. Phil. 2:9

GEORGE W. BETHUNE   WILLIAM B. BRADBURY

1. There is no name so sweet on earth, No name so sweet in heav - en,
2. And when He hung up - on the tree, They wrote this name a - bove Him;
3. So now, up - on His Fa - ther's throne, Al - might - y to re - lease us
4. O Je - sus, by that match-less name, Thy grace shall fail us nev - er;

The name, be - fore His won-drous birth To Christ the Sav - ior giv - en.
That all might see the rea - son we For - ev - er - more must love Him.
From sin and pain, He glad - ly reigns, The Prince and Sav - ior, Je - sus.
To - day as yes - ter - day the same, Thou art the same for - ev - er.

Chorus

We love to sing of Christ our King, And hail Him, bless - ed Je - sus;

For there's no word ear ev - er heard So dear, so sweet as "Je - sus."

278 His Eye Is on the Sparrow

Ye are of more value than many sparrows. Matt. 10:31

CIVILLA D. MARTIN   CHARLES H. GABRIEL

Unison

1. Why should I feel dis-cour-aged, Why should the shad-ows come,
2. "Let not your heart be trou-bled," His ten-der word I hear,
3. When-ev-er I am temp-ted, When-ev-er clouds a-rise,

Why should my heart be lone-ly And long for Heav'n and home, When
And rest-ing on His good-ness, I lose my doubts and fears; Tho'
When songs give place to sing-ing, When hope with-in me dies, I

Je-sus is my por-tion? My con-stant Friend is He: His eye is
by the path He lead-eth But one step I may see: His eye is
draw the clo-ser to Him, From care He sets me free; His eye is

on the spar-row, And I know He watch-es me; His eye is on the
on the spar-row, And I know He watch-es me; His eye is on the
on the spar-row, And I know He cares for me; His eye is on the

Chorus

spar-row, And I know He watch-es me. I sing be-cause I'm

hap - py (I'm hap - py), I sing be - cause I'm free (I'm free),

For His eye is on the spar - row, And I know He watch - es me.

Just a Closer Walk with Thee 279

Let the weak say, I am strong. Joel 3:10

Source unknown

Source unknown

Unison

1. I am weak, but Thou art strong; Je - sus, keep me from all wrong;
2. Thro' this world of toil and snares, If I fal - ter, Lord, who cares?
3. When my fee - ble life is o'er, Time for me will be no more;
Ch. Just a clos - er walk with Thee, Grant it, Je - sus, is my plea,

D. C. Chorus

I'll be sat - is - fied as long As I walk, let me walk close to Thee.
Who with me my bur - den shares? None but Thee, dear Lord, none but Thee.
Guide me gent - ly, safe - ly o'er To Thy king - dom shore, to Thy shore.
Dai - ly walk - ing close to Thee, Let it be, dear Lord, let it be.

280 Sweeter as the Years Go By

The unsearchable riches of Christ. Eph. 3:8

LELIA N. MORRIS   LELIA N. MORRIS

1. Of Jesus' love that sought me When I was lost in sin—
2. He trod in old Judea Life's pathway long ago—
3. 'Twas wondrous love which led Him For us to suffer loss—

Of wondrous grace that brought me Back to His fold again—
The people thronged about Him His saving grace to know;
To bear without a murmur The anguish of the cross;

Of heights and depths of mercy Far deeper than the sea
He healed the broken-hearted And caused the blind to see;
With saints redeemed in glory Let us our voices raise,

And higher than the heavens, My theme shall ever be.
And still His great heart yearneth In love for even me.
Till heav'n and earth re-echo With our Redeemer's praise.

Chorus

Sweeter as the years go by, Sweeter as the years go by;
Sweeter as the years go by, 'Tis sweeter as the years go by;

Copyright 1912. Renewed 1940 by Nazarene Publishing House. Used by permission.

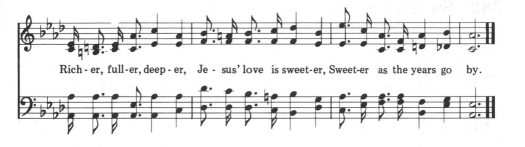

Rich-er, full-er, deep-er, Je-sus' love is sweet-er, Sweet-er as the years go by.

O, How I Love Jesus 281

We love Him, because He first loved us. I John 4:19

FREDERICK WHITFIELD

Traditional American melody

1. There is a name I love to hear, I love to sing its
2. It tells me of a Sav-ior's love, Who died to set me
3. It tells me what my Fa-ther hath In store for ev-ery
4. It tells of One whose lov-ing heart Can feel my deep-est

worth; It sounds like mu-sic in my ear, The sweet-est name on earth.
free; It tells me of His pre-cious blood, The sin-ner's per-fect plea.
day, And though I tread a dark-some path, Yields sun-shine all the way.
woe, Who in each sor-row bears a part, That none can bear be-low.

Chorus

O, how I love Je-sus, O, how I love Je-sus,

O, how I love Je-sus, Be-cause He first loved me!

282 Surely Goodness and Mercy

Surely goodness and mercy shall follow me all the days of my life. Psa. 23:6

JOHN W. PETERSON AND
ALFRED B. SMITH
Based on PSALM 23

JOHN W. PETERSON AND
ALFRED B. SMITH

1. A pil-grim was I and a-wan-d'ring, In the cold night of
2. He re-stor-eth my soul when I'm wea-ry, He giv-eth me
3. When I walk thro' the dark lone-some val-ley, My Sav-ior will

sin I did roam, When Je-sus the kind Shep-herd found me, And
strength day by day; He leads me be-side the still wa-ters, He
walk with me there; And safe-ly His great hand will lead me To the

Chorus

now I am on my way home.
guards me each step of the way. Sure-ly good-ness and mer-cy shall
man-sions He's gone to pre-pare.

fol-low me All the days, all the days of my life; Sure-ly good-ness

and mer-cy shall fol-low me All the days, all the days of my life.

© Copyright 1958 by Singspiration, Inc. All rights reserved. Used by permission.

Coda

And I shall dwell in the house of the Lord for - ev - er, And I shall feast at the

ta - ble spread for me; Sure - ly good-ness and mer-cy shall fol - low me

All the days, all the days of my life, All the days, all the days of my life.

Are You Weary, Heavy Laden?   283

Come unto Me, all ye that labor and are heavy laden . . . Matt. 11:28

JOHN M. NEALE
Based on an early Greek hymn

HENRY W. BAKER

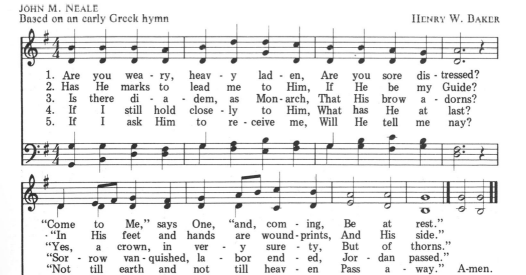

1. Are you wea - ry, heav - y lad - en, Are you sore dis - tressed?
2. Has He marks to lead me to Him, If He be my Guide?
3. Is there di - a - dem, as Mon - arch, That His brow a - dorns?
4. If I still hold close - ly to Him, What has He at last?
5. If I ask Him to re - ceive me, Will He tell me nay?

"Come to Me," says One, "and, com - ing, Be at rest."
-"In His feet and hands are wound - prints, And His side."
"Yes, a crown, in ver - y sure - ty, But of thorns."
"Sor - row van - quished, la - bor end - ed, Jor - dan passed."
"Not till earth and not till heav - en Pass a - way." A-men.

284 We Have an Anchor

And that Rock was Christ. I Cor. 10:4

PRISCILLA J. OWENS

WILLIAM J. KIRKPATRICK

1. Will your an-chor hold in the storms of life, When the clouds un-fold
2. It is safe-ly moored, 'twill the storms with-stand, For 'tis well se-cured
3. It will firm-ly hold in the straits of fear, When the break-ers have told
4. When our eyes be-hold thro' the gath-'ring night The cit-y of gold,

their wings of strife? When the strong tides lift, and the ca-bles strain,
by the Sav-ior's hand; And the ca-bles passed from His heart to mine,
the reef is near; Tho' the tem-pest rave and the wild winds blow,
our har-bor bright, We shall an-chor fast by the heav'n-ly shore,

Chorus

Will your an-chor drift, or firm re-main?
Can de-fy that blast, thro' strength di-vine.
Not an **an-gry** wave shall our bark o'er-flow. We have an an-chor that
With the storms all past for - ev - er - more.

keeps the soul Stead-fast and sure while the bil-lows roll, Fas-tened to the

Rock which can-not move, Ground-ed firm and deep in the Sav-ior's love.

Trust in the Lord 285

Trust in the Lord with all thine heart . . . Prov. 3:5

THOMAS O. CHISHOLM

WENDELL P. LOVELESS

1. Trust in the Lord with all your heart, This is God's gra-cious com-mand;
2. Trust in the Lord who rul - eth all, See - eth all things as they are,
3. Trust in the Lord—His eye will guide All thro' your path-way a - head,

In all your ways ac-knowl-edge Him, So shall you dwell in the land.
Be it a bird-ling in its nest, Or yon-der ut-ter-most star.
He hath re-deemed and He will keep, Trust Him and be not a - fraid.

Chorus

Trust in the Lord, O trou-bled soul, Rest in the arms of His care; What-
care, of His care;

ev - er your lot, it mat-ter-eth not, For noth-ing can trou-ble you there;

Trust in the Lord, O trou-bled soul, Noth-ing can trou-ble you there.

Copyright 1937. Renewal 1965. Hope Publishing Co., owner. All rights reserved.

286 The Love of God

Behold, what manner of love the Father hath bestowed upon us . . . I John 3:1

FREDERICK M. LEHMAN
St. 3, ATTR. TO MEIR BEN ISAAC NEHORAL

FREDERICK M. LEHMAN
ARR. BY CLAUDIA LEHMAN MAYS

1. The love of God is great-er far Than tongue or pen can
2. When hoar-y time shall pass a-way, And earth-ly thrones and
3. Could we with ink the o-cean fill, And were the skies of

ev-er tell, It goes be-yond the high-est star, And reach-es
king-doms fall; When men who here re-fuse to pray, On rocks and
parch-ment made, Were ev-ery stalk on earth a quill And ev-ery

to the low-est hell; The guilt-y pair, bowed down with care,
hills and moun-tains call; God's love, so sure, shall still en-dure,
man a scribe by trade; To write the love of God a-bove

God gave His Son to win; His err-ing child He rec-on-ciled,
All meas-ure-less and strong; Re-deem-ing grace to Ad-am's race—
Would drain the o-cean dry; Nor could the scroll con-tain the whole,

Chorus

And par-doned from his sin.
The saints' and an-gels' song. Oh love of God, how rich and
Tho' stretched from sky to sky.

Copyright 1917. Renewed 1945 by Nazarene Publishing House. Used by permission.

pure! How meas - ure - less and strong! It shall for -
ev - er - more en - dure, The saints' and an - gels' song.

On the Cross for Me 287

He . . . became obedient unto death, even the death of the cross. Phil. 2:8

PAUL HUTCHENS   PAUL HUTCHENS

On the cross for me, On the cross for me; See Him
dy - ing there for me; (for me;) Je - sus paid the price;
Him - self the sac - ri - fice, On the cross for me.

Copyright 1927. Renewal 1955. Hope Publishing Co., owner. All rights reserved.

288 There's a New Song in My Heart

And he hath put a new song in my mouth . . . Psa. 40:3

JOHN W. PETERSON

JOHN W. PETERSON

1. Once my life was filled with dis-cord, Sad - ness reigned with - in,
2. What a won-drous trans - for - ma - tion In my life was wrought,
3. Some-day I will go to Heav - en Where the an - gels sing,
4. I shall nev - er cease in prais - ing Je - sus Christ my Lord,

For my heart was heav - y lad - en With a weight of sin.
When I trust - ed Christ as Sav - ior And His par - don sought.
And I'll join their hap - py cho - rus Prais - ing Christ the King.
For the won - der - ful sal - va - tion That he did ac - cord.

Chorus

There's a new song in my heart Since the Sav - ior set me free; There's a new song in my heart— 'Tis a heav'n - ly har - mo - ny! All my sins are washed a -

© Copyright 1955 by Singspiration, Inc. All rights reserved. Used by permission.

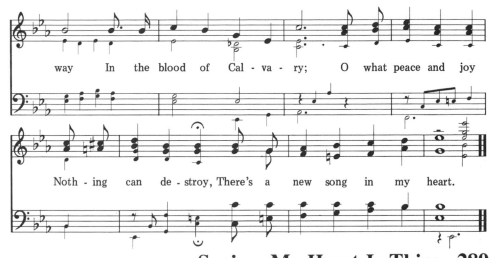

way In the blood of Cal - va - ry; O what peace and joy

Noth - ing can de - stroy, There's a new song in my heart.

Savior, My Heart Is Thine 289

Glorify God in your body, and in your spirit, which are God's. I Cor. 6:20

Author unknown
ALT. BY GEORGE C. STEBBINS

GEORGE C. STEBBINS

1. Sav - ior, my heart is Thine, Keep it for me; May ev - ery
2. Sav - ior, my will is Thine, Keep it for me; May ev - ery
3. Sav - ior, my life is Thine, Keep it for me; May ev - ery
4. Sav - ior, my all is Thine, Keep it for me; May all I

thought of mine Glo - ri - fy Thee. Glo - ri - fy Thee,
act of mine Be done for Thee. Be done for Thee,
hour of mine Be lived for Thee. Be lived for Thee,
have, O Lord, Be used for Thee. Be used for Thee,

Glo - ri - fy Thee; May ev - ery thought of mine Glo - ri - fy Thee.
Be done for Thee; May ev - ery act of mine Be done for Thee.
Be lived for Thee; May ev - ery hour of mine Be lived for Thee.
Be used for Thee; May all I have, O Lord, Be used for Thee.

Copyright 1953. Hope Publishing Co., owner. International copyright secured. All rights reserved.

290 Victory in Jesus

Victory . . . through our Lord Jesus Christ. I Cor. 15:57

EUGENE M. BARTLETT   EUGENE M. BARTLETT

1. I heard an old, old sto - ry, how a Sav - ior came from glo - ry,
2. I heard a - bout His heal - ing, of His cleans - ing pow'r re - veal - ing,
3. I heard a - bout a man - sion He has built for me in glo - ry,

How He gave his life on Cal - va - ry to save a wretch like me;
How He made the lame to walk a - gain and caused the blind to see;
And I heard a - bout the streets of gold be - yond the crys - tal sea;

I heard a - bout His groan - ing, of His pre - cious blood's a - ton - ing,
And then I cried "Dear Je - sus, come and heal my bro - ken spir - it,"
A - bout the an - gels sing - ing, and the old re - demp - tion sto - ry,

Then I re - pent - ed of my sins and won the vic - to - ry.
And some - how Je - sus came and bro't to me the vic - to - ry.
And some sweet day I'll sing up there the song of vic - to - ry.

Copyright 1939 by E. M. Bartlett. © Copyright 1967 by Mrs. E. M. Bartlett, Renewal. Assigned to Albert E. Brumley & Sons. All rights reserved. Used by permission.

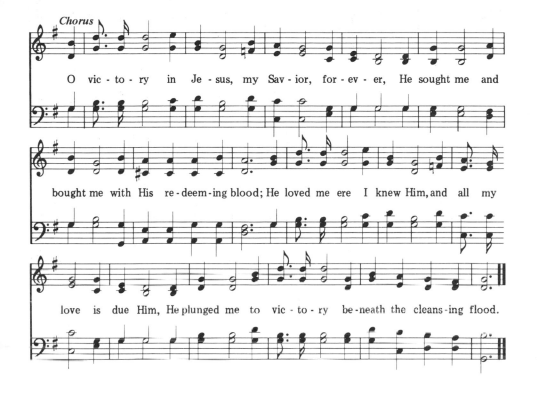

Chorus

O vic-to-ry in Je-sus, my Sav-ior, for-ev-er, He sought me and bought me with His re-deem-ing blood; He loved me ere I knew Him, and all my love is due Him, He plunged me to vic-to-ry be-neath the cleans-ing flood.

Jesus Calls Us; o'er the Tumult 291

He saith unto them, Follow Me. Matt. 4:19

CECIL F. ALEXANDER

WILLIAM H. JUDE

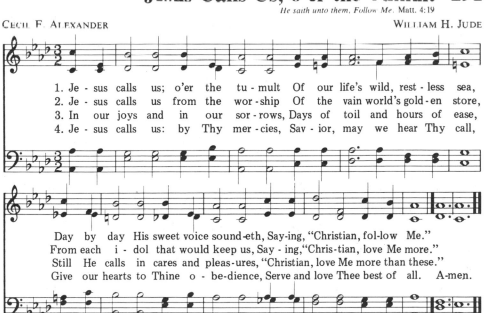

1. Je - sus calls us; o'er the tu - mult Of our life's wild, rest - less sea,
2. Je - sus calls us from the wor -ship Of the vain world's gold - en store,
3. In our joys and in our sor - rows, Days of toil and hours of ease,
4. Je - sus calls us: by Thy mer - cies, Sav - ior, may we hear Thy call,

Day by day His sweet voice sound-eth, Say-ing, "Christian, fol-low Me."
From each i - dol that would keep us, Say-ing, "Chris-tian, love Me more."
Still He calls in cares and pleas-ures, "Christian, love Me more than these."
Give our hearts to Thine o - be-dience, Serve and love Thee best of all. A-men.

292 It's Just Like His Great Love

For his great love wherewith He loved us . . . Eph. 2:4

EDNA H. WORRELL

CLARENCE B. STROUSE

1. A friend I have called Je - sus, Whose love is strong and true, And
2. Some-times the clouds of troub - le Be - dim the sky a - bove, I
3. When sor - row's clouds o'er - take me, And break up - on my head, When
4. Oh, I could sing for - ev - er Of Je - sus' love di - vine, Of

nev - er fails how - e'er 'tis tried, No mat - ter what I do; I've
can - not see my Sav - ior's face, I doubt His won - drous love; But
life seems worse than use - less, And I were bet - ter dead; I
all His care and ten - der - ness For this poor life of mine; His

sinned a - gainst this love of His, But when I knelt to pray, Con-
He, from Heav - en's mer - cy seat, Be - hold - ing my de - spair, In
take my grief to Je - sus then, Nor do I go in vain, For
love is in and o - ver all, And wind and waves o - bey When

fess - ing all my guilt to Him, The sin - clouds rolled a - way.
pit - y bursts the clouds be - tween, And shows me He is there.
heav'n - ly hope He gives that cheers Like sun - shine aft - er rain.
Je - sus whis - pers "Peace, be still!" And rolls the clouds a - way.

Chorus

It's just like Je-sus to roll the clouds a-way, It's just like Je-sus to keep me day by day. It's just like Je-sus all a-long the way, It's just like His great love.

I Am Trusting Thee, Lord Jesus 293

Trust ye in the Lord for ever . . . Isa. 26:4

FRANCES R. HAVERGAL ETHELBERT W. BULLINGER

1. I am trust-ing Thee, Lord Je-sus, Trust-ing on-ly Thee;
2. I am trust-ing Thee to guide me; Thou a-lone shalt lead,
3. I am trust-ing Thee for pow-er: Thine can nev-er fail;
4. I am trust-ing Thee, Lord Je-sus; Nev-er let me fall;

Trust-ing Thee for full sal-va-tion, Great and free.
Ev-ery day and hour sup-ply-ing All my need.
Words which Thou Thy-self shalt give me Must pre-vail.
I am trust-ing Thee for-ev-er, And for all. A-men.

294 Is My Name Written There?

. . . They which are written in the Lamb's book of life. Rev. 21:27

MARY A. KIDDER

FRANK M. DAVIS

1. Lord, I care not for rich - es, nei - ther sil - ver nor gold—
2. Lord, my sins they are man - y, like the sands of the sea,
3. O that beau - ti - ful cit - y with its man - sions of light,

I would make sure of heav - en, I would en - ter the fold.
But Thy blood, O my Sav - ior, is suf - fi - cient for me;
With its glo - ri - fied be - ings in pure gar - ments of white;

In the book of Thy king - dom with its pa - ges so fair,
For Thy prom - ise is writ - ten in bright let - ters that glow,
Where no e - vil thing com - eth to de - spoil what is fair,

Tell me, Je - sus, my Sav - ior, is my name writ - ten there?
"Tho' your sins be as scar - let, I will make them like snow."
Where the an - gels are watch - ing— yes, my name's writ - ten there.

1,2. Is my name writ - ten there On the page white and fair?
3. Yes, my name's writ - ten there On the page white and fair;

In the book of Thy king - dom, Is my name writ - ten there?
In the book of Thy king - dom, Yes, my name's writ - ten there.

Into My Heart 295

If any man . . . open the door, I will come in . . . Rev. 3:20

HARRY D. CLARKE   HARRY D. CLARKE

In - to my heart, in - to my heart, Come in - to my heart, Lord Je - sus;

Come in to - day, come in to stay, Come in - to my heart, Lord Je - sus.

Copyright 1924. Renewal 1952. Hope Publishing Co., owner. All rights reserved.

296 My Redeemer

Jesus Christ, who gave Himself for us, that He might redeem us. Titus 2:13, 14

PHILIP P. BLISS

JAMES McGRANAHAN

1. I will sing of my Re-deem-er, And His won-drous love to me;
2. I will tell the won-drous sto-ry, How my lost es-tate to save,
3. I will praise my dear Re-deem-er, His tri-um-phant pow'r I'll tell,
4. I will sing of my Re-deem-er, And His heav'n-ly love to me;

On the cru-el cross He suf-fered, From the curse to set me free.
In His bound-less love and mer-cy, He the ran-som free-ly gave.
How the vic-to-ry He giv-eth O-ver sin, and death, and hell.
He from death to life hath bro't me, Son of God with Him to be.

Chorus

Sing, oh, sing of my Re-deem-er,
of my Re-deem-er, Sing, oh, sing of my Re-deem-er,

With His blood He pur-chased me,
He pur-chased me, With His blood He pur-chased me,

On the cross He sealed my par - don,
He sealed my par - don, On the cross He sealed my par - don,

Paid the debt, and made me free.
and made me free, and made me free.

I'll Live for Him 297

That they might live . . . unto Him which died for them. II Cor. 5:15

RALPH E. HUDSON   C. R. DUNBAR

1. My life, my love I give to Thee, Thou Lamb of God who died for me;
2. I now be-lieve Thou dost re-ceive, For Thou hast died that I might live;
3. O Thou who died on Cal - va - ry, To save my soul and make me free,
Ch. — I'll live for Him who died for me, How hap - py then my life shall be!

D. C. Chorus

O may I ev - er faith - ful be, My Sav - ior and my God!
And now hence-forth I'll trust in Thee, My Sav - ior and my God!
I'll con - se - crate my life to Thee, My Sav - ior and my God!
I'll live for Him who died for me, My Sav - ior and my God!

298 I Will Sing of the Mercies of the Lord

I will sing of the mercies of the Lord forever . . . Psa. 89:1

PSALM 89:1

Source unknown

I will sing of the mer-cies of the Lord for-ev-er, I will sing, I will sing, I will sing of the mer-cies of the Lord for-ev-er, I will sing of the mer-cies of the Lord. With my mouth will I make known Thy faith-ful-ness, Thy faith-ful-ness, With my mouth will I make known Thy

faith - ful - ness to all gen - er - a - tions, I will sing of the mer - cies of the

Lord for - ev - er, I will sing of the mer - cies of the Lord.

I Have Decided to Follow Jesus 299

Master, I will follow Thee whithersoever Thou goest. Matt. 8:19

Source unknown

Folk melody from India

Unison

1. I have de - cid - ed to fol - low Je - sus, I have de -
2. The world be - hind me, the cross be - fore me; The world be -
3. Tho' none go with me, I still will fol - low, Tho' none go
4. Will you de - cide now to fol - low Je - sus? Will you de -

cid - ed to fol - low Je - sus, I have de - cid - ed to fol - low
hind me, the cross be - fore me; The world be - hind me, the cross be -
with me, I still will fol - low, Tho' none go with me, I still will
cide now to fol - low Je - sus? Will you de - cide now to fol - low

Je - sus, No turn - ing back, no turn - ing back.
fore me, No turn - ing back, no turn - ing back.
fol - low, No turn - ing back, no turn - ing back.
Je - sus? No turn - ing back, no turn - ing back.

300 I Am Praying for You

He ever liveth to make intercession for them. Heb. 7:25

S. O'Malley Clough

Ira D. Sankey

1. I have a Sav-ior, He's plead-ing in glo-ry, A dear, lov-ing Sav-ior, tho' earth-friends be few; And now He is watch-ing in ten-der-ness o'er me, But O, that my Sav-ior were your Sav-ior too!

2. I have a Fa-ther; to me He has giv-en A hope for e-ter-ni-ty, bless-ed and true; And soon He will call me to meet Him in heav-en, But O, that He'd let me bring you with me too!

3. I have a peace; it is calm as a riv-er, A peace that the friends of this world nev-er knew: My Sav-ior a-lone is its au-thor and giv-er, And O, could I know it was giv-en for you.

4. When He has found you, tell oth-ers the sto-ry, That my lov-ing Sav-ior is your Sav-ior, too; Then pray that your Sav-ior may bring them to glo-ry, And prayer will be an-swered—'twas an-swered for you!

Chorus

For you I am pray-ing, For you I am pray-ing, For you I am pray-ing, I'm pray-ing for you.

What Will You Do with Jesus? 301

What shall I do then with Jesus which is called Christ? Matt. 27:22

ALBERT B. SIMPSON

M. L. STOCKS

1. Je - sus is stand - ing in Pi - late's hall— Friend - less, for -
2. Je - sus is stand - ing on tri - al still, You can be
3. Will you e - vade Him as Pi - late tried? Or will you
4. Will you, like Pe - ter, your Lord de - ny? Or will you
5. "Je - sus, I give Thee my heart to - day! Je - sus, I'll

sak - en, be - trayed by all: Heark - en! what mean - eth the
false to Him if you will, You can be faith - ful thro'
choose Him, what - e'er be - tide? Vain - ly you strug - gle from
scorn from His foes to fly, Dar - ing for Je - sus to
fol - low Thee all the way, Glad - ly o - bey - ing Thee!"

sud - den call! What will you do with Je - sus?
good or ill: What will you do with Je - sus?
Him to hide! What will you do with Je - sus?
live or die? What will you do with Je - sus?
will you say. "This will I do with Je - sus!"

Chorus

What will you do with Je - sus? Neu - tral you can - not be;

Some day your heart will be ask - ing, "What will He do with me?"

302 I Believe in a Hill Called Mount Calvary

It pleased God . . . to save them that believe. I Cor. 1:21

DALE OLDHAM,
GLORIA GAITHER AND
WILLIAM J. GAITHER

WILLIAM J. GAITHER

1 There are things, as we trav-el this earth's shift-ing sands, That tran-
2. I be-lieve that the Christ who was slain on that cross Has the
3. I be-lieve that this life with its great mys-ter-ies Sure-ly

scend all the rea-son of man; But the things that mat-ter the
pow-er to change lives to-day; For He changed me com-plete-ly— a
some-day will come to an end; But faith will con-quer the

most in this world, They can nev-er be held in our hand.
new life is mine, That is why by the cross I will stay.
dark-ness and death, And will lead me at last to my Friend.

I be-lieve in a hill called Mount Cal-v'ry— I'll be-lieve what-

ev-er the cost; And when time has sur-ren-dered and

© Copyright 1968 by William J. Gaither. International copyright secured. All rights reserved. Used by permission.

earth is no more, I'll still cling to that old rug - ged cross.

Nearer, My God, to Thee 303

It is good for me to draw near to God . . . Psa. 73:28

SARAH F. ADAMS
Based on GEN. 28:10-22

LOWELL MASON

1. Near - er, my God, to Thee, Near - er to Thee! E'en though it
2. Though like the wan - der - er, The sun gone down, Dark - ness be
3. There let the way ap - pear Steps un - to heav'n; All that Thou
4. Then, with my walk ing thoughts Bright with Thy praise, Out of my
5. Or if on joy - ful wing, Cleav - ing the sky, Sun, moon, and

be a cross That rais - eth me; Still all my song shall be, Near - er, my
o - ver me, My rest a stone; Yet in my dreams I'd be Near - er, my
send - est me In mer - cy giv'n; An - gels to beck - on me Near - er, my
ston - y griefs, Beth - el I'll raise; So by my woes to be Near - er, my
stars for - got, Up - ward I fly, Still all my song shall be Near - er, my

God, to Thee, Near - er, my God, to Thee, Near - er to Thee. A - men.

304 Sweet Peace, the Gift of God's Love

For He is our peace . . . Eph. 2:14

PETER P. BILHORN   PETER P. BILHORN

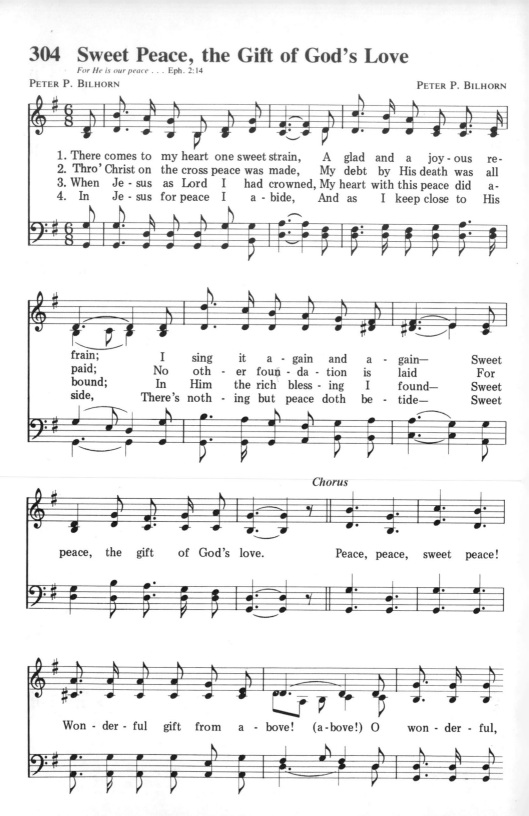

1. There comes to my heart one sweet strain, A glad and a joy-ous re-
2. Thro' Christ on the cross peace was made, My debt by His death was all
3. When Je-sus as Lord I had crowned, My heart with this peace did a-
4. In Je-sus for peace I a-bide, And as I keep close to His

frain; I sing it a-gain and a-gain— Sweet
paid; No oth-er foun-da-tion is laid For
bound; In Him the rich bless-ing I found— Sweet
side, There's noth-ing but peace doth be-tide— Sweet

Chorus

peace, the gift of God's love.   Peace, peace, sweet peace!

Won-der-ful gift from a-bove! (a-bove!) O won-der-ful,

won - der - ful peace! Sweet peace, the gift of God's love!

Keep Praising 305

At midnight Paul and Silas prayed and sang praises unto God. Acts 16:25

WENDELL P. LOVELESS

WENDELL P. LOVELESS

Keep prais ing, keep prais - ing, When the days are dark and drear; Keep

prais - ing, keep prais - ing, God will guide you, nev - er fear; Keep

prais - ing, keep prais - ing, Thank-ful hearts to Him be rais - ing; Has the

Lord not said, There is glo - ry on a - head—So keep on prais - ing Him.

Copyright 1934. Renewal 1962. Hope Publishing Co., owner. All rights reserved.

306 You May Have the Joybells

Making melody in your heart to the Lord. Eph. 5:19

J. EDWARD RUARK

WILLIAM J. KIRKPATRICK

1. You may have the joy-bells ring-ing in your heart, And a peace that
2. Love of Je - sus in its full - ness you may know, And this love to
3. You will meet with tri - als as you jour - ney home; Grace suf - fi - cient
4. Let your life speak well of Je - sus ev - ery day; Own His right to

from you nev - er will de - part; Walk the straight and nar - row way,
those a - round you sweet - ly show; Words of kind - ness al - ways say,
He will give to o - ver - come; Tho' un - seen by mor - tal eye,
ev - ery serv - ice you can pay; Sin - ners you can help to win

Live for Je - sus ev - ery day, He will keep the joy - bells
Deeds of mer - cy do each day, Then He'll keep the joy - bells
He is with you ev - er nigh, And He'll keep the joy - bells
If your life is pure and clean, And you keep the joy - bells

Chorus

ring - ing in your heart.
ring - ing in your heart. Joy - bells ring - ing in your heart,
ring - ing in your heart.
ring - ing in your heart.

Joy - bells ring - ing in your heart; Take the Sav - ior here be - low

With you ev - ery-where you go; He will keep the joy-bells ring-ing in your heart.

Rejoice in the Lord Always 307

Rejoice in the Lord alway; and again I say, Rejoice. Phil. 4:4

PHIL. 4:4

Traditional

Re - joice in the Lord al - ways, a - gain I say, re - joice! Re -

joice in the Lord al - ways, a - gain I say, re-joice! Re-joice, re-joice, a -

gain I say, re - joice! Re-joice, re - joice, a - gain I say, re - joice!

308 Love Lifted Me

And Jesus took him by the hand, and lifted him up. Mark 9:27

JAMES ROWE

HOWARD E. SMITH

1. I was sink-ing deep in sin, Far from the peace-ful shore, Ver - y deep-ly
2. All my heart to Him I give, Ev - er to Him I'll cling, In His bless - ed
3. Souls in dan- ger, look a-bove, Je - sus com-plete-ly saves; He will lift you

stained with-in, Sink-ing to rise no more; But the Mas - ter of the sea
pres - ence live, Ev - er His prais - es sing. Love so might - y and so true
by His love Out of the an - gry waves. He's the Mas - ter of the sea,

Heard my des-pair - ing cry, From the wa - ters lift - ed me, Now safe am I.
Mer - its my soul's best songs; Faith-ful, lov- ing serv-ice too To Him be - longs.
Bil-lows His will o - bey; He your Sav-ior wants to be— Be saved to - day.

Chorus

Love lift - ed me! Love lift - ed me! When noth - ing
e - ven me! e - ven me!

else could help, Love lift - ed me. Love lift - ed me!
e - ven me!

© 1911 and renewed 1939 by John T. Benson, Jr. Copyright extended. International copyright secured. All rights reserved. Printed by permission of The Benson Company, 365 Great Circle Road, Nashville, TN 37228.

Love lift-ed me! When noth-ing else could help, Love lift-ed me!
e - ven me!

Lord, I'm Coming Home 309

I will arise and go to my father . . . Luke 15:18

WILLIAM J. KIRKPATRICK

WILLIAM J. KIRKPATRICK

1. I've wan-dered far a - way from God, Now I'm com - ing home;
2. I've wast - ed man - y pre - cious years, Now I'm com - ing home;
3. I've tired of sin and stray - ing, Lord, Now I'm com - ing home;
4. My soul is sick, my heart is sore, Now I'm com - ing home;

The paths of sin too long I've trod, Lord, I'm com - ing home.
I now re - pent with bit - ter tears, Lord, I'm com - ing home.
I'll trust Thy love, be - lieve Thy word, Lord, I'm com - ing home.
My strength re - new, my hope re - store, Lord, I'm com - ing home.

Chorus

Com - ing home, com - ing home, Nev - er more to roam,

O - pen wide Thine arms of love, Lord, I'm com - ing home.

310 The Lily of the Valley

I am the rose of Sharon, and the lily of the valleys. S. of S. 2:1

CHARLES W. FRY

Traditional melody
ARR. BY WILLIAM S. HAYS

1. I have found a friend in Je-sus—He's ev-ery-thing to me,
2. He all my griefs has tak-en and all my sor-rows borne,
3. He will nev-er, nev-er leave me nor yet for-sake me here,

He's the fair-est of ten thou-sand to my soul; The
In temp-ta-tion He's my strong and might-y tow'r; I have
While I live by faith and do His bless-ed will; A

Lil-y of the Val-ley— in Him a-lone I see
all for Him for-sak-en, and all my i-dols torn
wall of fire a-bout me, I've noth-ing now to fear—

All I need to cleanse and make me ful-ly whole.
From my heart, and now He keeps me by His pow'r.
With His man-na He my hun-gry soul shall fill.

In sor - row He's my com - fort, in trou - ble He's my stay,
Tho' all the world for - sake me and Sa - tan tempt me sore,
Then sweep - ing up to glo - ry I'll see His bless - ed face,

He tells me ev - ery care on Him to roll; He's the
Thro' Je - sus I shall safe - ly reach the goal; He's the
Where riv - ers of de - light shall ev - er roll; He's the

Hal - le - lu - jah!

Lil - y of the Val - ley, the Bright and Morn - ing Star,

He's the fair - est of ten thou - sand to my soul.

311 This World Is Not My Home

These all died in faith . . . and confessed that they were strangers and pilgrims on the earth. Heb. 11:13

ALBERT E. BRUMLEY

ALBERT E. BRUMLEY

1. This world is not my home, I'm just a pass-ing through My
2. They're all ex-pect-ing me, and that's one thing I know, My
3. I have a lov-ing Sav-ior up in glo-ry-land, I
4. Just up in glo-ry-land we'll live e-ter-nal-ly, The

treas-ures are laid up some-where be-yond the blue; The
Sav-ior par-doned me and now I on-ward go; I
don't ex-pect to stop un-til I with Him stand, He's
saints on ev-ery hand are shout-ing vic-to-ry, Their

an-gels beck-on me from heav-en's o-pen door, And I
know He'll take me thro' tho' I am weak and poor, And I
wait-ing now for me in heav-en's o-pen door, And I
songs of sweet-est praise drift back from heav-en's shore, And I

can't feel at home in this world an-y-more.

Chorus

O Lord, you know I
have no friend like you, If heav-en's not my home, then

Arr. Copyright 1937 by Albert E. Brumley. Renewal Copyright 1965 by Albert E. Brumley & Sons. All rights reserved. Used by permission.

Lord what will, I do? The an-gels beck-on me from heav-en's

o-pen door, And I can't feel at home in this world an-y-more.

Only Trust Him 312

He is able also to save them to the uttermost . . . Heb. 7:25

JOHN H. STOCKTON

JOHN H. STOCKTON

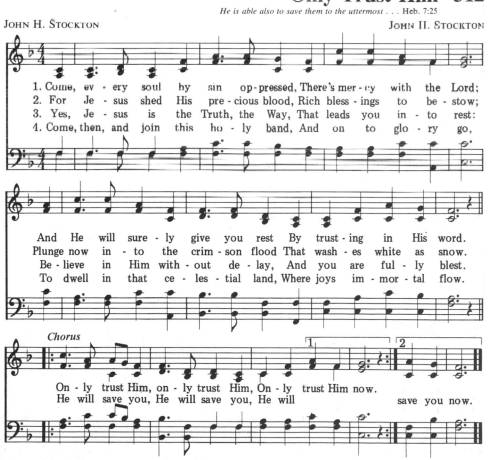

1. Come, ev-ery soul by sin op-pressed, There's mer-cy with the Lord;
2. For Je-sus shed His pre-cious blood, Rich bless-ings to be-stow;
3. Yes, Je-sus is the Truth, the Way, That leads you in-to rest:
4. Come, then, and join this ho-ly band, And on to glo-ry go,

And He will sure-ly give you rest By trust-ing in His word.
Plunge now in-to the crim-son flood That wash-es white as snow.
Be-lieve in Him with-out de-lay, And you are ful-ly blest.
To dwell in that ce-les-tial land, Where joys im-mor-tal flow.

Chorus

On-ly trust Him, on-ly trust Him, On-ly trust Him now.
He will save you, He will save you, He will save you now.

313 Sunlight

Who hath called you out of darkness into his marvelous light. 1 Pet. 2:9

JUDSON W. VAN DEVENTER

WINFIELD S. WEEDEN

1. I wan-dered in the shades of night, Till Je - sus came to me,
2. Tho' clouds may gath - er in the sky, And bil - lows round me roll,
3. While walk - ing in the light of God, I sweet com-mun - ion find;
4. I cross the wide ex - tend - ed fields, I jour - ney o'er the plain,
5. Soon I shall see Him as He is, The light that came to me;

And with the sun - light of His love Bid all my dark - ness flee.
How - ev - er dark the world may be I've sun - light in my soul.
I press with ho - ly vig - or on, And leave the world be - hind.
And in the sun - light of His love I reap the gold - en grain.
Be - hold the bright-ness of His face, Thro' - out e - ter - ni - ty.

Chorus

Sun - light, sun - light in my soul to - day,
to - day, yes,

Sun - light, sun - light

all a - long the way;
nar - row way;

Since the Sav - ior found me,

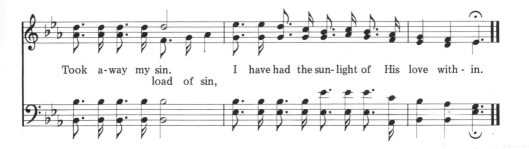

Took a-way my sin.   I have had the sun-light of His love with-in.
load of sin,

Lead Me to Some Soul Today 314

Now that we are ambassadors for Christ . . . II Cor. 5:20

WILL H. HOUGHTON   WENDELL P. LOVELESS

Lead me to some soul to-day, O teach me, Lord, just what to say;

Friends of mine are lost in sin, And can-not find their way.

Few there are who seem to care, And few there are who pray;
who pray;

Melt my heart and fill my life, Give me one soul to-day.

Copyright 1936. Renewal 1964. Hope Publishing Co., owner. All rights reserved.

315 Tell Me the Old, Old Story

Tell them how great things the Lord hath done for thee . . . Mark 5:19

A. CATHERINE HANKEY   WILLIAM H. DOANE

1. Tell me the Old, Old Sto - ry, Of un - seen things a -
bove, Of Je - sus and His glo - ry, Of Je - sus and His love;
Tell me the sto - ry sim - ply, As to a lit - tle child, For
I am weak and wea - ry, And help - less and de - filed.

2. Tell me the sto - ry slow - ly, That I may take it
in— That won - der - ful re - demp - tion, God's rem - e - dy for sin;
Tell me the sto - ry oft - en, For I for - get so soon, The
"ear - ly dew" of morn - ing Has passed a - way at noon.

3. Tell me the sto - ry soft - ly, With ear - nest tones and
grave; Re - mem - ber I'm the sin - ner Whom Je - sus came to save;
Tell me the sto - ry al - ways, If you would real - ly be, In
an - y time of troub - le, A com - fort - er to me.

4. Tell me the same old sto - ry, When you have cause to
fear That this world's emp - ty glo - ry Is cost - ing me too dear;
Yes, and when that world's glo - ry Is dawn - ing on my soul, Tell
me the Old, Old Sto - ry: "Christ Je - sus makes thee whole."

Chorus

Tell me the Old, Old Sto - ry, Tell me the Old, Old Sto - ry,

Tell me the Old, Old Sto - ry Of Je - sus and His love.

Jesus, Savior, All I Have Is Thine 316

. . . A vessel unto honor . . . meet for the Master's use. II Tim. 2:21

HERMAN VOSS   HERMAN VOSS

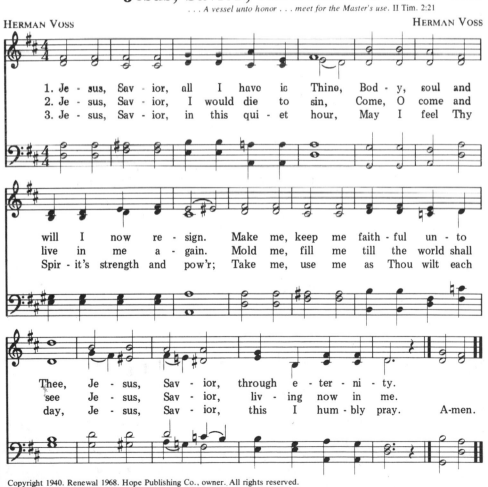

1. Je - sus, Sav - ior, all I have is Thine, Bod - y, soul and
2. Je - sus, Sav - ior, I would die to sin, Come, O come and
3. Je - sus, Sav - ior, in this qui - et hour, May I feel Thy

will I now re - sign. Make me, keep me faith - ful un - to
live in me a - gain. Mold me, fill me till the world shall
Spir - it's strength and pow'r; Take me, use me as Thou wilt each

Thee, Je - sus, Sav - ior, through e - ter - ni - ty.
'see Je - sus, Sav - ior, liv - ing now in me.
day, Je - sus, Sav - ior, this I hum - bly pray. A-men.

Copyright 1940. Renewal 1968. Hope Publishing Co., owner. All rights reserved.

317 Wonderful Peace

Now the Lord of peace himself give you peace . . . II Thess. 3:16

W. D. CORNELL, ALT.

W. G. COOPER

1. Far a - way in the depths of my spir - it to - night Rolls a
2. What a treas - ure I have in this won - der - ful peace, Bur - ied
3. I am rest - ing to - night in this won - der - ful peace, Rest - ing
4. And me - thinks when I rise to that Cit - y of peace, Where the
5. Ah! soul, are you here with - out com - fort or rest, March - ing

mel - o - dy sweet - er than psalm; In ce - les - tial - like strains it un -
deep in the heart of my soul; So se - cure that no pow - er can
sweet - ly in Je - sus' con - trol; For I'm kept from all dan - ger by
Au - thor of peace I shall see, That one strain of the song which the
down the rough path - way of time? Make Je - sus your friend ere the

ceas - ing - ly falls O'er my soul like an in - fi - nite calm.
mine it a - way, While the years of e - ter - ni - ty roll.
night and by day, And His glo - ry is flood - ing my soul.
ran - somed will sing, In that heav - en - ly king - dom shall be:
shad - ows grow dark; Oh, ac - cept this sweet peace so sub - lime.

Chorus

Peace! peace! won - der - ful peace, Com - ing down from the Fa - ther a - bove; Sweep

o - ver my spir-it for - ev - er, I pray, In fath-om-less bil-lows of love.

They That Know Thy Name   318

. . . And his name shall be called Wonderful, Counsellor, The mighty God, The everlasting Father, The Prince of Peace.

Isa. 9:6

PSALM 9:10

E. MARGARET CLARKSON

They that know Thy Name will put their trust in Thee, Their

trust in Thee, their trust in Thee, They that know Thy

Fine

Name will put their trust in Thee. For Thy Name is God!

D.C. al Fine

Won - der - ful, Coun - sel - lor, Might - y God art Thou.

Copyright © 1975. Hope Publishing Co., owner. International copyright secured. All rights reserved.

319 The Haven of Rest

. . . He bringeth them unto their desired haven. Psa. 107:30

HENRY L. GILMOUR

GEORGE D. MOORE

1. My soul in sad ex - ile was out on life's sea, So
2. I yield - ed my - self to His ten - der em - brace, And
3. The song of my soul, since the Lord made me whole, Has
4. How pre - cious the thought that we all may re - cline, Like
5. Oh, come to the Sav - ior, He pa - tient - ly waits To

bur - dened with sin and dis - trest, Till I heard a sweet voice say - ing,
faith tak - ing hold of the Word, My fet - ters fell off, and I
been the old sto - ry so blest, Of Je - sus, who'll save who - so -
John the be - lov - ed and blest, On Je - sus' strong arm, where no
save by His pow - er di - vine; Come, an - chor your soul in the

"Make me your choice;" And I en - tered the "Ha - ven of Rest!"
an - chored my soul; The "Ha - ven of Rest" is the Lord.
ev - er will have A home in the "Ha - ven of Rest!"
tem - pest can harm, Se - cure in the "Ha - ven of Rest!"
"Ha - ven of Rest," And say, "My Be - lov - ed is mine."

Chorus

I've an - chored my soul in the "Ha - ven of Rest," I'll

sail the wide seas no more; The tem-pest may sweep o'er the wild, storm-y deep, In Je - sus I'm safe ev - er - more.

Sweep over My Soul 320

They were all filled with the Holy Ghost. Acts 2:4

HARRY D. CLARKE

HARRY D. CLARKE

1. Sweep o - ver my soul, Sweep o - ver my soul;
2. Fill my life with *joy, Fill my life with *joy,

Come, gra - cious Spir - it, Sweep o - ver my soul.
Come, gra - cious Spir - it, Fill my life with *joy.

*3. love, 4. peace.

Copyright 1927. Renewal 1955. Hope Publishing Co., owner. All rights reserved.

321 Look and Live

When he looketh upon it, he shall live. Num. 21:8

William A. Ogden

William A. Ogden

1. I've a mes-sage from the Lord, Hal-le-lu-jah! The mes-sage un-to you I'll
2. I've a mes-sage full of love, Hal-le-lu-jah! A mes-sage, O my friend, for
3. Life is of-fered un-to you, Hal-le-lu-jah! E-ter-nal life your soul shall

give; 'Tis re-cord-ed in His word, Hal-le-lu-jah! It is
you; 'Tis a mes-sage from a-bove, Hal-le-lu-jah! Je-sus
have, If you'll on-ly look to Him, Hal-le-lu-jah! Look to

Chorus

on-ly that you "look and live."
said it and I know 'tis true. Look and live, O sin-ner,
Je-sus, who a-lone can save. Look and live, O sin-ner,

live, Look to Je-sus now and live; 'Tis re-
live, Look and live,

cord-ed in His word, Hal-le-lu-jah! It is on-ly that you look and live.

He's Only a Prayer Away 322

Then shalt thou call, and the Lord will answer . . . Isa. 58:9

JOHNNY LANGE AND
HAROLD L. GRAHAM

JOHNNY LANGE AND
HAROLD L. GRAHAM

1. There's Some-one who loves ev-ery sin-ner, He's call-ing, O
2. He has an in-fin-ite pow-er, And so man-y
3. When oth-ers for-sake and de-sert you, And you're in the

hear Him to-day; 'Tis Je-sus, our bless-ed re-deem-er, He's
things He can do; He'll al-ways be read-y to help you, Just
depth of de-spair; Let God share your bur-den and sor-row, Just

Chorus

on-ly a prayer a-way.
ask Him to come to you. He's on-ly a
seek Him and He'll be there.

prayer a-way, He's on-ly a prayer a-way;

God will be with you when-ev-er you pray, He's on-ly a prayer a-way.

Copyright © 1954 by BULLS-EYE MUSIC, INC., P.O. Box 1589, Hollywood, CA 90028. International copyright secured. All rights reserved. Used by permission.

323 For Those Tears I Died

And God shall wipe away all tears from their eyes. Rev. 7:17

MARSHA J. STEVENS

MARSHA J. STEVENS

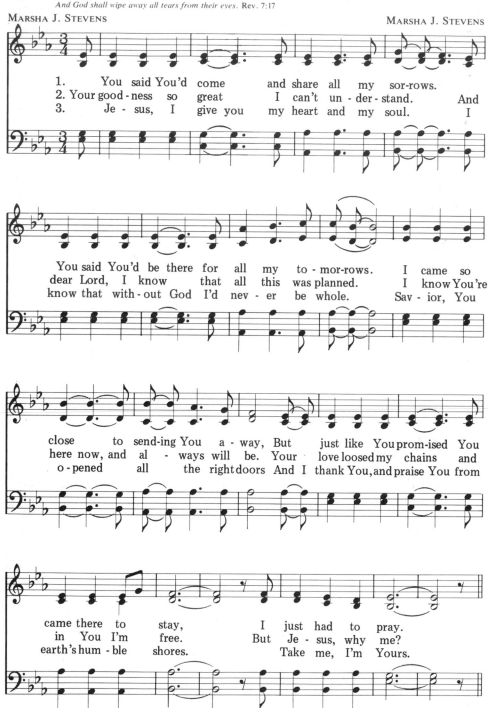

1. You said You'd come and share all my sor-rows.
2. Your good-ness so great I can't un-der-stand. And
3. Je-sus, I give you my heart and my soul. I

You said You'd be there for all my to-mor-rows. I came so
dear Lord, I know that all this was planned. I know You're
know that with-out God I'd nev-er be whole. Sav-ior, You

close to send-ing You a-way, But just like You prom-ised You
here now, and al-ways will be. Your love loosed my chains and
o-pened all the right doors And I thank You, and praise You from

came there to stay, I just had to pray.
in You I'm free. But Je-sus, why me?
earth's hum-ble shores. Take me, I'm Yours.

© Copyright 1969 by LEXICON MUSIC, INC. ASCAP. All rights reserved. International copyright secured. Used by special permission.

324 He Was There All the Time

The Lord is nigh unto them that are of a broken heart. Psa. 34:18

GARY S. PAXTON   GARY S. PAXTON

1. Time af-ter time I went search-ing for peace in some void,
2. Nev-er a-gain will I look for a fake rain-bow's end,

I was try-ing to blame all my ills on this world I was in;
Now that I have the an-swer, my life is just start-ing to rhyme;

Sur-face re-la-tion-ships used me till I was done in,
Shar-ing each new day with Him is a cup of new life,

Chorus

And all the while some-one was beg-ging to free me from sin.
O, what I missed! He's been wait-ing right there all the time.

He was there all the time, He was there all the time; Wait-ing

© Copyright 1975 by New Pax Music Press, 803 18th Ave., So., Nashville, TN 37202. International copyright secured. All rights reserved. Made in U.S.A. Used by permission.

pa - tient - ly in line, He was there all the time.

Have Thine Own Way, Lord 325

We are the clay, and Thou our potter . . . Isa. 64:8

ADELAIDE A. POLLARD   GEORGE C. STEBBINS

1. Have Thine own way, Lord! Have Thine own way! Thou art the
2. Have Thine own way, Lord! Have Thine own way! Search me and
3. Have Thine own way, Lord! Have Thine own way! Wound - ed and
4. Have Thine own way, Lord! Have Thine own way! Hold o'er my

1. Pot - ter, I am the clay. Mold me and make me aft - er Thy
2. try me, Mas - ter, to - day! Whit - er than snow, Lord, wash me just
3. wea - ry, help me, I pray! Pow - er— all pow - er— sure - ly is
4. be - ing ab - so - lute sway! Fill with Thy Spir - it till all shall

1. will, While I am wait - ing yield - ed and still.
2. now, As in Thy pres - ence hum - bly I bow.
3. Thine! Touch me and heal me, Sav - ior di - vine!
4. see Christ on - ly, al - ways, liv - ing in me! A - men.

Copyright 1907. Renewal 1935 extended. Hope Publishing Co., owner. All rights reserved.

326 Tho' Your Sins Be as Scarlet

Though your sins be as scarlet, they shall be as white as snow. Isa. 1:18

FANNY J. CROSBY

WILLIAM H. DOANE

1. "Tho' your sins be as scar-let, They shall be as white as snow;
2. Hear the voice that en-treats you, O re-turn ye un-to God!
3. He'll for-give your trans-gres-sions, And re-mem-ber them no more;

Tho' your sins be as scar-let, They shall be as white as snow;
Hear the voice that en-treats you, O re-turn ye un-to God!
He'll for-give your trans-gres-sions, And re-mem-ber them no more;

Tho' they be red like crim-son, They shall be as wool!"
He is of great com-pas-sion, And of won-drous love;
"Look un-to Me, ye peo-ple," Saith the Lord your God!

1. Tho' they be red

"Tho' your sins be as scar-let, Tho' your sins be as scar-let,
Hear the voice that en-treats you, Hear the voice that en-treats you,
He'll for-give your trans-gres-sions, He'll for-give your trans-gres-sions,

They shall be as white as snow, They shall be as white as snow."
O re-turn ye un-to God! O re-turn ye un-to God!
And re-mem-ber them no more, And re-mem-ber them no more.

Almost Persuaded 327

Almost thou persuadest me to be a Christian. Acts 26:28

PHILIP P. BLISS

PHILIP P. BLISS

1. "Al - most per - suad - ed," now to be - lieve;
2. "Al - most per - suad - ed," come, come to - day;
3. "Al - most per - suad - ed," har - vest is past!

"Al - most per - suad - ed," Christ to re - ceive;
"Al - most per - suad - ed," turn not a - way;
"Al - most per - suad - ed," doom comes at last!

Seems now some soul to say, "Go, Spir - it, go Thy way,
Je - sus in - vites you here, An - gels are ling - 'ring near,
"Al - most" can - not a - vail; "Al - most" is but to fail!

Some more con - ven - ient day On Thee I'll call."
Prayers rise from hearts so dear, O wan - d'rer, come.
Sad, sad, that bit - ter wail, "Al - most," but lost.

328 In Times Like These

Can ye not discern the signs of the times? Matt. 16:3

RUTH CAYE JONES   RUTH CAYE JONES

1. In times like these you need a Sav - ior, In times like
2. In times like these you need the Bi - ble, In times like
3. In times like these I have a Sav - ior, In times like

these you need an an - chor; Be ver - y sure, be ver - y
these O be not i - dle; Be ver - y sure, be ver - y
these I have an an - chor; I'm ver - y sure, I'm ver - y

sure Your an - chor holds and grips the Sol - id Rock!
sure Your an - chor holds and grips the Sol - id Rock!
sure My an - chor holds and grips the Sol - id Rock!

Chorus

This Rock is Je - sus, Yes, He's the One; This Rock is

Copyright 1944. Renewal 1972 by Ruth Caye Jones. Assigned to Zondervan Music Publishers. All rights reserved. Used by permission.

Je - sus, The on - ly One! 1,2. Be ver - y sure, be ver - y
3. I'm ver - y sure, I'm ver - y

sure Your an - chor holds and grips the Sol - id Rock!
sure My an - chor holds and grips the Sol - id Rock!

O for a Closer Walk with God 329

What doth the Lord require of thee . . . to walk humbly with thy God. Micah 6:8

WILLIAM COWPER

JOHN B. DYKES

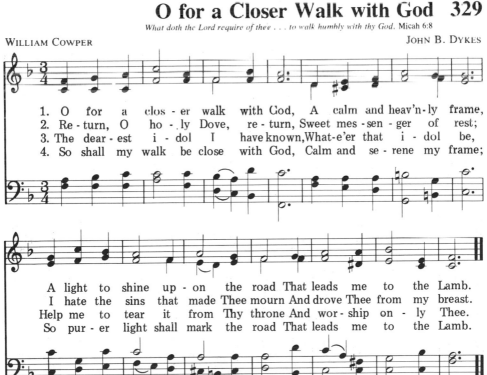

1. O for a clos - er walk with God, A calm and heav'n - ly frame,
2. Re - turn, O ho - ly Dove, re - turn, Sweet mes - sen - ger of rest;
3. The dear - est i - dol I have known, What - e'er that i - dol be,
4. So shall my walk be close with God, Calm and se - rene my frame;

A light to shine up - on the road That leads me to the Lamb.
I hate the sins that made Thee mourn And drove Thee from my breast.
Help me to tear it from Thy throne And wor - ship on - ly Thee.
So pur - er light shall mark the road That leads me to the Lamb.

330 Are You Washed in the Blood?

Wash me, and I shall be whiter than snow. Psa. 51:7

ELISHA A. HOFFMAN   ELISHA A. HOFFMAN

1. Have you been to Je - sus for the cleans - ing pow'r? Are you
2. Are you walk - ing dai - ly by the Sav - ior's side? Are you
3. When the Bride - groom com - eth, will your robes be white? Are you
4. Lay a - side the gar - ments that are stained with sin, And be

washed in the blood of the Lamb? Are you ful - ly trust - ing in His
washed in the blood of the Lamb? Do you rest each mo - ment in the
washed in the blood of the Lamb? Will your soul be read - y for the
washed in the blood of the Lamb; There's a foun - tain flow - ing for the

grace this hour? Are you washed in the blood of the Lamb?
Cru - ci - fied? Are you washed in the blood of the Lamb?
man - sions bright, And be washed in the blood of the Lamb?
soul un - clean, O be washed in the blood of the Lamb?

Chorus

Are you washed in the blood, In the
Are you washed in the blood,

soul-cleans - ing blood of the Lamb? Are your gar - ments
of the Lamb?

spot-less? Are they white as snow? Are you washed in the blood of the Lamb?

Why Do You Wait? 331

My Spirit shall not always strive with man . . . Gen. 6:3

GEORGE F. ROOT

GEORGE F. ROOT

1. Why do you wait, dear broth-er, Oh, why do you tar-ry so long?
2. What do you hope, dear broth-er, To gain by a fur-ther de-lay?
3. Do you not feel, dear broth-er, His Spir-it now striv-ing with-in?
4. Why do you wait, dear broth-er, The har-vest is pass-ing a-way;

Your Sav-ior is wait-ing to give you A place in His sanc-ti-fied throng.
There's no one to save you but Je-sus, There's no oth-er way but His way.
Oh, why not ac-cept His sal-va-tion, And throw off your bur-den of sin?
Your Sav-ior is long-ing to bless you, There's dan-ger and death in de-lay.

Chorus

Why not? why not? Why not come to Him now?

Why not? why not? Why not come to Him now?

332 Rock of Ages

I will put thee in a clift of the rock, and will cover thee . . . Exo. 33:22

AUGUSTUS M. TOPLADY

THOMAS HASTINGS

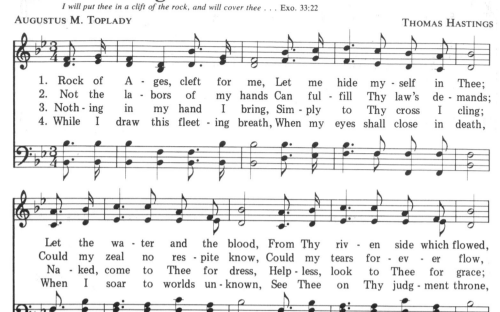

1. Rock of A - ges, cleft for me, Let me hide my - self in Thee;
2. Not the la - bors of my hands Can ful - fill Thy law's de - mands;
3. Noth - ing in my hand I bring, Sim - ply to Thy cross I cling;
4. While I draw this fleet - ing breath, When my eyes shall close in death,

Let the wa - ter and the blood, From Thy riv - en side which flowed,
Could my zeal no res - pite know, Could my tears for - ev - er flow,
Na - ked, come to Thee for dress, Help - less, look to Thee for grace;
When I soar to worlds un - known, See Thee on Thy judg - ment throne,

Be of sin the dou - ble cure, Cleanse me from its guilt and pow'r.
All for sin could not a - tone; Thou must save and Thou a - lone.
Foul, I to the foun - tain fly, Wash me, Sav - ior, or I die!
Rock of A - ges, cleft for me, Let me hide my - self in Thee. A-men.

333 I Am Not Skilled to Understand

Him hath God exalted with His right hand to be a . . . Savior. Acts 5:31

DORA GREENWELL

WILLIAM J. KIRKPATRICK

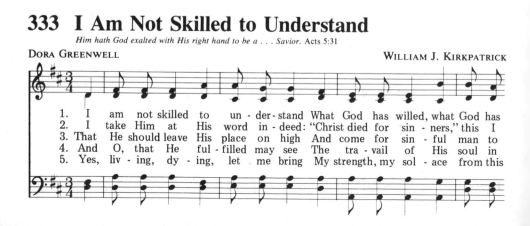

1. I am not skilled to un - der - stand What God has willed, what God has
2. I take Him at His word in - deed: "Christ died for sin - ners," this I
3. That He should leave His place on high And come for sin - ful man to
4. And O, that He ful - filled may see The tra - vail of His soul in
5. Yes, liv - ing, dy - ing, let me bring My strength, my sol - ace from this

planned; I on - ly know at His right hand Is One who is my **Sav - ior!**
read; For in my heart I find a need Of Him to be my Sav - ior!
die, You count it strange? so once did I, Be - fore I knew my Sav - ior!
me, And with His work con - tent - ed be, As I with my dear Sav - ior!
spring; That He who lives to be my King Once died to be my Sav - ior!

Just As I Am, Without One Plea 334

Him that cometh to Me I will in no wise cast out. John 6:37

CHARLOTTE ELLIOTT   WILLIAM B. BRADBURY

1. Just as I am, with - out one plea But that Thy blood was
2. Just as I am, and wait - ing not To rid my soul of
3. Just as I am, though tossed a - bout With man - y a con - flict,
4. Just as I am, poor, wretch - ed, blind; Sight, rich - es, heal - ing
5. Just as I am, Thou wilt re - ceive, Wilt wel - come, par - don,

shed for me, And that Thou bidd'st me come to Thee, O
one dark blot, To Thee whose blood can cleanse each spot, O
man - y a doubt, Fight-ings and fears with - in, with - out, O
of the mind, Yea, all I need, in Thee I find, O
cleanse, re - lieve; Be - cause Thy prom - ise I be - lieve, O

Coda (after last stanza)

Lamb of God, I come! I come!
Lamb of God, I come! I come!
Lamb of God, I come! I come!
Lamb of God, I come! I come!
Lamb of God, I come! I come! O Lamb of God, I come. A-men.

335 Reach Out to Jesus

In the time of trouble . . . Thou wilt answer me. Psa. 86:7

RALPH CARMICHAEL   RALPH CARMICHAEL

1. Is your bur-den heav-y as you bear it all a-lone?
2. Is the life you're liv-ing filled with sor-row and de-spair?

Does the road you trav-el har-bor dan-ger yet un-known?
Does the fu-ture press you with its wor-ry and its care?

Are you grow-ing wea-ry in the strug-gle of it all?
Are you tired and friend-less, have you al-most lost your way?

Je-sus will help you when on His name you call.
Je-sus will help you, just come to Him to-day.

© Copyright 1968 by LEXICON MUSIC, INC. ASCAP. All rights reserved. International copyright secured. Used by special permission.

Chorus

He is al - ways there, hear - ing ev - ery prayer, faith - ful and true;

Walk - ing by our side, in His love we hide all the day through.

When you get dis - cour - aged, just re - mem - ber what to do—

Reach out to Je - sus, He's reach - ing out to you.

336 He Is Able to Deliver Thee

Is thy God . . . able to deliver thee . . . ? Dan. 6:20

WILLIAM A. OGDEN

WILLIAM A. OGDEN

1. 'Tis the grand-est theme thro' the a - ges rung; 'Tis the grand-est theme
2. 'Tis the grand-est theme in the earth or main; 'Tis the grand-est theme
3. 'Tis the grand-est theme, let the ti - dings roll, To the guilt - y heart,

for a mor - tal tongue; 'Tis the grand - est theme that the
for a mor - tal strain; 'Tis the grand - est theme, tell the
to the sin - ful soul; Look to God in faith, He will

world e'er sung, "Our God is a - ble to de - liv - er thee."
world a - gain, "Our God is a - ble to de - liv - er thee."
make thee whole, "Our God is a - ble to de - liv - er thee."

Chorus

He is a - ble to de - liv - er thee, He is
a - ble, He is a - ble

a - ble to de - liv - er thee; Tho' by sin op-**pressed,**
a - ble, He is a - ble

Go to Him for rest; "Our God is a-ble to de-liv-er thee."

I Am Coming, Lord 337

Come unto Me . . . and I will give you rest. Matt. 11:28

LEWIS HARTSOUGH

LEWIS HARTSOUGH

1. I hear Thy wel-come voice, That calls me, Lord, to Thee For
2. Tho' com-ing weak and vile, Thou dost my strength as-sure; Thou
3. 'Tis Je-sus calls me on To per-fect faith and love, To

cleans-ing in Thy pre-cious blood That flowed on Cal-va-ry.
dost my vile-ness ful-ly cleanse, Till spot-less all and pure.
per-fect hope, and peace, and trust, For earth and heav'n a-bove.

Chorus

I am com-ing, Lord! Com-ing now to Thee!

Wash me, cleanse me in the blood That flowed on Cal-va-ry!

338 The Savior Is Waiting

Today if ye will hear His voice, harden not your hearts ... Heb. 3:7,8

RALPH CARMICHAEL   RALPH CARMICHAEL

1. The Sav-ior is wait-ing to en-ter your heart, Why don't you
2. If you'll take one step t'ward the Sav-ior, my friend, You'll find His

let Him come in? There's noth-ing in this world to keep you a-part,
arms o-pen wide; Re-ceive Him, and all of your dark-ness will end,

Chorus

What is your an-swer to Him? Time af-ter time He has
With-in your heart He'll a-bide.

wait-ed be-fore, And now He is wait-ing a-gain To

see if you're will-ing to o-pen the door, O, how He wants to come in.

© Copyright 1958 by Sacred Songs (A Division of Word, Inc.). All rights reserved. Used by permission.

Look to the Lamb of God 339

Behold the Lamb of God, which taketh away the sin of the world. John 1:29

H. G. JACKSON

JAMES M. BLACK

1. If you from sin are long - ing to be free, Look to the Lamb of God;
2. When Sa-tan tempts, and doubts and fears as - sail, Look to the Lamb of God;
3. Are you a - wea - ry, does the way seem long? Look to the Lamb of God;
4. Fear not when shad-ows on your path-way fall, Look to the Lamb of God;

He, to re - deem you, died on Cal - va - ry, Look to the Lamb of God.
You in His strength shall o - ver all pre - vail, Look to the Lamb of God.
His love will cheer and fill your heart with song, Look to the Lamb of God.
In joy or sor - row Christ is all in all, Look to the Lamb of God.

Chorus

Look to the Lamb of God,
the Lamb of God,
Look to the Lamb of God,
the Lamb of God,

For He a-lone is a - ble to save you—Look to the Lamb of God.

340 Christ Receiveth Sinful Men

This man receiveth sinners . . . Luke 15:2

ERDMANN NEUMEISTER
TRANS. BY EMMA F. BEVAN

JAMES McGRANAHAN

1. Sin - ners Je - sus will re - ceive; Sound this word of grace to all
2. Come, and He will give you rest; Trust Him, for His word is plain;
3. Now my heart con-demns me not, Pure be - fore the law I stand;
4. Christ re - ceiv - eth sin - ful men, E - ven me with all my sin;

Who the heav'n-ly path-way leave, All who lin - ger, all who fall.
He will take the sin - ful - est; Christ re - ceiv - eth sin - ful men.
He who cleansed me from all spot, Sat - is - fied its last de - mand.
Purged from ev - ery spot and stain, Heav'n with Him I en - ter in.

Chorus

Sing it o'er and o'er a - gain, Christ re -
Sing it o'er and o'er a - gain,

ceiv - eth sin - ful men; Make the mes - sage
Christ re - ceiv - eth sin - ful men; Make the mes -

clear and plain, Christ re - ceiv - eth sin - ful men.
sage clear and plain,

Have You Any Room for Jesus? 341

Today if ye will hear His voice, harden not your hearts . . . Heb. 3:15

Source unknown
Adapt. by Daniel W. Whittle

C. C. Williams

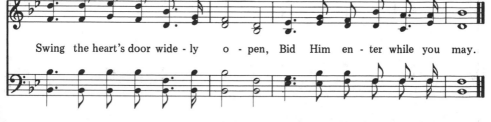

1. Have you an-y room for Je-sus, He who bore your load of sin?
2. Room for pleas-ure, room for busi-ness, But for Christ the Cru-ci-fied,
3. Have you an-y room for Je-sus, As in grace He calls a-gain?
4. Room and time now give to Je-sus, Soon will pass God's day of grace;

As He knocks and asks ad-mis-sion, Sin-ner, will you let Him in?
Not a place that He can en-ter, In the heart for which He died?
O, to-day is time ac-cept-ed, You will nev-er call in vain.
Soon your heart left cold and si-lent, And the Sav-ior's plead-ing cease.

Chorus

Room for Je-sus, King of glo-ry! Has-ten now, His word o-bey;

Swing the heart's door wide-ly o-pen, Bid Him en-ter while you may.

342 Lord, I Want to Be a Christian

Desire the sincere milk of the Word, that ye may grow thereby. I Pet. 2:2

Traditional Spiritual   Traditional Spiritual

1. Lord, I want to be a Chris-tian In-a my heart, in-a my heart, Lord, I want to be a Chris-tian In-a my heart.
2. Lord, I want to be more lov-ing In-a my heart, in-a my heart, Lord, I want to be more lov-ing In-a my heart.
3. Lord, I want to be more ho-ly In-a my heart, in-a my heart, Lord, I want to be more ho-ly In-a my heart.
4. Lord, I want to be like Je-sus In-a my heart, in-a my heart, Lord, I want to be like Je-sus In-a my heart.

Chorus

In-a my heart, In-a my heart, In-a my heart, In-a my heart,

1. Lord, I want to be a Chris-tian In-a my heart.
2. Lord, I want to be more lov-ing In-a my heart.
3. Lord, I want to be more ho-ly In-a my heart.
4. Lord, I want to be like Je-sus In-a my heart.

I Heard the Voice of Jesus Say 343

Come unto Me, all ye that labor . . . and I will give you rest. Matt. 11:28

HORATIUS BONAR

JOHN B. DYKES

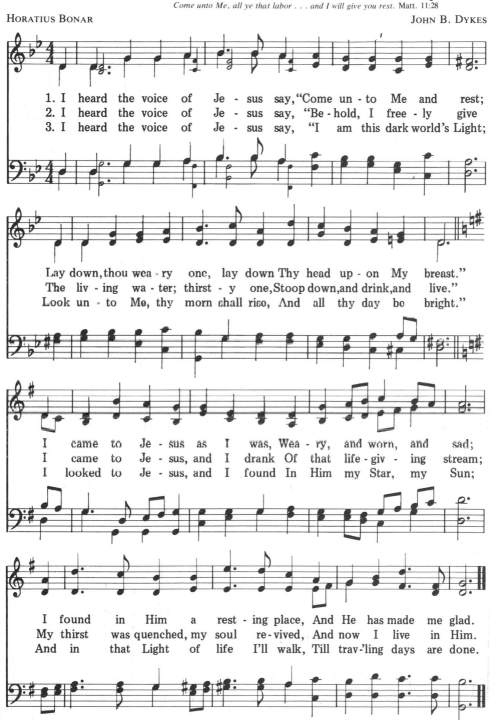

1. I heard the voice of Je - sus say, "Come un - to Me and rest;
2. I heard the voice of Je - sus say, "Be - hold, I free - ly give
3. I heard the voice of Je - sus say, "I am this dark world's Light;

Lay down, thou wea - ry one, lay down Thy head up - on My breast."
The liv - ing wa - ter; thirst - y one, Stoop down, and drink, and live."
Look un - to Me, thy morn shall rise, And all thy day be bright."

I came to Je - sus as I was, Wea - ry, and worn, and sad;
I came to Je - sus, and I drank Of that life - giv - ing stream;
I looked to Je - sus, and I found In Him my Star, my Sun;

I found in Him a rest - ing place, And He has made me glad.
My thirst was quenched, my soul re - vived, And now I live in Him.
And in that Light of life I'll walk, Till trav - 'ling days are done.

344 I Asked the Lord

I will not leave you comfortless: I will come to you. John 14:18

JOHNNY LANGE AND
JIMMY DUNCAN

JOHNNY LANGE AND
JIMMY DUNCAN

I asked the Lord to com-fort me when things weren't go-ing my way,

He said to me, "I will com-fort you, and lift your cares a - way."

I asked the Lord to walk with me, when dark-ness was all that I knew,

He said to me, "Nev - er be a - fraid, for I will see you

through." I did - n't ask for rich - es, He gave me wealth un-

Copyright © 1955 by BULLS-EYE MUSIC, INC., P.O. Box 1589, Hollywood, CA 90028. International copyright secured. All rights reserved. Used by permission.

told, The moon, the stars, the sun, the sky, And gave me eyes to be - hold. I thank the Lord for ev - ery-thing, and I count my bless - ings each day. He came to me when I need - ed Him, I on - ly had to pray, And He'll come to you if you ask Him to, He's on - ly a prayer a - way.

345 Jesus, I Come

He hath sent Me . . . to proclaim liberty to the captives . . . Isa. 61:1

WILLIAM T. SLEEPER

GEORGE C. STEBBINS

1. Out of my bond-age, sor-row and night, Je - sus, I come, Je - sus, I come;
2. Out of my shame-ful fail-ure and loss, Je - sus, I come, Je - sus, I come;
3. Out of un-rest and ar - ro-gant pride, Je - sus, I come, Je - sus, I come;
4. Out of the fear and dread of the tomb, Je - sus, I come, Je - sus, I come;

In - to Thy free-dom, glad-ness and light, Je - sus, I come to Thee.
In - to the glo-rious gain of Thy cross, Je - sus, I come to Thee.
In - to Thy bless-ed will to a - bide, Je - sus, I come to Thee.
In - to the joy and light of Thy home, Je - sus, I come to Thee.

Out of my sick-ness in - to Thy health, Out of my want and in - to Thy wealth,
Out of earth's sor-rows in - to Thy balm, Out of life's storms and in - to Thy calm,
Out of my-self to dwell in Thy love, Out of de-spair in-to rap-tures a-bove,
Out of the depths of ru - in un-told, In - to the peace of Thy shel-ter-ing fold,

Out of my sin and in - to Thy-self, Je - sus, I come to Thee.
Out of dis-tress to ju - bi-lant psalm, Je - sus, I come to Thee.
Up - ward for aye on wings like a dove, Je - sus, I come to Thee.
Ev - er Thy glo-rious face to be-hold, Je - sus, I come to Thee.

Once for All 346

Chirst hath redeemed us from the curse of the law. Gal. 3:13

PHILIP P. BLISS

PHILIP P. BLISS

1. Free from the law, O hap-py con-di-tion, Je-sus hath
2. Now are we free—there's no con-dem-na-tion, Je-sus pro-
3. Chil-dren of God, O glo-ri-ous call-ing, Sure-ly His

bled, and there is re-mis-sion; Cursed by the law and bruised by the
vides a per-fect sal-va-tion; "Come un-to Me," O hear His sweet
grace will keep us from fall-ing; Pass-ing from death to life at His

Chorus

fall, Grace hath re-deemed us once for all.
call, Come, and He saves us once for all. Once for all— O sin-ner, re-
call, Bless-ed sal-va-tion once for all.

ceive it; Once for all — O broth-er, be-lieve it; Cling to the

cross, the bur-den will fall, Christ hath re-deemed us once for all.

347 Softly and Tenderly Jesus Is Calling

Come unto Me, all ye that labor and are heavy laden . . . Matt. 11:28

WILL L. THOMPSON   WILL L. THOMPSON

1. Soft - ly and ten - der - ly Je - sus is call - ing, Call - ing for
2. Why should we tar - ry when Je - sus is plead - ing, Plead - ing for
3. Time is now fleet - ing, the mo - ments are pass - ing, Pass - ing from
4. O for the won - der - ful love He has prom - ised, Prom - ised for

you and for me; See, on the por - tals He's wait - ing and watch - ing,
you and for me? Why should we lin - ger and heed not His mer - cies,
you and from me; Shad - ows are gath - er - ing, death's night is com - ing,
you and for me! Though we have sinned, He has mer - cy and par - don,

Chorus

Watch - ing for you and for me.
Mer - cies for you and for me?
Com - ing for you and for me.
Par - don for you and for me.

Come home,   come home,
Come home,   come home,

Ye who are wea - ry, come home; Ear - nest - ly, ten - der - ly,

Je - sus is call - ing, Call - ing, O sin - ner, come home!

Jesus Is Calling 348

Today if ye will hear His voice, harden not your hearts . . . Heb. 3:15

FANNY J. CROSBY   GEORGE C. STEBBINS

1. Je - sus is ten - der - ly call - ing you home, Call - ing to - day,
2. Je - sus is call - ing the wea - ry to rest, Call - ing to - day,
3. Je - sus is wait - ing, O come to Him now, Wait - ing to - day,
4. Je - sus is plead - ing, O list to His voice: Hear Him to - day,

call - ing to - day, Why from the sun - shine of love will you roam
call - ing to - day, Bring Him your bur - den and you shall be blest;
wait - ing to - day, Come with your sins, at His feet low - ly bow;
hear Him to - day, They who be - lieve on His name shall re - joice;

Chorus

Far - ther and far - ther a - way? Call - ing to - day,
He will not turn you a - way,
Come, and no long - er de - lay.
Quick - ly a - rise and a - way. Call - ing, call - ing to - day, to - day,

Call - ing to - day, Je - sus is
Call - ing, call - ing to - day, to - day, Je - sus is ten - der - ly

call - ing, Is ten - der - ly call - ing to - day.
call - ing to - day,

349 Believe on the Lord Jesus Christ

Believe on the Lord Jesus Christ, and thou shalt be saved . . . Act. 16:31

AVIS B. CHRISTIANSEN

HARRY D. CLARKE

1. "What must I do?" the trem-bling jail - or cried, When dazed by
2. What must I do! O wea - ry, trem - bling soul, Just turn to-
3. His blood is all your plea for sav - ing grace, The pre - cious

fear and won - der; "Be - lieve on Christ!" was all that Paul re - plied,
day to Je - sus; He will re - ceive, for - give and make you whole—
fount of cleans - ing! O come, ac - cept His love, be - hold His face,

Chorus

"And you shall be saved from sin." Be - lieve on the
Christ a - lone can set you free. Be - lieve
And be saved for - ev - er - more.

Lord Je - sus Christ, Be - lieve on the Lord Je - sus Christ, Be -
Be - lieve

lieve on the Lord Je - sus Christ, And you shall be saved!
Be - lieve

Copyright 1920. Renewal 1948 extended. Hope Publishing Co., owner. All rights reserved.

Whosoever Will 350

Whosoever will, let him take the water of life freely. Rev. 22:17

PHILIP P. BLISS   PHILIP P. BLISS

1. "Who-so-ev-er hear-eth," shout, shout the sound! Spread the bless-ed ti-dings
2. Who-so-ev-er com-eth need not de-lay, Now the door is o-pen,
3. "Who-so-ev-er will," the prom-ise is se-cure; "Who-so-ev-er will," for-

all the world a-round; Tell the joy-ful news wher-ev-er man is found,
en-ter while you may; Je-sus is the true, the on-ly Liv-ing Way:
ev-er must en-dure; "Who-so-ev-er will," 'tis life for-ev-er-more;

Chorus

"Who-so-ev-er will may come." Who-so-ev-er will, who-so-ev-er will!

Send the proc-la-ma-tion o-ver vale and hill; 'Tis a lov-ing

Fa-ther calls the wan-d'rer home: "Who-so-ev-er will may come."

351 Let Jesus Come into Your Heart

Behold, now is the accepted time . . . now is the day of salvation. II Cor. 6:2

LELIA N. MORRIS

LELIA N. MORRIS

1. If you are tired of the load of your sin, Let Je-sus come
2. If 'tis for pu-ri-ty now that you sigh, Let Je-sus come
3. If there's a tem-pest your voice can-not still, Let Je-sus come
4. If you would join the glad songs of the blest, Let Je-sus come

in-to your heart; If you de-sire a new life to be-gin,
in-to your heart; Foun-tains for cleans-ing are flow-ing near by,
in-to your heart; If there's a void this world nev-er can fill,
in-to your heart; If you would en-ter the man-sions of rest,

Chorus

Let Je-sus come in-to your heart. Just now your

doubt-ings give o'er; Just now re-ject Him no more; Just now throw

o-pen the door; Let Je-sus come in-to your heart.

Ye Must Be Born Again 352

Except a man be born again, he cannot see the kingdom of God. John 3:3

William T. Sleeper   George C. Stebbins

1. A rul-er once came to Je-sus by night To ask Him the way of sal-va-tion and light; The Mas-ter made an-swer in words true and plain,
2. Ye chil-dren of men, at-tend to the word So sol-emn-ly ut-tered by Je-sus the Lord; And let not this mes-sage to you be in vain,
3. O ye who would en-ter that glo-ri-ous rest, And sing with the ran-somed the song of the blest; The life ev-er-last-ing if ye would ob-tain,

Chorus

"Ye must be born a-gain." "Ye must be born a-gain, a-gain," Ye must be born a-gain; I ver-i-ly, ver-i-ly say un-to thee, Ye must be born a-gain." a-gain."

353 Burdens Are Lifted at Calvary

Cast thy burden upon the Lord, and He shall sustain thee. Psa. 55:22

JOHN M. MOORE

JOHN M. MOORE

1. Days are filled with sor-row and care, Hearts are lone-ly and drear;
2. Cast your care on Je-sus to-day, Leave your wor-ry and fear;
3. Trou-bled soul, the Sav-ior can see Ev-ery heart-ache and tear;

Bur-dens are lift-ed at Cal-va-ry, Je-sus is ver-y near.
Bur-dens are lift-ed at Cal-va-ry, Je-sus is ver-y near.
Bur-dens are lift-ed at Cal-va-ry, Je-sus is ver-y near.

Chorus

Bur-dens are lift-ed at Cal-va-ry, Cal-va-ry, Cal-va-ry;

Bur-dens are lift-ed at Cal-va-ry, Je-sus is ver-y near.

Copyright 1952. Renewal 1980 by Singspiration, Inc. All rights reserved. Used by permission.

O Jesus, Thou Art Standing 354

If any man . . . open the door, I will come in to him. Rev. 3:20

WILLIAM W. HOW

JUSTIN H. KNECHT AND
EDWARD HUSBAND

1. O Je - sus, Thou art stand - ing Out - side the fast - closed door,
2. O Je - sus, Thou art knock - ing; And lo! that hand is scarred,
3. O Je - sus, Thou art plead - ing In ac - cents meek and low,

In low - ly pa - tience wait - ing To pass the thresh - old o'er:
And thorns Thy brow en - cir - cle, And tears Thy face have marred:
"I died for you, My chil - dren, And will ye treat Me so?"

Shame on us, Chris - tian bro - thers, His Name and sign who bear,
O love that pass - eth knowl - edge, So pa - tient - ly to wait!
O Lord, with shame and sor - row We o - pen now the door;

O shame, thrice shame up - on us, To keep Him stand - ing there!
O sin that hath no e - qual, So fast to bar the gate!
Dear Sav - ior, en - ter, en - ter, And leave us nev - er - more! A - men.

355 Throw Open the Door of Your Heart

Behold, I stand at the door, and knock . . . Rev. 3:20

HARRY D. CLARKE

HARRY D. CLARKE

1. Throw o-pen the door of your heart to-day, The Sav-ior stands
2. Throw o-pen the door of your heart to-day, And bid the dear
3. Throw o-pen the door of your heart to-day, Be-fore the dear

wait-ing out-side; He'll cleanse you from sin, bring you peace with-in,
Sav-ior come in; His pres-ence will drive all the gloom a-way,
Sav-ior de-parts; E-ter-ni-ty waits you, your doom is sure,

Chorus

Throw o-pen the door of your heart. O-pen the door,
o-pen the door, Throw o-pen the door of your heart; Why not ac-
cept Him? Oh, do not re-ject Him! Throw o-pen the door of your heart.

Copyright 1924. Renewal 1952. Hope Publishing Co., owner. All rights reserved.

Room at the Cross for You 356

The Lord . . . is longsuffering . . . that all should come to repentance. II Pet. 3:9

IRA F. STANPHILL

IRA F. STANPHILL

1. The cross up-on which Je - sus died Is a shel - ter in
2. Tho' mil - lions have found Him a friend And have turned from the
3. The hand of my Sav - ior is strong, And the love of my

which we can hide; And its grace so free is suf -
sins they have sinned, The Sav - ior still waits to
Sav - ior is long; Through sun - shine or rain, through

fi - cient for me, And deep is its foun-tain— as wide as the sea.
o - pen the gates And wel - come a sin - ner be - fore it's too late.
loss or in gain, The blood flows from Cal - v'ry to cleanse ev - ery stain.

Chorus

There's room at the cross for you, There's room at the cross for you; Tho'

mil-lions have come, there's still room for one—Yes, there's room at the cross for you.

Copyright 1946. Renewal 1974 by Ira Stanphill. Assigned to Singspiration, Inc. All rights reserved. Used by permission.

357 When I See the Blood

When I see the blood, I will pass over you . . . Exo. 12:13

JOHN FOOTE

J. G. FOOTE

1. Christ our Re-deem-er died on the cross, Died for the sin-ner,
2. Chief-est of sin-ners, Je-sus will save; All He has prom-ised,
3. Judg-ment is com-ing, all will be there, Each one re-ceiv-ing
4. O great com-pas-sion! O bound-less love! O lov-ing kind-ness,

paid all his due; Sprin-kle your soul with the blood of the Lamb,
that He will do; Wash in the foun-tain o-pened for sin,
just-ly his due; Hide in the sav-ing sin-cleans-ing blood,
faith-ful and true! Find peace and shel-ter un-der the blood,

And I will pass, will pass o-ver you. When I see the

When I

blood, When I see the blood, When I see the

see the blood, When I see the blood, When I

blood, I will pass, I will pass o-ver you.

see the blood, o-ver you.

Kneel at the Cross 358

I dwell . . . with him also that is of a contrite and humble spirit . . . Isa. 57:15

CHARLES E. MOODY

CHARLES E. MOODY
ARR. BY WILLIAM J. FLOYD

1. Kneel at the cross, Christ will meet you there, Come while He waits for you;
2. Kneel at the cross, There is room for all Who would His glo - ry share;
3. Kneel at the cross, Give your i - dols up, Look un - to realms a - bove;

List' to His voice, Leave with Him your care, And start your life a - new.
Bliss there a - waits, Harm can ne'er be - fall Those who are an - chored there.
Turn not a - way To life's spark-ling cup, Trust on - ly in His love.

Chorus

Kneel at the cross,
at the cross,
Leave ev - ery care,
Kneel oh kneel
at the cross,
at the cross,
Je - sus will meet you there.
meet you there.

Copyright © 1964. Hope Publishing Co., owner. International copyright secured. All rights reserved.

359 Why Not Now?

Today if ye will hear his voice, harden not your hearts . . . Heb. 3:7,8

DANIEL W. WHITTLE

CHARLES C. CASE

1. While we pray and while we plead, While you see your soul's deep
2. You have wan-dered far a - way— Do not risk an - oth - er
3. In the world you've failed to find Aught of peace for trou - bled
4. Come to Christ, con - fes - sion make— Come to Christ and par - don

need, While your Fa - ther calls you home, Will you
day; Do not turn from God your face, But to -
mind; Come to Christ, on Him be - lieve— Peace and
take; Trust in Him from day to day— He will

Chorus

not, my broth - er, come?
day ac - cept His grace. Why not now? Why not
joy you shall re - ceive. Why not now?
keep you all the way.

now? Why not come to Je - sus now? Je - sus now?
Why not now?

I Would Be Like Jesus 360

We . . . are changed into the same image from glory to glory. II Cor. 3:18

JAMES ROWE

BENTLEY D. ACKLEY

1. Earth-ly pleas-ures vain - ly call me, I would be like Je - sus;
2. He has bro-ken ev - ery fet - ter, I would be like Je - sus;
3. All the way from earth to glo - ry, I would be like Je - sus;
4. That in heav - en He may meet me, I would be like Je - sus;
   would be like Je - sus;

Noth - ing world - ly shall en - thrall me, I would be like Je - sus.
That my soul may serve Him bet - ter, I would be like Je - sus.
Tell - ing o'er and o'er the sto - ry, I would be like Je - sus.
That His words "Well done" may greet me, I would be like Je - sus.
   would be like Je - sus.

Chorus

Be like Je - sus, this my song, In the home and in the throng;

Be like Je - sus, all day long! I would be like Je - sus.

Copyright 1912 in "Make Christ King." The Hope Publishing Co., owner. © Renewed 1940 The Rodeheaver Co., owner. Used by permission.

361 Pass Me Not

Lord, I believe; help Thou mine unbelief. Mark 9:24

FANNY J. CROSBY

WILLIAM H. DOANE

1. Pass me not, O gen - tle Sav - ior— Hear my hum - ble cry!
2. Let me at a throne of mer - cy Find a sweet re - lief;
3. Trust - ing on - ly in Thy mer - it, Would I seek Thy face;
4. Thou the spring of all my com - fort, More than life to me!

While on oth - ers Thou art call - ing, Do not pass me by.
Kneel - ing there in deep con - tri - tion, Help my un - be - lief.
Heal my wound - ed, bro - ken spir - it, Save me by Thy grace.
Whom have I on earth be - side Thee? Whom in heav'n but Thee?

Chorus

Sav - ior, Sav - ior, Hear my hum - ble cry!

While on oth - ers Thou art call - ing, Do not pass me by.

Make Me a Captive, Lord 362

He that loseth his life for My sake shall find it. Matt. 10:39

GEORGE MATHESON

DONALD P. HUSTAD

1. Make me a cap-tive, Lord, And then I shall be free;
2. My heart is weak and poor Un-til it mas-ter find;
3. My pow'r is faint and low Till I have learned to serve;
4. My will is not my own Till Thou hast made it Thine;

Force me to ren-der up my sword, And I shall con-queror be;
It has no spring of ac-tion sure— It va-ries with the wind;
It wants the need-ed fire to glow, It wants the breeze to nerve;
If it would reach the mon-arch's throne It must its crown re-sign:

I sink in life's a-larms When by my-self I stand;
It can-not free-ly move Till Thou has wrought its chain;
It can-not drive the world Un-til it-self be driv'n;
It on-ly stands un-bent, A-mid the clash-ing strife,

Im-pris-on me with-in Thine arms, And strong shall be my hand.
En-slave it with Thy match-less love, And death-less it shall reign.
Its flag can on-ly be un-furled When Thou shalt breathe from heav'n.
When on Thy bos-om it has leaned, And found in Thee its life.

Copyright 1953. Hope Publishing Co., owner. International copyright secured. All rights reserved.

363 Living for Jesus

That ye might walk worthy of the Lord . . . Col. 1:10

THOMAS O. CHISHOLM

C. HAROLD LOWDEN

1. Liv - ing for Je - sus a life that is true, Striv - ing to please Him in
2. Liv - ing for Je - sus who died in my place, Bear - ing on Cal - v'ry my
3. Liv - ing for Je - sus wher - ev - er I am, Do - ing each du - ty in
4. Liv - ing for Je - sus through earth's lit - tle while, My dear - est treas - ure, the

all that I do; Yield - ing al - le - giance, glad - heart - ed and free,
sin and dis - grace; Such love con - strains me to an - swer His call,
His ho - ly name; Will - ing to suf - fer af - flic - tion and loss,
light of His smile; Seek - ing the lost ones He died to re - deem,

Chorus

This is the path - way of bless - ing for me.
Fol - low His lead - ing and give Him my all.
Deem - ing each tri - al a part of my cross. O Je - sus, Lord and
Bring - ing the wea - ry to find rest in Him.

Sav - ior, I give my - self to Thee, For Thou, in Thy a - tone - ment, Didst

give Thy - self for me; I own no oth - er Mas - ter, My heart shall be Thy

Copyright 1917 by Heidelberg Press. © Renewed 1945 by C. Harold Lowden. Assigned to The Rodeheaver Co. Used by permission.

throne; My life I give, hence-forth to live, O Christ, for Thee a - lone.

Near the Cross 364

God forbid that I should glory, save in the cross . . . Gal. 6:14

FANNY J. CROSBY

WILLIAM H. DOANE

1. Je - sus, keep me near the cross, There a pre - cious foun - tain
2. Near the cross, a trem - bling soul, Love and mer - cy found me;
3. Near the cross! O Lamb of God, Bring its scenes be - fore me;
4. Near the cross I'll watch and wait, Hop - ing, trust - ing ev - er,

Free to all, a heal - ing stream, Flows from Cal - v'ry's moun - tain.
There the Bright and Morn - ing Star Sheds its beams a - round me.
Help me walk from day to day With its shad - ows o'er me.
Till I reach the gold - en strand Just be - yond the riv - er.

Chorus

In the cross, in the cross Be my glo - ry ev - er;

Till my rap - tured soul shall find Rest be - yond the riv - er.

365 More Like the Master

That . . . ye might be partakers of the divine nature . . . II Pet. 1:4

CHARLES H. GABRIEL   CHARLES H. GABRIEL

1. More like the Mas-ter I would ev-er be, More of His meek-ness,
2. More like the Mas-ter is my dai-ly prayer, More strength to car-ry
3. More like the Mas-ter I would live and grow, More of His love to

more hu-mil-i-ty; More zeal to la-bor, more cour-age to be true,
cross-es I must bear; More ear-nest ef-fort to bring His king-dom in,
oth-ers I would show; More self-de-ni-al like His in Gal-i-lee,

Chorus

More con-se-cra-tion for work He bids me do.
More of His Spir-it, the wan-der-er to win.   Take Thou my
More like the Mas-ter I long to ev-er be.   Take my heart, O

heart, I would be Thine a-lone; Take Thou my heart and
take my heart, I would be Thine a-lone; Take my heart, O take my heart and

make it all Thine own. Purge me from sin, O Lord, I now im-
make it all Thine own. Purge Thou me from ev-ery sin, O Lord, I

plore, Wash me and keep me Thine for - ev - er - more.
now im - plore, Wash and keep, O wash and keep me Thine for - ev - er - more.

Near to the Heart of God 366

Draw nigh to God, and He will draw nigh to you. James 4:8

CLELAND B. MCAFEE

CLELAND B. MCAFEE

1. There is a place of qui - et rest Near to the heart of God,
2. There is a place of com - fort sweet Near to the heart of God,
3. There is a place of full re - lease Near to the heart of God,

A place where sin can - not mo - lest, Near to the heart of God.
A place where we our Sav - ior meet, Near to the heart of God.
A place where all is joy and peace, Near to the heart of God.

Chorus

O Je - sus, blest Re - deem - er Sent from the heart of God,

Hold us who wait be - fore Thee Near to the heart of God.

367 His Way with Thee

Yield yourselves unto God . . . Rom. 6:13

CYRUS S. NUSBAUM   CYRUS S. NUSBAUM

1. Would you live for Je - sus, and be al - ways pure and good?
2. Would you have Him make you free, and fol - low at His call?
3. Would you in His king - dom find a place of con - stant rest?

Would you walk with Him with - in the nar - row road? Would you have Him bear your
Would you know the peace that comes by giv - ing all? Would you have Him save you,
Would you prove Him true in prov - i - den - tial test? Would you in His serv - ice

bur - den, car - ry all your load? Let Him have His way with thee.
so that you need nev - er fall? Let Him have His way with thee.
la - bor al - ways at your best? Let Him have His way with thee.

Chorus

His pow'r can make you what you ought to be; His blood can cleanse your

heart and make you free; His love can fill your soul, and

you will see 'Twas best for Him to have His way with thee.

Savior, More Than Life to Me 368

They forsook all, and followed Him. Luke 5:11

FANNY J. CROSBY

WILLIAM H. DOANE

1. Sav - ior, more than life to me, I am cling - ing, cling - ing close to Thee;
2. Thro' this chang - ing world be - low, Lead me gen - tly, gen - tly as I go;
3. Let me love Thee more and more Till this fleet - ing, fleet - ing life is o'er;

Let Thy **pre - cious** blood, ap - plied, Keep me ev - er, ev - er near Thy side.
Trust - ing Thee, I can - not stray— I can nev - er, nev - er lose my way.
Till my soul is lost in love In a bright - er, bright - er world a - bove.

Chorus

Ev - ery day, ev - ery hour, Let me feel Thy cleans - ing pow'r;
Ev - ery day and hour, ev - ery day and hour,

May Thy ten - der love to me Bind me clos - er, clos - er, Lord, to Thee.

369 Is Your All on the Altar?

Present your bodies a living sacrifice, holy, acceptable unto God . . . Rom. 12:1

ELISHA A. HOFFMAN

ELISHA A. HOFFMAN

1. You have longed for sweet peace and for faith to in-crease, And have earn-est-ly, fer-vent-ly prayed; But you can-not have rest or be per-fect-ly blest Un-til all on the al-tar is laid.

2. Would you walk with the Lord in the light of His Word, And have peace and con-tent-ment al - way? You must do His sweet will to be free from all ill— On the al - tar your all you must lay.

3. O we nev - er can know what the Lord will be-stow Of the bless-ings for which we have prayed, Till our bod - y and soul He doth ful - ly con-trol, And our all on the al - tar is laid.

4. Who can tell all the love He will send from a - bove, And how hap - py our hearts will be made, Of the fel - low-ship sweet we shall share at His feet When our all on the al - tar is laid!

Chorus

Is your all on the al - tar of sac - ri - fice laid? Your

heart does the Spir-it con-trol? You can on-ly be blest and have

peace and sweet rest As you yield Him your bod-y and soul.

We Give Thee but Thine Own 370

All things come of Thee, and of Thine own have we given Thee. II Chron. 29.14

WILLIAM W. HOW

From Mason and Webb's
Cantica Laudis, 1850

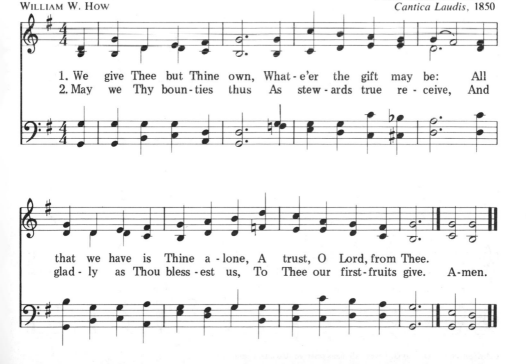

1. We give Thee but Thine own, What-e'er the gift may be: All
2. May we Thy boun-ties thus As stew-ards true re-ceive, And

that we have is Thine a-lone, A trust, O Lord, from Thee.
glad-ly as Thou bless-est us, To Thee our first-fruits give. A-men.

371 A Passion for Souls

My heart's desire and prayer to God . . . is, that they might be saved. Rom. 10:1

HERBERT G. TOVEY

FOSS L. FELLERS

1. Give me a pas-sion for souls, dear Lord, A pas-sion to save the lost;
2. Though there are dan-gers un-told and stern Con-front-ing me in the way,
3. How shall this pas-sion for souls be mine? Lord, make Thou the an-swer clear;

O that Thy love were by all a-dored, And wel-comed at an-y cost.
Will-ing-ly still would I go, nor turn, But trust Thee for grace each day.
Help me to throw out the old life-line To those who are strug-gling near.

Chorus

Je-sus, I long, I long to be win-ning Men who are lost, and con-stant-ly sin-ning; O may this hour be one of be-gin-ning The sto-ry of par-don to tell.

Copyright 1953 by Herbert G. Tovey. All rights reserved. Used by permission.

"Are Ye Able," Said the Master 372

Jesus said . . . Can ye drink of the cup that I drink of? Mark 10:38

EARL MARLATT

HARRY S. MASON

1. "Are ye a - ble," said the Mas - ter, "To be cru - ci - fied with me?"
2. "Are ye a - ble," to re - mem - ber, When a thief lifts up his eyes,
3. "Are ye a - ble," when the shad - ows Close a - round you with the sod,
4. "Are ye a - ble?" still the Mas - ter Whis - pers down e - ter - ni - ty,

"Yea," the stur - dy dream - ers an - swered, "To the death we fol - low Thee."
That his par - doned soul is wor - thy Of a place in par - a - dise?
To be - lieve that spir - it tri - umphs, To com - mend your soul to God?
And he - ro - ic spir - its an - swer Now, as then in Gal - i - lee.

Chorus

"Lord, we are a - ble," our spir - its are Thine. Re - mold them, make us like Thee, di - vine: Thy guid - ing ra - diance a - bove us shall be A bea - con to God, To love and loy - al - ty. A - men.

373 Does Jesus Care?

Casting all your care upon Him; for He careth for you. I Pet. 5:7

FRANK E. GRAEFF

J. LINCOLN HALL

1. Does Je - sus care when my heart is pained Too deep - ly for
2. Does Je - sus care when my way is dark With a name - less
3. Does Je - sus care when I've tried and failed To re - sist some temp-
4. Does Je - sus care when I've said good - by To the dear - est on

mirth and song; As the bur - dens press and the cares dis - tress, And the
dread and fear? As the day - light fades in - to deep night shades, Does He
ta - tion strong; When for my deep grief I find no re - lief, Though my
earth to me, And my sad heart aches till it near - ly breaks—Is it

Chorus

way grows wea - ry and long?
care e - nough to be near?
tears flow all the night long? O yes, He cares; I know He cares, His
aught to Him? Does He see?

heart is touched with my grief; When the days are wea - ry, the

long nights drear - y, I know my Sav - ior cares. (He cares).

Whiter Than Snow 374

Wash me, and I shall be whiter than snow. Psa. 51:7

JAMES L. NICHOLSON

WILLIAM G. FISCHER

1. Lord Je - sus, I long to be per - fect - ly whole; I want You for - ev - er to
2. Lord Je - sus, look down from Your throne in the skies, And help me to make a com-
3. Lord Je - sus, for this I most hum - bly en - treat, I wait, bless - ed Lord, at Your
4. Lord Je - sus, You see that I pa - tient - ly wait, Come now, and with - in me a

live in my soul, Break down ev - ery i - dol, cast out ev - ery foe;
plete sac - ri - fice; I give up my - self, and what - ev - er I know,
cru - ci - fied feet; By faith, for my cleans-ing I see Your blood flow,
new heart cre - ate;. To those who have sought You, You nev - er said "No,"

Chorus

Now wash me and I shall be whit - er than snow. Whit - er than snow, yes,

whit - er than snow; Now wash me, and I shall be whit - er than snow.

375 Draw Me Nearer

Let us draw near with a true heart . . . Heb. 10:22

FANNY J. CROSBY

WILLIAM H. DOANE

1. I am Thine, O Lord, I have heard Thy voice, And it
2. Con - se - crate me now to Thy serv - ice, Lord, By the
3. O, the pure de - light of a sin - gle hour That be -
4. There are depths of love that I can - not know Till I

told Thy love to me; But I long to rise in the arms of faith,
pow'r of grace di - vine; Let my soul look up with a stead - fast hope,
fore Thy throne I spend, When I kneel in prayer, and with Thee, my God,
cross the nar - row sea; There are heights of joy that I may not reach

Chorus

And be clos - er drawn to Thee.
And my will be lost in Thine.
I com - mune as friend with friend!   Draw me near - er,
Till I rest in peace with Thee.

near - er, bless - ed Lord, To the cross where Thou hast died; Draw me

near - er, near - er, near - er, bless - ed Lord, To Thy pre - cious, bleed - ing side.

Give Me Thy Heart 376

My son, give Me thine heart . . . Prov. 23:26

Eliza E. Hewitt

William J. Kirkpatrick

1. "Give Me thy heart," says the Fa-ther a-bove, No gift so pre-cious to
2. "Give Me thy heart," says the Sav-ior of men, Call-ing in mer-cy a-
3. "Give Me thy heart," says the Spir-it di-vine, "All that thou hast, to My

Him as our love; Soft-ly He whis-pers, wher-ev-er thou art,
gain and a-gain; "Turn now from sin, and from e-vil de-part,
keep-ing re-sign; Grace more a-bound-ing is Mine to im-part,

Chorus

"Grate-ful-ly trust Me, and give Me thy heart."
Have I not died for thee? give Me thy heart." "Give Me thy heart,
Make full sur-ren-der and give Me thy heart."

give Me thy heart," Hear the soft whis-per, wher-ev-er thou art: From this dark

world He would draw thee a-part; Speak-ing so ten-der-ly, "Give Me thy heart."

377 Till You Know Jesus

To make in Himself of twain one new man, so making peace. Eph. 2:15

WENDELL P. LOVELESS   WENDELL P. LOVELESS

You'll nev- er know real peace till you know Je - sus,   No

mat - ter how or where you try;   For life is but loss with - out

Him— Je - sus,   Je - sus. He died on Cal-v'ry's cross to win our

par - don,   He rose to jus - ti - fy;   He is com - ing

soon to take us,   to reign with Him on high.

Copyright 1934. Renewal 1962. Hope Publishing Co., owner. All rights reserved.

I Surrender All 378

Lo, we have left all, and have followed Thee. Mark 10:28

JUDSON W. VANDEVENTER

WINFIELD S. WEEDEN

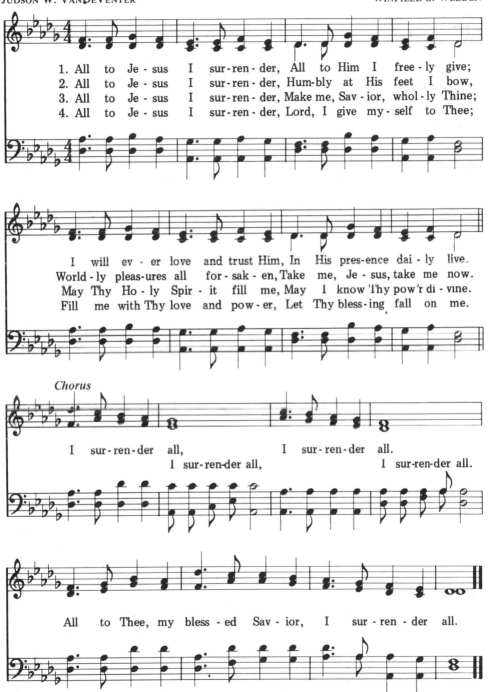

1. All to Je-sus I sur-ren-der, All to Him I free-ly give;
2. All to Je-sus I sur-ren-der, Hum-bly at His feet I bow,
3. All to Je-sus I sur-ren-der, Make me, Sav-ior, whol-ly Thine;
4. All to Je-sus I sur-ren-der, Lord, I give my-self to Thee;

I will ev-er love and trust Him, In His pres-ence dai-ly live.
World-ly pleas-ures all for-sak-en, Take me, Je-sus, take me now.
May Thy Ho-ly Spir-it fill me, May I know Thy pow'r di-vine.
Fill me with Thy love and pow-er, Let Thy bless-ing fall on me.

Chorus

I sur-ren-der all, I sur-ren-der all.
I sur-ren-der all, I sur-ren-der all.

All to Thee, my bless-ed Sav-ior, I sur-ren-der all.

379 Dear Lord and Father of Mankind

. . . Sitting at the feet of Jesus, clothed, and in His right mind. Luke 8:35

JOHN G. WHITTIER

FREDERICK C. MAKER

1. Dear Lord and Fa - ther of man - kind, For - give our fool - ish
2. In sim - ple trust like theirs who heard, Be - side the Syr - ian
3. Drop Thy still dews of qui - et - ness, Till all our striv - ings
4. Breathe through the heats of our de - sire Thy cool - ness and Thy

ways! Re - clothe us in our right - ful mind; In pur - er
Sea, The gra - cious call - ing of the Lord, Let us, like
cease; Take from our souls the strain and stress, And let our
balm; Let sense be dumb, let flesh re - tire; Speak through the

lives Thy serv - ice find, In deep - er rev - 'rence, praise.
them, with - out a word, Rise up and fol - low Thee.
or - dered lives con - fess The beau - ty of Thy peace.
earth - quake, wind, and fire, O still small voice of calm! A-men.

380 Take My Life and Let It Be

Ye are bought with a price; therefore glorify God in your body . . . I Cor. 6:20

FRANCES R. HAVERGAL

HENRI A. CÉSAR MALAN

1. Take my life and let it be Con - se - crat - ed, Lord, to Thee; Take my hands and
2. Take my feet and let them be Swift and beau - ti - ful for Thee; Take my voice and
3. Take my lips and let them be Filled with mes - sa - ges for Thee; Take my sil - ver
4. Take my love, my God, I pour At Thy feet its treas-ure store; Take my-self and

let them move At the im-pulse of Thy love, At the im - pulse of Thy love.
let me sing Al - ways, on - ly, for my King, Al - ways, on - ly, for my King.
and my gold, Not a mite would I with-hold, Not a mite would I with-hold.
I will be Ev - er, on - ly, all for Thee, Ev - er, on - ly, all for Thee.

Come, Ye Disconsolate 381

Let us then with confidence draw near to the throne of grace . . . Heb. 4:16

ST. 1, 2, THOMAS MOORE
ST. 3, THOMAS HASTINGS

SAMUEL WEBBE

1. Come, ye dis - con - so - late, wher - e'er ye lan - guish; Come to the
2. Joy of the des - o - late, Light of the stray - ing, Hope of the
3. Here see the Bread of Life; see wa - ters flow - ing Forth from the

mer - cy - seat, fer - vent - ly kneel; Here bring your wound - ed hearts, here tell your
pen - i - tent, fade - less and pure, Here speaks the Com - fort - er, ten - der - ly
throne of God, pure from a - bove; Come to the feast of love; come, ev - er

an - guish; Earth has no sor - row that heav'n can - not heal.
say - ing, "Earth has no sor - row that heav'n can - not cure."
know - ing Earth has no sor - row but heav'n can re - move. A - men.

382 I Would Be True

Be thou an example of the believers . . . I Tim. 4:12

HOWARD A. WALTER

JOSEPH Y. PEEK

1. I would be true, for there are those who trust me; I would be pure, for there are those who care: I would be strong, for there is much to suf-fer; I would be brave, for there is much to dare; I would be brave, for there is much to dare.

2. I would be friend of all— the foe, the friend-less; I would be giv-ing, and for-get the gift; I would be hum-ble, for I know my weak-ness; I would look up, and laugh, and love, and lift; I would look up, and laugh, and love, and lift.

3. I would be learn-ing day by day the les-sons My heav'n-ly Fa-ther gives me in His Word; I would be quick to hear His light-est whis-per, And prompt and glad to do the things I've heard; And prompt and glad to do the things I've heard.

4. I would be prayer-ful through each bus-y mo-ment; I would be con-stant-ly in touch with God; I would be tuned to hear His slight-est whis-per, I would have faith to keep the path Christ trod; I would have faith to keep the path Christ trod. A-men.

More About Jesus 383

But grow in grace, and in the knowledge of our Lord and Savior Jesus Christ. II Pet. 3:18

ELIZA E. HEWITT   JOHN R. SWENEY

1. More a - bout Je - sus would I know, More of His grace to oth - ers show;
2. More a - bout Je - sus let me learn, More of His ho - ly will dis - cern;
3. More a - bout Je - sus; in His Word, Hold-ing com-mun-ion with my Lord;
4. More a - bout Je - sus on His throne, Rich-es in glo - ry all His own;

More of His sav - ing ful - ness see, More of His love who died for me.
Spir - it of God, my teach - er be, Show-ing the things of Christ to me.
Hear - ing His voice in ev - ery line, Mak-ing each faith - ful say - ing mine.
More of His king-dom's sure in-crease; More of His com-ing, Prince of Peace.

Chorus

More, more a - bout Je - sus, More, more a - bout Je - sus;

More of His sav - ing ful - ness see, More of His love who died for me.

384 Yes, God Is Real

Thou art near, O Lord . . . Psa. 119:151

PHILLIP LANDGRAVE

PHILLIP LANDGRAVE

1. Yes, God is real, don't you feel His pres-ence here?
2. Yes, God will care, share with Him what's on your heart.
3. Yes, God will lead, firm but gen - tle His com-mand.

Yes, God is real, don't you know His pow'r is near? God is
Yes, God will care, dare to tell Him ev - ery part. God will
Yes, God will lead, let Him lead you by the hand. God will

here, won't you be - lieve it? Here in love, won't you re -
heal your deep - est sor - row, He will help you face to -
guide, tho' rough the way may seem; He will guide be - yond your

ceive it? Sim - ply trust Him and you will know that God is
mor - row, Sim - ply trust Him and you will know that God will
high-est dream. Sim - ply trust Him and you will know that God will

Copyright © 1969. Hope Publishing Co.. owner. International copyright secured. All rights reserved.

real.
care.
lead,   for He will care,

rit.

for God   is   real.

Where He Leads Me   385

Master, I will follow Thee whithersoever Thou goest. Matt. 8:19

E. W. BLANDY   JOHN S. NORRIS

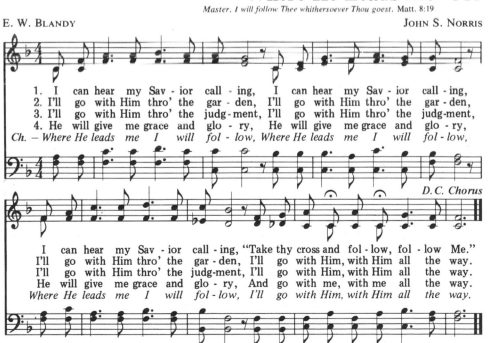

1. I   can hear my Sav - ior call - ing,   I   can hear my Sav - ior call - ing,
2. I'll go with Him thro' the gar - den, I'll go with Him thro' the gar - den,
3. I'll go with Him thro' the judg-ment, I'll go with Him thro' the judg-ment,
4. He will give me grace and glo - ry, He will give me grace and glo - ry,
Ch. — Where He leads me   I   will   fol - low, Where He leads   me   I   will   fol - low,

D. C. Chorus

I   can hear my Sav - ior call - ing, "Take thy cross and fol - low, fol - low Me."
I'll go with Him thro' the gar - den, I'll go with Him, with Him all the way.
I'll go with Him thro' the judg-ment, I'll go with Him, with Him all the way.
He will give me grace and glo - ry, And go with me, with me all the way.
Where He leads me   I   will fol - low, I'll go with Him, with Him all   the way.

386 Nothing Between

Sell all that thou hast . . . and come, follow me. Luke 18:22

C. Albert Tindley

C. Albert Tindley
Arr. by F. A. Clark

1. Noth-ing be-tween my soul and the Sav-ior, Naught of this world's de-
2. Noth-ing be-tween, like world-ly pleas-ure, Hab-its of life though
3. Noth-ing be-tween, like pride or sta-tion, Self or friends shall
4. Noth-ing be-tween, e'en man-y hard tri-als, Tho' the whole world a-

lu - sive dream; I have re-nounced all sin - ful pleas-ure,
harm-less they seem, Must not my heart from Him e'er sev - er,
not in - ter-vene, Tho' it may cost me much trib - u - la-tion,
gainst me con-vene; Watch-ing with prayer and much self - de - ni-al,

Chorus

Je - sus is mine; there's noth - ing be - tween.
He is my all; there's noth - ing be - tween. Noth-ing be-tween my
I am re - solved; there's noth - ing be - tween.
Tri - umph at last, with noth - ing be - tween.

soul and the Sav - ior, So that His bless - ed face may be seen; Noth-ing pre-

vent-ing the least of His fa - vor, Keep the way clear! Let noth-ing be-tween.

The Rock That Is Higher Than I 387

Lead me to the rock that is higher than I. Psa. 61:2

ERASTUS JOHNSON

WILLIAM G. FISCHER

1. O some-times the shad-ows are deep, And rough seems the path to the goal,
2. O some-times how long seems the day, And some-times how wea-ry my feet;
3. O near to the Rock let me keep, If bless-ings or sor-rows pre-vail;

And sor-rows, some-times how they sweep Like tem-pests down o-ver the soul!
But toil-ing in life's dust-y way, The Rock's bless-ed shad-ow, how sweet!
Or climb-ing the moun-tain way steep, Or walk-ing the shad-ow-y vale.

Chorus

O then to the Rock let me fly,
let me fly,
To the Rock that is high-er than I;
is high-er than I;
O then to the Rock let me fly,
let me fly,
To the Rock that is high-er than I!

388 Where He Leads I'll Follow

How sweet are Thy words unto my taste! Psa. 119:103

WILLIAM A. OGDEN

WILLIAM A. OGDEN

1. Sweet are the prom - is - es, Kind is the word,
2. Sweet is the ten - der love Je - sus hath shown,
3. List' to His lov - ing words, "Come un - to Me;"

Dear - er far than an - y mes - sage man ev - er heard;
Sweet - er far than an - y love that mor - tals have known;
Wea - ry, heav - y - la - den, there is sweet rest for thee;

Pure was the mind of Christ, Sin - less I see;
Kind to the err - ing one, Faith - ful is He;
Trust in His prom - is - es, Faith - ful and sure;

He the great ex - am - ple is, and pat - tern for me.
He the great ex - am - ple is, and pat - tern for me.
Lean up - on the Sav - ior, and thy soul is se - cure.

389 I Will Follow Thee

Lord, I will follow Thee. Luke 9:61

Johnson Oatman, Jr.

Edwin O. Excell

1. Sav - ior, I will fol - low Thee; Thou art all the world to me;
2. Sav - ior, I will fol - low Thee, Tho' it lead me to the cross;
3. Sav - ior, I will fol - low Thee, Tho' it lead through toil and tears;
4. Sav - ior, I will fol - low Thee Till the toils of life are o'er;

Tho' the way I can - not see, Sav - ior, I will fol - low Thee.
Count - ing all things here but dross, Sav - ior, I will fol - low Thee.
Through the long and wea - ry years, Sav - ior, I will fol - low Thee.
Till I reach the gold - en shore, Sav - ior, I will fol - low Thee.

Chorus

Fol - low Thee, I will fol - low Thee, Fol - low Thee,
Fol - low, I will fol - low Thee, fol - low Thee, Fol - low, I will fol - low

I will fol - low Thee; Fol - low till the day is done,
Thee, fol - low Thee;

Fol - low till the crown is won, Sav - ior, I will fol - low Thee.

Copyright © 1921. Renewal 1949 extended. Hope Publishing Co., owner. All rights reserved.

Jesus, Lover of My Soul 390

Thou hast been . . . a refuge from the storm . . . Isa. 25:4

CHARLES WESLEY   SIMEON B. MARSH

1. Je - sus, Lov - er of my soul, Let me to Thy bos - om fly,
2. Oth - er ref - uge have I none, Hangs my help - less soul on Thee;
3. Thou, O Christ, art all I want; More than all in Thee I find;
4. Plen - teous grace with Thee is found, Grace to cov - er all my sin;

While the near - er wa - ters roll, While the tem - pest still is high;
Leave, ah, leave me not a - lone, Still sup - port and com - fort me.
Raise the fall - en, cheer the faint, Heal the sick, and lead the blind.
Let the heal - ing streams a - bound; Make and keep me pure with - in

Hide me, O my Sav - ior, hide, Till the storm of life is past;
All my trust on Thee is stayed, All my help from Thee I bring;
Just and ho - ly is Thy name, I am all un - right-eous - ness;
Thou of life the foun - tain art, Free - ly let me take of Thee;

Safe in - to the ha - ven guide, O re - ceive my soul at last.
Cov - er my de - fense - less head With the shad - ow of Thy wing.
Vile and full of sin I am, Thou art full of truth and grace.
Spring Thou up with - in my heart, Rise to all e - ter - ni - ty.

391 All for Jesus

Present your bodies a living sacrifice . . . Rom. 12:1

MARY D. JAMES   Source unknown

1. All for Je-sus, all for Je-sus! All my be-ing's ran-somed pow'rs:
2. Let my hands per-form His bid - ding, Let my feet run in His ways;
3. Since my eyes were fixed on Je - sus, I've lost sight of all be - side;
4. Oh, what won-der! how a - maz - ing! Je - sus, glo-rious King of kings,

All my tho'ts and words and do - ings, All my days and all my hours.
Let my eyes see Je - sus on - ly, Let my lips speak forth His praise.
So en-chained my spir - it's vi - sion, Look - ing at the Cru - ci - fied.
Deigns to call me His be - lov - ed, Lets me rest be - neath His wings.

All for Je-sus! all for Je-sus! All my days and all my hours; hours.
All for Je-sus! all for Je-sus! Let my lips speak forth His praise; praise.
All for Je-sus! all for Je-sus! Look-ing at the Cru - ci - fied; fied.
All for Je-sus! all for Je-sus! Rest-ing now be-neath His wings; wings.

392 Must Jesus Bear the Cross Alone?

If any man will come after Me, let him . . . take up his cross. Matt. 16:24

THOMAS SHEPHERD AND OTHERS   GEORGE N. ALLEN

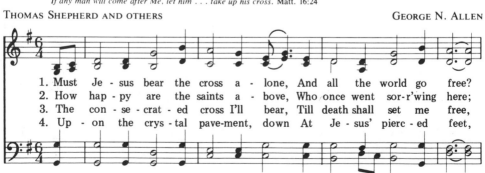

1. Must Je - sus bear the cross a - lone, And all the world go free?
2. How hap - py are the saints a - bove, Who once went sor - r'wing here;
3. The con - se - crat - ed cross I'll bear, Till death shall set me free,
4. Up - on the crys - tal pave - ment, down At Je - sus' pierc - ed feet,

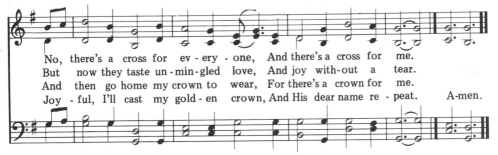

No, there's a cross for ev-ery-one, And there's a cross for me.
But now they taste un-min-gled love, And joy with-out a tear.
And then go home my crown to wear, For there's a crown for me.
Joy-ful, I'll cast my gold-en crown, And His dear name re-peat. A-men.

All That Thrills My Soul 393

My Beloved is . . . the chiefest among ten thousand. S. of S. 5:10

THORO HARRIS   THORO HARRIS

1. Who can cheer the heart like Je-sus, By His pres-ence all di-vine?
2. Love of Christ so free-ly giv-en, Grace of God be-yond de-gree,
3. What a won-der-ful re-demp-tion! Nev-er can a mor-tal know
4. Ev-ery need His hand sup-ply-ing, Ev-ery good in Him I see;
5. By the crys-tal flow-ing riv-er With the ran-somed I will sing,

True and ten-der, pure and pre-cious, O how blest to call Him mine!
Mer-cy high-er than the heav-en, Deep-er than the deep-est sea.
How my sin, tho' red like crim-son, Can be whit-er than the snow.
On His strength di-vine re-ly-ing, He is all in all to me.
And for-ev-er and for-ev-er, Praise and glo-ri-fy the King.

Chorus

All that thrills my soul is Je-sus, He is more than life to me.(to me);

And the fair-est of ten thou-sand In my bless-ed Lord I see.

Copyright 1931. Renewed 1959 by Mrs. Thoro Harris. Nazarene Publishing House, owner. Used by permission.

394 Only Jesus

They saw no man, save Jesus only. Matt. 17:8

AVIS B. CHRISTIANSEN

LANCE B. LATHAM

1. I've found a ref - uge from life's care in Je - sus, I am
2. I've found a pre - cious joy in know - ing Je - sus, Nev - er
3. I've found a bless - ed hope di - vine in Je - sus, 'Tis a

hid - ing in His love di - vine; He ful - ly un - der - stands my
dreamed of in this world of woe; No clouds, how - ev - er dark, can
Day Star ev - er shin - ing bright; It fills my earth - ly way with

soul's deep long - ing, And He whis - pers soft - ly, "Thou art mine."
dim the ra - diance Of the heav'n - ly light He doth be - stow.
heav'n - ly glo - ry, And it turns life's dark - ness in - to light.

Chorus

On - ly Je - sus! On - ly Je - sus! On - ly He can sat - is - fy;

Ev - ery bur - den be - comes a bless - ing, When I know my Lord is nigh.

Copyright 1920. Renewal 1948 extended. Hope Publishing Co., owner. All rights reserved.

Moment by Moment 395

Who are kept by the power of God through faith unto salvation. I Pet. 1:5

DANIEL W. WHITTLE

MAY WHITTLE MOODY

1. Dy - ing with Je - sus, by death reck-oned mine; Liv - ing with Je - sus a
2. Nev - er a tri - al that He is not there, Nev - er a bur - den that
3. Nev - er a heart-ache and nev - er a groan, Nev - er a tear-drop and
4. Nev - er a weak-ness that He doth not feel, Nev - er a sick-ness that

new life di - vine; Look-ing to Je - sus till glo - ry doth shine, Mo-ment by
He doth not bear, Nev - er a sor - row that He doth not share, Mo-ment by
nev - er a moan; Nev - er a dan - ger, but there on the throne, Mo-ment by
He can - not heal; Mo-ment by mo-ment, in woe or in weal, Je - sus my

Chorus

mo - ment, O Lord, I am Thine.
mo - ment, I'm un - der His care. Mo-ment by mo-ment I'm kept in His love;
mo - ment, He thinks of His own.
Sav - ior a - bides with me still.

Mo - ment by mo - ment I've life from a - bove; Look-ing to Je - sus till

glo - ry doth shine; Mo - ment by mo - ment, O Lord, I am Thine.

396 Jesus, I My Cross Have Taken

Lo, we have left all, and have followed Thee. Mark 10:28

Leavitt's *The Christian Lyre*, 1831
ATTR. TO WOLFGANG A. MOZART
ARR. BY HUBERT P. MAIN

HENRY F. LYTE

1. Je - sus, I my cross have tak - en, All to leave and fol - low Thee;
2. Let the world de - spise and leave me, They have left my Sav - ior too;
3. Man may trou - ble and dis - tress me, 'Twill but drive me to Thy breast;
4. Has - ten on from grace to glo - ry, Armed by faith and winged by prayer;

Des - ti - tute, de - spised, for - sak - en, Thou from hence my all shalt be:
Hu - man hearts and looks de - ceive me; Thou art not, like man, un - true;
Life with tri - als hard may press me, Heav'n will bring me sweet - er rest.
Heav'n's e - ter - nal day's be - fore me, God's own hand shall guide me there.

Per - ish ev - ery fond am - bi - tion, All I've sought, and hoped, and known;
And, while Thou shalt smile up - on me, God of wis - dom, love, and might,
O 'tis not in grief to harm me, While Thy love is left to me;
Soon shall close my earth - ly mis - sion, Swift shall pass my pil - grim days,

Yet how rich is my con - di - tion, God and heav'n are still my own!
Foes may hate and friends may shun me; Show Thy face, and all is bright.
O 'twere not in joy to charm me, Were that joy un - mixed with Thee.
Hope shall change to glad fru - i - tion, Faith to sight, and prayer to praise. A - men.

More Like Jesus Would I Be 397

Abide in Me, and I in you. As the branch cannot bear fruit of itself . . . John 15:4

FANNY J. CROSBY   WILLIAM H. DOANE

1. More like Je - sus would I be, Let my Sav - ior dwell in me;
2. If He hears the rav - en's cry, If His ev - er watch - ful eye
3. More like Je - sus when I pray, More like Je - sus day by day;

Fill my soul with peace and love, Make me gen - tle as a dove;
Marks the spar - rows when they fall, Sure - ly He will hear my call:
May I rest me by His side, Where the tran - quil wa - ters glide;

More like Je - sus while I go, Pil - grim in this world be - low;
He will teach me how to live, All my sin - ful thoughts for - give;
Born of Him, through grace re - newed, By His love my will sub - dued,

Poor in spir - it would I be; Let my Sav - ior dwell in me.
Pure in heart I still would be; Let my Sav - ior dwell in me.
Rich in faith I still would be; Let my Sav - ior dwell in me.

398 Hiding in Thee

Lead me to the rock that is higher than I. Psa. 61:2

WILLIAM O. CUSHING

IRA D. SANKEY

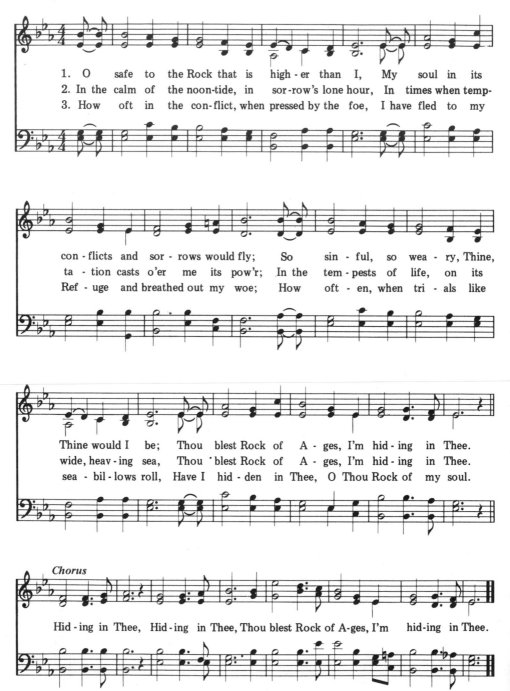

1. O safe to the Rock that is high-er than I, My soul in its con-flicts and sor-rows would fly; So sin-ful, so wea-ry, Thine, Thine would I be; Thou blest Rock of A-ges, I'm hid-ing in Thee.

2. In the calm of the noon-tide, in sor-row's lone hour, In times when temp-ta-tion casts o'er me its pow'r; In the tem-pests of life, on its wide, heav-ing sea, Thou blest Rock of A-ges, I'm hid-ing in Thee.

3. How oft in the con-flict, when pressed by the foe, I have fled to my Ref-uge and breathed out my woe; How oft-en, when tri-als like sea-bil-lows roll, Have I hid-den in Thee, O Thou Rock of my soul.

Chorus

Hid-ing in Thee, Hid-ing in Thee, Thou blest Rock of A-ges, I'm hid-ing in Thee.

Yield Not to Temptation 399

Jesus the Son of God . . . was in all points tempted like as we are . . . Heb. 4:14, 15

HORATIO R. PALMER   HORATIO R. PALMER

1. Yield not to temp-ta-tion, For yield-ing is sin, Each vic-t'ry will
2. Shun e-vil com-pan-ions, Bad lan-guage dis-dain, God's name hold in
3. To him that o'er-com-eth God giv-eth a crown, Thro' faith we shall

help you Some oth-er to win; Fight man-ful-ly on-ward,
rev-'rence, Nor take it in vain; Be thought-ful and ear-nest,
con-quer, Though of-ten cast down; He, who is our Sav-ior,

Dark pas-sions sub-due, Look ev-er to Je-sus, He will car-ry you through.
Kind-heart-ed and true, Look ev-er to Je-sus, He will car-ry you through.
Our strength will re-new, Look ev-er to Je-sus, He will car-ry you through.

Chorus

Ask the Sav-ior to help you, Com-fort, strength-en, and keep you,

He is will-ing to aid you, He will car-ry you through.

400 Unto the Hills

I will lift up mine eyes unto the hills. Psa. 121:1

PSALM 121
JOHN D. S. CAMPBELL

CHARLES H. PURDAY

1. Un-to the hills a-round do I lift up My long-ing eyes;
2. He will not suf-fer that thy foot be moved: Safe shalt thou be.
3. Je-ho-vah is Him-self thy keep-er true, Thy change-less shade;
4. From ev-ery e-vil shall He keep thy soul, From ev-ery sin;

O whence for me shall my sal-va-tion come, From whence a-rise?
No care-less slum-ber shall His eye-lids close, Who keep-eth thee.
Je-ho-vah thy de-fense on thy right hand Him-self hath made.
Je-ho-vah shall pre-serve thy go-ing out, Thy com-ing in.

From God the Lord doth come my cer-tain aid,
Be-hold our God the Lord, He slum-bereth ne'er,
And thee no sun by day shall ev-er smite;
A-bove thee watch-ing, He whom we a-dore

From God the Lord who heav'n and earth hath made.
Who keep-eth Is-rael in His ho-ly care.
No moon shall harm thee in the si-lent night.
Shall keep thee hence-forth, yea, for-ev-er-more. A-men.

Wherever He Leads I'll Go 401

Whosoever will come after Me, let him . . . take up his cross and follow Me. Mark 8:34

B. B. McKinney

B. B. McKinney

1. "Take up thy cross and fol-low Me," I heard my Mas-ter say;
2. He drew me clos-er to His side, I sought His will to know,
3. It may be through the shad-ows dim, Or o'er the storm-y sea,
4. My heart, my life, my all I bring To Christ who loves me so;

"I gave My life to ran-som thee, Sur-ren-der your all to-day."
And in that will I now a-bide, Wher-ev-er He leads I'll go.
I take my cross and fol-low Him, Wher-ev-er He lead-eth me.
He is my Mas-ter, Lord, and King, Wher-ev-er He leads I'll go.

Chorus

Wher-ev-er He leads I'll go, Wher-ev-er He leads I'll go,

I'll fol-low my Christ who loves me so, Wher-ev-er He leads I'll go.

© Copyright 1936. Renewal 1964 Broadman Press. All rights reserved. Used by permission.

402 O to Be Like Thee!

. . . To be conformed to the image of His Son. Rom. 8:29

THOMAS O. CHISHOLM

WILLIAM J. KIRKPATRICK

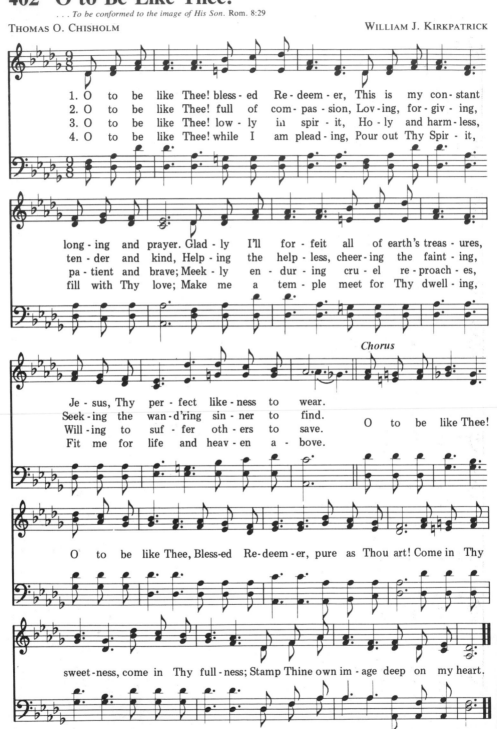

1. O to be like Thee! bless-ed Re-deem-er, This is my con-stant
2. O to be like Thee! full of com-pas-sion, Lov-ing, for-giv-ing,
3. O to be like Thee! low-ly in spir-it, Ho-ly and harm-less,
4. O to be like Thee! while I am plead-ing, Pour out Thy Spir-it,

long-ing and prayer. Glad-ly I'll for-feit all of earth's treas-ures,
ten-der and kind, Help-ing the help-less, cheer-ing the faint-ing,
pa-tient and brave; Meek-ly en-dur-ing cru-el re-proach-es,
fill with Thy love; Make me a tem-ple meet for Thy dwell-ing,

Chorus

Je-sus, Thy per-fect like-ness to wear.
Seek-ing the wan-d'ring sin-ner to find.
Will-ing to suf-fer oth-ers to save.
Fit me for life and heav-en a-bove.

O to be like Thee!

O to be like Thee, Bless-ed Re-deem-er, pure as Thou art! Come in Thy

sweet-ness, come in Thy full-ness; Stamp Thine own im-age deep on my heart.

Jesus Led Me All the Way 403

For Thy name's sake lead me, and guide me. Psa. 31:3

JOHN W. PETERSON   JOHN W. PETERSON

1. Some day life's jour-ney will be o'er, And I shall reach that
2. If God should let me there re-view The wind-ing paths of
3. And hith-er-to my Lord hath led, To-day He guides each

dis-tant shore; I'll sing while en-t'ring heav-en's door, "Je-sus
earth I knew, It would be prov-en clear and true— Je-sus
step I tread; And soon in heav'n it will be said, "Je-sus

Chorus

led me all the way."
led me all the way."   Je-sus led me all the way,
led me all the way."

Led me step by step each day; I will tell the saints and an-gels

as I lay my bur-dens down, "Je-sus led me all the way."

8va

Copyright 1954 by Singspiration, Inc. Arr. © 1965 by Singspiration. All rights reserved. Used by permission.

404 The Way of the Cross Leads Home

The preaching of the cross . . . is the power of God. 1 Cor. 1:18

JESSIE B. POUNDS

CHARLES H. GABRIEL

1. I must needs go home by the way of the cross, There's no oth-er
2. I must needs go on in the blood-sprin-kled way, The path that the
3. Then I bid fare-well to the way of the world, To walk in it

way but this; I shall ne'er get sight of the Gates of Light,
Sav-ior trod; If I ev-er climb to the heights sub-lime,
nev-er more; For my Lord says "Come," and I seek my home,

Chorus

If the way of the cross I miss.
Where the soul is at home with God. The way of the cross leads
Where He waits at the o-pen door.

home, The way of the cross leads home; It is
leads home, leads home;

sweet to know as I on-ward go, The way of the cross leads home.

The Touch of His Hand on Mine 405

And Jesus put forth His hand and touched him . . . Matt. 8:3

JESSIE B. POUNDS

HENRY P. MORTON

1. There are days so dark that I seek in vain For the face of my
2. There are times, when tired of the toil-some road, That for ways of the
3. When the way is dim, and I can-not see Thro' the mist of His
4. In the last sad hour, as I stand a-lone Where the pow-ers of

Friend di - vine; But tho' dark-ness hide, He is there to guide
world I pine; But He draws me back to the up-ward track
wise de - sign, How my glad heart yearns and my faith re - turns
death com-bine, While the dark waves roll He will guide my soul

Chorus

By the touch of His hand on mine. Oh, the touch of His hand on

mine, Oh, the touch of His hand on mine! There is grace and

pow'r, in the try - ing hour, In the touch of His hand on mine.

Copyright 1913. Renewal 1941 extended. Hope Publishing Co., owner. All rights reserved.

406 In the Hollow of His Hand

And he arose . . . and said to the sea, Peace, be still. Mark 4:39

WILLIAM M. RUNYAN   GEORGE S. SCHULER

Solo, Duet or Trio

1. Our God hath giv-en prom-ise— And His grace for this hath planned;
2. O soul, be thou not troub-led, Tho' thou dost not un-der-stand;
3. E'en tho' stern du-ty call thee, And each day make full de-mand,
4. The joy that pass-eth knowl-edge, Peace that none can un-der-stand,

His child shall rest se-cure-ly   In the hol-low of His hand.
No tur-moil shall mo-lest thee   In the hol-low of His hand.
The soul may find its shel-ter   In the hol-low of His hand.
For thee, for thee are wait-ing   In the hol-low of His hand.

Chorus

Let come what may—or wave, or tem-pest—"Peace, be still!" 'tis His com-mand;

My soul is held in peace e-ter-nal In the hol-low of His hand.

Copyright 1929. Renewal 1957. Hope Publishing Co., owner. All rights reserved.

No One Understands Like Jesus 407

He knoweth our frame; He remembereth that we are dust. Psa. 103:14

JOHN W. PETERSON

JOHN W. PETERSON

1. No one un-der-stands like Je-sus, He's a friend be-yond com-pare;
2. No one un-der-stands like Je-sus, Ev-ery woe He sees and feels;
3. No one un-der-stands like Je-sus, When the foes of life as-sail;
4. No one un-der-stands like Je-sus, When you falt-er on the way;

Meet Him at the throne of mer-cy, He is wait-ing for you there.
Ten-der-ly He whis-pers com-fort, And the bro-ken heart He heals.
You should nev-er be dis-cour-aged, Je-sus cares and will not fail.
Tho' you fail Him, sad-ly fail Him, He will par-don you to-day.

Chorus

No one un-der-stands like Je-sus, When the days are dark and grim;

No one is so near, so dear as Je-sus, Cast your ev-ery care on Him.

© 1952, Norman Clayton Publishing Co. Used by permission.

408 Savior, Like a Shepherd Lead Us

When He putteth forth His own sheep, He goeth before them. John 10:4

Hymns for the Young, 1836
ATTR. TO DOROTHY A. THRUPP

WILLIAM B. BRADBURY

1. Sav - ior, like a shep-herd lead us, Much we need Thy ten-der care;
2. We are Thine, do Thou be-friend us, Be the guard-ian of our way;
3. Thou hast prom-ised to re-ceive us, Poor and sin-ful though we be;
4. Ear - ly let us seek Thy fa - vor, Ear - ly let us do Thy will;

In Thy pleas-ant pas-tures feed us, For our use Thy folds pre-pare:
Keep Thy flock, from sin de - fend us, Seek us when we go a - stray:
Thou hast mer - cy to re - lieve us, Grace to cleanse, and pow'r to free:
Bless - ed Lord and on - ly Sav - ior, With Thy love our bos-oms fill:

Bless - ed Je - sus, bless - ed Je - sus, Thou hast bought us, Thine we are;
Bless - ed Je - sus, bless - ed Je - sus, Hear, O hear us when we pray;
Bless - ed Je - sus, bless - ed Je - sus, Ear - ly let us turn to Thee;
Bless - ed Je - sus, bless - ed Je - sus, Thou hast loved us, love us still;

Bless - ed Je - sus, bless - ed Je - sus, Thou hast bought us, Thine we are.
Bless - ed Je - sus, bless - ed Je - sus, Hear, O hear us when we pray.
Bless - ed Je - sus, bless - ed Je - sus, Ear - ly let us turn to Thee.
Bless - ed Je - sus, bless - ed Je - sus, Thou hast loved us, love us still.

Lead, Kindly Light 409

Thou wilt show me the path of life: at Thy right hand there are pleasures for evermore. Psa. 16:11

JOHN H. NEWMAN   JOHN B. DYKES

1. Lead, kind-ly Light, a - mid th' en - cir - cling gloom,   Lead Thou me on;
2. I was not ev - er thus, nor prayed that Thou   Shouldst lead me on;
3. So long Thy pow'r hath blest me, sure it still   Will lead me on,

The night is dark, and I am far from home;   Lead Thou me on:
I loved to choose and see my path; but now   Lead Thou me on.
O'er moor and fen, o'er crag and tor - rent, till   The night is gone;

Keep Thou my feet; I do not ask to see
I loved the gar - ish day, and, spite of fears,
And with the morn those an - gel fac - es smile,

The dis - tant scene—one step e - nough for me.
Pride ruled my will: re - mem - ber not past years.
Which I have loved long since, and lost a - while. A - men.

410 He Leadeth Me

I am the Lord thy God . . . which leadeth thee . . . Isa. 48:17

JOSEPH H. GILMORE

WILLIAM B. BRADBURY

1. He lead-eth me, O bless-ed thought! O words with heav'n-ly
2. Some-times 'mid scenes of deep-est gloom, Some-times where E - den's
3. Lord, I would clasp Thy hand in mine, Nor ev - er mur - mur
4. And when my task on earth is done, When by Thy grace the

com - fort fraught! What - e'er I do, wher - e'er I be, Still
bow - ers bloom, By wa - ters still, o'er trou - bled sea, Still
nor re - pine; Con - tent, what - ev - er lot I see, Since
vic - t'ry's won, E'en death's cold wave I will not flee, Since

Chorus

'tis God's hand that lead - eth me.
'tis His hand that lead - eth me. He lead - eth me, He
'tis my God that lead - eth me.
God through Jor - dan lead - eth me.

lead - eth me! By His own hand He lead - eth me! His

faith - ful fol - l'wer I would be, For by His hand He lead-eth me.

Be Still, My Soul 411

Be still and know that I am God. Psa. 46:10

KATHARINA VON SCHLEGEL
TRANS. BY JANE L. BORTHWICK

JEAN SIBELIUS

1. Be still, my soul: the Lord is on thy side; Bear pa-tient-ly the
2. Be still, my soul: thy God doth un-der-take To guide the fu-ture
3. Be still, my soul: the hour is hast-'ning on When we shall be for-

cross of grief or pain; Leave to thy God to or-der and pro-vide;
as He has the past. Thy hope, thy con-fi-dence let noth-ing shake;
ev-er with the Lord, When dis-ap-point-ment, grief, and fear are gone,

In ev-ery change He faith-ful will re-main. Be still, my soul: thy
All now mys-te-rious shall be bright at last. Be still, my soul: the
Sor-row for-got, love's pur-est joys re-stored. Be still, my soul: when

best, thy heav'n-ly Friend Thro' thorn-y ways leads to a joy-ful end.
waves and wind still know His voice who ruled them while He dwelt be-low.
change and tears are past, All safe and bless-ed we shall meet at last.

412 Stepping in the Light

Leaving us an example, that ye should follow His steps. I Pet. 2:21

ELIZA E. HEWITT   WILLIAM J. KIRKPATRICK

1. Try - ing to walk in the steps of the Sav - ior, Try - ing to fol -
2. Press - ing more close - ly to Him who is lead - ing, When we are tempt -
3. Walk - ing in foot - steps of gen - tle for - bear - ance, Foot - steps of faith -
4. Try - ing to walk in the steps of the Sav - ior, Up - ward, still up -

low our Sav - ior and King; Shap - ing our lives by His
ed to turn from the way; Trust - ing the arm that is
ful - ness, mer - cy and love, Look - ing to Him for the
ward we'll fol - low our Guide; When we shall see Him, "the

bless - ed ex - am - ple, Hap - py, how hap - py, the songs that we bring.
strong to de - fend us, Hap - py, how hap - py, our prais - es each day.
grace free - ly prom - ised, Hap - py, how hap - py, our jour - ney a - bove.
King in His beau - ty," Hap - py, how hap - py, our place at His side.

Chorus

How beau - ti - ful to walk in the steps of the Sav - ior,

Step - ping in the light, Step - ping in the light; How beau - ti - ful to walk

in the steps of the Sav - ior, Led in paths of light.

Lord, I Hear of Showers of Blessing 413

. . . The times of refreshing shall come from the presence of the Lord. Acts 3:19

ELIZABETH CODNER

WILLIAM B. BRADBURY

1. Lord, I hear of show'rs of bless - ing Thou art scat - t'ring full and free;
2. Pass me not, O gra - cious Fa - ther, Sin - ful though my heart may be;
3. Pass me not, O ten - der Sav - ior, Let me love and cling to Thee;
4. Love of God, so pure and change - less, Blood of Christ, so rich, so free,

Show'rs the thirst - y land re - fresh - ing; Let some drops now fall on me;
Thou mightst leave me, but the rath - er Let Thy mer - cy light on me;
I am long - ing for Thy fa - vor; While Thou'rt call - ing, O call me,
Grace of God, so strong and bound - less, Mag - ni - fy them all in me,

E - ven me, E - ven me, Let some drops now fall on me.
E - ven me, E - ven me, Let Thy mer - cy light on me.
E - ven me, E - ven me, While Thou'rt call - ing, O call me.
E - ven me, E - ven me, Mag - ni - fy them all in me. A - men.

414 It's Not an Easy Road

As the sufferings . . . our consolation also aboundeth by Christ. II Cor. 1:5

JOHN W. PETERSON   JOHN W. PETERSON

1. It's not an eas-y road we are trav-'ling to heav-en, For
2. It's not an eas-y road— there are tri-als and trou-bles, And
3. Tho' I am oft-en foot-sore and wea-ry from trav-el, Tho'

man-y are the thorns on the way; It's not an eas-y
man-y are the dan-gers we meet; But Je-sus guards and
I am oft-en bowed down with care, A bet-ter day is

road, but the Sav-ior is with us, His pres-ence gives us
keeps so that noth-ing can harm us, And smooths the rug-ged
com-ing when home in the glo-ry We'll rest in per-fect

Chorus

joy ev-ery day.
path for our feet. No, no, it's not an eas-y road,
peace o-ver there.

No, no, it's not an eas-y road; But Je-sus walks be-side me and

Copyright 1952 by Singspiration, Inc. All rights reserved. Used by permission.

bright- ens the jour - ney, And light - ens ev - ery heav - y load.

Take Time to Be Holy 415

Follow peace with all men, and holiness . . . Heb. 12:14

WILLIAM D. LONGSTAFF

GEORGE C. STEBBINS

1. Take time to be ho - ly, Speak oft with thy Lord; A - bide in Him
2. Take time to be ho - ly, The world rush - es on; Much time spend in
3. Take time to be ho - ly, Let Him be thy guide, And run not be -
4. Take time to be ho - ly, Be calm in thy soul; Each thought and each

al - ways, And feed on His Word. Make friends of God's chil - dren; Help
se - cret With Je - sus a - lone; By look - ing to Je - sus, Like
fore Him What - ev - er be - tide; In joy or in sor - row Still
mo - tive Be - neath His con - trol; Thus led by His Spir - it To

those who are weak; For - get - ting in noth - ing His bless - ing to seek.
Him thou shalt be; Thy friends in thy con - duct His like - ness shall see.
fol - low thy Lord, And, look - ing to Je - sus, Still trust in His Word.
foun - tains of love, Thou soon shalt be fit - ted For ser - vice a - bove.

416 Each Step I Take

He leadeth me in the paths of righteousness for His names's sake. Psa. 23:3

W. Elmo Mercer   W. Elmo Mercer

1. Each step I take my Savior goes before me, And with His
2. At times I feel my faith begin to waver, When up a-
3. I trust in God, no matter come what may, For life e-

lov-ing hand He leads the way. And with each breath I whis-per
head I see a chas-m wide. It's then I turn and look up
ter-nal is in His hand. He holds the key that o-pens

"I a-dore Thee"; Oh, what joy to walk with Him each day.
to my Sav-ior, I am strong when He is by my side.
up the way, That will lead me to the prom-ised land.

Chorus

Each step I take I know that He will guide me; To high-er

ground He ev-er leads me on. Un-til some day the last step will be

© 1953 by John T. Benson Publishing Company, a division of The Benson Company, 365 Great Circle Road, Nashville, TN 37228. International copyright secured. All rights reserved. Printed by permission.

tak - en, Each step I take just leads me clos - er home.

I Gave My Life for Thee 417

He died for all, that they . . . should not henceforth live unto themselves . . . II Cor. 5:15

FRANCES R. HAVERGAL

PHILIP P. BLISS

1. I gave My life for thee, My pre - cious blood I shed,
2. My Fa - ther's house of light, My glo - ry - cir - cled throne
3. I suf - fered much for thee, More than thy tongue can tell,
4. And I have brought to thee, Down from My home a - bove,

That thou might ran - somed be, And quick - ened from the dead;
I left for earth - ly night, For wan - d'rings sad and lone;
Of bit - terest ag - o - ny, To res - cue thee from hell;
Sal - va - tion full and free, My par - don and My love;

I gave, I gave My life for thee, What hast thou given for Me?
I left, I left it all for thee, Hast thou left aught for Me?
I've borne, I've borne it all for thee, What hast thou borne for Me?
I bring, I bring rich gifts to thee, What hast thou brought to Me?

418 Never Alone!

I will not leave you comfortless: I will come to you. John 14:18

Source unknown

Source unknown
ARR. BY FRED JACKY

1. I've seen the light-ning flash-ing, I've heard the thun-der
2. The world's fierce winds are blow-ing; Temp-ta-tion sharp and
3. When in af-flic-tion's val-ley I tread the road of
4. He died on Cal-v'ry's moun-tain, For me they pierced His

roll, I've felt sin's break-ers dash-ing, Which al-most con-quered my
keen; I have a peace in know-ing My Sav-ior stands be-
care, My Sav-ior helps me to car-ry The cross so heav-y to
side, For me He o-pened that foun-tain, The crim-son, cleans-ing

soul; I've heard the voice of my Sav-ior Bid-ding me
tween— He stands to shield me from dan-ger When my
bear; Tho' all a-round me is dark-ness, Earth-ly
tide; For me He wait-eth in glo-ry, Seat-ed up-

still to fight on; He prom-ised nev-er to leave me,
friends are all gone; He prom-ised nev-er to leave me,
joys all flown; My Sav-ior whis-pers His prom-ise,
on His throne; He prom-ised nev-er to leave me,

Chorus

Nev - er to leave me a - lone!
Nev - er to leave me a - lone! No, nev - er a - lone,
Nev - er to leave me a - lone! No, nev - er a - lone,
Nev - er to leave me a - lone!

No, nev - er a - lone, He prom - ised nev - er to
No, no, nev - er a - lone,

leave me, He'll claim me for His own. No, nev - er a -
No,

lone, No, nev - er a - lone, He
nev - er a - lone, No, no, nev - er a - lone,

prom - ised nev - er to leave me, Nev - er to leave me a - lone.

419 Master, the Tempest Is Raging

He commandeth even the winds and water, and they obey Him. Luke 8:25

HORATIUS R. PALMER
ARR. BY FRED JACKY

MARY A. BAKER

1. Mas-ter, the tem-pest is rag-ing! The bil-lows are toss-ing high!
2. Mas-ter, with an-guish of spir-it I bow in my grief to-day;
3. Mas-ter, the ter-ror is o-ver, The el-e-ments sweet-ly rest;

The sky is o'er-shad-owed with black-ness, No shel-ter or help is nigh;
The depths of my sad heart are trou-bled; O wak-en and save, I pray!
Earth's sun in the calm lake is mir-rored, And heav-en's with-in my breast.

(Hum)
"Car-est Thou not that we per-ish?" How canst Thou lie a-sleep,
Tor-rents of sin and of an-guish Sweep o'er my sink-ing soul!
Lin-ger, O bless-ed Re-deem-er, Leave me a-lone no more;
(Hum)

When each mo-ment so mad-ly is threat-'ning A grave in the an-gry deep?
And I per-ish! I per-ish, dear Mas-ter; O has-ten, and take con-trol!
And with joy I shall make the blest har-bor, And rest on the bliss-ful shore.

Copyright 1941. Renewal 1969. Hope Publishing Co., owner. All rights reserved.

Chorus

(Hum)
"The winds and the waves shall o-bey My will. Peace be still!
Peace, be still! Peace, be still!
(Hum)

(Hum)
Wheth-er the wrath of the storm-tossed sea, Or de-mons, or men, or what-
(Hum)

ev-er it be, No wa-ter can swal-low the ship where lies The Mas-ter of

o-cean and earth and skies; They all shall sweet-ly o-bey My will; Peace, be still!

Peace, be still! They all shall sweet-ly o-bey My will; Peace, peace, be still!"

420 All the Way My Savior Leads Me

I will guide thee with Mine eye. Psa. 32:8

FANNY J. CROSBY   ROBERT LOWRY

1. All the way my Sav-ior leads me; What have I to ask be - side?
2. All the way my Sav-ior leads me; Cheers each wind-ing path I tread;
3. All the way my Sav-ior leads me; O the full-ness of His love!

Can I doubt His ten-der mer - cy, Who through life has been my guide?
Gives me grace for ev - ery tri - al, Feeds me with the liv-ing bread;
Per-fect rest to me is prom-ised In my Fa-ther's house a - bove;

Heav'n-ly peace, di - vin-est com-fort, Here by faith in Him to dwell!
Though my wea - ry steps may fal - ter, And my soul a-thirst may be,
When my spir - it, clothed im - mor-tal, Wings its flight to realms of day,

For I know, what-e'er be-fall me, Je - sus do - eth all things well;
Gush-ing from the rock be-fore me, Lo! a spring of joy I see,
This my song through end-less a - ges, Je - sus led me all the way.

For I know, what-e'er be-fall me, Je-sus do-eth all things well.
Gush-ing from the rock be-fore me, Lo! a spring of joy I see.
This my song through end-less a-ges, Je-sus led me all the way.

Jesus, Savior, Pilot Me 421

And He . . . rebuked the wind and said unto the sea, Peace be still. Mark 4:39

EDWARD HOPPER

JOHN E. GOULD

1. Je - sus, Sav - ior, pi - lot me O - ver life's tem - pes-tuous sea;
2. As   a moth-er stills her child, Thou canst hush the o - cean wild;
3. When at last I near the shore, And the fear - ful break-ers roar

Un-known waves be-fore me roll, Hid - ing rock and treacherous shoal;
Boisterous waves o - bey Thy will When Thou say'st to them "Be still!"
'Twixt me and the peace-ful rest, Then, while lean-ing on Thy breast,

Chart and com - pass came from Thee: Je - sus, Sav - ior, pi - lot me.
Won-drous Sov-'reign of the sea, Je - sus, Sav - ior, pi - lot me.
May I hear Thee say to me, "Fear not, I will pi - lot thee."

422 Day After Day

Every day will I bless Thee. Psa. 145:2

WENDELL P. LOVELESS

WENDELL P. LOVELESS

Day af-ter day He loves me, and day af-ter day He leads; Day af-ter day He gra-cious-ly sup-plies my needs, all my needs. Day af-ter day He guards me, I need nev-er have a fear; Day af-ter day He

He leads;

my needs,

a fear;

Copyright 1946. Renewal 1974. Hope Publishing Co.. owner. All rights reserved.

423 The New 23rd

The Lord is my shepherd; I shall not want. Psa. 23:1

RALPH CARMICHAEL
Based on PSALM 23

RALPH CARMICHAEL

Be - cause the Lord is my Shep - herd, I have ev - ery - thing that I need. He lets me rest in mead-ows green and leads me be - side the qui - et stream. He keeps on giv - ing life to me, and helps me to do what hon - ors Him the most. E - ven when walk-ing thro' the dark val - ley of death, val - ley of death, I will nev - er

© Copyright 1969 by LEXICON MUSIC, INC. ASCAP. All rights reserved. International copyright secured. Used by special permission.

9-29-85 *You can cut time is directing but do it other way til we learn*

424 Until Then

In hope of eternal life which God . . . promised before the world began. Titus 1:2

STUART HAMBLEN   STUART HAMBLEN

1. My heart can sing when I pause to re - mem - ber A heart-ache
2. The things of earth will dim and lose their val - ue If we re -
3. This wear - y world, with all its toil and strug - gle, May take its

here is but a step - ping stone A - long a trail that's wind - ing
call they're bor-rowed for a while; And things of earth that cause the
toll of mis - er - y and strife; The soul of man is like a

al - ways up - wards; This trou-bled world is not my fi - nal home.
heart to trem - ble, Re - mem-bered there will on - ly bring a smile.
wait - ing fal - con, When it's re - leased it's des-tined for the skies.

Chorus

But un - til then my heart will go on sing - ing, Un - til

then with joy I'll car - ry on; Un - til the day my

© Copyright 1958 by Hamblen Music Company. International copyright secured. All rights reserved. Used by permission.

eyes be-hold the cit - y, Un - til the day God calls me home.

In the Hour of Trial 425

God is faithful, who will not suffer you to be tempted above that ye are able . . . I Cor. 10:13

JAMES MONTGOMERY   SPENCER LANE

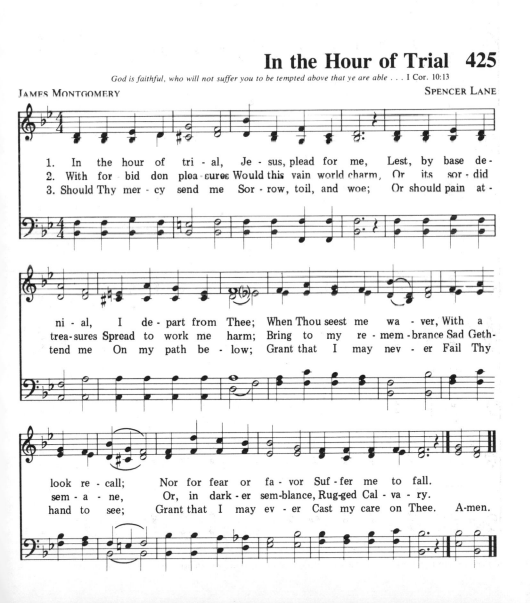

1. In the hour of tri - al, Je - sus, plead for me, Lest, by base de-
2. With for - bid don plea - sures Would this vain world charm, Or its sor - did
3. Should Thy mer - cy send me Sor - row, toil, and woe; Or should pain at-

ni - al, I de - part from Thee; When Thou seest me wa - ver, With a
trea - sures Spread to work me harm; Bring to my re - mem - brance Sad Geth-
tend me On my path be - low; Grant that I may nev - er Fail Thy

look re - call; Nor for fear or fa - vor Suf - fer me to fall.
sem - a - ne, Or, in dark - er sem - blance, Rug - ged Cal - va - ry.
hand to see; Grant that I may ev - er Cast my care on Thee. A - men.

426 God Will Take Care of You

Casting all your care on Him; for He careth for you. I Pet. 5:7

CIVILLA D. MARTIN

W. STILLMAN MARTIN

1. Be not dis-mayed what-e'er be-tide, God will take care of you;
2. Through days of toil when heart doth fail, God will take care of you;
3. All you may need He will pro-vide, God will take care of you;
4. No mat-ter what may be the test, God will take care of you;

Be-neath His wings of love a-bide, God will take care of you.
When dan-gers fierce your path as-sail, God will take care of you.
Noth-ing you ask will be de-nied, God will take care of you.
Lean, wea-ry one, up-on His breast, God will take care of you.

Chorus

God will take care of you, Through ev-ery day, o'er all the way;

He will take care of you, God will take care of you.

Under His Wings I Am Safely Abiding 427

Under His wings shalt thou trust. Psa. 91:4

WILLIAM O. CUSHING

IRA D. SANKEY

1. Un - der His wings I am safe - ly a - bid - ing; Though the night
2. Un - der His wings, what a ref - uge in sor - row! How the heart
3. Un - der His wings, O what pre - cious en - joy - ment! There will I

deep - ens and tem - pests are wild, Still I can trust Him— I
yearn - ing - ly turns to His rest! Oft - en when earth has no
hide till life's tri - als are o'er; Shel - tered, pro - tect - ed, no

know He will keep me; He has re - deemed me and I am His child.
balm for my heal - ing, There I find com - fort and there I am blest.
e - vil can harm me; Rest - ing in Je - sus I'm safe ev - er - more.

Chorus

Un - der His wings, un - der His wings, Who from His love can sev - er?

Un - der His wings my soul shall a - bide, Safe - ly a - bide for - ev - er.

428 Heavenly Sunlight

He that followeth Me shall not walk in darkness . . . John 8:12

HENRY J. ZELLEY

GEORGE H. COOK

1. Walk-ing in sun-light all of my jour-ney, O-ver the moun-tains, through the deep vale; Je-sus has said, "I'll nev-er for-sake thee," Prom-ise di-vine that nev-er can fail.

2. Shad-ows a-round me, shad-ows a-bove me Nev-er con-ceal my Sav-ior and Guide; He is the Light, in Him is no dark-ness; Ev-er I'm walk-ing close to His side.

3. In the bright sun-light, ev-er re-joic-ing, Press-ing my way to man-sions a-bove; Sing-ing His prais-es glad-ly I'm walk-ing, Walk-ing in sun-light, sun-light of love.

Chorus

Heav-en-ly sun-light, heav-en-ly sun-light, Flood-ing my soul with glo-ry di-vine; Hal-le-lu-jah! I am re-joic-ing, Sing-ing His prais-es, Je-sus is mine.

Anywhere with Jesus 429

Lo, I am with you always . . . Matt. 28:20

ST. 1, 2, JESSIE B. POUNDS
ST. 3, BY HELEN C. DIXON

DANIEL B. TOWNER

1. An-y-where with Je-sus I can safe-ly go; An-y-where He
2. An-y-where with Je-sus I am not a-lone, Oth-er friends may
3. An-y-where with Je-sus o-ver land and sea, Tell-ing souls in

leads me in this world be-low; An-y-where with-out Him dear-est
fail me, He is still my own; Though His hand may lead me o-ver
dark-ness of sal-va-tion free; Read-y as He sum-mons me to

joys would fade; An-y-where with Je-sus I am not a-fraid.
drear-y ways, An-y-where with Je-sus is a house of praise.
go or stay, An-y-where with Je-sus when He points the way.

Chorus

An-y-where! an-y-where! Fear I can-not know;

An-y-where with Je-sus I can safe-ly go.

430 I Need Jesus

One thing is needful: and Mary hath chosen that good part . . . Luke 10:42

GEORGE O. WEBSTER   CHARLES H. GABRIEL

1. I need Je - sus, my need I now con - fess; No friend like Him in
2. I need Je - sus, I need a friend like Him, A friend to guide when
3. I need Je - sus, I need Him to the end; No one like Him, He

times of deep dis - tress; I need Je - sus, the need I glad - ly own; Tho'
paths of life are dim; I need Je - sus, when foes my soul as - sail; A-
is the sin - ner's Friend; I need Je - sus, no oth - er friend will do; So

some may bear their load a - lone, Yet I need Je - sus.
lone I know I can but fail, So I need Je - sus.
con - stant, kind, so strong and true, Yes, I need Je - sus.

Chorus

I need Je - sus, I need Je - sus, I need Je - sus ev - ery
I need Je - sus with me, I need Je - sus al - ways,

day; Need Him in the sun - shine hour, Need Him when the
ev - ery day;

Copyright 1924 by Homer A. Rodeheaver. © Renewed 1952, The Rodeheaver Co. All rights reserved. Used by permission.

storm-clouds low'r; Ev - ery day a - long my way, Yes, I need Je - sus.

I Need Thee Every Hour   431

Bow down Thine ear, O Lord, and hear me: for I am poor and needy. Psa. 86:1

ANNIE S. HAWKS   ROBERT LOWRY

1. I need Thee ev - ery hour, Most gra - cious Lord; No ten - der voice like
2. I need Thee ev - ery hour, Stay Thou near by; Temp - ta - tions lose their
3. I need Thee ev - ery hour In joy or pain; Come quick - ly and a -
4. I need Thee ev - ery hour, Most Ho - ly One; O make me Thine in -

Chorus

Thine Can peace af - ford.
pow'r When Thou art nigh.   I need Thee, O I need Thee; Ev - ery hour I
bide Or life is vain.
deed, Thou bless - ed Son!

need Thee; O bless me now, my Sav - ior, I come to Thee!

432 God Leads Us Along

I am the Lord thy God . . . which leadeth thee . . . Isa. 48:17

G. A. YOUNG

G. A. YOUNG

1. In shad-y, green pas-tures, so rich and so sweet, God
2. Some-times on the mount where the sun shines so bright, God
3. Tho' sor-rows be-fall us and Sa-tan op-pose, God
4. A-way from the mire and a-way from the clay, God

leads His dear chil-dren a-long; Where the wa-ter's cool
leads His dear chil-dren a-long; Some - times in the
leads His dear chil-dren a-long; Through grace we can
leads His dear chil-dren a-long; A - way up in

flow bathes the wea-ry one's feet, God leads His dear chil-dren a-long.
val-ley, in dark-est of night, God leads His dear chil-dren a-long.
con-quer, de-feat all our foes, God leads His dear chil-dren a-long.
glo-ry, e-ter-ni-ty's day, God leads His dear chil-dren a-long.

Chorus

Some thro' the wa-ters, some thro' the flood, Some thro' the fire,

but all thro' the blood; Some thro' great sor-row, but

God gives a song, In the night sea-son and all the day long.

God Is So Good 433

Truly God is good . . . to such as are of a clean heart. Psa. 73:1

Traditional   Traditional

1. God is so good, God is so good,
2. He cares for me, He cares for me,
3. I'll do His will, I'll do His will,
4. He loves me so, He loves me so,

God is so good, He's so good to me.
He cares for me, He's so good to me.
I'll do His will, He's so good to me.
He loves me so, He's so good to me.

434 Follow On

My sheep hear my voice . . . and they follow me. John 10:27

WILLIAM O. CUSHING

ROBERT LOWRY

1. Down in the val-ley with my Sav-ior I would go,
2. Down in the val-ley with my Sav-ior I would go,
3. Down in the val-ley or up-on the moun-tain steep,

Where the flowers are bloom-ing and the sweet wa-ters flow;
Where the storms are sweep-ing and the dark wa-ters flow;
Close be-side my Sav-ior would my soul ev-er keep;

Ev-ery-where He leads me I would fol-low, fol-low on,
With His hand to lead me I will nev-er, nev-er fear,
He will lead me safe-ly in the path that He has trod,

Walk-ing in His foot-steps till the crown be won.
Dan-ger can-not fright me if my Lord is near.
Up to where they gath-er on the hills of God.

Chorus

Fol - low! fol - low! I would fol - low Je - sus! An - y - where, ev - ery-where,

I would fol - low on! Ev - ery-where He leads me I would fol - low on!

Praise Him, All Ye Little Children 435

Both . . . old men and children: let them praise the name of the Lord. Psa. 148.12, 13

ANNA B. WARNER, ALT.

WILLIAM B. BRADBURY

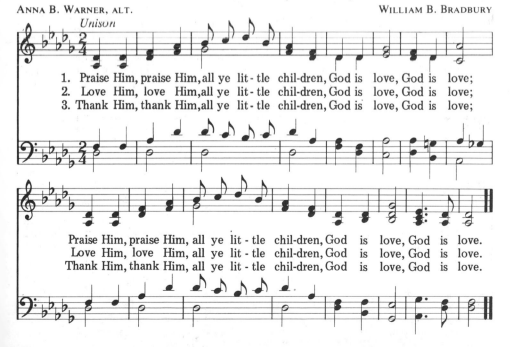

Unison

1. Praise Him, praise Him, all ye lit - tle chil-dren, God is love, God is love;
2. Love Him, love Him, all ye lit - tle chil-dren, God is love, God is love;
3. Thank Him, thank Him, all ye lit - tle chil-dren, God is love, God is love;

Praise Him, praise Him, all ye lit - tle chil-dren, God is love, God is love.
Love Him, love Him, all ye lit - tle chil-dren, God is love, God is love.
Thank Him, thank Him, all ye lit - tle chil-dren, God is love, God is love.

436 Learning to Live Like a Child of the King

That ye may know . . . the riches of the glory of His inheritance . . . Eph. 1:18

GARY S. PAXTON,
GLORIA GAITHER AND
WILLIAM J. GAITHER

GARY S. PAXTON,
GLORIA GAITHER AND
WILLIAM J. GAITHER

1. Learn-ing to live like a child of the King, Learn-ing to lose
2. Learn-ing to bathe in the warmth of His love, Spir-it-filled calm-
3. Learn-ing to be all He wants me to be, Learn-ing to feel
4. Learn-ing to live like a child of the King, Grace so a-maz-

just to find ev-ery-thing; Ac-cept-ing His wealth tho' I had
ness in a world I'm not of; Mak-ing down pay-ments on my
what it means to be free; Learn-ing to live life with
ing is the new song I sing; Shar-ing my song with the

1,3 | **2,4** *Fine*

noth-ing to bring, Learn-ing to live free and hap-py.
home up a-bove, Learn-ing to live free and hap-py.
great cer-tain-ty, Learn-ing to live free and hap-py.
beg-gars I bring, Learn-ing to live free and hap-py.

Be-ing an heir to all I do not de-serve, Learn-ing to mas-

ter by the way that I serve; Be-ing de-pen-dent on His

© Copyright 1976 by Paragon Music Corp. and New Pax Music Press, 803 18th Ave., So., Nashville, TN 37202. International copyright secured. All rights reserved. Made in U.S.A. Used by permission.

D.C. al Fine

bless-ing re - serve, I gave Him my soul, He's got tot - al con - trol.

Learning to Lean 437

Come unto me . . . and I will give you rest. Matt. 11:28

JOHN STALLINGS   JOHN STALLINGS

I'm learn-ing to lean, learn-ing to lean, Learn-ing to lean on

Je - sus; Find-ing more pow-er than I'd ev - er

dreamed, I'm learn - ing to lean on Je - sus.

© 1977 by HeartWarming Music, a division of The Benson Company, 365 Great Circle Road, Nashville, TN 37228. International copyright secured. All rights reserved. Printed by permission.

438 I Never Walk Alone

I will not leave you comfortless: I will come to you. John 14:18

ALFRED H. ACKLEY

ALFRED H. ACKLEY

1. I nev - er walk a - lone, I have the Sav - ior, Who walks be -
2. I nev - er walk a - lone, in storm - y wea - ther, When winds of

side me ev - ery-where I go; My heart re - joic - es in His
trou - ble sweep a - bout my head; I know I'm safe, be - cause we

lov - ing fa - vor, And all who will His sav - ing grace may know.
are to - geth - er, And 'round me His pro - tect - ing love is spread.

Chorus

I nev - er walk a - lone, Christ walks be - side me, He is the

dear - est Friend I've ev - er known, With such a Friend to com - fort

© Copyright 1952, The Rodeheaver Co. All rights reserved. Used by permission.

and to guide me, I nev-er, no, I nev-er walk a-lone.

O Thou, in Whose Presence 439

I am the good Shepherd, and know my sheep . . . John 10:14

JOSEPH SWAIN

FREEMAN LEWIS

1. O Thou, in whose pres-ence my soul takes de-light, On
2. Where dost Thou, dear Shep-herd, re-sort with Thy sheep, To
3. O why should I wan-der, an al-ien from Thee, Or
4. He looks! and ten thou-sands of an-gels re-joice, And
5. Dear Shep-herd! I hear, and will fol-low Thy call; I

whom in af-flic-tion I call, My com-fort by day and my
feed them in pas-tures of love? Say, why in the val-ley of
cry in the des-ert for bread? Thy foes will re-joice when my
myr-i-ads wait for His word; He speaks! and e-ter-ni-ty,
know the sweet sound of Thy voice; Re-store and de-fend me, for

song in the night, My hope, my sal-va-tion, my all.
death should I weep, Or a-lone in this wil-der-ness rove?
sor-rows they see, And smile at the tears I have shed.
filled with His voice, Re-ech-oes the praise of the Lord.
Thou art my all, And in Thee I will ev-er re-joice.

440 Trusting Jesus

Commit thy way unto the Lord; trust also in Him . . . Psa. 37:5

EDGAR P. STITES

IRA D. SANKEY

1. Sim - ply trust - ing ev - er - y day, Trust - ing through a storm - y way;
2. Bright - ly doth His Spir - it shine In - to this poor heart of mine;
3. Sing - ing if my way is clear, Pray - ing if the path be drear;
4. Trust - ing Him while life shall last, Trust - ing Him till earth be past;

E - ven when my faith is small, Trust - ing Je - sus—that is all.
While He leads I can - not fall, Trust - ing Je - sus—that is all.
If in dan - ger, for Him call, Trust - ing Je - sus—that is all.
Till with - in the jas - per wall, Trust - ing Je - sus—that is all.

Chorus

Trust - ing as the mo - ments fly, Trust - ing as the days go by;

Trust - ing Him what - e'er be - fall, Trust - ing Je - sus—that is all.

There's Joy in Following Jesus 441

Jesus said unto him, Follow me . . . Matt. 8:22

WENDELL P. LOVELESS

WENDELL P. LOVELESS

There's joy in fol - low - ing Je - sus, Ev - ery mo - ment of the. day; There's joy in fol - low - ing Je - sus, Ev - ery step a - long life's rug - ged way, yes, I'll go where-ev - er He leads me, On the land, or o'er the sea; There's joy in fol - low - ing Je - sus, And He lead - eth me.

Copyright 1936. Renewal 1964. Hope Publishing Co., owner. All rights reserved

442 My Anchor Holds

Which hope we have as an anchor of the soul . . . Heb. 6:19

W. C. MARTIN

DANIEL B. TOWNER

1. Tho' the an - gry sur - ges roll On my tem - pest - driv - en soul,
2. Might - y tides a - bout me sweep, Per - ils lurk with - in the deep,
3. I can feel the an - chor fast As I meet each sud - den blast,
4. Troub - les al - most 'whelm the soul; Griefs like bil - lows o'er me roll;

I am peace - ful, for I know, Wild - ly though the winds may blow,
An - gry clouds o'er - shade the sky, And the tem - pest ris - es high;
And the ca - ble, though un - seen, Bears the heav - y strain be - tween;
Tempt - ers seek to lure a - stray; Storms ob - scure the light of day:

I've an an - chor safe and sure, That can ev - er - more en - dure.
Still I stand the tem - pest's shock, For my an - chor grips the Rock.
Thro' the storm I safe - ly ride, Till the turn - ing of the tide.
But in Christ I can be bold, I've an an - chor that shall hold.

Chorus

And it holds, my an - chor holds; Blow your wild - est, then, O
And it holds, my an - chor holds; Blow your wild - est,

gale, On my bark so small and frail; By His grace I shall not

then, O gale,

fail, For my an - chor holds, my an - chor holds.

For my an - chor holds, it firm - ly holds,

Peace, Perfect Peace 443

Thou wilt keep Him in perfect peace, whose mind is stayed on Thee. Isa. 26:3

EDWARD H. BICKERSTETH

GEORGE T. CALDBECK
ARR. BY CHARLES J. VINCENT

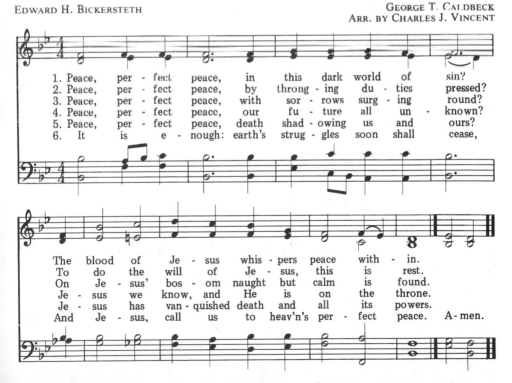

1. Peace, per - fect peace, in this dark world of sin?
2. Peace, per - fect peace, by throng - ing du - ties pressed?
3. Peace, per - fect peace, with sor - rows surg - ing round?
4. Peace, per - fect peace, our fu - ture all un - known?
5. Peace, per - fect peace, death shad - owing us and ours?
6. It is e - nough: earth's strug - gles soon shall cease,

The blood of Je - sus whis - pers peace with - in.
To do the will of Je - sus, this is rest.
On Je - sus' bos - om naught but calm is found.
Je - sus we know, and He is on the throne.
Je - sus has van - quished death and all its powers.
And Je - sus, call us to heav'n's per - fect peace. A - men.

444 I Know Who Holds Tomorrow

Ye know not what shall be on the morrow. James 4:14

IRA STANPHILL   IRA STANPHILL

1. I don't know a - bout to - mor - row, I just live from day to
2. Ev - ery step is get - ting bright - er, As the gold - en stairs I
3. I don't know a - bout to - mor - row, It may bring me pov - er -

day. I don't bor - row from its sun - shine, For its
climb; Ev - ery bur - den's get - ting light - er; Ev - ery
ty; But the one who feeds the spar - row, Is the

skies may turn to gray. I don't wor - ry o'er the fu - ture,
cloud is sil - ver lined. There the sun is al - ways shin - ing,
one who stands by me. And the path that be my por - tion,

For I know what Je - sus said, And to - day
There no tear will dim the eye, At the end -
May be through the flame or flood, But His pres -

I'll walk be - side Him, For He knows what is a - head.
ing of the rain - bow, Where the moun - tains touch the sky.
ence goes be - fore me, And I'm cov - ered with His blood.

Copyright 1950 by Singspiration, Inc. All rights reserved. Used by permission.

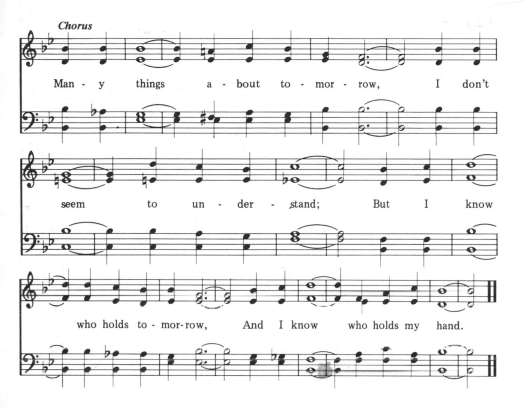

Chorus

Man-y things a-bout to-mor-row, I don't
seem to un-der-stand; But I know
who holds to-mor-row, And I know who holds my hand.

O Master, Let Me Walk with Thee 445

He appeared . . . unto two of them, as they walked . . . Mark 16.12

WASHINGTON GLADDEN

H. PERCY SMITH

1. O Mas-ter, let me walk with Thee   In low-ly paths of ser-vice free;
2. Help me the slow of heart to move   By some clear, win-ning word of love;
3. Teach me Thy pa-tience! still with Thee   In clos-er, dear-er com-pa-ny,
4. In hope that sends a shin-ing ray   Far down the fu-ture's broad'ning way,

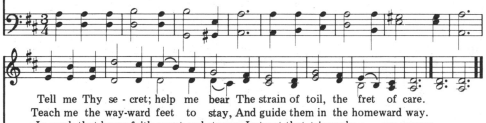

Tell me Thy se-cret; help me bear   The strain of toil, the fret of care.
Teach me the way-ward feet to stay, And guide them in the homeward way.
In work that keeps faith sweet and strong, In trust that tri-umphs o - ver wrong;
In peace that on-ly Thou canst give, With Thee, O Mas-ter, let me live. A-men.

446 Something for Thee

. . . Faith which worketh by love. Gal. 5:6

SYLVANUS D. PHELPS

ROBERT LOWRY

1. Sav-ior, Thy dy-ing love Thou gav-est me, Nor should I
2. At the blest mer-cy-seat Plead-ing for me, My fee-ble
3. Give me a faith-ful heart, Like-ness to Thee, That each de-
4. All that I am and have— Thy gifts so free— In joy, in

aught with-hold, Dear Lord, from Thee: In love my soul would bow, My heart ful-
faith looks up, Je-sus, to Thee: Help me the cross to bear, Thy won-drous
part-ing day Henceforth may see Some work of love be-gun, Some deed of
grief, thro' life, Dear Lord, for Thee! And when Thy face I see, My ran-somed

fill its vow, Some of-fering bring Thee now, Some-thing for Thee.
love de-clare, Some song to raise, or prayer, Some-thing for Thee.
kind-ness done, Some wan-d'rer sought and won, Some-thing for Thee.
soul shall be Through all e-ter-ni-ty, Some-thing for Thee. A-men.

447 Seek Ye First

Seek ye first the kingdom of God and His righteousness . . . Matt. 6:33

MATT. 6:33

KAREN LAFFERTY

Seek ye first the King-dom of God, And His right-eous-ness.

© 1972 Maranatha! Music. All rights reserved. International copyright secured. Use by permission only. P.O. Box 1396, Costa Mesa, California, 92626, U.S.A.

And all these things shall be ad - ded un - to you! Al - le - lu, al - le - lu - ia!

Open My Eyes, That I May See 448

Open Thou mine eyes, that I may behold wondrous things out of Thy law. Psa. 119:18

CLARA H. SCOTT   CLARA H. SCOTT

1. O - pen my eyes, that I may see Glimps-es of truth Thou hast for me;
2. O - pen my ears, that I may hear Voic - es of truth Thou send-est clear;
3. O - pen my mouth, and let me bear Glad - ly the warm truth ev - ery-where;

Place in my hands the won - der - ful key That shall un - clasp and set me free.
And while the wave notes fall on my ear, Ev - ery-thing false will dis - ap - pear.
O - pen my heart, and let me pre - pare Love with Thy chil-dren thus to share.

Chorus

Si - lent - ly now I wait for Thee, Read - y, my God, Thy will to see;

O - pen my eyes, il - lu - mine me, Spir - it di - vine!
O - pen my ears, il - lu - mine me, Spir - it di - vine!
O - pen my heart, il - lu - mine me, Spir - it di - vine! A - men.

449 What God Hath Promised

In the world ye shall have tribulation: but be of good cheer . . . John 16:33

ANNIE JOHNSON FLINT

WILLIAM M. RUNYAN

1. God hath not prom-ised skies al - ways blue, Flow - er-strewn path-ways
2. God hath not prom-ised we shall not know Toil and temp - ta - tion,
3. God hath not prom-ised smooth roads and wide, Swift, eas - y trav - el,

all our lives through; God hath not prom - ised sun with - out rain,
trou - ble and woe; He hath not told us we shall not bear
need - ing no guide; Nev - er a moun - tain rock - y and steep,

Chorus

Joy with - out sor - row, peace with - out pain.
Man - y a bur - den, man - y a care. But God hath prom - ised
Nev - er a riv - er tur - bid and deep.

strength for the day, Rest for the la - bor, light for the way; Grace for the

tri - als, help from a - bove, Un - fail - ing sym - pa - thy, un - dy - ing love.

Copyright 1919. Renewal 1947. Hope Publishing Co., owner. All rights reserved.

Lo, I Am with You Always 450

Lo, I am with you alway . . . Matt. 28:20

LORETTA ELLENBERGER

LORETTA ELLENBERGER

"Lo, I am with you al - ways, Lo, I am with you al - ways,

Fine

Lo, I am with you al - ways; Spread the Good News thro'-out the land!"

Unison

1. Go and make dis - ci - ples thro' - out the land, Heal the sick, reach the
2. Je - sus is our help - er, He is our friend, He has shown how to
3. If you live for Je - sus a life that's true, You will find you've a

poor the way that God planned; Be the peo - ple of God, work for
love a love with -out end! Go to Him when you're down, He will
chal-lenge to meas-ure up to; Find your whole-ness in God and the

D. C.

peace a - mong men, Spread the Good News thro'-out the land. For He says,
lis - ten to you, Give you pow - er to see it thro'. For He says,
king-dom at hand, Help-ing peo - ple thro'-out the land. For He says,

Copyright © 1973 by Hope Publishing Company. International copyright secured. All rights reserved.

451 Gentle Shepherd

And when he putteth forth His own sheep, He goeth before them . . . John 10:4

GLORIA GAITHER AND
WILLIAM J. GAITHER

WILLIAM J. GAITHER

Gen-tle Shep-herd, come and lead us, For we need You to help us find our way. Gen-tle Shep-herd, come and feed us, For we need Your strength from day to day. There's no oth-er we can turn to Who can help us face an-oth-er day; Gen-tle Shep-herd, come and lead us, For we need You to help us find our way.

© Copyright 1974 by William J. Gaither. International copyright secured. All rights reserved. Used by permission.

Let the Lower Lights Be Burning 452

Among whom ye shine as lights in the world. Phil. 2:15

Philip P. Bliss   Philip P. Bliss

1. Bright-ly beams our Fa-ther's mer-cy From His light-house ev-er-more,
2. Dark the night of sin has set-tled, Loud the an-gry bil-lows roar;
3. Trim your fee-ble lamp, my broth-er! Some poor sail-or, tem-pest-tossed,

But to us He gives the keep-ing Of the lights a-long the shore.
Ea-ger eyes are watch-ing, long-ing, For the lights a-long the shore.
Try-ing now to make the har-bor, In the dark-ness may be lost.

Chorus

Let the low-er lights be burn-ing! Send a gleam a-cross the wave!

Some poor faint-ing, strug-gling sea-man You may res-cue, you may save.

453 If Jesus Goes with Me

Master, I will follow Thee whithersoever Thou goest. Matt. 8:19

C. Austin Miles

C. Austin Miles

1. It may be in the val-ley,where count-less dan-gers hide; It may be in the
2. It may be I must car-ry the bless-ed word of life A-cross the burn-ing
3. But if it be my por-tion to bear my cross at home, While oth-ers bear their
4. It is not mine to ques-tion the judg-ments of my Lord, It is but mine to

sun-shine that I, in peace, a-bide; But this one thing I know— if
des-erts to those in sin-ful strife; And tho' it be my lot to
bur-dens be-yond the bil-low's foam, I'll prove my faith in Him— con-
fol-low the lead-ings of His Word; But if to go or stay, or

it be dark or fair, If Je-sus is with me, I'll go an-y-where!
bear my col-ors there, If Je-sus goes with me, I'll go an-y-where!
fess His judg-ments fair, And, if He stays with me, I'll stay an-y-where!
wheth-er here or there, I'll be, with my Sav-ior, Con-tent an-y-where!

Chorus

If Je-sus goes with me, I'll go An-y-where! 'Tis hea-ven to me, Wher-
I'll go

Copyright 1908 by Hall-Mack Co. © Renewed 1936. The Rodeheaver Co. Used by permission.

e'er I may be, If He is there! I count it a priv - i - lege here His
His cross, His

cross to bear; If Je - sus goes with me, I'll go An - y - where!
cross, His cross to bear;

Am I a Soldier of the Cross? 454

. . . Endure hardness, as a good soldier of Jesus Christ. II Tim. 2:3

ISAAC WATTS

THOMAS A. ARNE

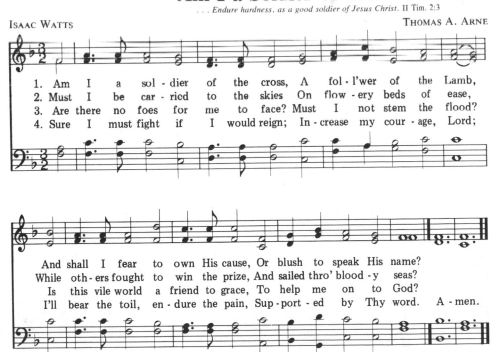

1. Am I a sol - dier of the cross, A fol - l'wer of the Lamb,
2. Must I be car - ried to the skies On flow - ery beds of ease,
3. Are there no foes for me to face? Must I not stem the flood?
4. Sure I must fight if I would reign; In - crease my cour - age, Lord;

And shall I fear to own His cause, Or blush to speak His name?
While oth - ers fought to win the prize, And sailed thro' blood - y seas?
Is this vile world a friend to grace, To help me on to God?
I'll bear the toil, en - dure the pain, Sup - port - ed by Thy word. A - men.

455 Faith Is the Victory

This is the victory that overcometh the world, even our faith. I John 5:4

JOHN H. YATES

IRA D. SANKEY

1. En-camped a - long the hills of light, Ye Chris - tian sol - diers, rise,
2. His ban - ner o - ver us is love, Our sword the Word of God;
3. On ev - ery hand the foe we find Drawn up in dread ar - ray;
4. To him that o - ver-comes the foe, White rai - ment shall be giv'n;

And press the bat - tle ere the night Shall veil the glow - ing skies.
We tread the road the saints a - bove With shouts of tri - umph trod.
Let tents of ease be left be - hind, And on - ward to the fray;
Be - fore the an - gels he shall know His name con-fessed in heav'n.

A - gainst the foe in vales be - low Let all our strength be hurled;
By faith they, like a whirl-wind's breath, Swept on o'er ev - ery field;
Sal - va - tion's hel - met on each head, With truth all girt a - bout,
Then on - ward from the hills of light, Our hearts with love a - flame,

Faith is the vic - to - ry, we know, That o - ver-comes the world.
The faith by which they con-quered death Is still our shin - ing shield.
The earth shall trem - ble 'neath our tread, And ech - o with our shout.
We'll van - quish all the hosts of night, In Je - sus' con-quering name.

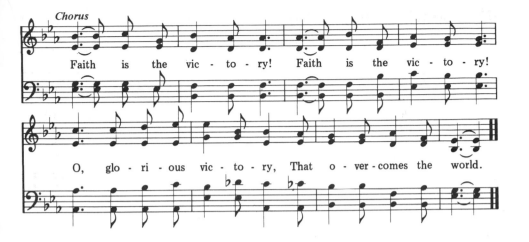

Chorus

Faith is the vic - to - ry! Faith is the vic - to - ry!

O, glo - ri - ous vic - to - ry, That o - ver - comes the world.

Teach Me Thy Will, O Lord 456

Teach me to do Thy will; for Thou art my God. Psa. 143:10

KATHERINE A. GRIMES   WILLIAM M. RUNYAN

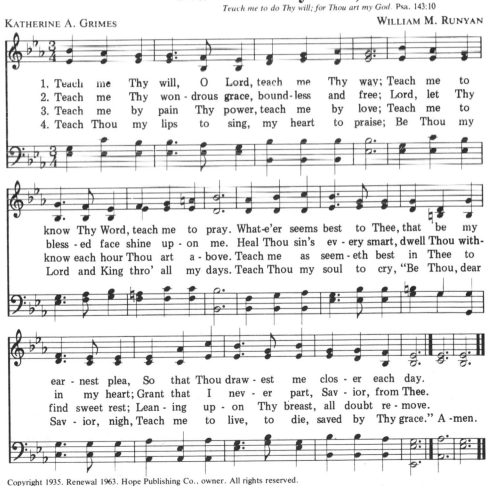

1. Teach me Thy will, O Lord, teach me Thy way; Teach me to
2. Teach me Thy won - drous grace, bound-less and free; Lord, let Thy
3. Teach me by pain Thy power, teach me by love; Teach me to
4. Teach Thou my lips to sing, my heart to praise; Be Thou my

know Thy Word, teach me to pray. What-e'er seems best to Thee, that be my
bless - ed face shine up - on me. Heal Thou sin's ev - ery smart, dwell Thou with-
know each hour Thou art a - bove. Teach me as seem - eth best in Thee to
Lord and King thro' all my days. Teach Thou my soul to cry, "Be Thou, dear

ear - nest plea, So that Thou draw - est me clos - er each day.
in my heart; Grant that I nev - er part, Sav - ior, from Thee.
find sweet rest; Lean - ing up - on Thy breast, all doubt re - move.
Sav - ior, nigh, Teach me to live, to die, saved by Thy grace." A -men.

Copyright 1935. Renewal 1963. Hope Publishing Co., owner. All rights reserved.

457 Work, for the Night Is Coming

The night cometh, when no man can work. John 9:4

ANNIE L. COGHILL

LOWELL MASON

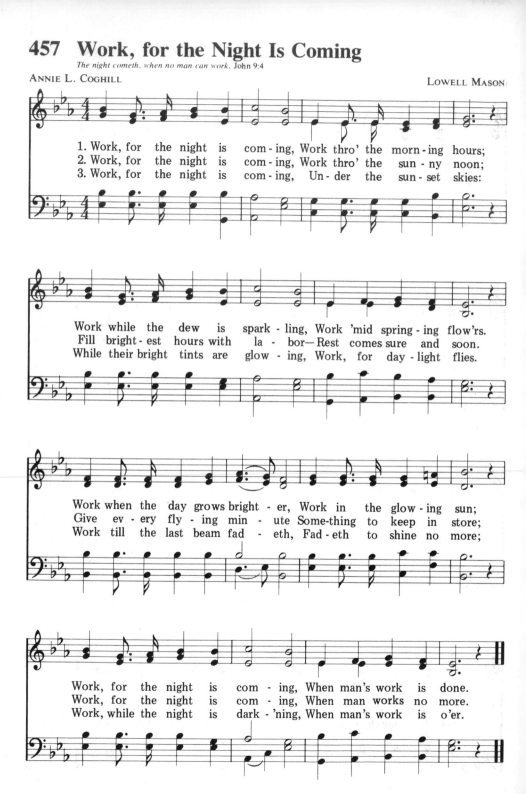

1. Work, for the night is com-ing, Work thro' the morn-ing hours;
2. Work, for the night is com-ing, Work thro' the sun-ny noon;
3. Work, for the night is com-ing, Un-der the sun-set skies:

Work while the dew is spark-ling, Work 'mid spring-ing flow'rs.
Fill bright-est hours with la-bor—Rest comes sure and soon.
While their bright tints are glow-ing, Work, for day-light flies.

Work when the day grows bright-er, Work in the glow-ing sun;
Give ev-ery fly-ing min-ute Some-thing to keep in store;
Work till the last beam fad-eth, Fad-eth to shine no more;

Work, for the night is com-ing, When man's work is done.
Work, for the night is com-ing, When man works no more.
Work, while the night is dark-'ning, When man's work is o'er.

Soldiers of Christ, Arise 458

Be strong in the Lord . . . Put on the whole armor of God. Eph. 6:10, 11

CHARLES WESLEY

GEORGE J. ELVEY

1. Sol - diers of Christ, a - rise And put your ar - mor on,
Strong in the strength which God sup - plies Through His e - ter - nal Son;
Strong in the Lord of hosts, And in His might - y pow'r, Who
in the strength of Je - sus trusts Is more than con - quer - or.

2. Stand then in His great might, With all His strength en - dued,
And take, to arm you for the fight, The pan - o - ply of God;
From strength to strength go on, Wres - tle and fight and pray; Tread
all the pow'rs of dark - ness down, And win the well - fought day.

3. Leave no un - guard - ed place, No weak - ness of the soul;
Take ev - ery vir - tue, ev - ery grace, And for - ti - fy the whole.
That hav - ing all things done, And all your con - flicts past, Ye
may o'er - come through Christ a - lone, And stand com - plete at last. A - men.

459 Lead on, O King Eternal

Henceforth there is laid up for me a crown of righteousness . . . II Tim. 4:8

ERNEST W. SHURTLEFF

HENRY T. SMART

1. Lead on, O King E - ter - nal, The day of march has come;
2. Lead on, O King E - ter - nal, Till sin's fierce war shall cease,
3. Lead on, O King E - ter - nal, We fol - low, not with fears;

Hence-forth in fields of con - quest Your tents shall be our home.
And ho - li - ness shall whis - per The sweet A - men of peace;
For glad - ness breaks like morn - ing Wher - e'er Your face ap - pears;

Through days of prep - a - ra - tion Your grace has made us strong,
For not with swords loud clash - ing, Nor roll of stir - ring drums,
Your cross is lift - ed o'er us; We jour - ney in its light:

And now, O King E - ter - nal, We lift our bat - tle song.
With deeds of love and mer - cy The heav'n - ly king - dom comes.
The crown a - waits the con - quest; Lead on, O God of might. A-men.

The Son of God Goes Forth to War 460

Can ye drink of the cup that I drink of . . . ? Mark 10:38

REGINALD HEBER

HENRY S. CUTLER

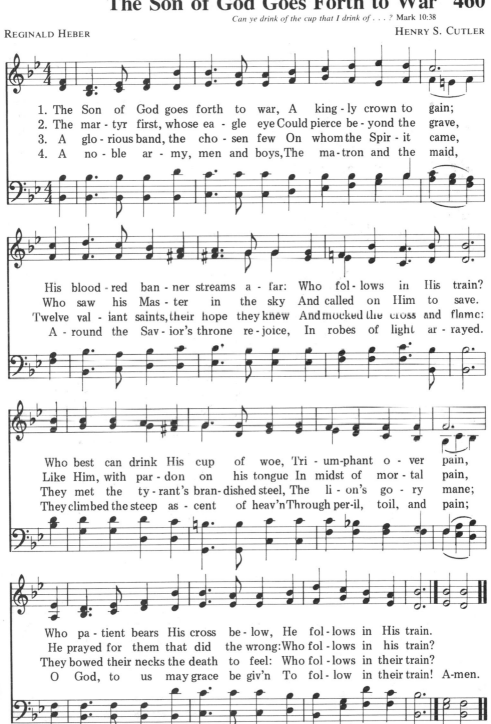

1. The Son of God goes forth to war, A king-ly crown to gain;
2. The mar-tyr first, whose ea-gle eye Could pierce be-yond the grave,
3. A glo-rious band, the cho-sen few On whom the Spir-it came,
4. A no-ble ar-my, men and boys, The ma-tron and the maid,

His blood-red ban-ner streams a-far: Who fol-lows in His train?
Who saw his Mas-ter in the sky And called on Him to save.
Twelve val-iant saints, their hope they knew And mocked the cross and flame:
A-round the Sav-ior's throne re-joice, In robes of light ar-rayed.

Who best can drink His cup of woe, Tri-um-phant o-ver pain,
Like Him, with par-don on his tongue In midst of mor-tal pain,
They met the ty-rant's bran-dished steel, The li-on's go-ry mane;
They climbed the steep as-cent of heav'n Through per-il, toil, and pain;

Who pa-tient bears His cross be-low, He fol-lows in His train.
He prayed for them that did the wrong: Who fol-lows in his train?
They bowed their necks the death to feel: Who fol-lows in their train?
O God, to us may grace be giv'n To fol-low in their train! A-men.

461 Loyalty to Christ

Be thou faithful unto death, and I will give thee a crown of life. Rev. 2:10

E. TAYLOR CASSEL

FLORA H. CASSEL

1. From o-ver hill and plain There comes the sig-nal strain, 'Tis
2. O hear, ye brave, the sound That moves the earth a-round, 'Tis
3. Come, join our loy-al throng, We'll rout the gi-ant wrong, 'Tis
4. The strength of youth we lay At Je-sus' feet to-day, 'Tis

loy-al-ty, loy-al-ty, loy-al-ty to Christ; Its mu-sic rolls a-
loy-al-ty, loy-al-ty, loy-al-ty to Christ; A-rise to dare and
loy-al-ty, loy-al-ty, loy-al-ty to Christ; Where Sa-tan's ban-ners
loy-al-ty, loy-al-ty, loy-al-ty to Christ; His gos-pel we'll pro-

long, The hills take up the song, Of loy-al-ty, loy-al-ty, Yes,
do, Ring out the watch-word true, Of loy-al-ty, loy-al-ty, Yes,
float We'll send the bu-gle note, Of loy-al-ty, loy-al-ty, Yes,
claim Through-out the world's do-main, Of loy-al-ty, loy-al-ty, Yes,

Chorus

loy-al-ty to Christ. "On to vic-to-ry! On to vic-to-ry!" Cries our

great Com-mand-er "On!"
great Com-mand-er "On!"
We'll move at His com-mand, We'll

soon pos-sess the land, Thro' loy-al-ty, loy-al-ty, Yes, loy-al-ty to Christ.

Footprints of Jesus 462

And when the people had heard . . . they followed Him on foot . . . Matt. 14:13

MARY B. C. SLADE

ASA B. EVERETT

1. Sweet - ly, Lord, have we heard Thee call - ing, "Come, fol - low
2. Tho' they lead o'er the cold, dark moun - tains, Seek - ing His
3. If they lead thro' the tem - ple ho - ly, Preach - ing the
4. Then at last, when on high He sees us, Our jour - ney

Me!" And we see where Thy foot - prints fall - ing
sheep, Or a - long by Si - lo - am's foun - tains,
Word, Or in homes of the poor and low - ly,
done, We will rest where the steps of Je - sus

Chorus

Lead us to Thee.
Help - ing the weak:
Serv - ing the Lord: Foot - prints of Je - sus, that make the path - way
End at His throne.

glow! We will fol - low the steps of Je - sus wher - e'er they go.

463 Bringing in the Sheaves

The sower soweth the word. Mark 4:14

KNOWLES SHAW　　　　　　　　　　　　　　　　　　　　　　**GEORGE A. MINOR**

1. Sow-ing in the morn-ing, sow-ing seeds of kind-ness, Sow-ing in the
2. Sow-ing in the sun-shine, sow-ing in the shad-ows, Fear-ing nei-ther
3. Go-ing forth with weep-ing, sow-ing for the Mas-ter, Tho' the loss sus-

noon-tide and the dew-y eve; Wait-ing for the har-vest,
clouds nor win-ter's chill-ing breeze; By and by the har-vest
tained our spir-it oft-en grieves; When our weep-ing's o-ver,

and the time of reap-ing, We shall come re-joic-ing, bring-ing in the sheaves.
and the la-bor end-ed, We shall come re-joic-ing, bring-ing in the sheaves.
He will bid us wel-come, We shall come re-joic-ing, bring-ing in the sheaves.

Chorus

Bring-ing in the sheaves, bring-ing in the sheaves, We shall come re-joic-ing,

bring-ing in the sheaves; Bring-ing in the sheaves, bring-ing in the sheaves,

We shall come re - joic - ing, bring - ing in the sheaves.

Bring Them In 464

The good Shepherd giveth His life for the sheep. John 10:11

ALEXCENAH THOMAS

WILLIAM A. OGDEN

1. Hark! 'tis the Shepherd's voice I hear, Out in the des - ert dark and drear,
2. Who'll go and help this Shepherd kind, Help Him the wand'ring ones to find?
3. Out in the des - ert hear their cry, Out on the mountains wild and high;

Call - ing the sheep who've gone a-stray, Far from the Shepherd's fold a - way.
Who'll bring the lost ones to the fold, Where they'll be sheltered from the cold?
Hark! 'tis the Mas - ter speaks to thee, "Go find my sheep wher-e'er they be."

Chorus

Bring them in, bring them in, Bring them in from the fields of sin;

Bring them in, bring them in, Bring the wand'ring ones to Je - sus.

465 I'll Go Where You Want Me to Go

Then said I, Here am I; send me. Isa. 6:8

CHARLES H. GABRIEL

CARRIE E. ROUNSEFELL

1. It may not be on the moun-tain's height, Or o - ver the storm - y
2. Per - haps to - day there are lov - ing words Which Je - sus would have me
3. There's sure - ly some-where a low - ly place In earth's har - vest-fields so

sea; It may not be at the bat - tle's front My
speak; There may be now, in the paths of sin, Some
wide, Where I may la - bor thro' life's short day For

Lord will have need of me; But if by a still, small
wan - d'rer whom I should seek. O Sav - ior, if Thou wilt
Je - sus, the Cru - ci - fied. So, trust - ing my all un -

voice He calls To paths I do not know, I'll
be my Guide, Tho' dark and rug - ged the way, My
to Thy care, I know Thou lov - est me! I'll

an - swer, dear Lord, with my hand in Thine, I'll go where you
voice shall ech - o the mes - sage sweet, I'll say what you
do Thy will with a heart sin - cere, I'll be what you

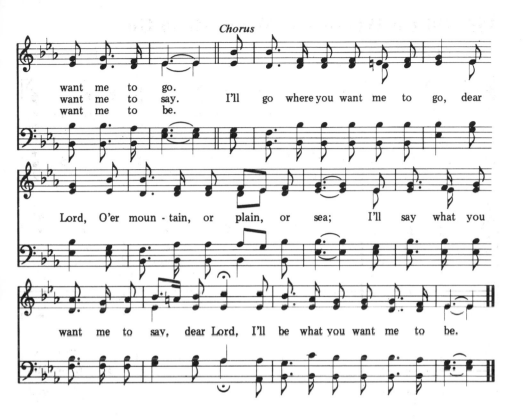

Chorus

want me to go.
want me to say. I'll go where you want me to go, dear
want me to be.

Lord, O'er moun-tain, or plain, or sea; I'll say what you

want me to say, dear Lord, I'll be what you want me to be.

My Soul, Be on Your Guard 466

Be sober, be vigilant . . . I Pet. 5:8

GEORGE HEATH

LOWELL MASON

1. My soul, be on your guard, Ten thou-sand foes a - rise; The
2. O watch and fight and pray, The bat - tle ne'er give o'er; Re -
3. Ne'er think the vic - t'ry won, Nor lay your ar - mor down; The
4. Fight on, my soul, till death Shall bring you to your God; He'll

hosts of sin are press - ing hard To draw you from the skies.
new it bold - ly ev - ery day, And help di - vine im - plore.
work of faith will not be done Till you ob - tain the crown.
take you at your part - ing breath, To His di - vine a - bode. A-men.

467 True-Hearted, Whole-Hearted

Let us draw near with a true heart . . . Heb. 10:22

FRANCES R. HAVERGAL

GEORGE C. STEBBINS

1. True-heart-ed, whole-heart-ed, faith-ful and loy-al, King of our
2. True-heart-ed, whole-heart-ed, full-est al-le-giance Yield-ing hence-
3. True-heart-ed, whole-heart-ed, Sav-ior all-glo-rious! Take Thy great

lives, by Thy grace we will be; Un-der the stan-dard ex-
forth to our glo-ri-ous King; Val-iant en-deav-or and
pow-er and reign there a-lone, O-ver our wills and af-

alt-ed and roy-al, Strong in Thy strength we will bat-tle for Thee.
lov-ing o-be-dience, Free-ly and joy-ous-ly now would we bring.
fec-tions vic-to-rious, Free-ly sur-ren-dered and whol-ly Thine own.

Chorus

Peal out the watch-word! si-lence it nev-er! Song of our
Peal out the watch-word! si-lence it nev-er! Song of our

spir-its, re-joic-ing and free Peal out the watch-word!
spir-its, re-joic-ing and free Peal out the watch-word!

loy - al for - ev - er, King of our lives, by Thy grace we will be.
loy - al for - ev - er, King of our lives, by Thy grace we will be.

Fishers of Men 468

Follow Me, and I will make you fishers of men. Matt. 4:19

HARRY D. CLARKE   HARRY D. CLARKE

1. I will make you fish - ers of men, Fish - ers of men,
2. Hear Christ call - ing, Come un - to Me, Come un - to Me,

fish - ers of men, I will make you fish - ers of men If you
Come un - to Me; Hear Christ call - ing, Come un - to Me, I will

fol - low Me; If you fol - low Me, If you fol - low Me,
give you rest; I will give you rest, I will give you rest;

I will make you fish - ers of men, If you fol - low Me.
Hear Christ call - ing, Come un - to Me, I will give you rest.

Copyright 1927. Renewal 1955. Hope Publishing Co., owner. All rights reserved.

469 Stand Up, Stand Up for Jesus

Watch ye, stand fast in the faith, quit you like men, be strong. I Cor. 16:13

GEORGE DUFFIELD

ADAM GEIBEL

1. Stand up, stand up for Je - sus, Ye sol - diers of the cross;
2. Stand up, stand up for Je - sus, The trum - pet call o - bey;
3. Stand up, stand up for Je - sus, The strife will not be long;

Lift high His roy - al ban - ner, It must not suf - fer loss:
Forth to the might - y con - flict In this His glo - rious day:
This day the noise of bat - tle, The next, the vic - tor's song:

From vic - t'ry un - to vic - t'ry His ar - my shall He lead,
"Ye that are men, now serve Him" A - gainst un - num-bered foes;
To Him that o - ver - com - eth A crown of life shall be;

Till ev - ery foe is van - quished And Christ is Lord in - deed.
Let cour - age rise with dan - ger, And strength to strength op - pose.
He with the King of glo - ry Shall reign e - ter - nal - ly.

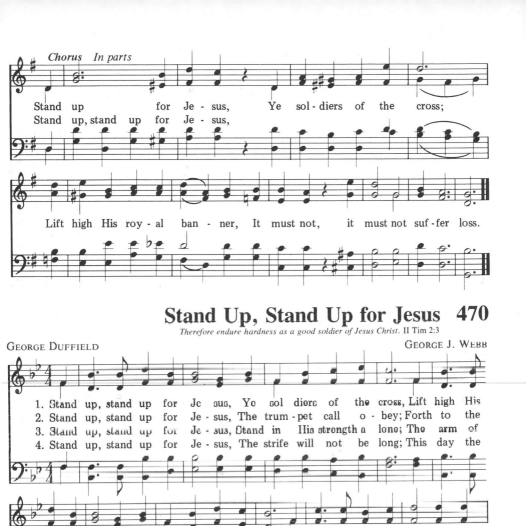

Chorus In parts

Stand up   for Je - sus, Ye sol - diers of the   cross;
Stand up, stand up for Je - sus,

Lift high His roy - al ban - ner, It must not,   it must not suf - fer loss.

Stand Up, Stand Up for Jesus 470

Therefore endure hardness as a good soldier of Jesus Christ. II Tim 2:3

GEORGE DUFFIELD   GEORGE J. WEBB

1. Stand up, stand up for Je - sus, Ye sol - diers of the cross, Lift high His
2. Stand up, stand up for Je - sus, The trum - pet call o - bey; Forth to the
3. Stand up, stand up for Je - sus, Stand in His strength a - lone; The arm of
4. Stand up, stand up for Je - sus, The strife will not be long; This day the

roy - al ban-ner, It must not suf - fer loss; From vic-tory un - to vic-tory His
might - y con-flict In this His glo - rious day. "Ye that are men, now serve Him" A-
flesh will fail you—Ye dare not trust your own; Put on the gos - pel ar - mor, Each
noise of bat - tle, The next, the vic - tor's song; To him that o - ver-com-eth A

ar - my shall He lead, Till ev - ery foe is van-quished And Christ is Lord in-deed.
gainst un - numbered foes; Let courage rise with dan - ger, And strength to strength oppose.
piece put on with prayer; Where duty calls, or dan - ger, Be nev - er want-ing there.
crown of life shall be; He with the King of glo - ry Shall reign e - ter - nal-ly.

471 "V" Is for Victory

God . . . giveth us the victory through our Lord Jesus Christ. I Cor. 15:57

WENDELL P. LOVELESS

WENDELL P. LOVELESS

"V" is for vic - to - ry! Sing it out, 'tis a glo - rious

word; "V" is for vic - to - ry! It is

ours through Christ our Lord. Some days may

be dark and drear, In Christ the way's "all clear,"

Copyright 1942. Renewal 1970. Hope Publishing Co., owner. All rights reserved.

472 It Pays to Serve Jesus

For My yoke is easy, and My burden is light. Matt. 11:30

FRANK C. HUSTON

FRANK C. HUSTON

1. The serv-ice of Je-sus true pleas-ure af-fords, In Him there is
2. It pays to serve Je-sus what-e'er may be-tide, It pays to be
3. Tho' some-times the shad-ows may hang o'er the way, And sor-rows may

joy with-out an al-loy; 'Tis heav-en to trust Him and rest on His
true what-e'er you may do; 'Tis rich-es of mer-cy in Him to a-
come to beck-on us home, Our pre-cious Re-deem-er each toil will re-

Chorus

words; It pays to serve Je-sus each day.
bide; It pays to serve Je-sus each day. It pays to serve Je-sus. it
pay; It pays to serve Je-sus each day.

pays ev-ery day, It pays ev-ery step of the way; Tho' the path-way to
ev-ery step of the way;

glo-ry may some-times be drear, You'll be hap-py each step of the way.

© 1937. Renewal by Standard Publishing. All rights reserved. Used by permission.

In the Service of the King 473

Both he that soweth and he that reapeth may rejoice . . . John 4:36

ALFRED H. ACKLEY

BENTLEY D. ACKLEY

1. I am hap-py in the serv-ice of the King, I am
2. I am hap-py in the serv-ice of the King, I am
3. I am hap-py in the serv-ice of the King, I am
4. I am hap-py in the serv-ice of the King, I am

hap-py, oh, so hap-py; I have peace and joy that
hap-py, oh, so hap-py; Thro' the sun-shine and the
hap-py, oh, so hap-py; To His guid-ing hand for-
hap-py, oh, so hap-py; All that I pos-sess to

noth-ing else can bring, In the serv-ice of the King.
shad-ow I can sing, In the serv-ice of the King.
ev-er I will cling, In the serv-ice of the King.
Him I glad-ly bring, In the serv-ice of the King.

Chorus

In the serv-ice of the King, Ev-ery tal-ent I will bring;

I have peace and joy and bless-ing In the serv-ice of the King.

Copyright 1912. © Renewed 1940, The Rodeheaver Co. Used by permission.

474 Onward, Christian Soldiers

Thou therefore endure hardness, as a good soldier of Jesus Christ. II Tim. 2:3

SABINE BARING-GOULD

ARTHUR S. SULLIVAN

1. On-ward, Chris-tian sol-diers, march-ing as to war, With the cross of Je-sus
2. Like a might-y ar-my moves the Church of God; Broth-ers, we are tread-ing
3. Crowns and thrones may perish, king-doms rise and wane, But the Church of Je-sus
4. On-ward, then, ye peo-ple, join our hap-py throng, Blend with ours your voices

go-ing on be-fore: Christ, the roy-al Mas-ter, leads a-gainst the foe;
where the saints have trod; We are not di-vid-ed, all one bod-y we,
con-stant will re-main; Gates of hell can nev-er 'gainst that Church pre-vail;
in the tri-umph song; Glo-ry, laud, and hon-or un-to Christ the King;

Chorus

For-ward in-to bat-tle, see His ban-ners go.
One in hope and doc-trine, one in char-i-ty.
We have Christ's own prom-ise, and that can-not fail.
This thro' count-less a-ges men and an-gels sing.

On-ward, Chris-tian sol-diers,

march-ing as to war, With the cross of Je-sus go-ing on be-fore.

We're Marching to Zion 475

Let the children of Zion be joyful in their King. Psa. 149:2

Isaac Watts
Refrain, Robert Lowry

Robert Lowry

1. Come, we that love the Lord, And let our joys be known,
2. Let those re - fuse to sing Who nev - er knew our God,
3. The hill of Zi - on yields A thou - sand sa - cred sweets
4. Then let our songs a - bound, And ev - ery tear be dry;

Join in a song with sweet ac - cord, Join in a song with sweet ac - cord
But chil - dren of the heav'n - ly King, But chil - dren of the heav'n - ly King
Be - fore we reach the heav'n - ly fields, Be - fore we reach the heav'n - ly fields
We're march - ing thro' Im-manuel's ground, We're march - ing thro' Im-manuel's ground

And thus sur - round the throne, And thus sur - round the throne.
May speak their joys a - broad, May speak their joys a - broad.
Or walk the gold - en streets, Or walk the gold - en streets.
To fair - er worlds on high, To fair - er worlds on high.

Chorus

We're march - ing to Zi - on, Beau - ti - ful, beau - ti - ful Zi - on;
We're march - ing on to Zi - on,

We're march - ing up - ward to Zi - on, The beau - ti - ful cit - y of God.

476 Make Me a Channel of Blessing

... A vessel unto honor, sanctified, and meet for the Master's use. II Tim. 2:21

HARPER G. SMYTH   HARPER G. SMYTH

1. Is your life a chan-nel of bless-ing? Is the love of God
2. Is your life a chan-nel of bless-ing? Are you bur-dened for
3. Is your life a chan-nel of bless-ing? Is it dai - ly
4. We can-not be chan-nels of bless-ing If our lives are not

flow - ing through you? Are you tell-ing the lost of the Sav - ior?
those who are lost? Have you urged up - on those who are stray-ing
tell - ing for Him? Have you spo - ken the word of sal - va - tion
free from known sin; We will bar - ri - ers be and a hin-drance

Chorus

Are you read - y His serv - ice to do?
The Sav - ior who died on the cross?
To those who are dy - ing in sin? Make me a chan - nel of
To those we are try - ing to win.

bless-ing to - day, Make me a chan-nel of bless-ing, I pray; My life pos-

sess-ing, my ser-vice bless-ing, Make me a chan-nel of bless-ing to - day.

Make Me a Blessing 477

So will I save you and ye shall be a blessing. Zech. 8:13

Ira B. Wilson

George S. Schuler

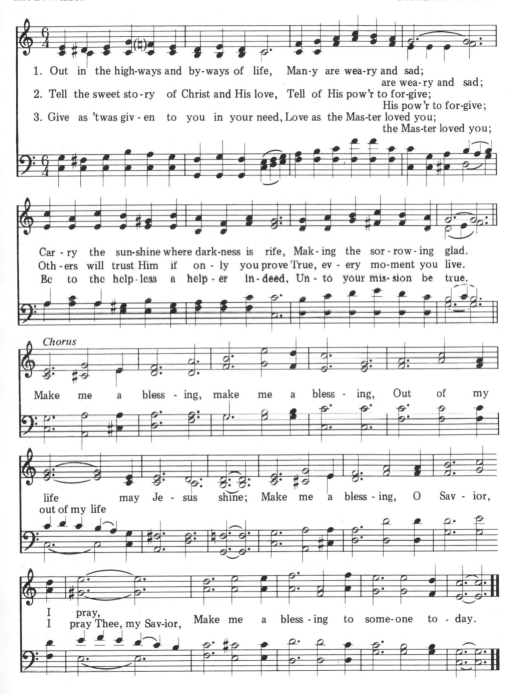

1. Out in the high-ways and by-ways of life, Man-y are wea-ry and sad;
   are wea-ry and sad;
2. Tell the sweet sto-ry of Christ and His love, Tell of His pow'r to for-give;
   His pow'r to for-give;
3. Give as 'twas giv-en to you in your need, Love as the Mas-ter loved you;
   the Mas-ter loved you;

Car-ry the sun-shine where dark-ness is rife, Mak-ing the sor-row-ing glad.
Oth-ers will trust Him if on-ly you prove True, ev-ery mo-ment you live.
Be to the help-less a help-er in-deed, Un-to your mis-sion be true.

Chorus

Make me a bless-ing, make me a bless-ing, Out of my
life may Je-sus shine; Make me a bless-ing, O Sav-ior,
out of my life

I pray,
I pray Thee, my Sav-ior, Make me a bless-ing to some-one to-day.

Copyright 1924 by Geo. S. Schuler. © Renewed 1952. The Rodeheaver Co. Used by permission.

478 Who Is on the Lord's Side?

Who is on the Lord's side? Exo. 32:26

FRANCES R. HAVERGAL

C. LUISE REICHARDT
ARR. BY JOHN GOSS

1. Who is on the Lord's side? Who will serve the King? Who will be His
2. Not for weight of glo - ry, Not for crown and palm, En - ter we the
3. Je - sus, Thou hast bought us, Not with gold or gem, But with Thine own
4. Fierce may be the con - flict, Strong may be the foe, But the King's own

help - ers, Oth - er lives to bring? Who will leave the world's side?
ar - my, Raise the war - rior psalm; But for love that claim - eth
life - blood, For Thy di - a - dem. With Thy bless - ing fill - ing
ar - my None can o - ver - throw. Round His stand - ard rang - ing

Who will face the foe? Who is on the Lord's side? Who for
Lives for whom He died; He whom Je - sus nam - eth Must be
Each who comes to Thee, Thou hast made us will - ing, Thou hast
Vic - t'ry is se - cure; For His truth un - chang - ing Makes the

Him will go? By Thy call of mer - cy, By Thy grace di - vine,
on His side. By Thy love con - strain - ing, By Thy grace di - vine,
made us free. By Thy grand re - demp - tion, By Thy grace di - vine,
tri - umph sure. Joy - ful - ly en - list - ing By Thy grace di - vine,

We are on the Lord's side, Sav - ior, we are Thine. A - men.

A Charge to Keep I Have 479

Walk worthy of the vocation wherewith ye are called. Eph. 4:1

CHARLES WESLEY

LOWELL MASON

1. A charge to keep I have, A God to glo - ri - fy, A
2. To serve the pres - ent age, My call - ing to ful - fill; O
3. Arm me with watch - ful care As in Thy sight to live, And
4. Help me to watch and pray, And still on Thee re - ly, O

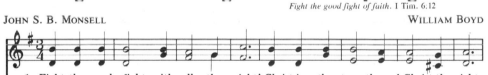

nev - er - dy - ing soul to save, And fit it for the sky.
may it all my pow'rs en - gage To do my Mas - ter's will!
now Thy serv - ant, Lord, pre - pare A strict ac - count to give!
let me not my trust be - tray, But press to realms on high. A - men.

Fight the Good Fight with All Thy Might 480

Fight the good fight of faith. 1 Tim. 6.12

JOHN S. B. MONSELL

WILLIAM BOYD

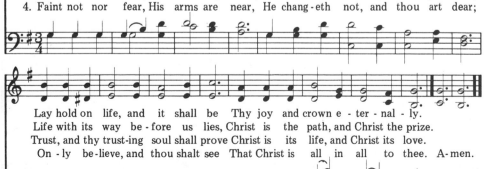

1. Fight the good fight with all thy might! Christ is thy strength, and Christ thy right;
2. Run the straight race thro' God's good grace, Lift up thine eyes, and seek His face;
3. Cast care a - side, lean on thy Guide, His bound-less mer - cy will pro - vide;
4. Faint not nor fear, His arms are near, He chang - eth not, and thou art dear;

Lay hold on life, and it shall be Thy joy and crown e - ter - nal - ly.
Life with its way be - fore us lies, Christ is the path, and Christ the prize.
Trust, and thy trust-ing soul shall prove Christ is its life, and Christ its love.
On - ly be - lieve, and thou shalt see That Christ is all in all to thee. A - men.

481 To the Work!

I must work the works of Him that sent me . . . John 9:4

FANNY J. CROSBY   WILLIAM H. DOANE

1. To the work! to the work! we are serv-ants of God, Let us fol-low the
2. To the work! to the work! let the hun-gry be fed; To the foun-tain of
3. To the work! to the work! there is la-bor for all; For the king-dom of
4. To the work! to the work! in the strength of the Lord, And a robe and a

path that our Mas-ter has trod; With the balm of His coun-sel our
life let the wea-ry be led; In the cross and its ban-ner our
dark-ness and er-ror shall fall; And the name of Je-ho-vah ex-
crown shall our la-bor re-ward; When the home of the faith-ful our

strength to re-new, Let us do with our might what our hands find to do.
glo-ry shall be, While we her-ald the ti-dings, "Sal-va-tion is free!"
alt-ed shall be, In the loud swell-ing cho-rus, "Sal-va-tion is free!"
dwell-ing shall be, And we shout with the ran-somed, "Sal-va-tion is free!"

Chorus

Toil-ing on, toil-ing on, Toil-ing on, toil-ing on;
Toil-ing on, toil-ing on, Toil-ing on, toil-ing on;

Let us hope, let us watch, And la-bor till the Mas-ter comes.
and trust, and pray,

We'll Work till Jesus Comes 482

Occupy till I come . . . Luke 19:13

ELIZABETH MILLS

WILLIAM MILLER

1. O land of rest, for thee I sigh! When will the mo-ment come
2. To Je-sus Christ I fled for rest; He bade me cease to roam,
3. I sought at once my Sav-ior's side, No more my steps shall roam;

When I shall lay my ar-mor by, And dwell in peace at home?
And lean for suc-cor on His breast Till He con-duct me home.
With Him I'll brave death's chill-ing tide, And reach my heav'n-ly home.

Chorus

We'll work till Je-sus comes, We'll work till Je-sus comes, We'll
We'll work   We'll work

work till Je-sus comes, And we'll be gath-ered home.
We'll work

483 I'll Be a Sunbeam

Ye shine as lights in the world. Phil. 2:15

NELLIE TALBOT

EDWIN O. EXCELL

1. Je - sus wants me for a sun - beam, To shine for Him each day;
2. Je - sus wants me to be lov - ing, And kind to all I see;
3. I will ask Je - sus to help me To keep my heart from sin,
4. I'll be a sun - beam for Je - sus; I can if I but try;

In ev - ery way try to please Him, At home, at school, at play.
Show - ing how pleas - ant and hap - py His lit - tle one can be.
Ev - er re - flect - ing His good - ness, And al - ways shine for Him.
Serv - ing Him mo - ment by mo - ment, Then live with Him on high.

Chorus

A sun - beam, a sun - beam, Je - sus wants me for a sun - beam; A

sun - beam, a sun - beam, I'll be a sun - beam for Him.

Help Somebody Today 484

As ye have done it unto one of . . . My brethren, ye have done it unto Me. Matt. 25:40

CARRIE E. BRECK   CHARLES H. GABRIEL

1. Look all a-round you, find some-one in need, Help some-bod-y to-day!
2. Man-y are 'wait-ing a kind, lov-ing word, Help some-bod-y to-day!
3. Man-y have bur-dens too heav-y to bear, Help some-bod-y to-day!
4. Some are dis-cour-aged and wea-ry in heart, Help some-bod-y to-day!

Tho' it be lit-tle— a neigh-bor-ly deed—Help some-bod-y to-day!
You have a mes-sage, O let it be heard, Help some-bod-y to-day!
Grief is the por-tion of some ev-ery-where, Help some-bod-y to-day!
Some-one the jour-ney to heav-en should start, Help some-bod-y to-day!

Chorus

Help some-bod-y to-day, Some-bod-y a-long life's way; Let
     to-day,   home-ward way;

sor-row be end-ed, the friend-less be-friend-ed, Oh, help some-bod-y to-day!

485 Will There Be Any Stars?

And they that turn many to righteousness as the stars . . . Dan. 12:3

ELIZA E. HEWITT

JOHN R. SWENEY

1. I am think-ing to-day of that beau-ti-ful land I shall reach when the
2. In the strength of the Lord let me la-bor and pray, Let me watch as a
3. Oh, what joy it will be when His face I be-hold, Liv-ing gems at His

sun go-eth down; When thro' won-der-ful grace by my Sav-ior I stand, Will there
win-ner of souls; That bright stars may be mine in the glo-ri-ous day, When His
feet to lay down; It would sweet-en my bliss in the cit-y of gold, Should there

Chorus

be an-y stars in my crown?
praise like the sea-bil-low rolls. Will there be an-y stars, an-y stars in my
be an-y stars in my crown.

crown When at eve-ning the sun go-eth down? When I wake with the blest
go-eth down?

in the man-sions of rest, Will there be an-y stars in my crown?
an-y stars in my crown?

I Am Resolved 486

I determined not to know anything . . . save Jesus Christ. I Cor. 2:2

PALMER HARTSOUGH

JAMES H. FILLMORE

1. I am re-solved no lon-ger to lin-ger, Charmed by the world's de-light;
2. I am re-solved to go to the Sav-ior, Leav-ing my sin and strife;
3. I am re-solved to fol-low the Sav-ior, Faith-ful and true each day;
4. I am re-solved to en-ter the King-dom, Leav-ing the paths of sin;

Things that are high-er, things that are no-bler, These have al-lured my sight.
He is the true One, He is the just One, He hath the words of life.
Heed what He say-eth, do what He will-eth, He is the liv-ing way.
Friends may op-pose me, foes may be-set me, Still will I en-ter in.

Chorus

I will has-ten, has-ten to Him, Has-ten so glad and free; Has-ten glad and free;

Je - sus, Great-est, High-est, I will come to Thee.
Je - sus, Je - sus,

487 Throw Out the Life-Line

He which converteth a sinner . . . shall save a soul from death . . . James 5:20

EDWARD S. UFFORD

EDWARD S. UFFORD
ARR. BY GEORGE C. STEBBINS

1. Throw out the Life-Line a-cross the dark wave, There is a broth-er whom
2. Throw out the Life-Line with hand quick and strong: Why do you tar-ry, why
3. Throw out the Life-Line to dan-ger-fraught men, Sink-ing in an-guish where
4. Soon will the sea-son of res-cue be o'er, Soon will they drift to e

some-one should save; Some-bod-y's broth-er! oh, who then will dare To
lin-ger so long? See! he is sink-ing; oh, has-ten to-day And
you've nev-er been: Winds of temp-ta-tion and bil-lows of woe Will
ter-ni-ty's shore, Haste then, my broth-er, no time for de-lay, But

Chorus

throw out the Life-Line, his per-il to share?
out with the Life-Boat! a-way, then, a-way!
soon hurl them out where the dark wa-ters flow.
throw out the Life-Line and save them to-day.

Throw out the Life-Line!

Throw out the Life-Line! Some-one is drift-ing a-way; Throw out the

Life-Line! Throw out the Life-Line! Some-one is sink-ing to-day.

Rescue the Perishing 488

The Son of man is come to seek and to save that which was lost. Luke 19:10

FANNY J. CROSBY

WILLIAM H. DOANE

1. Res - cue the per - ish - ing, care for the dy - ing, Snatch them in pit - y from
2. Though they are slight-ing Him, still He is wait - ing, Wait-ing the pen - i - tent
3. Down in the hu - man heart, crushed by the tempt-er, Feel-ings lie bur - ied that
4. Res - cue the per - ish - ing, du - ty de-mands it; Strength for thy la - bor the

sin and the grave; Weep o'er the err - ing one, lift up the fall - en,
child to re - ceive; Plead with them ear - nest - ly, plead with them gen - tly,
grace can re - store; Touched by a lov - ing heart, wak - ened by kind - ness,
Lord will pro - vide; Back to the nar - row way pa - tient - ly win them;

Chorus

Tell them of Je - sus the might - y to save.
He will for-give if they on - ly be - lieve.
Cords that are bro - ken will vi - brate once more.   Res - cue the per - ish - ing,
Tell the poor wan - d'rer a Sav - ior has died.

care for the dy - ing; Je - sus is mer - ci - ful, Je - sus will save.

489 The Banner of the Cross

Thou hast given a banner to them . . . that it may be displayed . . . Psa. 60:4

DANIEL W. WHITTLE   JAMES McGRANAHAN

1. There's a roy-al ban-ner giv-en for dis-play To the sol-diers of the King; As an en-sign fair we lift it up to-day, While as ran-somed ones we sing.
2. Though the foe may rage and gath-er as the flood, Let the stand-ard be dis-played; And be-neath its folds, as sol-diers of the Lord For the truth be not dis-mayed!
3. O-ver land and sea, wher-ev-er man may dwell, Make the glo-rious ti-dings known; Of the crim-son ban-ner now the sto-ry tell, While the Lord shall claim His own!
4. When the glo-ry dawns—'tis draw-ing ver-y near— It is has-tening day by day; Then be-fore our King the foe shall dis-ap-pear, And the cross the world shall sway!

Chorus

March-ing on, march-ing on, on, on, For Christ count ev-ery-thing but loss! And to crown Him King, we'll toil and sing 'Neath the ban-ner of the cross!

Sound the Battle Cry 490

Fight the good fight of faith . . . I Tim. 6:12

WILLIAM F. SHERWIN

WILLIAM F. SHERWIN

1. Sound the bat-tle cry! See, the foe is nigh; Raise the stan-dard high
2. Strong to meet the foe, March-ing on we go, While our cause we know,
3. O! Thou God of all, Hear us when we call, Help us one and all

for the Lord; Gird your ar-mor on, Stand firm, ev-ery-one; Rest your
must pre-vail; Shield and ban-ner bright, Gleam-ing in the light; Bat-tling
by Thy grace; When the bat-tle's done, And the vic-t'ry's won, May we

Chorus

cause up-on His ho-ly word.
for the right we ne'er can fail. Rouse, then, sol-diers, ral-ly round the
wear the crown be-fore Thy face.

ban-ner, Read-y, stead-y, pass the word a-long; On-ward, for-ward,

shout a-loud Ho-san-na! Christ is Cap-tain of the might-y throng.

491 Pass It On

If God so loved us, we ought also to love one another. I John 4:11

KURT KAISER

KURT KAISER

Unison

1. It on - ly takes a spark to get a fire go - ing,
2. What a won - drous time is spring when all the trees are bud - ding,
3. I wish for you, my friend, this hap - pi-ness that I've found,

And soon all those a-round can warm up in its glow-ing.
The birds be - gin to sing, the flow - ers start their bloom-ing,
You can de-pend on Him, it mat - ters not where you're bound.

That's how it is with God's love once you've ex-pe-ri-enced it;
That's how it is with God's love once you've ex-pe-ri-enced it;
I'll shout it from the moun-tain top— I want my world to know;

You spread His love to ev -ery one; You want to pass it on.
You want to sing, it's fresh like spring, You want to pass it on.
The Lord of love has come to me, I want to pass it on.

© Copyright 1969 by LEXICON MUSIC. INC. ASCAP. All rights reserved. International copyright secured. Used by special permission.

Lonely Voices 492

I . . . am as a sparrow alone upon the housetop. Psa. 102:7

BILLIE HANKS, JR.

BILLIE HANKS, JR.

1. Lone-ly voic-es cry-ing in the cit - y, Lone-ly voic-es
2. Lone-ly fac-es look-ing for the sun - rise, Just to find an-
3. Lone-ly eyes, I see them in the sub - way, Bur-dened by the
4. A - bund-ant life He came to tru - ly give man, But so few His

sound-ing like a child, Lone-ly voic-es come from bus - y peo - ple,
oth - er bus - y day. Lone-ly fac-es all a-round the cit - y,
wor - ries of the day: Men at lei - sure, but they're so un-hap - py,
gift of grace re - ceive, Lone-ly peo - ple live in ev - ery cit - y,

Too dis-turbed to stop a lit - tle while. Lone-ly voic - es
Men a - fraid, but too a-shamed to pray. Lone-ly fac - es
Tired of fool - ish roles they try to play. Lone-ly peo - ple
Men who face a dark and lone - ly grave. Lone-ly fac - es

fill my dreams, Lone-ly voic-es haunt my mem - o - ry.
do I see, Lone-ly fac-es haunt my mem - o - ry.
do I see, Lone-ly peo-ple haunt my mem - o - ry.
do I see, Lone-ly voic-es call - ing out to me.

Copyright © 1967. Hope Publishing Co., owner. International copyright secured. All rights reserved.

493 From Greenland's Icy Mountains

Come over . . . and help us. Acts 16:9

REGINALD HEBER

LOWELL MASON

1. From Green-land's i - cy moun-tains, From In - dia's cor - al strand,
2. What though the spic - y breez - es Blow soft o'er Cey-lon's isle;
3. Shall we, whose souls are light - ed With wis - dom from on high,
4. Waft, waft, ye winds, His sto - ry, And you, ye wa - ters, roll,

Where Af - ric's sun - ny foun - tains Roll down their gold - en sand,
Though ev - ery pros - pect pleas - es, And on - ly man is vile?
Shall we to men be - night - ed The lamp of life de - ny?
Till, like a sea of glo - ry, It spreads from pole to pole:

From man - y an an - cient riv - er, From man - y a palm - y plain,
In vain with lav - ish kind - ness The gifts of God are strown;
Sal - va - tion! O sal - va - tion! The joy - ful sound pro - claim,
Till o'er our ran-somed na - ture The Lamb for sin - ners slain,

They call us to de - liv - er Their land from er - ror's chain.
The hea - then in his blind - ness Bows down to wood and stone.
Till earth's re - mot - est na - tion Has learned Mes - si - ah's name.
Re - deem - er, King, Cre - a - tor, In bliss re - turns to reign. A - men.

Jesus Saves! 494

Tell of His salvation from day to day. Declare His glory . . . Psa. 96:2, 3

PRISCILLA J. OWENS

WILLIAM J. KIRKPATRICK

1. We have heard the joy - ful sound: Je - sus saves! Je - sus saves!
2. Waft it on the roll - ing tide; Je - sus saves! Je - sus saves!
3. Sing a - bove the bat - tle strife, Je - sus saves! Je - sus saves!
4. Give the winds a might - y voice, Je - sus saves! Je - sus saves!

Spread the ti - dings all a - round: Je - sus saves! Je - sus saves!
Tell to sin - ners far and wide: Je - sus saves! Je - sus saves!
By His death and end - less life, Je - sus saves! Je - sus saves!
Let the na - tions now re - joice— Je - sus saves! Je - sus saves!

Bear the news to ev - ery land, Climb the steeps and cross the waves;
Sing, ye is - lands of the sea; Ech - o back, ye o - cean caves;
Sing it soft - ly through the gloom, When the heart for mer - cy craves;
Shout sal - va - tion full and free, High - est hills and deep - est caves;

On - ward! 'tis our Lord's com - mand; Je - sus saves! Je - sus saves!
Earth shall keep her ju - bi - lee: Je - sus saves! Je - sus saves!
Sing in tri - umph o'er the tomb— Je - sus saves! Je - sus saves!
This our song of vic - to - ry— Je - sus saves! Je - sus saves!

495 Where Cross the Crowded Ways of Life

Whosoever shall give . . . a cup of cold water . . . shall in no wise lose his reward. Matt. 10:42

FRANK M. NORTH

William Gardiner's *Sacred Melodies*, 1815

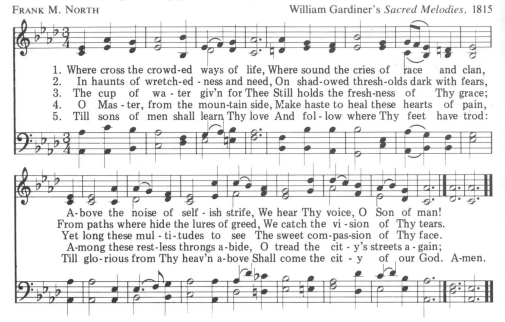

1. Where cross the crowd-ed ways of life, Where sound the cries of race and clan,
2. In haunts of wretch-ed - ness and need, On shad-owed thresh-olds dark with fears,
3. The cup of wa - ter giv'n for Thee Still holds the fresh-ness of Thy grace;
4. O Mas - ter, from the moun-tain side, Make haste to heal these hearts of pain,
5. Till sons of men shall learn Thy love And fol - low where Thy feet have trod:

A - bove the noise of self - ish strife, We hear Thy voice, O Son of man!
From paths where hide the lures of greed, We catch the vi - sion of Thy tears.
Yet long these mul - ti-tudes to see The sweet com-pas-sion of Thy face.
A-mong these rest-less throngs a-bide, O tread the cit - y's streets a - gain;
Till glo-rious from Thy heav'n a-bove Shall come the cit - y of our God. A-men.

496 Jesus Shall Reign Where'er the Sun

All kings shall fall down before Him: all nations shall serve Him. Psa. 72:11

ISAAC WATTS
Based on PSALM 72

JOHN HATTON

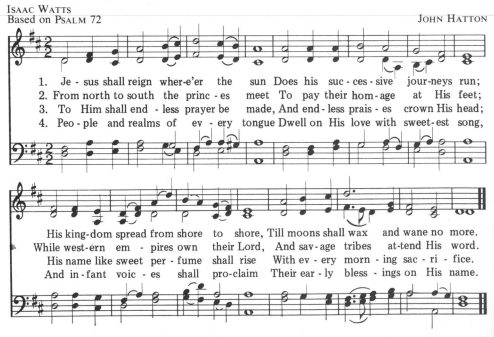

1. Je - sus shall reign wher-e'er the sun Does his suc-ces-sive jour-neys run;
2. From north to south the princ - es meet To pay their hom-age at His feet;
3. To Him shall end - less prayer be made, And end-less prais - es crown His head;
4. Peo - ple and realms of ev - ery tongue Dwell on His love with sweet-est song,

His king-dom spread from shore to shore, Till moons shall wax and wane no more.
While west-ern em - pires own their Lord, And sav-age tribes at-tend His word.
His name like sweet per - fume shall rise With ev - ery morn - ing sac - ri - fice.
And in-fant voic - es shall pro-claim Their ear - ly bless - ings on His name.

So Send I You 497

As My Father hath sent Me, even so send I you. John 20:21

E. Margaret Clarkson

John W. Peterson

1. So send I you to la - bor un - re - ward - ed, To serve un-
2. So send I you to bind the bruised and bro - ken, O'er wand - 'ring
3. So send I you to lone - li - ness and long - ing, With heart a-
4. So send I you to leave your life's am - bi - tion, To die to
5. So send I you to hearts made hard by ha - tred, To eyes made

paid, un - loved, un - sought, un - known, To bear re - buke, to suf - fer
souls to work, to weep, to wake, To bear the bur - dens of a
hung - 'ring for the loved and known, For - sak - ing home and kin - dred,
dear de - sire, self - will re - sign, To la - bor long, and love where
blind be - cause they will not see, To spend, though it be blood, to

scorn and scoff - ing— So send I you to toil for Me a - lone.
world a - wea - ry— So send I you to suf - fer for My sake.
friend and dear one— So send I you to know My love a - lone.
men re - vile you— So send I you to lose your life in Mine.
spend and spare not— So send I you to taste of Cal - va - ry.

Chorus (following the final stanza)

"As the Fa - ther hath sent me, So send I you."

Copyright 1954 by Singspiration, Inc. All rights reserved. Used by permission.

498 Go Ye into All the World

Go ye into all the world, and preach the gospel . . . Mark 16:15

JAMES McGRANAHAN   JAMES McGRANAHAN

1. Far, far a - way, in death and dark-ness dwell-ing, Mil-lions of souls for-
2. See o'er the world wide o - pen doors in - vit - ing, Sol-diers of Christ, a -
3. "Why will ye die?" the voice of God is call - ing, "Why will ye die?" re-
4. God speed the day, when those of ev - ery na - tion "Glo - ry to God!" tri-

ev - er may be lost; Who, who will go, sal - va-tion's sto - ry tell - ing,
rise and en - ter in! Chris-tians, a - wake! your forc - es all u - nit - ing,
ech - o in His name; Je - sus hath died to save from death ap - pall - ing,
um-phant - ly shall sing; Ran-somed, re-deemed, re-joic - ing in sal - va - tion,

Chorus

Look-ing to Je - sus, mind-ing not the cost?
Send forth the gos - pel, break the chains of sin. "All pow'r is giv - en un - to Me,
Life and sal - va - tion there-fore go pro-claim.
Shout Hal - le - lu - jah, for the Lord is King.

All pow'r is giv - en un - to Me, Go ye in - to all the world and

preach the gos - pel, And lo, I am with you al - way."

We've a Story to Tell to the Nations 499

And this gospel . . . shall be preached in all the world for a witness unto all nations. Matt. 24:14

E. ERNEST NICHOL

H. ERNEST NICHOL

1. We've a sto - ry to tell to the na - tions That shall
2. We've a song to be sung to the na - tions That shall
3. We've a mes - sage to give to the na - tions That the
4. We've a Sav - ior to show to the na - tions Who the

turn their hearts to the right, A sto - ry of truth and mer - cy,
lift their hearts to the Lord, A song that shall con - quer e - vil
Lord who reign - eth a - bove Hath sent us His Son to save us,
path of sor - row hath trod, That all of the world's great peo - ples

A sto - ry of peace and light, A sto - ry of peace and light.
And shat - ter the spear and sword, And shat - ter the spear and sword.
And show us that God is love, And show us that God is love.
Might come to the truth of God, Might come to the truth of God.

Chorus

For the dark-ness shall turn to dawn-ing, And the dawn-ing to noon-day bright,

And Christ's great king-dom shall come to earth, The king-dom of love and light.

500 O Zion, Haste

We declare unto you glad tidings. Acts 13:32

MARY A. THOMSON

JAMES WALCH

1. O Chris-tian, haste, your mis-sion high ful - fill - ing, To tell to all the
2. Be - hold how man - y thou-sands still are ly - ing, Bound in the dark-some
3. Pro-claim to ev - ery peo - ple, tongue and na - tion That God, in whom they
4. Give of your sons to bear the mes-sage glo-rious; Give of your wealth to

world that God is Light; That He who made all na - tions is not will - ing
pris - on-house of sin, With none to tell them of the Sav-ior's dy - ing,
live and move, is love: Tell how He stooped to save His lost cre - a - tion,
speed them on their way; Pour out your soul for them in prayer vic - to-rious;

Chorus

One soul should per - ish, lost in shades of night.
Or of the life He died for them to win.
And died on earth that man might live a - bove. Pub - lish glad ti - dings,
And all your spend-ing Je - sus will re - pay.

ti - dings of peace; Ti - dings of Je - sus, re - demp-tion, and re - lease.

Give of Your Best to the Master 501

Unto whomsoever much is given, of him shall be much required. Luke 12:48

HOWARD B. GROSE

CHARLOTTE A. BARNARD

1. Give of your best to the Mas-ter, Give of the strength of your youth;
2. Give of your best to the Mas-ter, Give Him first place in your heart;
3. Give of your best to the Mas-ter, Naught else is wor-thy His love;
Ch. Give of your best to the Mas-ter, Give of the strength of your youth;

Throw your soul's fresh, glow-ing ar-dor In - to the bat-tle for truth.
Give Him first place in your serv - ice, Con - se-crate ev - ery part.
He gave Him - self for your ran - som, Gave up His glo-ry a - bove;
Clad in sal - va-tion's full ar - mor, Join in the bat-tle for truth.

Je - sus has set the ex - am - ple—Daunt-less was He, young and brave;
Give, and to you shall be giv - en— God His be - lov - ed Son gave;
Laid down His life with-out mur - mur, You from sin's ru - in to save;

Give Him your loy - al de - vo - tion, Give Him the best that you have.
Grate-ful - ly seek-ing to serve Him, Give Him the best that you have.
Give Him your heart's ad-o - ra - tion, Give Him the best that you have.

502 I'll Tell the World That I'm a Christian

Tell them how great things the Lord hath done for thee. Mark 5:19

BAYNARD L. FOX   BAYNARD L. FOX

1. I'll tell the world that I'm a Christ-ian— I'm not a-shamed
2. I'll tell the world that He is com-ing— It may be near

His name to bear; I'll tell the world that I'm a Christ-ian—
or far a-way; But we must live as if His com-ing

I'll take Him with me an-y-where. I'll tell the world
Would be to-mor-row or to-day. For when He comes

how Je-sus saved me, And how He gave me a life brand-new;
and life is o-ver, For those who love Him, there's more to be;

© Copyright 1958. 1963 by Fox Music Publications. All rights reserved. Used by permission.

And I know   that if you trust Him   That all He gave me
Eyes have nev - er seen the won - ders   That He's pre -par - ing

He'll give to you.   I'll tell the world   that He's my Sav -ior,
for you and me.   O tell the world   that you're a Christ-ian,

No oth - er   one   could love me   so;   My life, my   all
Be not a - shamed   His name to   bear;   O tell   the world

is His for - ev - er,   And where He leads me   I will go.
that you're a Christ-ian,   And take Him with you   ev - ery-where.

503 Send the Light!

The light of the glorious gospel of Christ . . . II Cor. 4:4

CHARLES H. GABRIEL   CHARLES H. GABRIEL

1. There's a call comes ring-ing o'er the rest-less wave, "Send the light!
2. We have heard the Mac - e - do - nian call to - day, "Send the light!
3. Let us pray that grace may ev-ery-where a-bound, Send the light!
4. Let us not grow wea - ry in the work of love, Send the light!

Send the light!

Send the light!"   There are souls to res - cue, there are souls to save,
Send the light!"   And a gold - en of-f'ring at the cross we lay,
Send the light!   And a Christ-like spir - it ev - ery-where be found,
Send the light!   Let us gath - er jew - els for a crown a - bove,

Send the light!

Chorus

Send the light!   Send the light!   Send the light,   the
Send the light!   Send the light!   Send the light,

1

bless - ed gos - pel light; Let it shine   from shore to
the bless - ed gos - pel light;   Let it shine

shore!   shine   for - ev - er - more!

from shore to shore!   Let   it shine   for - ev - er-more!

Jesus Bids Us Shine 504

Let your light so shine before men . . . Matt. 5:16

SUSAN WARNER

EDWIN O. EXCELL

1. Je - sus bids us shine, with a clear, pure light, Like a lit - tle
2. Je - sus bids us shine, first of all for Him; Well He sees and
3. Je - sus bids us shine, then, for all a - round Man - y kinds of
4. Je - sus bids us shine, as we work for Him, Bring - ing those that

can - dle burn - ing in the night; In this world of dark - ness
knows it if our light is dim; He looks down from heav - en,
dark - ness in this world a - bound— Sin, and want, and sor - row:
wan - der from the paths of sin; He will ev - er help us,

we must shine, You in your small cor - ner, and I in mine.
sees us shine, You in your small cor - ner, and I in mine.
we must shine, You in your small cor - ner, and I in mine.
if we shine, You in your small cor - ner, and I in mine.

505 Rise Up, O Men of God

Yet a little while, and He . . . will come, and will not tarry. Heb. 10:37

WILLIAM P. MERRILL

AARON WILLIAMS

1. Rise up, O men of God! Have done with less - er things;
2. Rise up, O men of God! His king - dom tar - ries long;
3. Rise up, O men of God! The Church for you doth wait,
4. Lift high the cross of Christ! Tread where His feet have trod;

Give heart and mind and soul and strength To serve the King of kings.
Bring in the day of broth - er - hood And end the night of wrong.
Her strength un - e - qual to her task; Rise up, and make her great!
As broth - ers of the Son of man, Rise up, O men of God!

Words used by permission of The Presbyterian Outlook, Richmond, Va. (USA)

506 The Savior's Wondrous Love

That they all may be one . . . John 17:21

Source unknown

WILLIAM H. WALTER

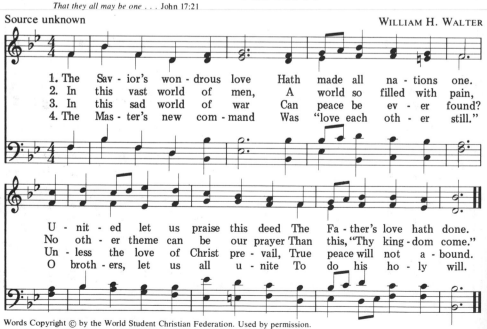

1. The Sav - ior's won - drous love Hath made all na - tions one.
2. In this vast world of men, A world so filled with pain,
3. In this sad world of war Can peace be ev - er found?
4. The Mas - ter's new com - mand Was "love each oth - er still."

U - nit - ed let us praise this deed The Fa - ther's love hath done.
No oth - er theme can be our prayer Than this, "Thy king - dom come."
Un - less the love of Christ pre - vail, True peace will not a - bound.
O broth - ers, let us all u - nite To do his ho - ly will.

Words Copyright © by the World Student Christian Federation. Used by permission.

Will Jesus Find Us Watching? 507

Watch therefore: for ye know not what hour your Lord doth come. Matt. 24:42

FANNY J. CROSBY

WILLIAM H. DOANE

1. When Je - sus comes to re - ward His serv - ants, Wheth - er it be
2. If, at the dawn of the ear - ly morn - ing, He shall call us
3. Have we been true to the trust He left us? Do we seek to
4. Bless - ed are those whom the Lord finds watch-ing, In His glo - ry

noon or night, Faith - ful to Him will He find us watch - ing,
one by one, When to the Lord we re - store our tal - ents,
do our best? If in our hearts there is naught con - demns us,
they shall share; If He shall come at the dawn or mid - night,

Chorus

With our lamps all trimmed and bright?
Will He an - swer thee—"Well done"? Oh, can we say we are
We shall have a glo - rious rest.
Will He find us watch - ing there?

read - y, broth - er? Read - y for the soul's bright home? Say, will He

find you and me still watch-ing, Wait - ing, wait - ing when the Lord shall come?

508 The Regions Beyond

To preach the gospel in the regions beyond . . . II Cor. 10:16

ALBERT B. SIMPSON

MARGARET M. SIMPSON

1. To the re - gions be - yond I must go, I must go, Where the
2. To the hard - est of plac - es He calls me to go, Not
3. Oh, ye that are spend - ing your lei - sure and pow'rs In
4. There are oth - er "lost sheep" that the Mas - ter must bring, And

sto - ry has nev - er been told (been told); To the mil - lions that nev -
think - ing of com - fort or ease (or ease); The world may pro-nounce
pleas - ures so fool - ish and fond (and fond); A - wake from your self -
they must the mes - sage be told (be told); He sends me to gath -

er have heard of His love, I must tell the sweet sto - ry of old (of old).
me a dream - er, a fool, E - nough if the Mas - ter I please (I please).
ish - ness, fol - ly and sin, And go to the re - gions be - yond (be-yond).
er them out of all lands, And wel-come them back to His fold (His fold).

Chorus

To the re - gions be-yond I must go,
I must go, I must go, To the re -

I must go, Till the world,
gions be - yond I must go, Till the world,

all the world, His sal - va - tion shall know.
all the world, His sal - va - tion shall know, shall know.

Beyond the Sunset 509

For there shall be no night there . . . Rev. 21:25

VIRGIL P. BROCK

BLANCHE KERR BROCK

1. Be - yond the sun - set, O bliss - ful morn - ing, When with our
2. Be - yond the sun - set no clouds will gath - er, No storms will
3. Be - yond the sun - set a hand will guide me To God, the
4. Be - yond the sun - set, O glad re - un - ion, With our dear

Sav - ior heav'n is be - gun. Earth's toil - ing end - ed, O glo - rious
threat - en, no fears an - noy; O day of glad - ness, O day un -
Fa - ther, whom I a - dore; His glo - rious pres - ence, His words of
loved ones who've gone be - fore; In that fair home - land we'll know no

dawn - ing; Be - yond the sun - set, when day is done.
end - ing, Be - yond the sun - set, e - ter - nal joy!
wel - come, Will be my por - tion on that fair shore.
part - ing, Be - yond the sun - set for ev - er - more!

Copyright 1936. The Rodeheaver Co. © Renewed 1964. The Rodeheaver Co. All rights reserved. Used by permission.

510 Shall We Gather at the River?

A pure river of water of life . . . proceeding out of the throne of God. Rev. 22:1

ROBERT LOWRY   ROBERT LOWRY

1. Shall we gath-er at the riv-er, Where bright an-gel feet have trod;
2. On the bos-om of the riv-er, Where the Sav-ior-King we own,
3. Ere we reach the shin-ing riv-er, Lay we ev-ery bur-den down;
4. Soon we'll reach the shin-ing riv-er, Soon our pil-grim-age will cease;

With its crys-tal tide for-ev-er Flow-ing by the throne of God?
We shall meet, and sor-row nev-er,'Neath the glo-ry of the throne.
Grace our spir-its will de-liv-er, And pro-vide a robe and crown.
Soon our hap-py hearts will quiv-er With the mel-o-dy of peace.

Chorus

Yes, we'll gath-er at the riv-er, The beau-ti-ful, the beau-ti-ful riv-er,

Gath-er with the saints at the riv-er That flows by the throne of God.

On Jordan's Stormy Banks 511

Ye are passed over Jordan into the land of Canaan. Num. 33:51

American Folk Hymn
ARR. BY REGION M. McINTOSH

SAMUEL STENNETT

1. On Jor-dan's storm-y banks I stand, And cast a wish-ful eye
2. All o'er those wide ex-tend-ed plains Shines one e-ter-nal day;
3. No chill-ing winds nor poi-s'nous breath Can reach that health-ful shore;
4. When shall I reach that hap-py place, And be for-ev-er blest?

To Ca-naan's fair and hap-py land, Where my pos-ses-sions lie.
There God the Son for-ev-er reigns And scat-ters night a-way.
Sick-ness and sor-row, pain and death Are felt and feared no more.
When shall I see my Fa-ther's face, And in His bos-om rest?

Chorus

I am bound for the prom-ised land, I am bound for the prom-ised land;

O who will come and go with me? I am bound for the prom-ised land.

512 The Sands of Time Are Sinking

Behold, the Bridegroom cometh, go ye out to meet Him. Matt. 25:6

ANNE R. COUSIN

CHRÉTIEN URHAN
ARR. BY EDWARD F. RIMBAULT

1. The sands of time are sink - ing, The dawn of heav - en breaks;
2. O Christ! He is the foun - tain, The deep, sweet well of love!
3. O, I am my Be - lov - ed's, And my Be - lov - ed's mine!
4. The Bride eyes not her gar - ment, But her dear Bride-groom's face;

The sum - mer morn I've sighed for, The fair, sweet morn a - wakes:
The streams on earth I've tast - ed, More deep I'll drink a - bove:
He brings a poor vile sin - ner In - to His "house of wine."
I will not gaze at glo - ry But on my King of grace.

Dark, dark hath been the mid - night, But day - spring is at hand,
There to an o - cean ful - ness His mer - cy doth ex - pand,
I stand up - on His mer - it, I know no oth - er stand,
Not at the crown He giv - eth But on His pierc - ed hand,

And glo - ry, glo - ry dwell - eth In Im - man - uel's land.
And glo - ry, glo - ry dwell - eth In Im - man - uel's land.
Not e'en where glo - ry dwell - eth In Im - man - uel's land.
The Lamb is all the glo - ry Of Im - man - uel's land. A - men.

Saved by Grace 513

Or ever the silver cord be loosed . . . Then shall the dust return to the earth. Eccl. 12:6, 7

FANNY J. CROSBY

GEORGE C. STEBBINS

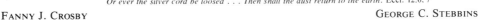

1. Some day the sil - ver cord will break, And I no more as now shall sing;
2. Some day my earth-ly house will fall, I can-not tell how soon 'twill be;
3. Some day, when fades the gold-en sun Be-neath the ro - sy - tint - ed west,
4. Some day: till then I'll watch and wait, My lamp all trimmed and burn-ing bright,

But oh, the joy when I shall wake With-in the pal-ace of the King!
But this I know—my All in All Has now a place in heav'n for me.
My bless-ed Lord will say, "Well done!" And I shall en - ter in - to rest.
That when my Sav-ior opes the gate, My soul to Him may take its flight.

Chorus

And I shall see Him face to face, And tell the sto - ry—Saved by grace;
shall see to face,

And I shall see Him face to face, And tell the sto - ry—Saved by grace.
shall see to face,

514 When the Roll Is Called Up Yonder

I . . . heard behind me a great voice, as of a trumpet. Rev. 1:10

JAMES M. BLACK

JAMES M. BLACK

1. When the trum - pet of the Lord shall sound, and time shall be no more, And the morn - ing breaks, e - ter - nal, bright and fair; When the saved of earth shall gath - er o - ver on the oth - er shore, And the roll is called up yon - der, I'll be there.

2. On that bright and cloud - less morn - ing when the dead in Christ shall rise, And the glo - ry of His res - ur - rec - tion share; When His cho - sen ones shall gath - er to their home be - yond the skies, And the roll is called up yon - der, I'll be there.

3. Let us la - bor for the Mas - ter from the dawn till set - ting sun, Let us talk of all His won - drous love and care; Then when all of life is o - ver, and our work on earth is done, And the roll is called up yon - der, I'll be there.

Chorus

When the roll   is called up
When the roll   is called up

yon - der, When the roll   is called up
yon - der, I'll   be there,   When the roll   is called up

yon - der, When the roll   is called up
yon - der, I'll   be there,   When the roll   is called up

yon - der, When the roll   is called up yon - der, I'll   be there.

515 The King Is Coming

Till they see the Son of man coming in His kingdom. Matt. 16:28

GLORIA GAITHER,
WILLIAM J. GAITHER AND
CHARLES MILHUFF

WILLIAM J. GAITHER

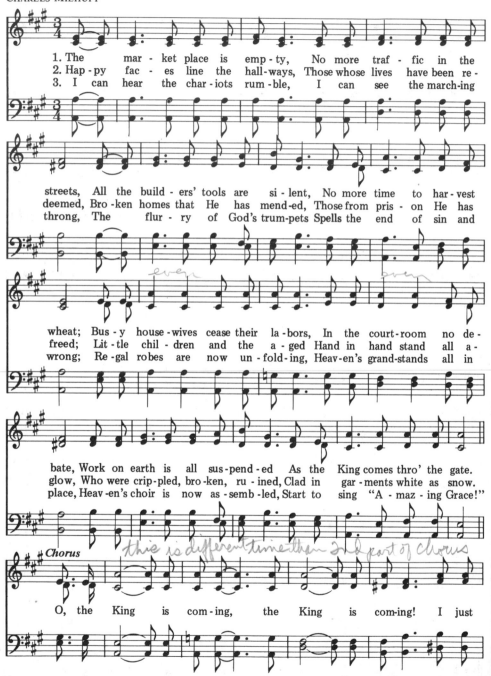

1. The mar-ket place is emp-ty, No more traf-fic in the streets, All the build-ers' tools are si-lent, No more time to har-vest wheat; Bus-y house-wives cease their la-bors, In the court-room no de-bate, Work on earth is all sus-pend-ed As the King comes thro' the gate.

2. Hap-py fac-es line the hall-ways, Those whose lives have been re-deemed, Bro-ken homes that He has mend-ed, Those from pris-on He has freed; Lit-tle chil-dren and the a-ged Hand in hand stand all a-glow, Who were crip-pled, bro-ken, ru-ined, Clad in gar-ments white as snow.

3. I can hear the char-iots rum-ble, I can see the march-ing throng, The flur-ry of God's trum-pets Spells the end of sin and wrong; Re-gal robes are now un-fold-ing, Heav-en's grand-stands all in place, Heav-en's choir is now as-sem-bled, Start to sing "A-maz-ing Grace!"

Chorus

O, the King is com-ing, the King is com-ing! I just

© Copyright 1970 by William J. Gaither. International copyright secured. All rights reserved. Used by permission.

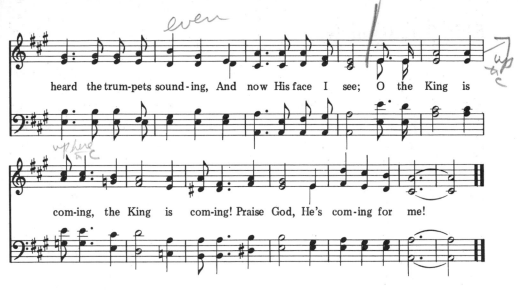

heard the trum-pets sound-ing, And now His face I see; O the King is
com-ing, the King is com-ing! Praise God, He's com-ing for me!

Alleluia! 516

Alleluia; salvation, and glory, and honor and power unto the Lord our God. Rev. 19:1

Source unknown

Source unknown

1. Al - le - lu - ia, al - le - lu - ia, al - le -
2. He's my Sav - ior, al - le - lu - ia, He's my
3. I will praise Him, al - le - lu - ia, I will
4. He is wor - thy, al - le - lu - ia, He is

lu - ia, al - le - lu - ia! Al - le - lu - ia, al - le -
Sav - ior, al - le - lu - ia; He's my Sav - ior, al - le -
praise Him, al - le - lu - ia; I will praise Him, al - le -
wor - thy, al - le - lu - ia; He is wor - thy, al - le -

lu - ia, al - le - lu - ia, al - le - lu - ia!
lu - ia, He's my Sav - ior, al - le - lu - ia.
lu - ia, I will praise Him, al - le - lu - ia.
lu - ia, He is wor - thy, al - le - lu - ia.

517 Beulah Land

Thy land (shall be called) Beulah; for the Lord delighteth in Thee. Isa. 62:4

EDGAR P. STITES

JOHN R. SWENEY

1. I've reached the land of corn and wine, And all its rich - es free - ly mine;
2. My Sav - ior comes and walks with me, And sweet com-mun - ion here have we;
3. A sweet per-fume up - on the breeze Is borne from ev - er - ver - nal trees;
4. The zeph - yrs seem to float to me, Sweet sounds of Heav-en's mel - o - dy,

Here shines un-dimmed one bliss - ful day, For all my night has passed a - way.
He gent - ly leads me by His hand, For this is Heav-en's bor - der-land.
And flow'rs that nev - er - fad - ing grow, Where streams of life for - ev - er flow.
As an - gels with the white-robed throng Join in the sweet re - demp-tion song.

Chorus

O Beu - lah Land, sweet Beu - lah Land, As on thy high - est mount I stand,

I look a - way a - cross the sea, Where man-sions are pre - pared for me, And

view the shin - ing glo - ry shore, My Heav'n, my home for - ev - er - more!

Sweet By and By 518

On either side of the river was there the tree of life ... Rev. 22:2

SANFORD F. BENNETT

JOSEPH P. WEBSTER

1. There's a land that is fair - er than day, And by faith we can
2. We shall sing on that beau - ti - ful shore The me - lo - di - ous
3. To our boun - ti - ful Fa - ther a - bove We will of - fer our

see it a - far, For the Fa - ther waits o - ver the way To pre -
songs of the blest; And our spir - its shall sor - row no more— Not a
trib - ute of praise, For the glo - ri - ous gift of His love And the

Chorus

pare us a dwell - ing place there.
sigh for the bless - ing of rest.
bless - ings that hal - low our days.

In the sweet by and

In the sweet

by, We shall meet on that beau - ti - ful shore; In the

by and by, by and by,

sweet by and by, We shall meet on that beau - ti - ful shore.

In the sweet by and by,

519 When We See Christ

The sufferings (of this present time) are not worthy to be compared with the glory . . . Rom. 8:18

ESTHER K. RUSTHOI   ESTHER K. RUSTHOI

1. Oft-times the day seems long, our tri-als hard to bear, We're tempt-ed to com-plain, to mur-mur and de-spair; But Christ will soon ap-pear to catch His Bride a-way, All tears for-ev-er o-ver in God's e-ter-nal day.

2. Some-times the sky looks dark with not a ray of light, We're tossed and driv-en on, no hu-man help in sight; But there is one in heav'n who knows our deep-est care, Let Je-sus solve your prob-lem— just go to Him in pray'r.

3. Life's day will soon be o'er, all storms for-ev-er past, We'll cross the great di-vide to glo-ry, safe at last; We'll share the joys of heav'n— a harp, a home, a crown, The tempt-er will be ban-ished, we'll lay our bur-den down.

Chorus

It will be worth it all when we see Je-sus, Life's trials will seem so small when we see Christ; One glimpse of His dear face

Copyright 1941. Renewal 1969 by Howard Rusthoi. Assigned to Singspiration, Inc. All rights reserved. Used by permission.

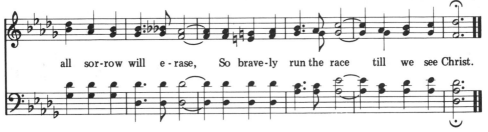

all sor-row will e-rase, So brave-ly run the race till we see Christ.

Face to Face 520

Now we see through a glass, darkly; but then face to face . . . I Cor. 13:12

CARRIE E. BRECK

GRANT C. TULLAR

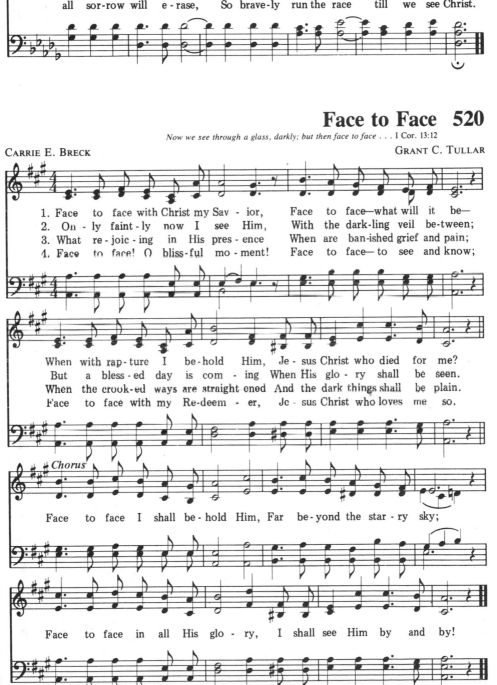

1. Face to face with Christ my Sav - ior, Face to face—what will it be—
2. On - ly faint-ly now I see Him, With the dark-ling veil be-tween;
3. What re-joic-ing in His pres-ence When are ban-ished grief and pain;
4. Face to face! O bliss-ful mo-ment! Face to face—to see and know;

When with rap-ture I be-hold Him, Je-sus Christ who died for me?
But a bless-ed day is com-ing When His glo-ry shall be seen.
When the crook-ed ways are straight-ened And the dark things shall be plain.
Face to face with my Re-deem-er, Je-sus Christ who loves me so.

Chorus

Face to face I shall be-hold Him, Far be-yond the star-ry sky;

Face to face in all His glo-ry, I shall see Him by and by!

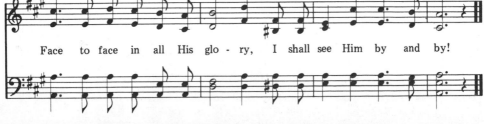

521 He'll Understand and Say, "Well Done"

Well done, thou good and faithful servant . . . Matt. 25:21

LUCY E. CAMPBELL

LUCY E. CAMPBELL
ARR. BY WILLIAM J. FLOYD

1. If when you give the best of your ser - vice, Tell - ing the
2. Mis - un - der - stood, the Sav - ior of sin - ners Hung on the
3. If when this life of la - bor is end - ed, And the re -
4. But if you try and fail in your try - ing, Hands sore and

world that the Sav - ior is come; Be not dis - mayed when men don't be -
cross; He was God's on - ly Son; Oh! hear Him call His Fa - ther in
ward of the race you have run; Oh! take the sweet rest pre - pared for
scarred from the work you've be - gun; Take up your cross, run quick - ly to

lieve you, He un - der - stands; He'll say, "Well done."
heav - en, "Let not my will, but Thine be done."
faith - ful, Will be His blest and fi - nal, "Well done."
meet Him, He'll un - der - stand; He'll say, "Well done."

Chorus

Oh when I come to the end of my jour - ney, Wea - ry of

life and the bat - tle is won; Car - ry - ing the staff and the

Copyright © 1964. Hope Publishing Co., owner. International copyright secured. All rights reserved.

cross of re-demp-tion, He'll un-der-stand and say, "Well done."

He the Pearly Gates Will Open 522

They that do His commandments . . . may enter in through the gates into the city. Rev. 22:14

FREDERICK A. BLOM
TRANS. BY NATHANIEL CARLSON

ATTR. TO ALFRED DULIN
ARR. BY ELSIE AHLWÉN

1. Love di-vine, so great and won-drous, Deep and might-y, pure, sub-lime;
2. Like a dove when hunt-ed, fright-ened, As a wound-ed fawn was I,
3. Love di-vine, so great and won-drous— All my sins He then for-gave,
4. In life's e-ven-tide, at twi-light, At His door I'll knock and wait;

Com-ing from the heart of Je-sus—Just the same thro' tests of time,
Bro-ken heart-ed, yet He healed me— He will heed the sin-ner's cry,
I will sing His praise for-ev-er, For His blood, His pow'r to save.
By the pre-cious love of Je-sus, I shall en-ter heav-en's gate.

Chorus

He the pearl-y gates will o-pen, So that I may en-ter in;

For He pur-chased my re-demp-tion, And for-gave me all my sin.

523 He Is Coming Again

Then shall they see the Son of man coming . . . with power and great glory. Luke 21:27

MABEL J. CAMP   MABEL J. CAMP

1. Lift up your heads, pil-grims a-wea-ry, See day's ap-proach now
2. Dark was the night, sin warred a-gainst us; Heav-y the load of
3. O bless-ed hope! O bliss-ful prom-ise! Fill-ing our hearts with
4. E-ven so come, pre-cious Lord Je-sus; Cre-a-tion waits re-

crim-son the sky; Night shad-ows flee, and your Be-lov-ed,
sor-row we bore; But now we see signs of His com-ing;
rap-ture di-vine; O day of days! hail Thy ap-pear-ing!
demp-tion to see; Caught up in clouds, soon we shall meet Thee;

A-wait-ed with long-ing, at last draw-eth nigh.
Our hearts glow with-in us, joy's cup run-neth o'er!
Thy tran-scen-dent glo-ry for-ev-er shall shine!
O bless-ed as-sur-ance, for-ev-er with Thee!

Chorus

He is com-ing a-gain, He is com-ing a-gain, The ver-y same

Je-sus, re-ject-ed of men; He is com-ing a-gain, He is com-ing a-gain,

Copyright 1913. Renewal 1941 by Norman H. Camp. Assigned to Singspiration, Inc. All rights reserved. Used by permission.

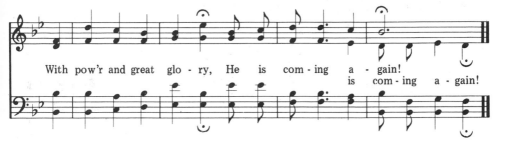

With pow'r and great glo - ry, He is com - ing a - gain!
is com - ing a - gain!

Where the Roses Never Fade 524

And the street of the city was pure gold . . . Rev. 21:21

Elsie, Jack and Jim

Elsie, Jack and Jim

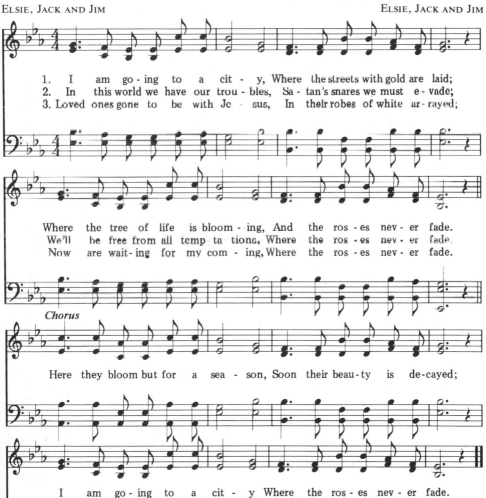

1. I am go - ing to a cit - y, Where the streets with gold are laid;
2. In this world we have our trou - bles, Sa - tan's snares we must e - vade;
3. Loved ones gone to be with Je - sus, In their robes of white ar - rayed;

Where the tree of life is bloom - ing, And the ros - es nev - er fade.
We'll be free from all temp - ta - tions, Where the ros - es nev - er fade.
Now are wait - ing for my com - ing, Where the ros - es nev - er fade.

Chorus

Here they bloom but for a sea - son, Soon their beau - ty is de - cayed;

I am go - ing to a cit - y Where the ros - es nev - er fade.

© Copyright 1942 by Stamps-Baxter Music & Ptg. Co. in "Blessed Hope".
©Copyright renewal 1970 by Stamps-Baxter Music & Ptg. Co. All rights reserved. Used by permission.

525 My Savior First of All

Then shall I know even as also I am known. I Cor. 13:12

FANNY J. CROSBY   JOHN R. SWENEY

1. When my life-work is end-ed and I cross the swell-ing tide,
2. O the soul-thrill-ing rap-ture when I view His bless-ed face
3. O the dear ones in glo-ry, how they beck-on me to come,
4. Thro' the gates to the cit-y, in a robe of spot-less white,

When the bright and glo-rious morn-ing I shall see, I shall know my Re-
And the lus-ter of His kind-ly beam-ing eye; How my full heart will
And our part-ing at the riv-er I re-call; To the sweet vales of
He will lead me where no tears will ev-er fall; In the glad song of

deem-er when I reach the oth-er side, And His smile will be the
praise Him for the mer-cy, love and grace That pre-pare for me a
E-den they will sing my wel-come home—But I long to meet my
a-ges I shall min-gle with de-light—But I long to meet my

Chorus

first to wel-come me.
man-sion in the sky. I shall know Him, I shall
Sav-ior first of all.
Sav-ior first of all. I shall know Him,

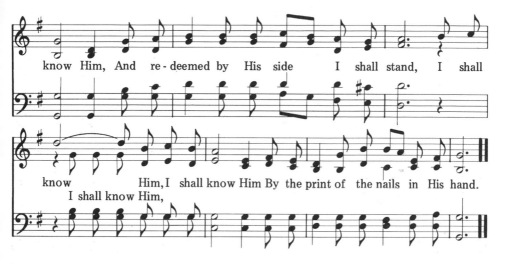

know Him, And re-deemed by His side I shall stand, I shall

know Him, I shall know Him By the print of the nails in His hand.
I shall know Him,

He's Coming Soon 526

Looking for . . . the glorious appearing of . . . our Savior Jesus Christ. Titus 2:13

THORO HARRIS

QUEEN LILIUOKALANI
'ARR. BY THORO HARRIS

He's com-ing soon, He's com-ing soon, With joy we

wel-come His re-turn-ing; It may be morn, it

may be night or noon, We know He's com-ing soon.

Copyright 1916 by Thoro Harris. Renewal 1944. The Rodeheaver Co. All rights reserved. Used by permission.

527 Safe in the Arms of Jesus

He shall gather the lambs with His arm . . . Isa. 40:11

FANNY J. CROSBY

WILLIAM H. DOANE

1. Safe in the arms of Je - sus, Safe on His gen - tle breast, There by His
2. Safe in the arms of Je - sus, Safe from cor - rod - ing care, Safe from the
3. Je - sus, my heart's dear ref - uge, Je - sus has died for me; Firm on the

love o'er - shad - ed, Sweet-ly my soul shall rest. Hark! 'tis the voice of
world's temp - ta - tions, Sin can - not harm me there. Free from the blight of
Rock of A - ges, Ev - er my trust shall be. Here let me wait with

an - gels, Borne in a song to me, O - ver the fields of glo - ry,
sor - row, Free from my doubts and fears; On - ly a few more tri - als,
pa - tience, Wait till the night is o'er; Wait till I see the morn - ing

Chorus

O - ver the jas - per sea.
On - ly a few more tears! Safe in the arms of Je - sus, Safe on His
Break on the gold - en shore.

gen - tle breast, There by His love o'er-shad - ed, Sweet-ly my soul shall rest.

I Won't Have to Cross Jordan Alone 528

Though I walk through the valley of the shadow of death . . . Psa. 23:4

THOMAS RAMSEY   CHARLES E. DURHAM

1. When I come to the riv-er at end-ing of day, When the last winds of
2. Oft-en-times I'm for-sak-en, and wea-ry and sad, When it seems that my
3. Tho' the bil-lows of sor-row and trou-ble may sweep, Christ the Sav-ior will

sor-row have blown; There'll be some-bod-y wait-ing to show me the way,
friends have all gone; There is one tho't that cheers me and makes my heart glad,
care for His own; Till the end of the jour-ney, my soul He will keep;

Chorus

I won't have to cross Jor-dan a - lone. I won't have to cross Jor-dan a-

lone, Je-sus died for my sins to a - tone; When the dark-ness I see,

He'll be wait-ing for me, I won't have to cross Jor-dan a - lone.

© Copyright 1934. Renewal 1962 Broadman Press. All rights reserved. Used by permission.

529 Jesus Is Coming Again

Watch therefore, for ye know neither the day nor the hour . . . Matt. 25:13

JOHN W. PETERSON   JOHN W. PETERSON

1. Mar - vel - ous mes - sage we bring, Glo - ri - ous car - ol we sing,
2. For - est and flow - er ex - claim, Moun - tain and mead - ow the same,
3. Stand - ing be - fore Him at last, Tri - al and trou - ble all past,

Won - der - ful word of the King— Je - sus is com - ing a - gain! (a - gain!)
All earth and heav - en pro - claim— Je - sus is com - ing a - gain! (a - gain!)
Crowns at His feet we will cast— Je - sus is com - ing a - gain! (a - gain!)

Chorus — Unison

Com - ing a - gain, Com - ing a -

gain; May - be morn - ing, may - be noon,

May - be eve - ning and may - be soon! Com - ing a -

© Copyright 1957 by Singspiration, Inc. All rights reserved. Used by permission.

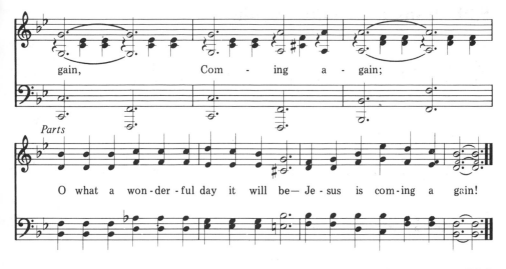

gain, Com - ing a - gain;

Parts

O what a won - der - ful day it will be— Je - sus is com - ing a - gain!

Nearer, Still Nearer 530

For to me to live is Christ, and to die is gain. Phil. 1:21

LELIA N. MORRIS   LELIA N. MORRIS

1. Near - er, still near - er, close to Thy heart, Draw me, my Sav - ior, so pre - cious Thou
2. Near - er, still near - er, noth - ing I bring, Naught as an of - f'ring to Je - sus my
3. Near - er, still near - er, Lord, to be Thine, Sin with its fol - lies I glad - ly re -
4. Near - er, still near - er, while life shall last, Till safe in glo - ry my an - chor is

art; Fold me, O fold me close to Thy breast, Shel - ter me safe in that
King; On - ly my sin - ful, now con - trite heart, Grant me the cleans - ing Thy
sign; All of its pleas - ures, pomp and its pride, Give me but Je - sus, my
cast; Thro' end - less a - ges, ev - er to be Near - er, my Sav - ior, still

"Ha - ven of Rest," Shel - ter me safe in that "Ha - ven of Rest."
blood doth im - part, Grant me the cleans - ing Thy blood doth im - part.
Lord cru - ci - fied, Give me but Je - sus, my Lord cru - ci - fied.
near - er to Thee, Near - er, my Sav - ior, still near - er to Thee. A - men.

531 What If It Were Today?

The Lord Himself shall descend from heaven with a shout . . . I Thess. 4:16

LELIA N. MORRIS

LELIA N. MORRIS

1. Je - sus is com - ing to earth a - gain, What if it were to - day?
2. Sa - tan's do - min - ion will soon be o'er, O, that it were to - day!
3. Faith-ful and true would He find us here, If He should come to - day?

Com - ing in pow - er and love to reign, What if it were to - day?
Sor - row and sigh - ing shall be no more, O, that it were to - day!
Watch-ing in glad-ness and not in fear, If He should come to - day?

Com - ing to claim His cho - sen Bride, All the re - deemed and pu - ri - fied,
Then shall the dead in Christ a - rise, Caught up to meet Him in the skies,
Signs of His com - ing mul - ti - ply, Morn - ing light breaks in east - ern sky,

O - ver this whole earth scat - tered wide, What if it were to - day?
When shall these glo - ries meet our eyes? What if it were to - day?
Watch, for that time is draw - ing nigh, What if it were to - day?

Copyright 1912. Renewal 1940 extended. Hope Publishing Co.. owner. All rights reserved.

Chorus

Glo - ry, glo - ry! Joy to my heart 'twill bring;
Joy to my heart 'twill bring;

Glo - ry, glo - ry! When we shall crown Him King;
When we shall crown Him King;

Glo - ry, glo - ry! Haste to pre - pare the way;
Haste to pre - pare the way;

Glo - ry, glo - ry! Je - sus will come some day.

532 O That Will Be Glory

We shall be like Him; for we shall see Him as He is. I John 3:2

CHARLES H. GABRIEL

CHARLES H. GABRIEL

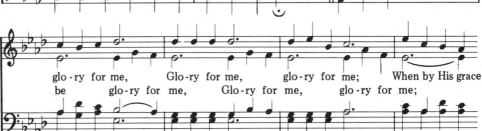

1. When all my la-bors and tri-als are o'er, And I am safe on that
2. When by the gift of His in-fi-nite grace, I am ac-cord-ed in
3. Friends will be there I have loved long a-go; Joy like a riv-er a-

beau-ti-ful shore, Just to be near the dear Lord I a-dore
heav-en a place, Just to be there and to look on His face
round me will flow; Yet, just a smile from my Sav-ior, I know,

Chorus

Will through the a-ges be glo-ry for me. O that will be

O that will

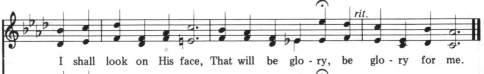

glo-ry for me, Glo-ry for me, glo-ry for me; When by His grace
be glo-ry for me, Glo-ry for me, glo-ry for me;

rit.

I shall look on His face, That will be glo-ry, be glo-ry for me.

When We All Get to Heaven 533

. . . At Thy right hand there are pleasures for evermore. Psa. 16:11

ELIZA E. HEWITT

EMILY D. WILSON

1. Sing the won-drous love of Je - sus, Sing His mer - cy
2. While we walk the pil - grim path - way Clouds will o - ver -
3. Let us then be true and faith - ful, Trust - ing, serv - ing
4. On - ward to the prize be - fore us! Soon His beau - ty

and His grace; In the man - sions bright and bless - ed He'll pre -
spread the sky; But when trav - 'ling days are o - ver, Not a
ev - ery day; Just one glimpse of Him in glo - ry Will the
we'll be - hold; Soon the pearl - y gates will o - pen, We shall

Chorus

pare for us a place.
sha - dow, not a sigh. When we all get to heav - en,
toils of life re - pay. When we all
tread the streets of gold.

What a day of re - joic - ing that will be! When we
What a day of re - joic - ing that will be!

all see Je - sus, We'll sing and shout the vic - to - ry.
When we all and shout the vic - to - ry.

534 Some Golden Daybreak

For the Lord Himself shall descend from heaven with a shout . . . I Thess. 4:16

CARL A. BLACKMORE   CARL A. BLACKMORE

1. Some glo-rious morn-ing sor-row will cease, Some glo-rious morn-ing
2. Sad hearts will glad-den, all shall be bright, Good-bye for-ev-er
3. Oh, what a meet-ing, there in the skies, No tears nor cry-ing

all will be peace; Heart-aches all end-ed, school-days all done,
to earth's dark night; Changed in a mo-ment, like Him to be,
shall dim our eyes; Loved ones u-nit-ed e-ter-nal-ly,

Chorus

Heav-en will o-pen— Je-sus will come.
Oh, glo-rious day-break, Je-sus I'll see. Some gold-en day-break
Oh, what a day-break that morn will be.

Je-sus will come; Some gold-en day-break, bat-tles all won, He'll shout the

vic-t'ry, break thro' the blue, Some gold-en day-break, for me, for you.

Copyright 1934 by Blackmore & Son. © Renewed 1962 by Carl A. Blackmore. The Rodeheaver Co., owner. Used by permission.

Christ Returneth 535

Ye shall see the Son of man . . . coming in the clouds of heaven. Mark 14:62

H. L. TURNER

JAMES McGRANAHAN

1. It may be at morn, when the day is a-wak-ing, When
2. It may be at mid-day, it may be at twi-light, It
3. While hosts cry Ho-san-na, from heav-en de-scend-ing, With
4. O joy! O de-light! should we go with-out dy-ing, No

sun-light through dark-ness and shad-ow is break-ing, That Je-sus will
may be, per-chance, that the black-ness of mid-night Will burst in-to
glo-ri-fied saints and the an-gels at-tend-ing, With grace on His
sick-ness, no sad-ness, no dread and no cry-ing, Caught up through the

come in the full-ness of glo-ry, To re-ceive from the world His own.
light in the blaze of His glo-ry, When Je-sus re-ceives His own.
brow, like a ha-lo of glo-ry, Will Je-sus re-ceive His own.
clouds with our Lord in-to glo-ry, When Je-sus re-ceives His own.

Chorus

O Lord Je-sus, how long, how long Ere we shout the glad song, Christ re-
turn-eth! Hal-le-lu-jah! hal-le-lu-jah! A-men, Hal-le-lu-jah! A-men.

9-22-85 choir

536 Mansion over the Hilltop

In my Father's house are many mansions . . . John 14:2

IRA STANPHILL   IRA STANPHILL

1. I'm sat - is - fied with just a cot - tage be - low, A lit - tle
2. Tho' oft - en temp - ted, tor - ment - ed and test - ed, And like the
3. Don't think me poor or de - sert - ed or lone - ly, I'm not dis -

sil - ver and a lit - tle gold; But in that ci - ty
proph - et, my pil - low a stone; And though I find here
cour - aged, I'm heav - en bound; I'm just a pil - grim

where the ran - somed will shine, I want a gold one
no per - ma - nent dwell - ing, I know He'll give me
in search of a ci - ty, I want a man - sion,

Chorus

that's sil - ver lined.
a man - sion my own.   I've got a man - sion just o - ver the
a robe and a crown.

hill - top, In that bright land where we'll nev - er grow old;

Copyright 1949. Renewal 1977 by Ira Stanphill. Assigned to Singspiration, Division of The Zondervan Corporation. All rights reserved. Used by permission.

And some day yon - der we will nev - er more wan - der, But walk the streets that are pur - est gold.

We Would See Jesus 537

Sir, we would see Jesus, John 12:21

ANNA B. WARNER

FELIX MENDELSSOHN

1. We would see Je - sus, for the shad - ows length - en A - cross this lit - tle land - scape of our life; We would see Je - sus, our weak faith to strength - en For the last wea - ri - ness, the fi - nal strife.

2. We would see Je - sus, the great rock foun - da - tion, Where - on our feet were set by sov - 'reign grace; Not life, nor death, with all their ag - i - ta - tion, Can thence re - move us, if we see His face.

3. We would see Je - sus, oth - er lights are pal - ing, Which for long years we have re - joiced to see; The bless - ings of our pil - grim - age are fail - ing; We would not mourn them, for we go to Thee.

4. We would see Je - sus; this is all we're need - ing; Strength, joy, and will - ing - ness come with the sight; We would see Je - sus, dy - ing, ris - en, plead - ing; Then wel - come, day! and fare - well, mor - tal night!

538 Sun of My Soul

The darkness and the light are both alike to Thee. Psa. 139:12

JOHN KEBLE

Arr. from *Katholisches Gesangbuch*, Vienna, c. 1774

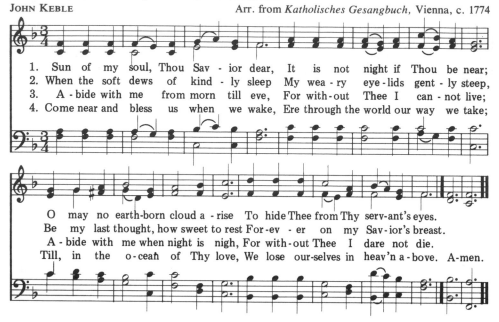

1. Sun of my soul, Thou Sav - ior dear, It is not night if Thou be near;
2. When the soft dews of kind - ly sleep My wea - ry eye - lids gent - ly steep,
3. A - bide with me from morn till eve, For with - out Thee I can - not live;
4. Come near and bless us when we wake, Ere through the world our way we take;

O may no earth-born cloud a - rise To hide Thee from Thy serv-ant's eyes.
Be my last thought, how sweet to rest For - ev - er on my Sav - ior's breast.
A - bide with me when night is nigh, For with - out Thee I dare not die.
Till, in the o - cean of Thy love, We lose our - selves in heav'n a - bove. A - men.

539 Now the Day Is Over

Thou shalt lie down, and thy sleep shall be sweet. Prov. 3:24

SABINE BARING-GOULD

JOSEPH BARNBY

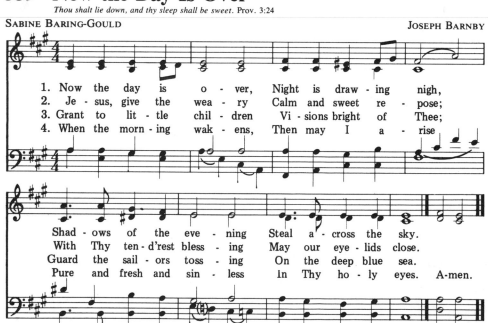

1. Now the day is o - ver, Night is draw - ing nigh,
2. Je - sus, give the wea - ry Calm and sweet re - pose;
3. Grant to lit - tle chil - dren Vi - sions bright of Thee;
4. When the morn - ing wak - ens, Then may I a - rise

Shad - ows of the eve - ning Steal a - cross the sky.
With Thy ten - d'rest bless - ing May our eye - lids close.
Guard the sail - ors toss - ing On the deep blue sea.
Pure and fresh and sin - less In Thy ho - ly eyes. A - men.

Day Is Dying in the West 540

Holy, holy, holy, is the Lord of Hosts . . . Isa. 6:3

MARY A. LATHBURY

WILLIAM F. SHERWIN

1. Day is dy - ing in the west, Heav'n is touch - ing earth with rest;
2. Lord of life, be - neath the dome Of the u - ni - verse, Thy home,
3. While the deep - 'ning shad - ows fall, Heart of Love, en - fold - ing all,
4. When for - ev - er from our sight Pass the stars, the day, the night,

Wait and wor - ship while the night Sets her eve - ning
Gath - er us, who seek Thy face, To the fold of
Thro' the glo - ry and the grace Of the stars that
Lord of an - gels, on our eyes Let e - ter - nal

Chorus

lamps a - light Thro' all the sky.
Thy em - brace, For Thou art nigh.
veil Thy face, Our hearts as - cend.
morn - ing rise, And shad - ows end!

Ho - ly, ho - ly,

ho - ly, Lord God of Hosts! Heav'n and earth are full of Thee!

Heav'n and earth are prais - ing Thee, O Lord most high! A - men.

541 Abide with Me

They constrained Him, saying, Abide with us. Luke 24:29

HENRY F. LYTE   WILLIAM H. MONK

1. A - bide with me: fast falls the e - ven - tide;
2. Swift to its close ebbs out life's lit - tle day;
3. I need Thy pres - ence ev - ery pass - ing hour;
4. I fear no foe, with Thee at hand to bless;
5. Hold Thou Thy cross be - fore my clos - ing eyes;

The dark - ness deep - ens; Lord, with me a - bide!
Earth's joys grow dim, its glo - ries pass a - way;
What but Thy grace can foil the tempt - er's power?
Ills have no weight, and tears no bit - ter - ness.
Shine through the gloom and point me to the skies:

When oth - er help - ers fail, and com - forts flee,
Change and de - cay in all a - round I see.
Who, like Thy - self, my guide and stay can be?
Where is death's sting? Where, grave, thy vic - to - ry?
Heav'n's morn - ing breaks, and earth's vain shad - ows flee;

Help of the help - less, O a - bide with me.
O Thou who chang - est not, a - bide with me.
Through cloud and sun - shine, Lord, a - bide with me.
I tri - umph still, if Thou a - bide with me.
In life, in death, O Lord, a - bide with me. A - men.

O Perfect Love 542

. . . And shall be joined unto his wife, and they two shall be one flesh. Eph. 5:31

DOROTHY F. GURNEY
ST. 4, JOHN ELLERTON

JOSEPH BARNBY

1. O per - fect Love, all hu - man thought tran - scend - ing,
2. O per - fect Life, be Thou their full as - sur - ance
3. Grant them the joy which bright - ens earth - ly sor - row;
4. Hear us, O Fa - ther, gra - cious and for - giv - ing,

Low - ly we kneel in prayer be - fore Thy throne,
Of ten - der char - i - ty and stead - fast faith,
Grant them the peace which calms all earth - ly strife,
Through Je - sus Christ, Thy co - e - ter - nal Word,

That theirs may be the love which knows no end - ing,
Of pa - tient hope, and qui - et, brave en - dur - ance,
And to life's day the glo - rious, un - known mor - row
Who, with the Ho - ly Ghost, by all things liv - ing

Whom Thou for - ev - er - more dost join in one.
With child - like trust that fears not pain nor death.
That dawns up - on e - ter - nal love and life.
Now and to end - less a - ges art a - dored. A - men.

Words by permission of Oxford University Press, London.

543 Come, Ye Thankful People, Come

The harvest is the end of the world; and the reapers are the angeles. Matt. 13:39

HENRY ALFORD   GEORGE J. ELVEY

1. Come, ye thank-ful peo-ple, come, Raise the song of har-vest-home:
2. All the world is God's own field, Fruit un-to His praise to yield;
3. For the Lord our God shall come, And shall take His har-vest home;
4. E-ven so, Lord, quick-ly come To Thy fi-nal har-vest-home;

All is safe-ly gath-ered in, Ere the win-ter storms be-gin;
Wheat and tares to-geth-er sown, Un-to joy or sor-row grown;
From His field shall in that day All of-fens-es purge a-way;
Gath-er Thou Thy peo-ple in, Free from sor-row, free from sin;

God, our Ma-ker, doth pro-vide For our wants to be sup-plied:
First the blade, and then the ear, Then the full corn shall ap-pear:
Give His an-gels charge at last In the fire the tares to cast;
There, for-ev-er pu-ri-fied, In Thy pres-ence to a-bide:

Come to God's own tem-ple, come, Raise the song of har-vest-home.
Lord of har-vest, grant that we Whole-some grain and pure may be.
But the fruit-ful ears to store In His gar-ner ev-er-more.
Come, with all Thine an-gels, come, Raise the glo-rious har-vest-home. A-men.

Now Thank We All Our God 544

Now therefore, our God, we thank Thee, and praise Thy Glorious name. I Chron. 29:13

MARTIN RINKART
TRANS. BY CATHERINE WINKWORTH

JOHANN CRÜGER

1. Now thank we all our God With heart and hands and voic - es,
2. O may this boun-teous God Through all our life be near us,
3. All praise and thanks to God The Fa - ther now be giv - en,

Who won-drous things hath done, In whom His world re - joic - es;
With ev - er joy - ful hearts And bless - ed peace to cheer us;
The Son, and Him who reigns With them in high - est heav - en,

Who, from our moth - er's arms, Hath blessed us on our way
And keep us in His grace And guide us when per - plexed,
The one e - ter - nal God Whom earth and heav'n a - dore;

With count-less gifts of love, And still is ours to - day.
And free us from all ills In this world and the next.
For thus it was, is now, And shall be ev - er - more. A - men.

545 Count Your Blessings

Many, O Lord my God, are Thy wonderful works . . . Psa. 40:5

JOHNSON OATMAN, JR.

EDWIN O. EXCELL

1. When up-on life's bil-lows you are tem-pest-tossed, When you are dis-
2. Are you ev-er bur-dened with a load of care? Does the cross seem
3. When you look at oth-ers with their lands and gold, Think that Christ has
4. So a-mid the con-flict, wheth-er great or small, Do not be dis-

cour-aged, think-ing all is lost, Count your man-y bless-ings—name them
heav-y you are called to bear? Count your man-y bless-ings— ev-ery
prom-ised you His wealth un-told; Count your man-y bless-ings—mon-ey
cour-aged—God is o-ver all; Count your man-y bless-ings— an-gels

one by one, And it will sur-prise you what the Lord has done.
doubt will fly, And you will be sing-ing as the days go by.
can-not buy Your re-ward in heav-en nor your home on high.
will at-tend, Help and com-fort give you to your jour-ney's end.

Chorus

Count your bless-ings—name them one by one; Count your
Count your man-y bless-ings— name them one by one; Count your man-y

bless-ings—see what God has done; Count your bless-ings—
bless-ings— see what God has done; Count your man-y bless-ings—

name them one by one; Count your man - y bless - ings—see what God has done.

We Gather Together 546

If God be for us, who can be against us? Rom. 8:31

Netherlands folk hymn
TRANS. BY THEODORE BAKER

Nederlandtsch Gedenckelanck, 1626
ARR. BY EDWARD KREMSER

1. We gath - er to - geth - er to ask the Lord's bless - ing;
2. Be - side us to guide us, our God with us join - ing,
3. We all do ex - tol Thee, Thou Lead - er tri - um - phant,

He chas - tens and has - tens His will to make known;
Or - dain - ing, main - tain - ing His king - dom di - vine;
And pray that Thou still our De - fend - er wilt be.

The wick - ed op - press - ing now cease from dis - tress - ing,
So from the be - gin - ning the fight we were win - ning:
Let Thy con - gre - ga - tion es - cape trib - u - la - tion:

Sing prais - es to His name: He for - gets not His own.
Thou, Lord, wast at our side, all glo - ry be Thine!
Thy name be ev - er praised! O Lord, make us free! A - men.

547 God of Our Fathers

The Lord of hosts is with us; the God of Jacob is our refuge. Psa. 46:7

DANIEL C. ROBERTS

GEORGE W. WARREN

1. God of our fa - thers, whose al - might - y
2. Thy love di - vine hath led us in the
3. From war's a - larms, from dead - ly pes - ti-
4. Re - fresh Thy peo - ple on their toil - some

hand   Leads forth in beau - ty all the star - ry
past;   In this free land by Thee our lot is
lence,   Be Thy strong arm our ev - er sure de-
way;   Lead us from night to nev - er - end - ing

band   Of shin - ing worlds in splen - dor through the
cast;   Be Thou our Rul - er, Guard - ian, Guide and
fense;   Thy true re - lig - ion in our hearts in-
day;   Fill all our lives with love and grace di-

skies,   Our grate - ful songs be - fore Thy throne a - rise.
Stay,   Thy Word our law, Thy paths our cho - sen way.
crease,   Thy boun - teous good - ness nour - ish us in peace.
vine;   And glo - ry, laud, and praise be ev - er Thine. A - men.

O Beautiful for Spacious Skies 548

Blessed is the nation whose God is the Lord. Psa. 33:12

KATHARINE L. BATES

SAMUEL A. WARD

1. O beau - ti - ful for spa - cious skies, For am - ber waves of grain,
2. O beau - ti - ful for pil - grim feet, Whose stern im - pas - sioned stress
3. O beau - ti - ful for he - roes proved In lib - er - at - ing strife,
4. O beau - ti - ful for pa - triot dream That sees be - yond the years

For pur - ple moun - tain maj - es - ties A - bove the fruit - ed plain!
A thor - ough - fare for free - dom beat A - cross the wil - der - ness!
Who more than self their coun - try loved, And mer - cy more than life!
Thine al - a - bas - ter cit - ies gleam, Un - dimmed by hu - man tears!

A - mer - i - ca! A - mer - i - ca! God shed His grace on thee,
A - mer - i - ca! A - mer - i - ca! God mend thine ev - ery flaw,
A - mer - i - ca! A - mer - i - ca! May God thy gold re - fine,
A - mer - i - ca! A - mer - i - ca! God shed His grace on thee,

And crown thy good with broth - er - hood From sea to shin - ing sea!
Con - firm thy soul in self - con - trol, Thy lib - er - ty in law!
Till all suc - cess be no - ble - ness, And ev - ery gain di - vine!
And crown thy good with broth - er - hood From sea to shin - ing sea! A - men.

549 The Star-Spangled Banner

It is better to trust in the Lord than to put confidence in princes. Psa. 118:9

FRANCIS SCOTT KEY

ATTR. TO JOHN STAFFORD SMITH

1. O say, can you see, by the dawn's ear - ly light, What so
2. O thus be it ev - er, when free men shall stand Be -

proud - ly we hailed at the twi - light's last gleam - ing, Whose broad
tween their loved homes and the war's des - o - la - tion! Blest with

stripes and bright stars, thro' the per - il - ous fight, O'er the
vic - t'ry and peace, may the heav'n - res - cued land Praise the

ram - parts we watched, were so gal - lant - ly stream - ing? And the
Pow'r that hath made and pre - served us a na - tion! Then

550 Faith of Our Fathers

Earnestly contend for the faith which was once delivered unto the saints. Jude 3

FREDERICK W. FABER

HENRI F. HEMY
ARR. BY JAMES G. WALTON

1. Faith of our fa - thers! liv - ing still In spite of dun - geon, fire and sword:
2. Our fa-thers, chained in pris - ons dark, Were still in heart and con-science free:
3. Faith of our fa - thers! we will strive To win all na - tions un - to thee,
4. Faith of our fa - thers! we will love Both friend and foe in all our strife:

O how our hearts beat high with joy When-e'er we hear that glo - rious word!
How sweet would be their chil-dren's fate, If they like them could die for thee!
And thro' the truth that comes from God, Man-kind shall then be tru - ly free.
And preach thee too as love knows how, By kind - ly words and vir - tuous life:

Faith of our fa - thers, ho - ly faith! We will be true to thee till death!
Faith of our fa - thers, ho - ly faith! We will be true to thee till death!
Faith of our fa - thers, ho - ly faith! We will be true to thee till death!
Faith of our fa - thers, ho - ly faith! We will be true to thee till death! A - men.

551 We Give Thee But Thine Own

Of Thine own have we given Thee. I Chron. 29:14

WILLIAM W. HOW

JOSEPH BARNBY

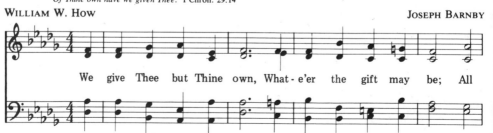

We give Thee but Thine own, What - e'er the gift may be; All

that we have is Thine a-lone, A trust, O Lord, from Thee. A-men.

My Country, 'Tis of Thee 552

Righteousness exalteth a nation: but sin is a reproach to any people. Prov. 14:34

SAMUEL F. SMITH

Thesaurus Masicus, c. 1745

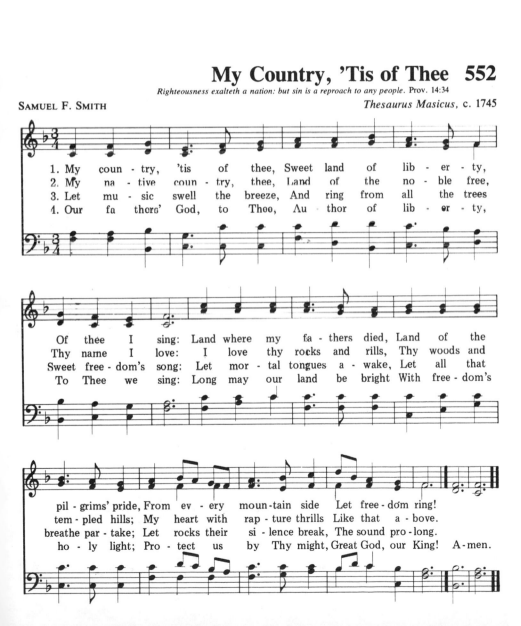

1. My coun-try, 'tis of thee, Sweet land of lib-er-ty,
Of thee I sing: Land where my fa-thers died, Land of the
pil-grims' pride, From ev-ery moun-tain side Let free-dom ring!

2. My na-tive coun-try, thee, Land of the no-ble free,
Thy name I love: I love thy rocks and rills, Thy woods and
tem-pled hills; My heart with rap-ture thrills Like that a-bove.

3. Let mu-sic swell the breeze, And ring from all the trees
Sweet free-dom's song: Let mor-tal tongues a-wake, Let all that
breathe par-take; Let rocks their si-lence break, The sound pro-long.

4. Our fa-thers' God, to Thee, Au-thor of lib-er-ty,
To Thee we sing: Long may our land be bright With free-dom's
ho-ly light; Pro-tect us by Thy might, Great God, our King! A-men.

553 Battle Hymn of the Republic

He is terrible to the kings of the earth. Psa. 76:12

JULIA W. HOWE

Traditional American melody

1. Mine eyes have seen the glo-ry of the com-ing of the Lord; He is
2. I have seen Him in the watch-fires of a hun-dred cir-cling camps; They have
3. He has sound-ed forth the trum-pet that shall nev-er sound re-treat; He is
4. In the beau-ty of the lil-ies, Christ was born a-cross the sea, With a

trampling out the vin-tage where the grapes of wrath are stored; He hath loosed the
build-ed Him an al-tar in the eve-ning dews and damps; I can read His
sift-ing out the hearts of men be-fore His judg-ment seat; O be swift, my
glo-ry in His bos-om that trans-fig-ures you and me; As He died to

fate-ful light-ning of His ter-ri-ble swift sword; His truth is march-ing on.
right-eous sen-tence by the dim and flar-ing lamps; His day is march-ing on.
soul, to an-swer Him! be ju-bi-lant, my feet! Our God is march-ing on.
make men ho-ly, let us live to make men free, While God is march-ing on.

Chorus

Glo-ry! glo-ry, hal-le-lu-jah! Glo-ry! glo-ry, hal-le-lu-jah!

Glo-ry! glo-ry, hal-le-lu-jah! Our God is march-ing on.

Praise God from Whom All Blessings 554

Let everything that hath breath praise the Lord. Psa. 150:6

DOXOLOGY
THOMAS KEN

Genevan Psalter, 1551

Praise God from whom all bless-ings flow; Praise Him, all crea-tures here be-low;

Praise Him a-bove, ye heav'n-ly host; Praise Fa-ther, Son, and Ho-ly Ghost. A-men.

God Be with You 555

And now, brethern, I commend you to God . . . Acts 20:32

JEREMIAH E. RANKIN

WILLIAM G. TOMER

1. God be with you till we meet a-gain; By His coun-sels guide, up-hold you,
2. God be with you till we meet a-gain; 'Neath His wings pro-tect-ing hide you,
3. God be with you till we meet a-gain; When life's per-ils thick con-found you,
4. God be with you till we meet a-gain; Keep love's ban-ner float-ing o'er you,

With His sheep se-cure-ly fold you; God be with you till we meet a-gain.
Dai-ly man-na still pro-vide you; God be with you till we meet a-gain.
Put His arms un-fail-ing round you; God be with you till we meet a-gain.
Smite death's threat'ning wave before you; God be with you till we meet a-gain.

556 The Lord Is in His Holy Temple

I will come into Thy house and . . . worship toward Thy holy temple. Psa. 5:7

HABAKKUK 2:20

GEORGE F. ROOT

The Lord is in His ho - ly tem - ple, The Lord is in His ho - ly tem - ple; Let all the earth keep si - lence, Let all the earth keep si - lence be - fore Him, Keep si - lence, keep si - lence be - fore Him. A - men.

557 All Things Come of Thee, O Lord

I CHRON. 29:14

JOHN F. WILSON

All things come of Thee, O Lord, And of Thine own have we giv - en Thee. A - men.

Copyright © 1967. Hope Publishing Co., owner. International copyright secured. All rights reserved.

Oh, How He Loves You and Me 558

...Behold how He loved him. John 11:36

KURT KAISER

KURT KAISER

Oh, how He loves you and me! Oh, how He
loves you and me! He gave His life, what
more could He give? Oh, how He loves you, Oh, how He
loves me, Oh, how He loves you and me!

Music copyright 1975, and words and arr. of music © 1975 by Word Music, Inc. International copyright secured. All rights reserved. Used by permission.

559 Glory Be to the Father

Give unto the Lord the glory due unto His name. I Chron. 16:29

Gloria Patri
Traditional

HENRY W. GREATOREX

Glo - ry be to the Fa - ther, and to the Son, and to the Ho - ly Ghost; As it was in the be - gin - ning, is now, and ev - er shall be, world with - out end. A - men, A - men.

560 Glory Be to the Father

Gloria Patri
Traditional

CHRISTOPH MEINEKE

Glo - ry be to the Fa - ther, and to the Son, and to the Ho - ly Ghost; As it was in the be - gin - ning, is now, and ev - er shall be, world with - out end. A - men, A - men.

SCRIPTURE READINGS

The text used for the readings is the King James Version. The readings are arranged, generally, as follows: God the Father, life of Christ, the Holy Spirit, the church, and the Christian life. An Index to Scripture Readings is on page 595.

562 GOD THE CREATOR

In the beginning God created the heaven and the earth.

And the earth was without form, and void; and darkness was upon the face of the deep.

And the Spirit of God moved upon the face of the waters. And God said, Let there be light: and there was light.

And God saw the light, that it was good: and God divided the light from the darkness.

And God called the light Day, and the darkness he called Night.

And the evening and the morning were the first day.
—Genesis 1:1-5.

By the word of the Lord were the heavens made; and all the host of them by the breath of his mouth.

He gathereth the waters of the sea together as an heap: he layeth up the depth in storehouses.

Let all the earth fear the Lord: let all the inhabitants of the world stand in awe of him.

For he spake, and it was done; he commanded, and it stood fast.
—Psalm 33:6-9.

Let us come before his presence with thanksgiving, and make a joyful noise unto him with psalms.

For the Lord is a great God, and a great King above all gods.

In his hand are the deep places of the earth: the strength of the hills is his also.

The sea is his, and he made it: and his hands formed the dry land.

O come, let us worship and bow down: let us kneel before the Lord our maker.

For he is our God; and we are the people of his pasture, and the sheep of his hand.   —Psalm 95:2-7.

563 GOD'S OMNISCIENCE

O Lord, thou hast searched me, and known me.

Thou knowest my downsitting and mine uprising, thou understandest my thought afar off.

Thou compassest my path and my lying down, and art acquainted with all my ways.

For there is not a word in my tongue, but, lo, O Lord, thou knowest it altogether.

Thou hast beset me behind and before, and laid thine hand upon me.

Such knowledge is too wonderful for me; it is high, I cannot attain unto it.

Whither shall I go from thy spirit? or whither shall I flee from thy presence?

If I ascend up into heaven, thou art there: if I make my bed in hell, behold, thou art there.

If I take the wings of the morning, and dwell in the uttermost parts of the sea;

Even there shall thy hand lead me, and thy right hand shall hold me.

If I say, Surely the darkness shall cover me; even the night shall be light about me.

Yea, the darkness hideth not from thee; but the night shineth as the day: the darkness and the light are both alike to thee.

I will praise thee; for I am fearfully and wonderfully made: marvellous are thy works; and that my soul knoweth right well.

Search me, O God, and know my heart: try me, and know my thoughts: and see if there be any wicked way in me, and lead me in the way everlasting.
—Psalm 139:1-12, 14, 23, 24.

564 GOD'S CARE

I will lift up mine eyes unto the hills, from whence cometh my help.

My help cometh from the Lord, which made heaven and earth.

He will not suffer thy foot to be moved: he that keepeth thee will not slumber.

Behold, he that keepeth Israel shall neither slumber nor sleep.

The Lord is thy keeper: the Lord is thy shade upon thy right hand.

The sun shall not smite thee by day, nor the moon by night.

The Lord shall preserve thee from all evil: he shall preserve thy soul.

The Lord shall preserve thy going out and thy coming in from this time forth, and even for evermore.
—Psalm 121.

565 THE SHEPHERD PSALM

The Lord is my shepherd; I shall not want.

He maketh me to lie down in green pastures: he leadeth me beside the still waters.

He restoreth my soul: he leadeth me in the paths of righteousness for his name's sake.

Yea, though I walk through the valley of the shadow of death, I will fear no evil:

For thou art with me; thy rod and thy staff they comfort me.

Thou preparest a table before me in the presence of mine enemies:

Thou anointest my head with oil; my cup runneth over.

Surely goodness and mercy shall follow me all the days of my life: and I will dwell in the house of the Lord for ever. —Psalm 23.

566 DIVINE PROVIDENCE

I will bless the Lord at all times: his praise shall continually be in my mouth.

My soul shall make her boast in the Lord: the humble shall hear thereof, and be glad.

O magnify the Lord with me, and let us exalt his name together.

I sought the Lord, and he heard me, and delivered me from all my fears.

They looked unto him, and were lightened: and their faces were not ashamed.

This poor man cried, and the Lord heard him, and saved him out of all his troubles.

The angel of the Lord encampeth round about them that fear him, and delivereth them.

O taste and see that the Lord is good: blessed is the man that trusteth in him.

O fear the Lord, ye his saints: for there is no want to them that fear him.

The young lions do lack, and suffer hunger: but they that seek the Lord shall not want any good thing.

The righteous cry, and the Lord heareth, and delivereth them out of all their troubles.

The Lord is nigh unto them that are of a broken heart; and saveth such as be of a contrite spirit.

Many are the afflictions of the righteous: but the Lord delivereth him out of them all.

The Lord redeemeth the soul of his servants: and none of them that trust in him shall be desolate.
—Psalm 34:1-10, 17-19, 22.

567 GOD'S COMMANDMENTS

I am the Lord thy God, which have brought thee out of the land of Egypt, out of the house of bondage. Thou shalt have no other gods before me.

Thou shalt not make unto thee any graven image, or any likeness of any thing that is in heaven above, or that is in the earth beneath, or that is in the water under the earth: thou shalt not bow down thyself to them, nor serve them:

Thou shalt not take the name of the Lord thy God in vain;

For the Lord will not hold him guiltless that taketh his name in vain.

Remember the sabbath day, to keep it holy. For in six days the Lord made heaven and earth, the sea, and all that in them is, and rested the seventh day:

Wherefore the Lord blessed the sabbath day, and hallowed it.

Honour thy father and thy mother: that thy days may be long upon the land which the Lord thy God giveth thee.

Thou shalt not kill.

Thou shalt not commit adultery.

Thou shalt not steal.

Thou shalt not bear false witness against thy neighbour.

Thou shalt not covet thy neighbour's house, thou shalt not covet thy neighbour's wife, nor his manservant, nor his maidservant, nor his ox, nor his ass, nor any thing that is thy neighbour's.
—Exodus 20:2-5, 7, 8, 11-17.

Thou shalt love the Lord thy God with all thy heart, and with all thy soul, and with all thy mind. This is the first and great commandment.

And the second is like unto it, Thou shalt love thy neighbour as thyself. On these two commandments hang all the law and the prophets.
—Matthew 22:37-40.

568 WORSHIP OF GOD

O sing unto the Lord a new song: sing unto the Lord, all the earth.

Sing unto the Lord, bless his name; shew forth his salvation from day to day.

Declare his glory among the heathen, his wonders among all people.

For the Lord is great, and greatly to be praised: he is to be feared above all gods.

For all the gods of the nations are idols: but the Lord made the heavens.

Honour and majesty are before him: strength and beauty are in his sanctuary.

Give unto the Lord, O ye kindreds of the people, give unto the Lord glory and strength.

Give unto the Lord the glory due unto his name: bring an offering, and come into his courts.

O worship the Lord in the beauty of holiness: fear before him, all the earth.

Say among the heathen that the Lord reigneth: the world also shall be established that it shall not be moved: he shall judge the people righteously.

Let the heavens rejoice, and let the earth be glad;

Let the sea roar, and the fulness thereof. Let the field be joyful, and all that is therein.

Then shall all the trees of the wood rejoice before the Lord: for he cometh, for he cometh to judge the earth:

He shall judge the world with rightousness, and the people with his truth. —Psalm 96.

569   THANKSGIVING TO GOD

Bless the Lord, O my soul: and all that is within me, bless his holy name.

Bless the Lord, O my soul, and forget not all his benefits:

Who forgiveth all thine iniquities; who healeth all thy diseases;

Who redeemeth thy life from destruction; who crowneth thee with lovingkindness and tender mercies;

Who satisfieth thy mouth with good things; so that thy youth is renewed like the eagle's.

The Lord executeth righteousness and judgment for all that are oppressed.

He made known his ways unto Moses, his acts unto the children of Israel.

The Lord is merciful and gracious, slow to anger, and plenteous in mercy.

He will not always chide: neither will he keep his anger for ever.

He hath not dealt with us after our sins; nor rewarded us according to our iniquities.

For as the heaven is high above the earth, so great is his mercy toward them that fear him.

As far as the east is from the west, so far hath he removed our transgressions from us.

Like as a father pitieth his children, so the Lord pitieth them that fear him.

Bless the Lord, all his works in all places of his dominion: bless the Lord, O my soul. —Psalm 103: 1-13, 22.

570   OBEDIENCE TO GOD

Thou hast commanded us to keep thy precepts diligently.

O that my ways were directed to keep thy statutes!

Then shall I not be ashamed, when I have respect unto all thy commandments.

I will praise thee with uprightness of heart, when I shall have learned thy righteous judgments.

I will keep thy statutes: O forsake me not utterly.

Wherewithal shall a young man cleanse his way? by taking heed thereto according to thy word.

With my whole heart have I sought thee: O let me not wander from thy commandments.

Thy word have I hid in mine heart, that I might not sin against thee.

Blessed art thou, O Lord: teach me thy statutes.

With my lips have I declared all the judgments of thy mouth.

I have rejoiced in the way of thy testimonies, as much as in all riches.

I will meditate in thy precepts, and have respect unto thy ways.

I will delight myself in thy statutes: I will not forget thy word.

Deal bountifully with thy servant, that I may live, and keep thy word.

Open thou mine eyes, that I may behold wondrous things out of thy law. —Psalm 119:4-18.

571 THE INCARNATE CHRIST

In the beginning was the Word, and the Word was with God, and the Word was God.

The same was in the beginning with God.

All things were made by him; and without him was not any thing made that was made.

In him was life; and the life was the light of men.

And the light shineth in darkness; and the darkness comprehended it not.

There was a man sent from God, whose name was John.

The same came for a witness, to bear witness of the Light, that all men through him might believe.

He was not that Light, but was sent to bear witness of that Light.

That was the true Light, which lighteth every man that cometh into the world.

He was in the world, and the world was made by him, and the world knew him not.

He came unto his own, and his own received him not.

But as many as received him, to them gave he power to become the sons of God, even to them that believe on his name:

Which were born, not of blood, nor of the will of the flesh, nor of the will of man, but of God.

And the Word was made flesh, and dwelt among us, (and we beheld his glory, the glory as of the only begotten of the Father,) full of grace and truth. —John 1:1-14.

For God so loved the world that he gave his only begotten Son, that whosoever believeth in him should not perish, but have everlasting life.

For God sent not his Son into the world to condemn the world; but that the world through him might be saved. —John 3:16, 17.

572 THE SAVIOUR'S ADVENT

And there were in the same country shepherds abiding in the field, keeping watch over their flock by night.

And, lo, the angel of the Lord came upon them, and the glory of the Lord shone round about them: and they were sore afraid.

And the angel said unto them, Fear not: for, behold, I bring you good tidings of great joy, which shall be to all people.

For unto you is born this day in the city of David a Saviour, which is Christ the Lord.

And this shall be a sign unto you; Ye shall find the babe wrapped in swaddling clothes, lying in a manger.

And suddenly there was with the angel a multitude of the heavenly host praising God, and saying,

Glory to God in the highest, and on earth peace, good will toward men.

And it came to pass, as the angels were gone away from them into heaven, the shepherds said one to another,

Let us now go even unto Bethlehem, and see this thing which is come to pass, which the Lord hath made known unto us.

And they came with haste, and found Mary, and Joseph, and the babe lying in a manger.

And when they had seen it, they made known abroad the saying which was told them concerning this child.

And all they that heard it wondered at those things which were told them by the shepherds.

But Mary kept all these things, and pondered them in her heart.

And the shepherds returned, glorifying and praising God for all the things that they had heard and seen, as it was told unto them.
—Luke 2:8-20.

573 ADORATION OF THE MAGI

Now when Jesus was born in Bethlehem of Judaea in the days of Herod the king, behold, there came wise men from the east to Jerusalem, saying,

Where is he that is born King of the Jews? for we have seen his star in the east, and are come to worship him.

When Herod the king had heard these things, he was troubled, and all Jerusalem with him.

And when he had gathered all the chief priests and scribes of the people together, he demanded of them where Christ should be born.

And they said unto him, In Bethlehem of Judaea: for thus it is written by the prophet,

And thou Bethlehem, in the land of Juda, art not the least among the princes of Juda: for out of thee shall come a Governor, that shall rule my people Israel.

Then Herod, when he had privily called the wise men, enquired of them diligently what time the star appeared. And he sent them to Bethlehem, and said,

Go and search diligently for the young child; and when ye have found him, bring me word again, that I may come and worship him also.

When they had heard the king, they departed; and, lo, the star, which they saw in the east, went before them, till it came and stood over where the young child was.

When they saw the star, they rejoiced with exceeding great joy. And when they were come into the house, they saw the young child with Mary his mother, and fell down, and worshipped him:

And when they had opened their treasures, they presented unto him gifts; gold, and frankincense, and myrrh.

And being warned of God in a dream that they should not return to Herod, they departed into their own country another way.
—Matthew 2:1-12.

574 BAPTISM OF JESUS

In those days came John the Baptist, preaching in the wilderness of Judaea, and saying,

Repent ye: for the kingdom of heaven is at hand.

For this is he that was spoken of by the prophet Esaias, saying, The voice of one crying in the wilderness, Prepare ye the way of the Lord, make his paths straight.

And the same John had his raiment of camel's hair, and a leathern girdle about his loins; and his meat was locusts and wild honey.

Then went out to him Jerusalem, and all Judaea, and all the region round about Jordan, and were baptized of him in Jordan, confessing their sins.

But when he saw many of the Pharisees and Sadducees come to his baptism, he said unto them,

O generation of vipers, who hath warned you to flee from the wrath to come? Bring forth therefore fruits meet for repentance:

I indeed baptize you with water unto repentance: but he that cometh after me is mightier than I, whose shoes I am not worthy to bear: he shall baptize you with the Holy Ghost, and with fire:

Then cometh Jesus from Galilee to Jordan unto John, to be baptized of him.

But John forbad him, saying, I have need to be baptized of thee, and comest thou to me?

And Jesus answering said unto him, Suffer it to be so now: for thus it becometh us to fulfil all righteousness. Then he suffered him.

And Jesus, when he was baptized, went up straightway out of the water:

And, lo, the heavens were opened unto him, and he saw the Spirit of God descending like a dove, and lighting upon him:

And lo a voice from heaven, saying, This is my beloved Son, in whom I am well pleased.
—Matthew 3:1-8, 11, 13-17.

575 THE LAMB OF GOD

Who hath believed our report? and to whom is the arm of the Lord revealed?

For he shall grow up before him as a tender plant, and as a root out of a dry ground: he hath no form nor comeliness; and when we shall see him, there is no beauty that we should desire him.

He is depised and rejected of men; a man of sorrows, and acquainted with grief: and we hid as it were our faces from him; he was despised, and we esteemed him not.

Surely he hath borne our griefs, and carried our sorrows: yet we did esteem him stricken, smitten of God, and afflicted.

But he was wounded for our transgressions, he was bruised for our iniquities: the chastisement of our peace was upon him; and with his stripes we are healed.

All we like sheep have gone astray; we have turned every one to his own way; and the Lord hath laid on him the iniquity of us all.

He was oppressed, and he was afflicted, yet he opened not his mouth: he is brought as a lamb to the slaughter, and as a sheep before her shearers is dumb, so he openeth not his mouth.

He was taken from prison and from judgment: and who shall declare his generation? for he was cut off out of the land of the living: for the transgression of my people was he stricken.

And he made his grave with the wicked, and with the rich in his death; because he had done no violence, neither was any deceit in his mouth.

Yet it pleased the Lord to bruise him; he hath put him to grief: when thou shalt make his soul an offering for sin, he shall see his seed, he shall prolong his days, and the pleasure of the Lord shall prosper in his hand.

He shall see of the travail of his soul, and shall be satisfied: by his knowledge shall my righteous servant justify many; for he shall bear their iniquities.

Therefore will I divide him a portion with the great, and he shall divide the spoil with the strong; because he hath poured out his soul unto death: and he was numbered with the transgressors; and he bare the sin of many, and made intercession for the transgressors. —Isaiah 53.

576 THE LAST SUPPER

And the disciples did as Jesus had appointed them; and they made ready the passover.

Now when the even was come, he sat down with the twelve.

And as they did eat, he said, Verily I say unto you, that one of you shall betray me.

And they were exceeding sorrowful, and began every one of them to say unto him, Lord, is it I?

And he answered and said, He that dippeth his hand with me in the dish, the same shall betray me.

The Son of man goeth as it is written of him: but woe unto that man by whom the Son of man is betrayed! it had been good for that man if he had not been born.

Then Judas, which betrayed him, answered and said, Master, is it I? He said unto him, Thou hast said.

And as they were eating, Jesus took bread, and blessed it, and brake it, and gave it to the disciples, and said, Take, eat; this is my body.

And he took the cup, and gave thanks, and gave it to them, saying, Drink ye all of it; for this is my blood of the new testament, which is shed for many for the remission of sins.

But I say unto you, I will not drink henceforth of this fruit of the vine, until that day when I drink it new with you in my Father's kingdom.
—Matthew 26:19-29.

577 THE TRIUMPHAL ENTRY

And when they came nigh to Jerusalem, unto Bethphage and Bethany, at the mount of Olives, he sendeth forth two of his disciples, and saith unto them,

Go your way into the village over against you: and as soon as ye be entered into it, ye shall find a colt tied, whereon never man sat; loose him, and bring him.

And if any man say unto you, Why do ye this? say ye that the Lord hath need of him; and straightway he will send him hither.

And they went their way, and found the colt tied by the door without in a place where two ways met; and they loose him.

And certain of them that stood there said unto them, What do ye, loosing the colt?

And they said unto them even as Jesus had commanded: and they let them go.

And they brought the colt to Jesus, and cast their garments on him; and he sat upon him.

And many spread their garments in the way: and others cut down branches off the trees, and strawed them in the way.

And they that went before, and they that followed, cried, saying, Hosanna; Blessed is he that cometh in the name of the Lord.

Blessed be the kingdom of our father David, that cometh in the name of the Lord: Hosanna in the highest. And Jesus entered into Jerusalem, and into the temple.
—Mark 11:1-11.

And when he was come into Jerusalem, all the city was moved, saying, Who is this?

And the multitude said, This is Jesus the prophet of Nazareth of Galilee. —Matthew 21: 10, 11.

578 CRUCIFIXION OF CHRIST

Then delivered he him therefore unto them to be crucified. And they took Jesus, and led him away.

And he bearing his cross went forth into a place called the place of a skull, which is called in the Hebrew Golgotha:

Where they crucified him, and two other with him, on either side one, and Jesus in the midst.

And Pilate wrote a title, and put it on the cross. And the writing was, JESUS OF NAZARETH THE KING OF THE JEWS.

Then the soliders, when they had crucified Jesus, took his garments, and made four parts, to every soldier a part; and also his coat: now the coat was without seam, woven from the top throughout.

They said therefore among themselves, Let us not rend it, but cast lots for it, whose it shall be: . . . These things therefore the soldiers did.

Now there stood by the cross of Jesus his mother, and his mother's sister, Mary the wife of Cleophas, and Mary Magdalene.

When Jesus therefore saw his mother, and the disciple standing by, whom he loved, he saith unto his mother, Woman, behold thy son!

Then saith he to the disciple, Behold thy mother! And from that hour that disciple took her unto his own home.

After this, Jesus knowing that all things were now accomplished, that the scripture might be fulfilled, saith, I thirst.

Now there was set a vessel full of vinegar: and they filled a sponge with vinegar, and put it upon hyssop, and put it to his mouth.

When Jesus therefore had received the vinegar, he said, It is finished: and he bowed his head, and gave up the ghost.
—John 19:16-19, 23-30.

579 THE RISEN LORD

In the end of the sabbath, as it began to dawn toward the first day of the week, came Mary Magdalene and the other Mary to see the sepulchre.

And, behold, there was a great earthquake: for the angel of the Lord descended from heaven, and came and rolled back the stone from the door, and sat upon it.

And the angel answered and said unto the women, Fear not ye: for I know that ye seek Jesus, which was crucified.

He is not here: for he is risen, as he said. Come, see the place where the Lord lay.

And go quickly, and tell his disciples that he is risen from the dead; and, behold, he goeth before you into Galilee; there shall ye see him: lo, I have told you.

And they departed quickly from the sepulchre with fear and great joy; and did run to bring his disciples word.

And as they went to tell his disciples, behold, Jesus met them, saying, All hail. And they came and held him by the feet, and worshipped him.

Then said Jesus unto them, Be not afraid: go tell my brethren that they go into Galilee, and there shall they see me. —Matthew 28:1, 2, 5-10.

Then the same day at evening, being the first day of the week, when the doors were shut where the disciples were assembled for fear of the Jews, came Jesus and stood in the midst, and saith unto them, Peace be unto you

And when he had so said, he shewed unto them his hands and his side. Then were the disciples glad, when they saw the Lord.
—John 20:19, 20.

580 THE GREAT COMMISSION

Then the eleven disciples went away into Galilee, into a mountain where Jesus had appointed them.

And when they saw him, they worshipped him: but some doubted.

And Jesus came and spake unto them, saying, All power is given unto me in heaven and in earth.

Go ye therefore, and teach all nations, baptizing them in the name of the Father, and of the Son, and of the Holy Ghost:

Teaching them to observe all things whatsoever I have commanded you: and, lo, I am with you alway, even unto the end of the world. —Matthew 28:16-20

[Jesus] said unto them, Thus it is written, and thus it behoved Christ to suffer, and to rise from the dead the third day:

And that repentance and remission of sins should be preached in his name among all nations, beginning at Jerusalem.

And ye are witnesses of these things.

And, behold, I send the promise of my Father upon you: but tarry ye in the city of Jerusalem, until ye be endued with power from on high.

They asked of him, saying, Lord, wilt thou at this time restore again the kingdom to Israel?

And he said unto them, It is not for you to know the times or the seasons, which the Father hath put in his own power.

But ye shall receive power, after that the Holy Ghost is come upon you:

And ye shall be witnesses unto me both in Jerusalem, and in all Judaea, and in Samaria, and unto the uttermost part of the earth.

And when he had spoken these things, while they beheld, he was taken up; and a cloud received him out of their sight. —Acts 1:6-9.

581 THE BEATITUDES

And seeing the multitudes, he went up into the mountain: and when he was set, his disciples came unto him:

And he opened his mouth, and taught them, saying,

Blessed are the poor in spirit: for theirs is the kingdom of heaven.

Blessed are they that mourn: for they shall be comforted.

Blessed are the meek: for they shall inherit the earth.

Blessed are they which do hunger and thirst after righteousness: for they shall be filled.

Blessed are the merciful: for they shall obtain mercy.

Blessed are the pure in heart: for they shall see God.

Blessed are the peacemakers: for they shall be called the children of God.

Blessed are they which are persecuted for righteousness' sake: for theirs is the kingdom of heaven.

Blessed are ye, when men shall revile you, and persecute you, and shall say all manner of evil against you falsely, for my sake.

Rejoice, and be exceeding glad: for great is your reward in heaven: for so persecuted they the prophets which were before you.

Ye are the light of the world.

Let your light so shine before men, that they may see your good works, and glorify your Father which is in heaven. —Matthew 5:1-12, 14, 16.

582   THE VINE AND BRANCHES

I am the true vine, and my Father is the husbandman.

Every branch in me that beareth not fruit he taketh away: and every branch that beareth fruit, he purgeth it, that it may bring forth more fruit.

Now ye are clean through the word which I have spoken unto you.

Abide in me, and I in you. As the branch cannot bear fruit of itself, except it abide in the vine; no more can ye, except ye abide in me.

I am the vine, ye are the branches: He that abideth in me, and I in him, the same bringeth forth much fruit: for without me ye can do nothing.

If a man abide not in me, he is cast forth as a branch, and is withered; and men gather them, and cast them into fire, and they are burned.

If ye abide in me, and my words abide in you, ye shall ask what ye will, and it shall be done unto you.

Herein is my Father glorified, that ye bear much fruit; so shall ye be my disciples.

These things have I spoken unto you, that my joy might remain in you, and that your joy might be full.

Ye are my friends, if ye do whatsoever I command you.

Henceforth I call you not servants; for the servant knoweth not what his lord doeth: but I have called you friends; for all things that I have heard of my Father I have made known unto you.

Ye have not chosen me, but I have chosen you, and ordained you, that ye should go and bring forth fruit, and that your fruit should remain: that whatsoever ye shall ask of the Father in my name, he may give it you. —John 15:1-8, 11, 14-16.

583   COMFORT FROM CHRIST

Let not your heart be troubled: ye believe in God, believe also in me.

In my Father's house are many mansions: if it were not so, I would have told you. I go to prepare a place for you.

And if I go and prepare a place for you, I will come again, and receive you unto myself; that where I am, there ye may be also.

And whither I go ye know, and the way ye know.

Thomas saith unto him, Lord, we know not whither thou goest; and how can we know the way?

Jesus saith unto him, I am the way, the truth, and the life: no man cometh unto the Father, but by me.

Philip saith unto him, Lord, shew us the Father, and it sufficeth us.

Jesus saith unto him, Have I been so long time with you, and yet hast thou not known me, Philip? he that hath seen me hath seen the Father; and how sayest thou then, Shew us the Father?

Believest thou not that I am in the Father, and the Father in me? the words that I speak unto you I speak not of myself; but the Father that dwelleth in me, he doeth the works.

Believe me that I am in the Father, and the Father in me: or else believe me for the very works' sake.

Verily, verily, I say unto you, He that believeth on me, the works that I do shall he do also; and greater works than these shall he do; because I go unto my Father.

Peace I leave with you, my peace I give unto you: not as the world giveth, give I unto you. Let not your heart be troubled, neither let it be afraid. —John 14:1-6, 8-12, 27.

584   THE HOLY SPIRIT

I will pray the Father, and he shall give you another Comforter, that he may abide with you for ever;

Even the Spirit of truth; whom the world cannot receive, because it seeth him not, neither knoweth him:

But ye know him; for he dwelleth with you, and shall be in you. I will not leave you comfortless: I will come to you.

Yet a little while, and the world seeth me no more; but ye see me: because I live, ye shall live also.
—John 14:16-19.

But because I have said these things unto you, sorrow hath filled your heart.

Nevertheless I tell you the truth; It is expedient for you that I go away:

For if I go not away, the Comforter will not come unto you; but if I depart, I will send him unto you.

And when he is come, he will reprove the world of sin, and of righteousness, and of judgment:

Of sin, because they believe not on me;

Of righteousness, because I go to my Father, and ye see me no more;

Of judgment, because the prince of this world is judged.

I have yet many things to say unto you, but ye cannot bear them now.

Howbeit when he, the Spirit of truth, is come, he will guide you into all truth:

For he shall not speak of himself; but whatsoever he shall hear, that shall he speak: and he will shew you things to come.

He shall glorify me: for he shall receive of mine, and shall shew it unto you.

These things I have spoken unto you, that in me ye might have peace. In the world ye shall have tribulation: but be of good cheer; I have overcome the world.
—John 16:6-14, 33.

585 THE HOLY SCRIPTURES

Knowing this first, that no prophecy of the scripture is of any private interpretation.

For the prophecy came not in old time by the will of man: but holy men of God spake as they were moved by the Holy Ghost.
—2 Peter 1:20, 21.

All scripture is given by inspiration of God, and is profitable for doctrine, for reproof, for correction, for instruction in righteousness:

That the man of God may be perfect, throughly furnished unto all good works. —2 Timothy 3:16, 17.

Study to shew thyself approved unto God, a workman that needeth not to be ashamed, rightly dividing the word of truth. —2 Timothy 2:15.

For whatsoever things were written aforetime were written for our learning, that we through patience and comfort of the scriptures might have hope. —Romans 15:4.

For ever, O Lord, thy word is settled in heaven.

Thy word is a lamp unto my feet, and a light unto my path.

The entrance of thy words giveth light; it giveth understanding unto the simple.

Great peace have they which love thy law: and nothing shall offend them. —Psalm 119:89, 105, 130, 165.

586 TRUE WISDOM

Happy is the man that findeth wisdom, and the man that getteth understanding.

For the merchandise of it is better than the merchandise of silver, and the gain thereof than fine gold.

She is more precious than rubies: and all the things thou canst desire are not to be compared unto her.

Length of days is in her right hand; and in her left hand riches and honour.

Her ways are ways of pleasantness, and all her paths are peace.

She is a tree of life to them that lay hold upon her: and happy is every one that retaineth her.

The Lord by wisdom hath founded the earth; by understanding hath he established the heavens.

By his knowledge the depths are broken up, and the clouds drop down the dew.

My son, let not them depart from thine eyes: keep sound wisdom and discretion:

So shall they be life unto thy soul, and grace to thy neck.

Then shalt thou walk in thy way safely, and thy foot shall not stumble.

When thou liest down, thou shalt not be afraid: yea, thou shalt lie down, and thy sleep shall be sweet.

Be not afraid of sudden fear, neither of the desolation of the wicked, when it cometh.

For the Lord shall be thy confidence, and shall keep thy foot from being taken.

Trust in the Lord with all thine heart; and lean not unto thine own understanding.

In all thy ways acknowledge him, and he shall direct thy paths.
—Proverbs 3:13-26, 5, 6.

When Jesus came into the coasts of Caesarea Philippi, he asked his disciples, saying, Whom do men say that I the Son of man am?

And they said, Some say that thou art John the Baptist: some, Elias; and others, Jeremias, or one of the prophets.

He saith unto them, But whom say ye that I am?

And Simon Peter answered and said, Thou art the Christ, the Son of the living God.

And Jesus answered and said unto him, Blessed art thou, Simon Bar-jona: for flesh and blood hath not revealed it unto thee, but my Father which is in heaven.

And I say also unto thee, That thou art Peter, and upon this rock I will build my church; and the gates of hell shall not prevail against it.
—Matthew 16:13-18.

Now therefore ye are no more strangers and foreigners, but fellowcitizens with the saints, and of the household of God;

And are built upon the foundation of the apostles and prophets, Jesus Christ himself being the chief corner stone;

In whom all the building fitly framed together groweth unto an holy temple in the Lord:

In whom ye also are builded together for an habitation of God through the Spirit.   —Ephesians 2:19-22.

There is one body, and one Spirit, even as ye are called in one hope of your calling;

One Lord, one faith, one baptism, one God and Father of all, who is above all, and through all, and in you all.   —Ephesians 4:4-6.

Whosoever shall call upon the name of the Lord shall be saved. How then shall they call on him in whom they have not believed?

And how shall they believe in him of whom they have not heard?

And how shall they hear without a preacher?

And how shall they preach, except they be sent?   —Romans 10:13-15.

For as we have many members in one body, and all members have not the same office: so we, being many, are one body in Christ, and every one members one of another.

Having then gifts differing according to the grace that is given to us, whether prophecy, let us prophesy according to the proportion of faith;

Or ministry, let us wait on our ministering:

Or he that teacheth, on teaching; or he that exhorteth, on exhortation.
—Romans 12:4-8.

As every man hath received the gift, even so minister the same one to another, as good stewards of the manifold grace of God. If any man speak, let him speak as the oracles of God;

If any man minister, let him do it as of the ability which God giveth: that God in all things may be glorified through Jesus Christ.
—1 Peter 4:10, 11.

589 CHRISTIAN UNITY

These words spake Jesus, and lifted up his eyes to heaven, and said, Father, the hour is come; glorify thy Son, that thy Son also may glorify thee:

I have manifested thy name unto the men which thou gavest me out of the world: thine they were, and thou gavest them me; and they have kept thy word.

I pray for them: I pray not for the world, but for them which thou hast given me; for they are thine.

And all mine are thine, and thine are mine; and I am glorified in them.

Neither pray I for these alone, but for them also which shall believe on me through their word; that they all may be one; as thou, Father, art in me, and I in thee.

That they also may be one in us: that the world may believe that thou hast sent me.

Now I beseech you, brethren, by the name of our Lord Jesus Christ, that ye all speak the same thing, and that there be no divisions among you;

But that ye be perfectly joined together in the same mind and in the same judgment. —1 Corinthians 1:10.

With all lowliness and meekness, with longsuffering, forbearing one another in love;

Endeavouring to keep the unity of the Spirit in the bond of peace.

There is one body, and one Spirit, even as ye are called in one hope of your calling;

One Lord, one faith, one baptism, one God and Father of all, who is above all, and through all, and in you all. —Ephesians 4:2-6.

590 SIN AND FORGIVENESS

Blessed is the man that endureth temptation: for when he is tried, he shall receive the crown of life, which the Lord hath promised to them that love him.

Let no man say when he is tempted, I am tempted of God: for God cannot be tempted with evil, neither tempteth he any man:

But every man is tempted, when he is drawn away of his own lust, and enticed.

Then when lust hath conceived, it bringeth forth sin: and sin, when it is finished, bringeth forth death.
—James 1:12-15

But if we walk in the light, as he is in the light, we have fellowship one with another, and the blood of Jesus Christ his Son cleanseth us from all sin.

If we say that we have no sin, we deceive ourselves, and the truth is not in us.

If we confess our sins, he is faithful and just to forgive us our sins, and to cleanse us from all unrighteousness. —1 John 1:7-9.

Blessed is he whose transgression is forgiven, whose sin is covered.

Blessed is the man unto whom the Lord imputeth not iniquity, and in whose spirit there is no guile.

I acknowledged my sin unto thee, and mine iniquity have I not hid. I said, I will confess my transgressions unto the Lord; and thou forgavest the iniquity of my sin.

Many sorrows shall be to the wicked: but he that trusteth in the Lord, mercy shall compass him about.

Be glad in the Lord, and rejoice, ye righteous: and shout for joy, all ye that are upright in heart.
—Psalm 32:1, 2, 5, 10, 11.

591 LAW AND GOSPEL

Now we know that what things soever the law saith, it saith to them who are under the law:

That every mouth may be stopped, and all the world may become guilty before God.

Therefore by the deeds of the law there shall no flesh be justified in his sight: for by the law is the knowledge of sin.

But now the righteousness of God without the law is manifested, being witnessed by the law and the prophets;

Even the righteousness of God which is by faith of Jesus Christ unto all and upon all them that believe: for there is no difference:

For all have sinned, and come short of the glory of God;

Being justified freely by his grace through the redemption that is in Christ Jesus   —Romans 3:19-24.

But before faith came, we were kept under the law, shut up unto the faith which should afterwards be revealed.

Wherefore the law was our schoolmaster to bring us unto Christ, that we might be justified by faith.

But after that faith is come, we are no longer under a school-master.

For ye are all the children of God by faith in Christ Jesus.

For as many of you as have been baptized into Christ have put on Christ.   —Galatians 3:23-27.

Therefore being justified by faith, we have peace with God through our Lord Jesus Christ:

By whom also we have access by faith into this grace wherein we stand, and rejoice in hope of the glory of God.   —Romans 5:1, 2.

592 GOD'S INVITATION

Ho, every one that thirsteth, come ye to the waters, and he that hath no money; come ye, buy, and eat; yea, come, buy wine and milk without money and without price.

Wherefore do ye spend money for that which is not bread? and your labour for that which satisfieth not? hearken diligently unto me, and eat ye that which is good, and let your soul delight itself in fatness.

Incline your ear, and come unto me: hear, and your soul shall live; and I will make an everlasting covenant with you, even the sure mercies of David.

Seek ye the Lord while he may be found, call ye upon him while he is near:

Let the wicked forsake his way, and the unrighteous man his thoughts: and let him return unto the Lord, and he will have mercy upon him; and to our God, for he will abundantly pardon.

For my thoughts are not your thoughts, neither are your ways my ways, saith the Lord.

So shall my word be that goeth forth out of my mouth: it shall not return unto me void, but it shall accomplish that which I please, and it shall prosper in the thing whereto I sent it.

For ye shall go out with joy, and be led forth with peace: the mountains and the hills shall break forth before you into singing, and all the trees of the field shall clap their hands.

Instead of the thorn shall come up the fir tree, and instead of the brier shall come up the myrtle tree:

And it shall be to the Lord for a name, for an everlasting sign that shall not be cut off.
    —Isaiah 55:1-3, 6-8, 11-13.

593 THE WAY OF LIFE

Blessed is the man that walketh not in the counsel of the ungodly, nor standeth in the way of sinners, nor sitteth in the seat of the scornful.

But his delight is in the law of the Lord; and in his law doth he meditate day and night.

And he shall be like a tree planted by the rivers of water, that bringeth forth his fruit in his season; his leaf also shall not wither; and whatsoever he doeth shall prosper.

The ungodly are not so: but are like the chaff which the wind driveth away.

Therefore the ungodly shall not stand in the judgment, nor sinners in the congregation of the righteous.

For the Lord knoweth the way of the righteous: but the way of the ungodly shall perish. —Psalm 1.

There is a way which seemeth right unto a man, but the end thereof are the ways of death. —Proverbs 14:12.

Trust in the Lord with all thine heart; and lean not unto thine own understanding.

In all thy ways acknowledge him, and he shall direct thy paths. —Proverbs 3:5, 6.

Enter ye in at the strait gate: for wide is the gate, and broad is the way, that leadeth to destruction, and many there be which go in thereat:

Because strait is the gate, and narrow is the way, which leadeth unto life, and few there be that find it. —Matthew 7:13, 14.

Jesus saith . . . I am the way, the truth, and the life: no man cometh unto the Father , but by me. —John 14:6.

594 FAITH IN CHRIST

Now faith is the substance of things hoped for, the evidence of things not seen.

But without faith it is impossible to please him: for he that cometh to God must believe that he is, and that he is a rewarder of them that diligently seek him. —Hebrews 11:1, 6.

And this is the will of him that sent me, that every one which seeth the Son, and believeth on him, may have everlasting life: and I will raise him up at the last day. —John 6:40.

For whatsoever is born of God overcometh the world: and this is the victory that overcometh the world, even our faith.

Who is he that overcometh the world, but he that believeth that Jesus is the Son of God?

And this is the record, that God hath given to us eternal life, and this life is in his Son.

These things have I written unto you that believe on the name of the Son of God; that ye may know that ye have eternal life, and that ye may believe on the name of the Son of God.

And we know that the Son of God is come, and hath given us an understanding, that we may know him that is true, and we are in him that is true, even in his Son Jesus Christ. This is the true God, and eternal life. —1 John 5:4, 5, 11, 13, 20.

595 PRAYER OF PENITENCE

Have mercy upon me, O God, according to thy lovingkindness:

According unto the multitude of thy tender mercies blot out my transgressions.

Wash me throughly from mine iniquity, and cleanse me from my sin.

For I acknowledge my transgressions: and my sin is ever before me.

Against thee, thee only, have I sinned, and done this evil in thy sight: that thou mightest be justified when thou speakest, and be clear when thou judgest.

Behold, I was shapen in iniquity; and in sin did my mother conceive me.

Behold, thou desirest truth in the inward parts: and in the hidden part thou shalt make me to know wisdom.

Purge me with hyssop, and I shall be clean: wash me, and I shall be whiter than snow.

Make me to hear joy and gladness; that the bones which thou hast broken may rejoice.

Hide thy face from my sins, and blot out all mine iniquities.

Create in me a clean heart. O God; and renew a right spirit within me.

Cast me not away from thy presence; and take not thy holy spirit from me.

Restore unto me the joy of thy salvation; and uphold me with thy free spirit.

Then will I teach transgressors thy ways; and sinners shall be converted unto thee.

O Lord, open thou my lips; and my mouth shall shew forth thy praise. For thou desirest not sacrifice; else would I give it: thou delightest not in burnt offering.

The sacrifices of God are a broken spirit: a broken and contrite heart, O God, thou wilt not despise. —Psalm 51:1-13, 15-17.

596 CONFESSION OF CHRIST

Whosever shall confess that Jesus is the Son of God, God dwelleth in him, and he in God. —1 John 4:15.

The word is nigh thee, even in thy mouth, and in thy heart: that is, the word of faith, which we preach;

That if thou shalt confess with thy mouth the Lord Jesus, and shalt believe in thine heart that God hath raised him from the dead, thou shalt be saved.

For with the heart man believeth unto righteousness; and with the mouth confession is made unto salvation. —Romans 10:8-10

Wherefore God also hath highly exalted him, and given him a name which is above every name: that at the name of Jesus every knee should bow, of things in heaven, and things in earth, and things under the earth;

And that every tongue should confess that Jesus Christ is Lord, to the glory of God the Father. —Philippians 2:9-11.

Whosoever shall confess me before men, him shall the Son of man also confess before the angels of God:

But he that denieth me before men shall be denied before the angels of God. —Luke 12:8, 9.

597 CHRISTIAN BAPTISM

And Jesus came and spake unto them, saying, All power is given unto me in Heaven and in earth. Go ye therefore, and teach all nations,

Baptizing them in the name of the Father, and of the Son, and of the Holy Ghost: teaching them to observe all things whatsoever I have commanded you: and, lo, I am with you alway, even unto the end of the world. —Matthew 28:18-20.

Therefore we are buried with him by baptism into death: that like as Christ was raised up from the dead by the glory of the Father, even so we also should walk in newness of life.

For if we have been planted together in the likeness of his death, we shall be also in the likeness of his resurrection:

Knowing this, that our old man is crucified with him, that the body of sin might be destroyed, that henceforth we should not serve sin.

For he that is dead is freed from sin. Now if we be dead with Christ, we believe that we shall also live with him:

Knowing that Christ being raised from the dead dieth no more; death hath no more dominion over him. For in that he died, he died unto sin once: but in that he liveth, he liveth unto God.

Likewise reckon ye also yourselves to be dead indeed unto sin, but alive unto God through Jesus Christ our Lord. —Romans 6:4-11.

598 THE MIND OF CHRIST

If there be therefore any consolation in Christ, if any comfort of love, if any fellowship of the Spirit, if any bowels and mercies,

Fulfil ye my joy, that ye be likeminded, having the same love, being of one accord, of one mind.

Let nothing be done through strife or vainglory; but in lowliness of mind let each esteem other better than themselves.

Look not every man on his own things, but every man also on the things of others.

Let this mind be in you, which was also in Christ Jesus:

Who, being in the form of God, thought it not robbery to be equal with God:

But made himself of no reputation, and took upon him the form of a servant, and was made in the likeness of men:

And being found in fashion as a man, he humbled himself, and became obedient unto death, even the death of the cross.

Wherefore God also hath highly exalted him, and given him a name which is above every name:

That at the name of Jesus every knee should bow, of things in heaven, and things in earth, and things under the earth;

And that every tongue should confess that Jesus Christ is Lord, to the glory of God the Father.

For it is God which worketh in you both to will and to do of his good pleasure.

Do all things without murmurings and disputings: that ye may be blameless and harmless, the sons of God, without rebuke, in the midst of a crooked and perverse nation,

Among whom ye shine as lights in the world; holding forth the word of life. —Philippians 2:1-11, 13-16.

599 GROWTH IN GRACE

Grace and peace be multiplied unto you through the knowledge of God, and of Jesus our Lord.

According as his divine power hath given unto us all things that pertain unto life and godliness, through the knowledge of him that hath called us to glory and virtue:

Whereby are given unto us exceeding great and precious promises: that by these ye might be partakers of the divine nature, having escaped the corruption that is in the world through lust.

And beside this, giving all diligence, add to your faith virtue; and to virtue knowledge;

And to knowledge temperance; and to temperance patience; and to patience godliness;

And to godliness brotherly kindness; and to brotherly kindness charity.

For if these things be in you, and abound, they make you that ye shall neither be barren nor unfruitful in the knowledge of our Lord Jesus Christ.

But he that lacketh these things is blind, and cannot see afar off, and hath forgotten that he was purged from his old sins.

Wherefore the rather, brethren, give diligence to make your calling and election sure: for if ye do these things, ye shall never fall:

For so an entrance shall be ministered unto you abundantly into the everlasting kingdom of our Lord and Savior Jesus Christ.
—2 Peter 1:2-11.

600 PRACTICAL CHRISTIANITY

I beseech you therefore, brethren, by the mercies of God, that ye present your bodies a living sacrifice, holy, acceptable unto God, which is your reasonable service.

And be not conformed to this world: but be ye transformed by the renewing of your mind, that ye may prove what is that good, and acceptable, and perfect, will of God.

For I say, through the grace given unto me, to every man that is among you, not to think of himself more highly than he ought to think; but to think soberly according as God hath dealt to every man the measure of faith.

Let love be without dissimulation. Abhor that which is evil; cleave to that which is good.

Be kindly affectioned one to another with brotherly love; in honour preferring one another;

Not slothful in business; fervent in spirit; serving the Lord;

Rejoicing in hope; patient in tribulation; continuing instant in prayer;

Distributing to the necessity of saints; given to hospitality.

Bless them which persecute you: bless, and curse not.

Rejoice with them that do rejoice, and weep with them that weep.

Be of the same mind one toward another. Mind not high things, but condescend to men of low estate. Be not wise in your own conceits.

Recompense to no man evil for evil. Provide things honest in the sight of all men. If it be possible, as much as lieth in you, live peaceably with all men.

Dearly beloved, avenge not yourselves, but rather give place unto wrath: for it is written, Vengeance is mine; I will repay, saith the Lord.

Therefore if thine enemy hunger, feed him; if he thirst, give him drink: for in so doing thou shalt heap coals of fire on his head. Be not overcome of evil, but overcome evil with good.—Romans 12:1-3, 9-21.

601 TEMPERANCE

Wine is a mocker, strong drink is raging: and whosoever is deceived thereby is not wise. —Proverbs 20:1.

Who hath woe? who hath sorrow? who hath contentions? who hath babbling? who hath wounds without cause? who hath redness of eyes?

They that tarry long at the wine; they that go to seek mixed wine. —Proverbs 23:29, 30.

For the flesh lusteth against the Spirit, and the Spirit against the flesh: and these are contrary the one to the other: so that ye cannot do the things that ye would.

But if ye be led of the Spirit, ye are not under the law.

Now the works of the flesh are manifest, which are these; Adultery, fornication, uncleanness, lasciviousness,

Idolatry, witchcraft, hatred, variance, emulations, wrath, strife, seditions, heresies, envyings, murders, drunkenness, revellings, and such like:

Of the which I tell you before, as I have also told you in time past, that they which do such things shall not inherit the kingdom of God.

But the fruit of the Spirit is love, joy, peace, longsuffering, gentleness, goodness, faith, meekness, temperance: against such there is no law. —Galatians 5:17-23.

And whatsoever ye do in word or deed, do all in the name of the Lord Jesus, giving thanks to God and the Father by him. —Colossians 3:17.

602 CHRISTIAN GIVING

Lay not up for yourselves treasures upon earth, where moth and rust doth corrupt, and where thieves break through and steal:

But lay up for yourselves treasures in heaven, where neither moth nor rust doth corrupt, and where thieves do not break through nor steal: for where your treasure is, there will your heart be also. —Matthew 6:19-21.

Upon the first day of the week let every one of you lay by him in store, as God hath prospered him. —1 Corinthians 16:2.

Therefore, as ye abound in every thing, in faith, and utterance, and knowledge, and in all diligence, and in your love to us, see that ye abound in this grace also.

I speak not by commandment, but by occasion of the forwardness of others, and to prove the sincerity of your love.

For ye know the grace of our Lord Jesus Christ, that, though he was rich, yet for your sakes he became poor, that ye through his poverty might be rich.
—2 Corinthians 8:7-9.

But this I say, He which soweth sparingly shall reap also sparingly; and he which soweth bountifully shall reap also bountifully.

Every man according as he purposeth in his heart, so let him give; not grudgingly, or of necessity: for God loveth a cheerful giver.
—2 Corinthians 9:6-7.

603 CHRISTIAN ASSURANCE

As many as are led by the Spirit of God, they are the sons of God.

For ye have not received the spirit of bondage again to fear; but ye have received the Spirit of adoption, whereby we cry, Abba, Father.

The Spirit itself beareth witness with our spirit, that we are the children of God:

And if children, then heirs; heirs of God, and joint-heirs with Christ; if so be that we suffer with him, that we may be also glorified together.

For I reckon that the sufferings of this present time are not worthy to be compared with the glory which shall be revealed in us.

And we know that all things work together for good to them that love God, to them who are the called according to his purpose.

What shall we then say to these things? If God be for us, who can be against us?

He that spared not his own Son, but delivered him up for us all, how shall he not with him also freely give us all things?

Who shall separate us from the love of Christ? shall tribulation, or distress, or persecution, or famine, or nakedness, or peril, or sword?

Nay, in all these things we are more than conquerors through him that loved us.

For I am persuaded, that neither death, nor life, nor angels, nor principalities, nor powers, nor things present, nor things to come,

Nor height, nor depth, nor any other creature, shall be able to separate us from the love of God, which is in Christ Jesus our Lord.
—Romans 8:14-18, 28, 31, 32, 35, 37-39.

604 LOVE

Though I speak with the tongues of men and of angels, and have not love, I am become as sounding brass, or a tinkling cymbal.

And though I have the gift of prophecy, and understand all mysteries, and all knowledge;

And though I have all faith, so that I could remove mountains, and have not love, I am nothing.

And though I bestow all my goods to feed the poor, and though I give my body to be burned, and have not love, it profiteth me nothing.

Love suffereth long, and is kind; love envieth not; love vaunteth not itself, is not puffed up,

Doth not behave itself unseemly, seeketh not her own, is not easily provoked, thinketh no evil;

Rejoiceth not in iniquity, but rejoiceth in the truth;

Beareth all things, believeth all things, hopeth all things, endureth all things.

Love never faileth: but whether there be prophecies, they shall fail; whether there be tongues, they shall cease; whether there be knowledge, it shall vanish away.

For we know in part, and we prophesy in part.

But when that which is perfect is come, then that which is in part shall be done away.

When I was a child, I spake as a child, I understood as a child, I thought as a child: but when I became a man, I put away childish things.

For now we see through a glass, darkly; but then face to face: now I know in part; but then shall I know even as also I am known.

And now abideth faith, hope, love, these three; but the greatest of these is love.   —1 Corinthians 13.

605 PRAYER

When ye pray, use not vain repetitions, as the heathen do: for they think that they shall be heard for their much speaking.

Be not ye therefore like unto them: for your Father knoweth what things ye have need of, before ye ask him.

After this manner therefore pray ye:

Our Father which art in heaven, Hallowed be thy name.

Thy kingdom come. Thy will be done in earth, as it is in heaven.

Give us this day our daily bread. And forgive us our debts, as we forgive our debtors.

And lead us not into temptation, but deliver us from evil:

For thine is the kingdom, and the power, and the glory, for ever. Amen. —Matthew 6:7-13.

Continue in prayer, and watch in the same with thanksgiving.
—Colossians 4:2.

Confess your faults one to another, and pray one for another, that ye may be healed. The effectual fervent prayer of a righteous man availeth much. —James 5:16.

Be careful for nothing; but in every thing by prayer and supplication with thanksgiving let your requests be made known unto God.

And the peace of God, which passeth all understanding, shall keep your hearts and minds through Christ Jesus. —Philippians 4:6, 7.

606 CIVIL POWER

Let every soul be subject unto the higher powers. For there is no power but of God: the powers that be are ordained of God.

Whosoever therefore resisteth the power, resisteth the ordinance of God: and they that resist shall receive to themselves damnation.

For rulers are not a terror to good works, but to the evil. Wilt thou then not be afraid of the power? do that which is good, and thou shalt have praise of the same:

For he is the minister of God to thee for good. But if thou do that which is evil, be afraid; for he beareth not the sword in vain: for he is the minister of God, a revenger to execute wrath upon him that doeth evil.

Wherefore ye must needs be subject, not only for wrath, but also for conscience sake.

For for this cause pay ye tribute also: for they are God's ministers, attending continually upon this very thing.

Render therefore to all their dues: tribute to whom tribute is due; custom to whom custom; fear to whom fear; honour to whom honour.

Owe no man any thing, but to love one another: for he that loveth another hath fulfilled the law.
—Romans 13:1-8.

607 SPIRITUAL WARFARE

Finally, my brethren, be strong in the Lord, and in the power of his might.

Put on the whole armour of God, that ye may be able to stand against the wiles of the devil.

For we wrestle not against flesh and blood, but against principalities, against powers, against the rulers of the darkness of this world, against spiritual wickedness in high places.

Wherefore take unto you the whole armour of God, that ye may be able to withstand in the evil day, and having done all, to stand.

Stand therefore, having your loins girt about with truth, and having on the breastplate of righteousness;

And your feet shod with the preparation of the gospel of peace;

Above all, taking the shield of faith, wherewith ye shall be able to quench all the fiery darts of the wicked.

And take the helmet of salvation, and the sword of the Spirit, which is the word of God:

Praying always with all prayer and supplication in the Spirit, and watching thereunto with all perseverance and supplication for all saints. Ephesians 6:10-18.

The night is far spent, the day is at hand: let us therefore cast off the works of darkness, and let us put on the armour of light.

Let us walk honestly, as in the day; not in rioting and drunkenness, not in chambering and wantonness, not in strife and envying.

But put ye on the Lord Jesus Christ, and make not provision for the flesh, to fulfil the lusts thereof.
—Romans 13:12-14.

608   THE RETURN OF CHRIST

But I would not have you to be ignorant, brethren, concerning them which are asleep, that ye sorrow not, even as others which have no hope.

For if we believe that Jesus died and rose again, even so them also which sleep in Jesus will God bring with him.

For this we say unto you by the word of the Lord, that we which are alive and remain unto the coming of the Lord shall not prevent them which are asleep.

For the Lord himself shall descend from heaven with a shout, with the voice of the archangel, and with the trump of God: and the dead in Christ shall rise first:

Then we which are alive and remain shall be caught up together with them in the clouds, to meet the Lord in the air: and so shall we ever be with the Lord.

Wherefore comfort one another with these words.

But of the times and seasons, brethren, ye have no need that I write unto you. For yourselves know perfectly that the day of the Lord so cometh as a thief in the night.

Therefore let us not sleep, as do others; but let us watch and be sober.

For they that sleep sleep in the night; and they that be drunken are drunken in the night.

But let us, who are of the day, be sober, putting on the breastplate of faith and love; and for an helmet, the hope of salvation.

For God hath not appointed us to wrath, but to obtain salvation by our Lord Jesus Christ,

Who died for us, that, whether we wake or sleep, we should live together with him.
—1 Thessalonians 4:13—5:2, 6-10.

609   CHRIST AND IMMORTALITY

Now is Christ risen from the dead, and become the firstfruits of them that slept.

For since by man came death, by man came also the resurrection of the dead.

For as in Adam all die, even so in Christ shall all be made alive.

And so it is written, The first man Adam was made a living soul; the last Adam was made a quickening spirit.

The first man is of the earth, earthy: the second man is the Lord from heaven.

As is the earthy, such are they also that are earthy: and as is the heavenly, such are they also that are heavenly.

And as we have borne the image of the earthy, we shall also bear the image of the heavenly.

For this corruptible must put on incorruption, and this mortal must put on immortality.

So when this corruptible shall have put on incorruption, and this mortal shall put on immortality, then shall be brought to pass the saying that is written, Death is swallowed up in victory.

O death, where is thy sting? O grave, where is thy victory?

The sting of death is sin; and the strength of sin is the law.

But thanks be to God, which giveth us the victory through our Lord Jesus Christ.
—1 Corinthians 15:20-22, 45, 47-49, 53-57.

610 THE JUDGMENT

And I saw a great white throne, and him that sat on it, from whose face the earth and the heaven fled away; and there was found no place for them.

And I saw the dead, small and great, stand before God; and the books were opened: and another book was opened, which is the book of life: and the dead were judged out of those things which were written in the books, according to their works.

And the sea gave up the dead which were in it; and death and hell delivered up the dead which were in them: and they were judged every man according to their works.

And death and hell were cast into the lake of fire. This is the second death.

And whosoever was not found written in the book of life was cast into the lake of fire. —Revelation 20:11-15.

As therefore the tares are gathered and burned in the fire; so shall it be in the end of this world.

The Son of man shall send forth his angels, and they shall gather out of his kingdom all things that offend, and them which do iniquity;

And shall cast them into a furnace of fire: there shall be wailing and gnashing of teeth.

Then shall the righteous shine forth as the sun in the kingdom of their Father. Who hath ears to hear, let him hear. —Matthew 13:40-43.

611 THE NEW CREATION

And I saw a new heaven and a new earth: for the first heaven and the first earth were passed away; and there was no more sea.

And I John saw the holy city, new Jerusalem, coming down from God out of heaven, prepared as a bride adorned for her husband.

And I heard a great voice out of heaven saying, Behold, the tabernacle of God is with men, and he will dwell with them, and they shall be his people, and God himself shall be with them, and be their God.

And God shall wipe away all tears from their eyes; and there shall be no more death, neither sorrow, nor crying, neither shall there be any more pain: for the former things are passed away.

And he that sat upon the throne said, Behold, I make all things new. And he said unto me, Write: for these words are true and faithful.

And he said unto me, It is done. I am Alpha and Omega, the beginning and the end. I will give unto him that is athirst of the fountain of the water of life freely.

He that overcometh shall inherit all things; and I will be his God, and he shall be my son.

And he carried me away in the spirit to a great and high mountain, and shewed me that great city, the holy Jerusalem, descending out of heaven from God,

Having the glory of God: and her light was like unto a stone most precious, even like a jasper stone, clear as crystal;

And I saw no temple therein: for the Lord God Almighty and the Lamb are the temple of it.

And the city had no need of the sun, neither of the moon, to shine in it: for the glory of God did lighten it, and the Lamb is the light thereof.

And the nations of them which are saved shall walk in the light of it: and the kings of the earth do bring their glory and honour into it.

And the gates of it shall not be shut at all by day: for there shall be no night there.

And they shall bring the glory and honour of the nations into it.

And there shall in no wise enter into it any thing that defileth,

Neither whatsover worketh abomination, or maketh a lie: but they which are written in the Lamb's book of life.
—Revelation 21:1-7, 10, 11, 22-27.

612 THE IDEAL MOTHER

Who can find a virtuous woman? for her price is far above rubies.

The heart of her husband doth safely trust in her, so that he shall have no need of spoil.

She will do him good and not evil all the days of her life.

She seeketh wool, and flax, and worketh willingly with her hands.

She is like the merchants' ships; she bringeth her food from afar.

She riseth also while it is yet night, and giveth meat to her household, and a portion to her maidens.

She considereth a field, and buyeth it: with the fruit of her hands she planteth a vineyard.

She girdeth her loins with strength, and strengtheneth her arms.

She perceiveth that her merchandise is good: her candle goeth not out by night.

She layeth her hands to the spindle, and her hands hold the distaff.

She stretcheth out her hand to the poor; yea, she reacheth forth her hands to the needy.

She is not afraid of the snow for her household: for all her household are clothed with scarlet.

She maketh herself coverings of tapestry; her clothing is silk and purple.

Her husband is known in the gates, when he sitteth among the elders of the land.

She maketh fine linen, and selleth it; and delivereth girdles unto the merchant.

Strength and honour are her clothing; and she shall rejoice in time to come.

She openeth her mouth with wisdom; and in her tongue is the law of kindness.

She looketh well to the ways of her household, and eateth not the bread of idleness.

Her children arise up, and call her blessed; her husband also, and he praiseth her.

Many daughters have done virtuously, but thou excellest them all.

Favour is deceitful, and beauty is vain: but a woman that feareth the Lord, she shall be praised.
—Proverbs 31: 10-30.

613 CHRIST AND CHILDREN

At the same time came the disciples unto Jesus, saying, Who is the greatest in the kingdom of heaven? And Jesus called a little child unto him, and set him in the midst of them, and said.

Verily I say unto you, Except ye be converted, and become as little children, ye shall not enter into the kingdom of heaven.

Whosoever therefore shall humble himself as this little child, the same is greatest in the kingdom of heaven. And whoso shall receive one such little child in my name receiveth me.

But whoso shall offend one of these little ones which believe in me, it were better for him that a millstone were hanged about his neck, and that he were drowned in the depth of the sea.

Take heed that ye despise not one of these little ones; for I say unto you, That in heaven their angels do always behold the face of my Father which is in heaven.   —Matthew 18:1-6, 10.

Whosoever shall receive one of such children in my name, receiveth me: and whosoever shall receive me, receiveth not me, but him that sent me.   —Mark 9:37.

And they brought young children to him, that he should touch them: and his disciples rebuked those that brought them.

But when Jesus saw it, he was much displeased, and said unto them, Suffer the little children to come unto me, and forbid them not: for of such is the kingdom of God.

Verily I say unto you, Whosoever shall not receive the kingdom of God as a little child, he shall not enter therein.

And he took them up in his arms, put his hands upon them, and blessed them.   —Mark 10:13-16.

TOPICAL INDEX OF SCRIPTURE READINGS

INDEX OF AUTHORS, COMPOSERS AND SOURCES

SCRIPTURAL ALLUSIONS AND QUOTATIONS IN HYMNS

COPYRIGHT OWNERS (Words and Music)

As mentioned in the foreword, we are indebted to the proprietors listed here for permission to include their copyrighted works in HYMNS OF FAITH. The right to use these copyrighted hymns and songs is restricted to this hymnal. Those wishing to use any of the copyrighted words or music contained herein must contact the appropriate owner whose name and address is listed below.

USED BY PERMISSION:

AFFILIATED MUSIC ENTERPRISES, INC. Box 1929, Melbourne, FL 32901—(305) 727-2500: Songs listed under names shown in copyright notices.

ALBERT E. BRUMLEY AND SONS Powell, MO 65730—(417) 435-2225: Hymns 290, 311.

BENSON COMPANY, THE 365 Great Circle Road, Nashville, TN 37228—(615) 259-9111: Songs listed under names shown in copyright notices.

BENSON, JOHN T., Jr.—contact The Benson Company: Hymns 149, 201, 235, 308, 416.

BOSTON MUSIC COMPANY 116-122 Boylston Street, Boston, MA 02116—(617) 426-5100: Hymn 203.

BROADMAN PRESS 127 Ninth Avenue North, Nashville, TN 37234—(615) 251-2000: Hymns 98, 224, 401, 528. (Affiliate of the Sunday School Board of the Southern Baptist Convention.)

BULLS-EYE MUSIC, INC. P.O. Box 1589, Hollywood, CA 90028—(213) 464-8697: Hymns 104, 322, 344.

CHANCEL MUSIC, INC. 8214 Hillside Avenue, Los Angeles, CA 90069—(213) 656-0666: Hymn 237.

CHARLES SCRIBNER'S SONS 587 Fifth Avenue, New York, NY 10017: Hymn 29.

CRESCENDO PUBLICATIONS, INC. P.O. Box 28218, Dallas, TX 75228—(214) 324-2451: Hymn 102.

DIMENSION MUSIC—contact The Benson Company: Hymn 89.

FOX MUSIC PUBLICATIONS—contact Paragon Associates, Inc.: Hymn 502.

GAITHER, WILLIAM J.—contact Paragon Associates, Inc.: Hymns 5, 67, 71, 75, 169, 177, 184, 206, 227, 302, 451, 515.

GOODLIFFE, DR. E. R. Mount Pleasant, Stoke St. Mary, Taunton, Somerset, England, TA3 5DE—Henlade 442090: Hymn 168.

G. SCHIRMER, INC. 866 Third Avenue, New York, NY 10022—(212) 935-5100: Hymn 61.

HAMBLEN MUSIC COMPANY—contact Paragon Associates, Inc.: Hymns 40, 106, 424.

HEARTWARMING MUSIC COMPANY—contact The Benson Company: Hymn 437.

HOPE PUBLISHING COMPANY Carol Stream, IL 60187—(312) 665-3200. Listed for your convenience.

J. CURWEN & SONS—contact G. Schirmer, Inc.: Hymn 12.

LANNY WOLFE MUSIC COMPANY—contact The Benson Company: Hymn 245.

LATTER RAIN MUSIC 19241 Ballinger, Northridge, CA 91324: Hymn 171.

LE FEVRE/SING PUBLISHING COMPANY P.O. Box 43703, Atlanta, GA 30336—(404) 696-6302: Hymn 176.

LEXICON MUSIC, INC. P.O. Box 296, Woodland Hills, CA 91365—(213) 884-0333: Hymns 4, 8, 34, 35, 194, 323, 335, 423, 491.

LILLENAS PUBLISHING COMPANY Box 527, Kansas City, MO 64141—(816) 931-1900: Hymns 65, 142, 212. Songs listed under names shown in copyright notices.

MANNA MUSIC, INC. P.O. Box 3257 (2111 Kenmere Avenue), Burbank, CA 91504—(213) 843-8100: Hymns 2, 42, 78, 248, 269.

MARANATHA! MUSIC PUBLISHING P.O. Box 1396, Costa Mesa, CA 92626—(714) 546-9210: Hymn 447.

MARSHALL, MORGAN & SCOTT PUBLICATIONS LTD. 1 Bath Street, London, EC1V 9QA, England—01-251-2925: Hymns 47, 225.

MOODY PRESS Moody Bible Institute, 820 North LaSalle Street, Chicago, IL 62610— (312) 329-4332: Hymn 83.

NAZARENE PUBLISHING HOUSE—contact Lillenas Publishing Company: Hymns 72, 99, 246, 280, 286, 393.

NEW PAX MUSIC PRESS—contact Paragon Associates, Inc.: Hymns 324, 436.

NORMAN CLAYTON PUBLISHING COMPANY—contact The Rodeheaver Company: Hymns 51, 170, 407.

OXFORD UNIVERSITY PRESS Ely House, 37 Dover Street, London, W1X 4AH, England—01-629-8494: Hymn 542.

PARAGON ASSOCIATES, INC. Box 23618 (19th Avenue North and Hayes), Nashville, TN 37202—(615) 327-2835. Songs listed under names shown in copyright notices.

PARAGON MUSIC CORPORATION—contact Paragon Associates, Inc.: Hymns 6, 436.

PRESBYTERIAN OUTLOOK, THE 512 East Main Street, Richmond, VA 23219—(703) 649-1371: Hymn 505.

RODEHEAVER COMPANY, THE Winona Lake, IN 46590—(219) 267-5116: Hymns 19, 138, 157, 167, 189, 198, 232, 253, 259, 360, 363, 430, 438, 453, 473, 477, 509, 526, 534. (Rodeheaver is affiliated with Word Music, Inc.)

SACRED SONGS (a division of Word, Inc.)—contact Word Music, Inc.: Hymns 220, 231, 338.

SINGSPIRATION, Division of the Zondervan Corporation 1415 Lake Drive SE, Grand Rapids, MI 49506—(616) 459-6900: Hymns 79, 87, 178, 183, 221, 241, 244, 252, 258, 267, 282, 288, 353, 356, 403, 414, 444, 497, 519, 523, 529, 536.

STAMPS-BAXTER MUSIC of The Zondervan Corporation P.O. Box 4007 (201-211 South Tyler), Dallas, TX 75208—(214) 943-1155: Hymn 524.

STANDARD PUBLISHING 8121 Hamilton Avenue, Cincinnati, OH 45231—(513) 931-4050: Hymn 472.

TOVEY, HERBERT G.—contact Affiliated Music Enterprises, Inc.: Hymn 371.

WEBB, MRS. DILYS 25 Groes Low, Rhiwbina, Cardiff, CF4 6JT, S. Glamorganshire, South Wales: Hymn 27.

WORD MUSIC, INC. 4800 West Waco Drive, Waco, TX 76703—(817) 772-7650: Hymns 220, 558.

WORK, MRS. JOHN W. III 1030 Seventeenth Avenue North, Nashville, TN 37208: Hymn 127.

WORLD STUDENT CHRISTIAN FEDERATION 37 quai Wilson, 1201 Geneva, Switzerland—(022) 31 61 35: Hymn 506.

ZONDERVAN MUSIC PUBLISHERS—contact Singspiration. Hymn 328.

TOPICAL INDEX OF HYMNS

ALPHABETICAL INDEX OF HYMNS

Page 619